GLOBAL OUTSOURCING WITH MICROSOFT VISUAL STUDIO 2005 TEAM SYSTEM

GLOBAL OUTSOURCING WITH MICROSOFT VISUAL STUDIO 2005 TEAM SYSTEM

JAMIL AZHER

CHARLES RIVER MEDIA
Boston, Massachusetts

Cover Design: The Printed Image

CHARLES RIVER MEDIA
25 Thomson Place
Boston, Massachusetts 02210
617-757-7900
617-757-7969 (FAX)
crm.info@thomson.com
www.charlesriver.com

This book is printed on acid-free paper.

Azher, Jamil. *Global Outsourcing with Microsoft Visul Studio 2005 Team System.*
ISBN: 1-58450-445-5

Printed in the United States of America
06 7 6 5 4 3 2 First Edition

CHARLES RIVER MEDIA titles are available for site license or bulk purchase by institutions, user groups, corporations, etc. For additional information, please contact the Special Sales Department at 800-347-7707.

The book is dedicated to my departed mother,
Dr. Sakina Azher, whose deep intellectual curiosity and grace
in the face of extreme adversity have inspired me to seek and fight.
There are no good-byes when you love.

Contents

Introduction

Enterprise software development is not a solo act. Enterprise applications are created through the collective efforts of many individuals, many of whom are increasingly dispersed geographically. The physical separation and non-overlapping work hours create unique challenges. However, traditionally, software development methodologies have not taken into account the sometimes novel problems associated with global outsourcing. As a result, many organizations function on an ad-hoc basis and fail to overcome inherent operational inefficiencies.

Microsoft's entrance in the software lifecycle tools market—via Visual Studio 2005 Team System (VSTS)—has presented new opportunities to streamline the global delivery model. VSTS contains built-in support for project management, issue tracking, source code management, quality control, architectural design, status reporting, and the like.

This book teaches how to use VSTS to manage outsourced projects. You'll learn how to improve visibility, ensure quality, minimize friction, and reduce execution risks. The information presented is based upon real-life experience of practitioners in this field. Yes, you'll need to make some up-front investments—in terms of infrastructure, process, and training—to set up a customized platform for your own organization. Your investments will pay rich dividends as you try to outsource increasingly large, complex, time-sensitive, and mission-critical projects.

Like life itself, this book represents a work-in-progress body of knowledge. The book can be enriched by your comments, criticisms, and suggestions—as you apply VSTS in your own scenario. We welcome your feedback and participation in improving the material.

WHO SHOULD READ THIS BOOK

This book is written for a variety of project stakeholders—project managers, process experts, team leads, developers, testers, and other IT professionals. Since an enterprise software project involves many parties—and VSTS aims to unify them—we have tried to keep the content broad, with technical deep-dives in selected areas.

HOW THIS BOOK IS ORGANIZED

In the first two chapters of the book, we discuss the nature of the outsourcing business and the need to come up with an effective methodology to streamline globally distributed development activities.

In the remaining chapters, we look at various aspects of VSTS from the perspective of managing outsourced projects. Starting with a general discussion about a particular problem area, in each chapter, we first look at the issue from a high level—using VSTS feature descriptions as well as walkthroughs. The material gets progressively more detailed. In some chapters, towards the end, we discuss source code examples and technical matters.

CONTACTING THE AUTHOR

We are interested in hearing from you! You can send me an email at *jamil@tfsinfo.com* or share your comments in the discussion board at *www.tfsinfo.com/outsourcingbook*. Your feedback will help improve the material presented in the book as well as benefit other readers. However, please note that technical support is not available from this site.

ACKNOWLEDGMENTS

Like enterprise software development itself, this book embodies the work of many people. I hope that I was able to convey in the book at least some of the passion and dedication that the team put in.

Thanks to Shafqat Ahmed, Omar Raihan, Momenul Islam, Shahed Huq, and Omar Al Zabir for enduring many hours of system crashes during the early days of VSTS and for providing key technical insights. Thanks to Manojit Paul and Moim Hossain for verifying the accuracy of the code. Thanks to Akther Ahmed for helping to arrange interviews with key outsourcing companies. Thanks to Hasan Arif for sharing his real-life perspectives.

Thanks to Iqbal Habib, Noele Lee, and Shihab Azhar for creating the graphic presentations. Their contributions enriched the content and breathed life to the concepts.

Thanks to the folks at Microsoft—Bindia Hallauer, Sonal Pardeshi, Rob Caron, Michael Leworthy, Eric Lee, and Amit Agarwal for their inspiration and guidance when the way forward seemed unclear. Thanks to Bill Essary, Tom Patton, Madhan Subhas, and Jason Barile for taking the time to perform technical reviews, despite their very busy schedules.

Thanks to the publishing team at Thomson Delmar Learning—Jim Walsh, Jenifer Niles, Jenifer Blaney, and Meg Dunkerley for their counsel and persistence. It was their behind-the-scenes magic that actually made it happen!

Thanks to Raffi Festekjian, CEO of PCi Corp, for giving me the freedom to embark upon this intellectual adventure.

Finally, special thanks to my dear wife, Rokeya Khan, for tolerating my crazy schedule and avoidance of family responsibilities. This book simply would not be possible without her understanding and support.

1 The Business of Outsourcing

INTRODUCTION

Global outsourcing has emerged as a dominant business trend in the twenty-first century. Thanks to revolutionary advances in global communication infrastructure, many services have become location-independent. The relocation of labor in the service industry is caused by the same economic forces that transformed manufacturing in the second half of the last century—leveraging the global labor pool and migrating production to cheaper locations. As 'sunset' industries move out of high-wage countries and get transplanted in emerging economies, fortunes are lost and built, dreams are destroyed and created, communities are devastated and enriched. However, in this chapter, we don't attempt to judge the merits of global capitalism; we merely present the facts and suggest how best to deal with the inevitable changes.

No matter how we might feel about outsourcing, we realize that it is here to stay and is gathering momentum. As such, the paradigm shift will increasingly affect the people working in the Information Technology (IT) industry, regardless of what kind of company they work for and what percentage of their work is outsourced. In this chapter, we present the motivation, context, and characteristics of the outsourcing industry. The information presented here will help you to construct an effective mental model as you deal with an increasingly global workforce.

We use the term "outsourcing" to mean offshore delivery of IT and IT-Enabled Services (ITES). To illustrate comparative scenarios, we have chosen the dominant player in this sector—India. With over 44-percent market share in the global outsourcing business [EconomicTimes05e] and 70-percent market share in the Business Process Outsourcing (BPO) market segment [EconomicTimes05a], India has become the largest solution provider in this space. Other emerging contenders include Argentina, Bangladesh, Canada, China, Czech Republic, Ireland, Malaysia, Mexico, Pakistan, Philippines, Poland, Russia, South Africa, Vietnam, and other countries (see Figure 1.1).

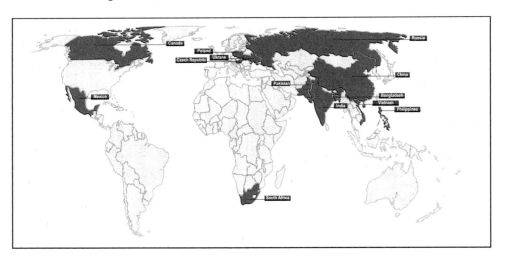

FIGURE 1.1   Representative outsourcing destinations.

WHY OUTSOURCE?

Why do companies outsource? The obvious answer is to save money. When a job is outsourced, in addition to the base salary, companies don't have to pay for health care, pensions, training or taxes (e.g., FICA, Medicare, or State and Federal unemployment tax). The company also saves on rent, equipment, utilities, and other expenses. Strategically speaking, the reasons for outsourcing are as follows:

Cost Savings: In a recent study of large U.S. corporations by Deloitte Consulting, 70 percent of the respondents cited cost savings as a key driver for outsourcing; 43 percent said cost was the primary factor [Deloitte05]. The difference between the wage rate of an IT worker in the U.S. versus in India—even after adding all the hidden costs—is substantial and indisputable. A programmer with a few years experience whose base salary is about $55,000 in the U.S. is available for approximately $15,000 in India (see Figure1.2). Numerous

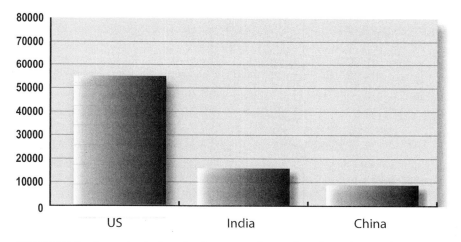

FIGURE 1.2 Annual salaries of software engineers in selected countries.

studies have shown overall cost savings to be in the range of 30 percent to 60 percent after adjusting for various hidden costs (see Figure 1.3 for indicative rates in various professions).

Competitive Pressure: When competitors reduce operational costs via offshoring, organizations often have no choice but to follow suit. Failure to do so usually means loss of competitive edge and pressure on operating margins.

Leverage Domain Expertise and Scale: When specialized work needs to be performed quickly and efficiently (e.g., a business-to-business exchange, validation of an automotive design, patent infringement investigation, etc.), low-cost vendors with flexible capacity and the required domain knowledge often can be found offshore. As science and engineering enrollments drop in the U.S.

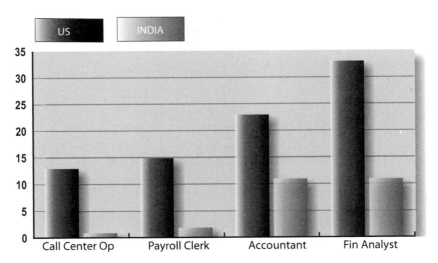

FIGURE 1.3 Average hourly wages (in U.S. dollars) of employees in the U.S. and India.

but rise in India and China, companies are increasingly likely to find themselves in this kind of situation. For example, the city of Bangalore in India is already bigger than Silicon Valley in terms of the number of IT workers. In 2005, the number of IT workers in Bangalore was estimated to be about 265,000 [Economist05], whereas the corresponding figure in Silicon Valley was less than 200,000 [Frauenheim04a].

'Commodity' Requirements: Organizations facing a time-boxed or cyclical need for contractors often turn to overseas vendors to meet critical time-to-market deadlines. If the work doesn't involve much specialized domain knowledge and involves mostly 'commodity' work (e.g., XML conversion), it can easily be outsourced.

Venture Capital Requirements: Venture Capitalists (VCs) increasingly require portfolio companies to follow a cost-saving outsourcing strategy and to use preferred offshore vendors. In order to reduce the burn-rate, many VCs now require start-ups to only have sales and marketing operations in the U.S., and to offshore all other activities—development as well as back office.

Pressure from Wall Street: All public companies are under shareholder and analyst pressure to meet or exceed expected earnings every quarter. One of the straightforward ways to achieve this goal is to aggressively cut costs, especially if increasing the top-line revenue looks challenging. It has gotten to the point where if a major company doesn't outsource at least its back-office operations, it is bound to face questions from Wall Street [BusinessWeek03b].

OUTSOURCING TRENDS

Outsourcing is causing sweeping changes in the IT and ITES industries. Forrester Research predicts that at least 3.3 million white-collar jobs (and $136 billion in wages) will be outsourced by 2015 [BusinessWeek03a]. According to Forrester, 830,000 service-sector jobs moved offshore in 2005 [MSNBC04]. AMR Research predicts that 15 percent of information technology jobs will be outsourced in the next six years [Frauenheim04b]. Gartner predicts that by 2015, the outsourcing rate of IT jobs in developed countries will increase to 30 percent from under 5·percent in 2006 [BostonGlobe06]. According to Frost and Sullivan, over $464 billion worth of IT services work was *cumulatively* sent offshore in 2004 from various developed countries [Frost04] (see Figure 1.4). In terms of dollar value, Japan is the largest outsourcer in the world, followed by the U.S.

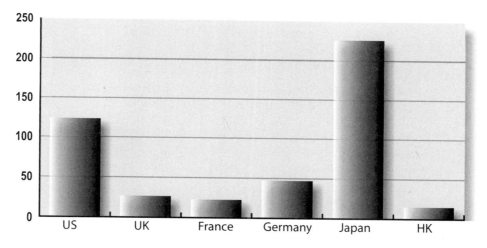

FIGURE 1.4 Cumulative total value (in billion dollars) of services sent offshore in 2004 by various countries (source: Frost and Sullivan).

Despite widespread adoption of offshore outsourcing, it is difficult to get an accurate estimate of the annual dollar figures involved. Various studies by consulting companies, trade associations, and government agencies report different numbers. A recent study by the World Trade Organization (WTO)—based upon an analysis of national balance-of-payment information as well as data from consulting companies and multilateral agencies—puts the total dollar value for global offshore services at around $45 billion in 2003 [WTO05]. Gartner estimates that global spending on offshore services will exceed $50 billion in 2007 [Gartner05]. The Indian IT industry organization NASSCOM predicts that the total global outsourcing market will exceed $100 billion by 2010 [EconomicTimes05i].

If you study the numbers, you'll realize that the outsourcing phenomenon has huge momentum and massive scale. Barring unexpected events, the outsourcing trend will accelerate; its effect on the global economy will be profound. However, it'll require new processes, benchmarks, attitudes, and tools to manage the new business reality and benefit from the emerging opportunities.

LONG-TERM DRIVERS OF OUTSOURCING

There are fundamental geodemographic and socioeconomic factors driving global outsourcing trends. Some of the underlying reasons are beyond the control of governments or multilateral trade organizations such as the WTO. The world economy is being restructured in ways that we are only beginning to fathom. The long-term consequences of the paradigm shift are unpredictable. Nevertheless, it is important to understand the core drivers of outsourcing in order to make sense of what's happening around us.

Demographics

As mentioned earlier in this chapter, the fundamental reason for migration of labor is, of course, cost. However, there is a deeper issue that merits exploration—demographic shifts. Lower fertility rates in developed countries are causing their overall population to age rapidly. These countries have a large proportion of old people compared to young people (see Figure 1.5). For instance, between 2005 and 2050,

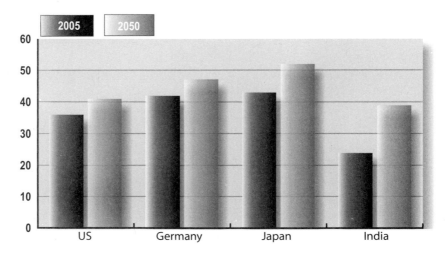

FIGURE 1.5 Median age in selected countries (source: United Nations Department of Economic and Social Affairs, Population Division).

the median age of people in Japan is projected to increase from 43 to 52. Over the same period, the median age of people in the U.S. will increase from 36 to 41. As you might have guessed, most developing countries have high fertility rates and do not share this trend. Among the large developing countries, China is the only exception. China's population is aging fast—the median age is projected to rise from 33 in 2005 to 45 in 2050 [UN04].

Although total global population will increase from 6.5 billion in 2005 to 9.1 billion in 2050, many industrialized countries will experience a negative population growth. Between 2005 and 2050, Japan will lose 15 million people. Russia's population will decrease by more than 30 million. Many countries in Eastern Europe will shrink by 15 percent to 40 percent. For example, Ukraine is projected to lose almost half its people between 2005 (population 46 million) and 2050 (projected population 26 million). Due to a slightly higher fertility rate (2.1 children per woman) and immigration, the U.S. will escape this demographic fate, and its population is projected to grow from 298 million in 2005 to 394 million in 2050 [UN04].

Simply speaking, the developing world has more working-age people (see Figure 1.6), and their populations (except China's) will continue to grow in the next 50 years. Over the same period of time, many developed countries (except the U.S.) will lose people. Many developed countries will also have a higher retiree (over age 65) to working-age population ratio, jeopardizing, among other things, senior citizen benefits such as pensions, health care, Social Security (U.S.), and so forth. These benefits are typically funded from the wages of the working population.

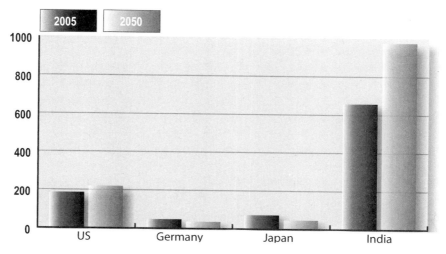

FIGURE 1.6 Number of people (in millions) in working-age group (15–59 years old) in selected countries (source: United Nations Department of Economic and Social Affairs, Population Division).

Developing countries that can leverage their demographic strength through effective mass education (e.g., low drop-out rates, meaningful curricula, and language training), business-friendly government policies, transparent legal systems, and similar efforts will become attractive outsourcing destinations.

Skilled Low-Cost Labor

The new global economy needs skilled workers at an increasing rate. The economic growth of China (currently at 9.9 percent) and India (currently at 6 percent)—countries that contain over 2 billion people between them—is generating unprecedented demand for goods and services. A large number of industrial sectors are undergoing explosive growth. The fast-growing industries include energy, steel, chemicals, cement, energy, automobiles, consumer appliances, cell phones, computers, textiles, aircraft, power plants, real estate, transportation, construction, and financial services. For example, the real-estate sector in China is experiencing a frenzied boom; in 2005, the country added a record 4.7 billion square feet of new occupancy space. In 2005, Shanghai added skyscrapers with more office and living space than there is in all the office buildings in New York City [IHT05]. Since both China and India are starting from a low base, and the per-capita income is abysmally low in both nations—$1,290 in China and $620 in India [WorldBank04] (see Figure 1.7)—a growth rate of 7–8 percent could be sustained for decades [BusinessWeek05d].

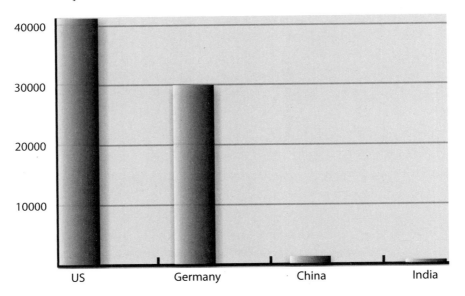

FIGURE 1.7   Gross National Income (GNI) per capita in selected countries (source: The World Bank).

The skyrocketing demand for goods and services in China, India and other developing countries is satisfied by indigenous as well as Western companies. Global as well as national corporations need an increasing number of skilled professionals to meet the surging consumer appetite. However, many companies are having trouble finding a sufficient supply of skilled labor at competitive rates in local or foreign markets. Furthermore, multinationals that depend on overseas markets for survival and growth are feeling the need to relocate staff closer to their overseas customers due to political, economic, and operational reasons.

Consequently, the demand for skilled manpower is fueled not only by the outsourcing practices of U.S., Western European, and Japanese companies, but also by rapid economic expansion of the Asian giants. However, there doesn't seem to be enough skilled people to go around. Demand exceeds supply even in China and India.

China and India produce far more technology professionals than the U.S. Together, China and India produce over 6 million college graduates per year; the U.S. produces just over a million [Fortune05] (see Figure 1.8). Out of this pool of young professionals, over 500,000 students in China and over 200,000 students in India

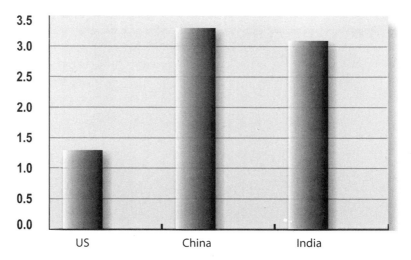

FIGURE 1.8   Total number (in millions) of college graduates per year in selected countries.

graduate in engineering disciplines, compared to only about 70,000 students in the U.S. [BostonGlobe05] (see Figure 1.9). What is worse, the number of engineering graduates in the U.S. is trending downward. The number of new undergraduate majors in computer science dropped by 23 percent in 2002–2003 and by another 10 percent in 2003–2004 [CRN05].

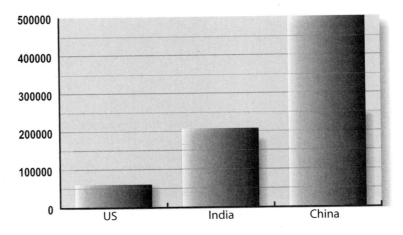

FIGURE 1.9   Number of engineering graduates per year in selected countries.

WHAT IS OUTSOURCED?

Broadly speaking, any business activity that does not involve looking a customer in the eye or shaking his hand is a candidate for outsourcing. Traditionally, outsourcing activities have been categorized into Application Development and Maintenance (ADM, 14 percent of global IT spending) and Business Process Outsourcing (BPO, 60 percent of global IT spending) sectors. (See Table 1.1 for representative types of services outsourced.) BPO typically includes call-center operations as well as back-office tasks, such as accounting, payroll processing, reconciliation, and documentation. The BPO industry in India was about $5 billion in 2005 and growing at the rate of about 40 percent annually [Nasscom05b]; it is projected to become a $20 billion business by 2008 [EconomicTimes05c]. Total Indian outsourcing exports are projected to rise to $50 billion by 2010 [Nasscom05b].

Offshore service providers are making a determined effort to move up the value chain, and they are succeeding. For example, in India, currently most of the BPO revenue comes from voice services, but it is estimated that by 2008, the nonvoice segment—dubbed Knowledge Process Outsourcing (KPO)—will jump to 50 percent of the total revenue [BusinessWorld05]. The KPO segment is projected to grow at the rate of 46 percent between now and 2010 [TimesofIndia05d]. The KPO space includes emerging growth sectors like system integration, infrastructure management, automotive and avionics design, engineering services, legal research, equity research, risk management, simulation, telemedicine, and human resources. By 2010, global KPO outsourcing business is expected to be about $16 billion, out

TABLE 1.1   Representative Types of Services Outsourced

Category	Name of Service
Software development and maintenance services	New application development Application or service integration End-of-life support Legacy application maintenance Legacy application conversion Software quality assurance
Contact management services	Call centers Customer support IT help desks Prospecting Telemarketing Mailing list management Web-based and email marketing
Data services	Database design and maintenance Data processing and mining Market research Legal research Analytics and statistical analysis Geographic Information Systems (GIS)
Financial services	Accounting, auditing, and bookkeeping Account payables, receivables processing Payroll processing Mortgage processing Credit/Debit card and check processing Insurance claims processing Debt collection and skip-tracing Transaction processing Fund management, back-office and mid-office services Portfolio analysis Investment research Equity research
Health-care services	Insurance form processing Medical transcription Radiology interpretation Biotech research Clinical trials Drug patent application management →

Category	Name of Service
Creative services	Web design
	Graphic design
	Animation design
	Advertising material creation
	Architectural services
	Video and online game development
	Automotive and aeronautical R&D and design
	Cell-phone 4G R&D and design
Miscellaneous	Desktop publishing
	Document management
	Hardware development and testing
	Litigation support
	Tax preparation
	Exam grading
	Logistics support
	Supply chain management
	Digitization and mapping
	Multimedia authoring
	Movie production support
	Industrial design
	Engineering services
	Human resources
	Network management

of which $12 billion is projected to be outsourced from India [TimesofIndia05f]. Some studies project even higher growth numbers for the KPO space; a recent study predicted that India's contract industrial engineering revenue alone will grow from $500 million in 2005 to about $10 billion in 2010 [BusinessWeek05f].

Research Process Outsourcing (RPO) in the biotech industry is another high-growth sector. It is currently a $120 million business in India, growing at the rate of 75 percent per year, and projected to hit the $1 billion mark by 2010 [TimesofIndia04a]. RPO includes basic research, drug discovery, clinical trials management, compound screening, bioinformatics, and regulatory submissions.

OUTSOURCING CHALLENGES

There is a tendency to think that outsourcing is a panacea. Just outsource the jobs, and the finished products will magically come back on time and the business processes will be executed reliably. The management strategy seems to be to outsource not only back office, middle office, and operations, but also R&D, development, and IT functions. If there are any employees left in the company besides executive management and janitorial staff, they are asked to focus on 'core competencies.'

This kind of outsourcing nirvana rarely happens in practice. No matter what credentials are touted by the outsourcing vendor, whether it be ISO 9000 or Capability Maturity Model Integration (CMMI), the reality is that there are likely to be problems, frustrations, and disappointments. You need to manage the outsourcing process carefully and continuously in order to derive the benefits. The path to the outsourcing promised land is littered with failed projects, cancelled contracts, cost overruns, angry arguments, and expensive lawsuits.

Many recent studies bear out the risks and failures associated with the outsourcing process. A recent Deloitte study of 25 large organizations reported that 70 percent of the participants had significant negative experiences with outsourcing; 25 percent of the respondents brought back some outsourced functions because they could be done better or cheaper in-house [Deloitte05]. Another report by Dun and Bradstreet stated that 20 percent of outsourcing relationships fail in the first two years, and 50 percent fail in the first five years [Deloitte05]. Despite the breakneck pace of outsourcing growth, you can't simply ignore the real-life issues faced by many large and small organizations. The process of outsourcing carries significant execution risk. In order to ensure success, the outsourcing process has to be managed wisely, closely, and continuously.

No matter what your contract says or the Service-Level Agreements (SLAs) stipulate, the inherent risks associated with software development do not simply migrate to the vendor when you outsource a project. At the end of the day, your neck is still on the line. You need to actively manage the engagement by investing time, effort, and resources. In a Deloitte study, 62 percent of participants found that it took more time and effort to manage the outsourcing process than they originally anticipated [Deloitte05]. A recent Gartner study reported that organizations do not achieve projected savings before investing one to two years in building the outsourcing relationship [Gartner05]. Moreover, many studies (including the ones by Deloitte and Gartner) show that the hidden costs end up being much higher than expected. You need to be aware of the structural and operational risks associated with sending work across the world. In the next sections, we look at a few common risk factors.

Communication

Effectively and efficiently communicating your requirements to a remote team, without adding massive documentation overhead, is often a big challenge and a source of much frustration. In theory, projects should have volumes of documents, spreadsheets, and screenshots describing the use cases, business workflow, and key algorithms. These artifacts are supposed to represent the complete set of functional and nonfunctional requirements.

However, in real life, specifications are rarely complete, current, and self-describing. There are usually gray areas, what-if scenarios, gaps in domain knowledge, unspoken assumptions, and unresolved ambiguities that need to be clarified. In a face-to-face scenario, a quick chat near the coffee machine is often all that's needed. In a remote context—without the presence of an onsite engagement manager who is flying back and forth (or a subject matter expert residing overseas)—lack of meaningful communication creates grave execution risks.

In some cases, the language barrier creates an additional layer of problems. It is not just the accent or linguistic skills; the problems go deeper and have to do with 'cultural' aspects. People who are intimately familiar with Western societies have an intrinsic understanding of their sociocultural norms and business practices. Since computer software is produced to interact with people in a given society, there are basic, common-sense, unspoken expectations regarding its functionality, look, and feel. It is much more efficient if the programmers automatically understand much of these nonverbalized requirements. Having to specify all the minutiae to the nth degree eats up precious bandwidth that most organizations simply don't have.

When a project manager feels that sense of vague unease when speaking to a foreign programmer who is thousands of miles away—often over a bad telephone connection full of random static noise—it is often a premonition of an impending problem. It is difficult to know whether the person at the other end actually 'got it.' You could try asking him to repeat what you've said, or ask him to send you a write-up demonstrating his actual understanding, but all these overhead steps take time and slow down implementation.

Time zone differences (approximately 9 hours from India to the East Coast and 12 hours to the West Coast; see Figure 1.10) result in both advantages as well as potential problems. The advantage is the possibility of creating a 24/7 development cycle. People in the U.S. can turn over their work to their overseas colleagues at the end of the business day, and the offshore team can do the same—potentially creating a round-the-clock delivery organization.

The problem is that often during the course of the day, issues come up that need instant feedback or fixes—when your remote colleagues are fast asleep. Many issues simply can't wait until the next business day without compromising efficiency and responsiveness to clients. Furthermore, people in both locations may

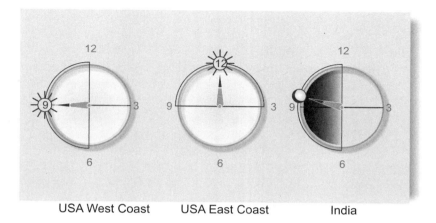

USA West Coast   USA East Coast   India

FIGURE 1.10   Time difference between U.S. and India (using U.S. standard time).

have to stay late or come in early to conduct teleconferences or virtual meetings—disrupting the normal flow of family and work life. Over time, it becomes a burden to deal with these anomalous schedules as well as to maintain normal office hours.

The asynchronous work pattern affects both parties. If an onsite developer needs a quick clarification to move forward, he can simply pick up the phone or walk over to the business analyst. When an offshore programmer needs an explanation, he has to wait until the next day or proceed based upon potentially erroneous assumptions. Moreover, no matter how efficient a person might be, he'll find it easier to explain an issue face-to-face to a local person. If he has to type an email explaining the business logic, he may not be able to manage the time or subconsciously postpone it until later. "Out of sight, out of mind" is a fundamental human trait.

Staff Turnover

Staff turnover in the vendor organization is a serious concern. If your software involves any amount of domain knowledge, you'll not want the developers—having invested time and money to train them up in your application space—to walk away or, worse, join a competitor's outsourcing operation.

No matter how thoroughly documented the software is, an experienced programmer is never just a 'resource'—to be switched at will without repercussions. The team members possess specialized knowledge of the domain models, vocabulary, oddities, workarounds, and exceptions. If the defecting programmers were local, you could probably offer them raises or additional stock options. At the minimum, you could try to prevent them from joining a competitor via a noncompete agreement. These strategies are harder to execute when the developers are not in your payroll. Moreover, the legal process in the foreign country might be inordinately lengthy or even dysfunctional.

Attrition is generally the result of high demand for skilled professionals compared to supply. The top 10 Indian BPO firms hire 40,000 to 48,000 people annually [EconomicTimes05f]. The Indian IT industry is projected to recruit about 100,000 in 2006 [EconomicTimes05l].

In addition to the supply-and-demand imbalance, attrition in the BPO sector is caused by simple exhaustion and lack of job satisfaction. Employees in the BPO industry are particularly vulnerable to rapid burn-out; work is often monotonous and people are required to stay up all night to serve clients in different time zones. An under-reported fact in the 24/7 BPO sector is how disruptive night shifts can be in an employee's life and can even affect his health. Studies have shown that when the normal human sleep-wake biological cycle is thrown off for an extended period, it can lead to clinical depression, high blood pressure, diabetes, and a host of other ailments [EconomicTimes05g]. Moreover, the employee's family and social lives are hampered by continuous all-nighters, often resulting in an unhappy and alienated workforce.

The attrition rate in top Indian software companies is between 7 percent and 20 percent [EconomicTimes05b, TimesofIndia04b, and EconomicTimes06]. The turnover is significantly higher in smaller companies. The attrition rate in Indian BPO companies is simply alarming—60 percent to 80 percent [BusinessWeek05c]. This level of talent loss, coupled with wage inflation of about 15 percent [EconomicTimes05b], is too disruptive for maintaining an efficient process. Furthermore, labor costs are rapidly rising; some companies in the BPO space experienced cost increase of about 35 percent in 2005 [EconomicTimes05h]. In the Deloitte study, 22 percent of the participants reported having problems related to vendor employee turnover [Deloitte05].

Faced with high attrition rates, some Indian BPO companies are hiring temporary workers to satisfy the growing demand for skilled personnel. Temporary workers are recruited not only to deal with high activity periods (such as the Christmas season), but for normal times as well. In 2005, temporary employees constituted approximately five percent of the BPO workforce [EconomicTimes05d]. The rate is projected to go up steadily. Relying on temporary workers introduces additional risks in terms of confidentiality, productivity, and quality.

Information Security and Privacy

In this day and age, protection of intellectual property and prevention of cyber crimes are of paramount importance. As more and more sensitive applications and data are sent offshore—where the legal framework and law-enforcement mechanisms tend to be not as efficient as in the U.S.—security and privacy issues become a top concern.

To be fair to offshore vendors, we need to keep in mind that cyber crime is not just an outsourcing issue; it takes place in the U.S. as well, and on a massive scale. According to the Federal Bureau of Investigation (FBI), more than 10 million Americans were victims of identity theft in 2004. Combined losses exceeded $50 billion in 2004 [FBI04]. In the U.S., scam artists regularly steal credit-card information, Social Security numbers, and personal identities—often causing a good deal of hassle and headache. The crooks are often able to achieve their nefarious aims due to mind-boggling incompetence and negligence on the part of some U.S. organizations. Security lapses include leaving sensitive data unencrypted and accessible to hackers, inadvertently selling customer information to fraudsters, losing financial files during shipment, failing to prevent insider manipulation, storing and then losing identity information that should not have been recorded in the first place, and so on [Newsweek05a]. Consequently, it doesn't make much sense to blame offshore BPO organizations for a relatively insignificant amount of data loss while billions of dollars in identity theft have not been prevented in the U.S.

Nevertheless, when a cyber crime is committed against an American citizen or business from overseas, it is more difficult to investigate, identify, and prosecute the offender. You have to deal with multiple legal systems and law enforcement organizations. Even if a company files a case in a U.S. court, in order to take legal action against an outsourcing company, *de novo* proceedings need to be filed in the foreign country under existing laws of the land [TimesofIndia05b].

Security problems in the offshore BPO industry stem from many causes (just as in the U.S.), but one of the main concerns is high staff turnover associated with the industry's breath-taking growth. In India, the BPO sector employs about 350,000 people [BusinessWeek05c, Nasscom05a], growing at over 45 percent [Business-World05]. To satisfy the explosive growth, the sector hires approximately 600 new workers daily. (See Figure 1.11 and Figure 1.12 to learn how fast the ITES industry has grown in India.) The average training period has been reduced to just two weeks, and attrition rates have gone sky high to as much as 80 percent [Business-Week05c]. In such a volatile environment, you do the math and figure out how reliably and securely your back-office work can be done. It is a testament to the average offshore worker's skill and integrity that most work is being performed without massive failures in quality, reliability, and security.

However, some high-profile security breaches have occurred in the offshore BPO industry, unnerving customers and generating anxiety. One of the most serious to date has been theft of funds (approximately $426,000) from Citibank's U.S. customers by ex-employees of an offshore BPO organization in April 2005; over 16 people were arrested in connection with this [BusinessWeek05c and TimesofIndia05c].

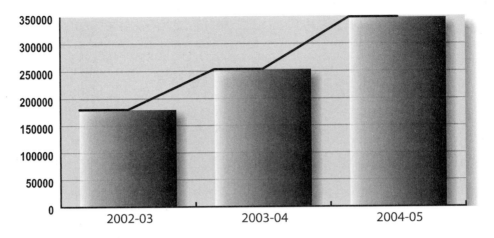

FIGURE 1.11   Personnel growth in Indian BPO industry (source: NASSCOM).

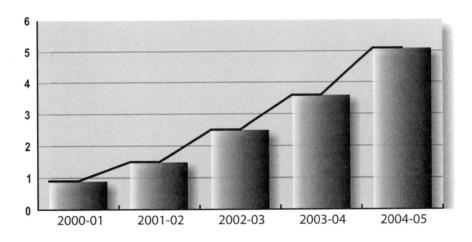

FIGURE 1.12   Growth (in billion dollars) of Indian BPO exports (source: NASSCOM).

In June 2005, another scandal broke out when an undercover reporter from a U.K. newspaper was able to obtain confidential bank account and credit-card information for over 1,000 British customers from a call-center employee for as little as $4,250 [AsiaTimes05]. Although the scale of these failures is miniscule compared to what routinely happens in the U.S. and Europe—losses from identity theft in 2004 was over $50 billion in the U.S. and over $5 billion in the U.K. [FBI04 and TimesofIndia05e]—as the offshore BPO business volume grows, both U.S. and offshore companies need to remain vigilant and continue to improve security audits, background checks, and surveillance procedures.

In addition to information piracy in offshore locations, there are concerns regarding security of the data while in transit. The security of the physical links and devices connecting the world—the infrastructure of the Internet—is susceptible to tampering. Furthermore, an increasing amount of the world's submarine cable network is being owned by foreign companies. For example, in the late 1990s, a U.S. company named Global Crossing spent $15 billion to create a transcontinental fiber-optic network that connected over 200 cities globally. After the dotcom bust, facing tumbling bandwidth prices and slumping demand, the company went bankrupt. In 2003, Singapore-based ST Telemedia bought a majority stake in Global Crossing for $250 million [ITAsiaOne03]. In 2004, India-based Reliance acquired FLAG Telecom, whose network spans the U.S., Europe, Middle East, and Asia [Newsweek04]. In 2005, India-based VSNL bought Tyco Global Network for $130 million. Tyco's submarine cable network spans the U.S., Europe, and the Asia-Pacific region [TelecomAsia05b]. The great telecom infrastructure sell-off is taking place at prices far below what it originally cost to create the networks—most sales have been made for five to ten cents on the dollar [TelecomAsia05a] and Newsweek04].

Given the transfer of ownership to foreign companies, what is there to guarantee the security of the sensitive traffic carried over submarine cables? Information traveling from the U.S. to offshore locations and back traverses multiple carrier circuits and crosses various countries. It is virtually impossible for average U.S. organizations to know who might be 'touching' their data as it zooms through transoceanic cables, landing stations, and overland loops. Although some networks provide stringent security guarantees, the fact of the matter is that there are inherent national security and commercial espionage concerns. These fears motivated the U.S. government to prevent Hong Kong tycoon Li Ka-shing from acquiring a big stake in Global Crossing in 2003 [ITAsiaOne03]. Nevertheless, large chunks of the American-built global 'information highway' are now under foreign ownership. Be careful when sending sensitive data through it.

Visibility

How closely can you watch what's being done offshore? In a maintenance scenario, you might not care that much, because the 'code churn' is limited. However, in new application development, instead of turning a blind eye to what's being done ("We don't care what's inside the software, as long as it looks and acts the way we want."), you need to be proactively involved in supervision and oversight at a more detailed level in order to ensure quality and to minimize execution risks.

Of course, this kind of proactive monitoring is much easier when the programmer is sitting in the next cubicle. You can simply have a quick chat or take a quick look over his shoulder. In remote situations, effective supervision requires extra effort and resources.

Geopolitical Risks

Although we don't usually worry about it, geopolitical risks tend to emerge at unexpected moments and complicate well-thought-out strategic plans. When the delivery organization is located in a distant land, you are susceptible to disturbances arising from all kinds of distant events. The possibilities include trade wars, anti-American sentiments, industrial actions, political uprisings, terrorist threats, wars, and natural disasters.

For example, the military standoff between India and Pakistan in the summer of 2002 raised the specter of a nuclear war in the subcontinent. The tensions were high enough for the U.S. Department of State to evacuate nonessential diplomatic staff and issue an advisory for Americans not to travel to the region. The unexpected events shocked many executives and forced them to make contingency plans. Although tensions between the two neighboring countries subsided—and many managers quickly forgot about making contingency plans and keeping them updated—geopolitical risks continue to pose a real threat when U.S. companies are increasingly dependent on overseas service providers for mission-critical operations.

Political problems don't just occur between countries; they can erupt between various communities within the same nation. China and India are both large multiethnic countries, and consist of a third of the planet's population. The differences in ethnic, religious, cultural, and economic backgrounds between groups constitute both strength and weakness—depending upon the situation. Wide income disparities in both countries between the numerically small ultra-rich and hundreds of millions of people living on less than a dollar a day (see Figure 1.13) could give rise to social tension and strife. Social unrest arising from economic deprivation and poverty is a real concern in both China and India. The stunning defeat of the ruling party in India in 2004 was attributed to the disenchantment of the poor who failed to reap the benefits of the country's economic boom. According to the Chinese government, there were 74,000 protests in 2004 alone [CNN05c]; the number and intensity of protests is expected to increase as the wealth gap widens and results in unpredictable social and political consequences.

Conflicts between various ethnic groups have also broken out frequently. As recently as 2002, over 1,000 people were killed in Hindu-Muslim riots in the Indian state of Gujarat. Kashmir and the northeast region in India remain political flashpoints. An armed conflict in the Taiwan (Formosa) Strait or widespread political challenge to the current authorities could greatly destabilize China.

Contingency plans and Business Continuity Practices (BCP) must be in place when outsourcing core operations—whether the risk of disruption seems imminent or not.

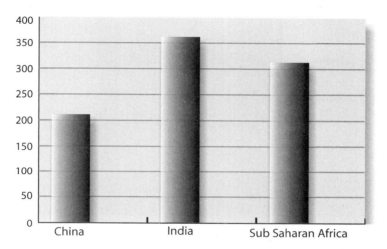

FIGURE 1.13   Number of people (in millions) earning $1 per day or less (source: The United Nations Development Program).

Environmental and Infrastructural Risks

Outsourcing to developing countries carries certain kinds of hidden risks that are often not immediately recognized by people living in Western countries. For example, most large outsourcing destinations in the developing countries suffer from population explosions in overcrowded cities—resulting in slums, unplanned housing, and unsanitary living conditions. Problems can be compounded by poor infrastructure, massive traffic congestion, inadequate and poorly maintained roads, unreliable power supply, contaminated water supply, poor drainage, deforestation, or a bad/nonexistent public transport systems. Degraded environmental conditions often create unsustainable living conditions, such as depletion of groundwater levels, overconstruction without regard to master plans or building codes, destruction of wetlands and forests, and elimination of green belts and natural water bodies. As an example, consider the fact that according to the World Health Organization, 7 out of the 10 most-polluted cities in the world are located in China [IHT05]. Poor public health systems make the task of infectious-disease management difficult. Consequently, problems that are easily managed in Western cities often get magnified in developing cities and cause disruptions.

Something as simple as heavy rainfall—given massive overconstruction, inadequate drainage systems, and destruction of natural drainage channels—can bring a city to standstill and cause significant loss of life. In the summer of 2005, record rainfall in the Indian city of Mumbai claimed more than 1,000 lives and caused massive business disruptions [CNN05b]. Many BPO operations in Mumbai had to close down. Large BPO organizations were able to re-route their calls to other cities like Bangalore, but smaller companies did not have such options.

An earthquake could cause unprecedented damage and loss of life in over-crowded cities because of loss of groundwater levels, rapid construction of high-rise office and residential buildings, weak enforcement of building codes, and ineffective postdisaster search and rescue capabilities. In October of 2005, an earthquake measuring 7.6 on the Richter scale killed over 80,000 people in Pakistan. The death toll will be many times higher if an earthquake strikes closer to a major South Asian population center. The Himalayan region—where the Indian plate collides with the Eurasian plate—is susceptible to strong earthquakes. It is estimated that about 50 million people are at risk of facing major Himalayan quakes [MSNBC05]. A serious bird flu epidemic—given lack of public health services and overcrowding—could cause millions of deaths in Asia [BusinessWeek05e].

Connectivity Problems

Given how ubiquitous the Internet has become worldwide, we often tend to forget that global connectivity is still dependent on cables and switches—hardware that is vulnerable to sabotage as well as normal failure. Many countries are connected to the Internet via a single fiber-optic cable. If the cable fails, the whole country could experience catastrophic loss of Internet service. This is what happened in Pakistan in June 2005 when the undersea cable (SEA-ME-WE-3) linking Pakistan with the rest of the world suddenly developed a fault somewhere under the Arabian Sea [CNN05a]. Although a strong effort was made to connect high-priority organizations to the Internet via satellite backup links, the performance was suboptimal. (Satellite provided about 100-Mbps bandwidth capacity, whereas cable bandwidth utilization was 775 Mbps [ITWorld05] prior to the crash.) The problem continued for days. The Call Center Association of Pakistan reported millions of dollars worth of direct and indirect business losses [Pak05]. A similar failure in the SEA-ME-WE-3 cable between Singapore and Jakarta in 2000 disrupted online traffic between Asia, Australia, and Europe [AsiaWeek00]. When offshoring your mission-critical 24/7 operations, make sure that there is guaranteed redundancy and a backup communication plan to deal with an unexpected loss of primary connectivity.

Brain Drain and Loss of Institutional Knowledge

When you outsource lock, stock, and barrel, you lose the domain knowledge painstakingly built up over time. Although it has become fashionable to say that implementation is a commodity process, many times it isn't. In any reasonable-size software development effort, alot of business knowledge is automatically passed to the development team. The embedded logic related to real-life quirks, outliers, exceptions, and boundary conditions are part of many business processes, and these need to be communicated to the development team. Over time, the 'balance of power' shifts to the vendor, especially if you have fired the in-house core technical staff. Switching vendors is easier said than done—it carries huge costs associated with reverse-knowledge transfer and is often dependent upon the original vendor's cooperation.

A related outcome of vendor lock-in is loss of effective control. In the absence of an actively engaged in-house technical team, over time you'll be more and more removed from the implementation details of the software. You'll lose the ability to judge whether the estimates are exaggerated, the targets are realistic, and the codebase is designed for easy maintenance and extensibility.

To prevent this kind of knowledge meltdown, you might want to consider the 80/20 rule. Develop the core modules in-house (20-percent work) and outsource what's routine (80-percent work), while maintaining close operational oversight. However, the global trend seems to be going in the opposite direction—even R&D and innovation are being outsourced. For example, both Boeing and Airbus have outsourced key aircraft navigation system design to Indian companies [Economist05 and TimesofIndia05g]. Leading Indian outsourcing companies expect their R&D revenue to increase from $1 billion in 2005 to $8 billion by 2008 [BusinessWeek05b]. The city of Bangalore expects to create about 100,000 jobs from biotech research in the next few years. Indian companies are involved in groundbreaking activities such as sophisticated bond analysis, advanced chip design, development of next-generation cell phones, Internet search-engine optimizations, automobile prototyping, protein analysis for life sciences, and other cutting-edge research.

Regulatory Requirements

In response to high-profile corporate scandals like Enron and WorldCom, terrorism concerns, and rising incidents of identity thefts, the U.S. Congress enacted various laws to protect shareholders, consumers, and average citizens. These regulations include the following:

Sarbanes-Oxley Act (SOX): Accuracy of corporate financial reporting by public companies.

Health Insurance Portability and Accountability Act (HIPAA): Access to health insurance coverage and privacy of patient information.

Gramm-Leach Bliley Act (GLBA): Protection of nonpublic personal information.

USA Patriot Act: Surveillance of communication and financial transactions.

Among the above-mentioned regulatory requirements, SOX—given its scope and implications—generates the most concern regarding a company's operations in general and outsourcing activities in particular. The Act requires a public company's executive officers as well as independent auditor(s) to certify each quarter and every year that adequate internal controls are in place to ensure the accuracy of the company's financial statements. They are also required to certify that those controls have been tested for effectiveness within the past 90 days. If you think about how many transactions a company typically does and the myriad business processes that are triggered by a given transaction, you'll realize the amount of overhead involved to ensure compliance with the Act. Furthermore, the internal controls need to be reasonably resistant to fraud, subversion, or efforts to bypass them.

When business processes are outsourced across the world, and the output of those processes could affect your financials, how do you make sure that stringent internal controls have been instituted and are being adhered to by your vendor? How do you ensure that when massive volumes of data are moved between your company's and the vendor's systems, the transmissions are error-free and tamper-proof? Even if the vendor uses your system (the vendor might be connecting remotely and working directly on your computers), you need to make sure that you have instituted and validated the safeguards necessary to ensure accuracy as well as to prevent unauthorized access. For example, you need to ensure that payments made by customers this quarter—and processed offshore—have been accounted for (assuming those payments have a material impact on your financial statement).

When it comes to vendor certification, it is going to require some sort of external audit (the industry might standardize on SAS 70 Type II) regarding a service provider's processes and risk-mitigation strategies. No matter what auditing and enforcement practice the industry ultimately adopts, SOX requirements will present significant challenges in the outsourcing environment. They will increase overhead and costs, complicate vendor selection, and expose your company to a variety of operational risks in foreign jurisdictions. Given the teeth of the Act (up to $5 million fine and up to 20 years in prison), failures will bite.

CONCLUSION

In this chapter, we have looked at the strategic backdrop of outsourcing as well as tactical operational issues. We have seen that outsourcing is a worldwide phenomenon with rapid growth—driven by advances in communication technology, demographic trends, and globalization of trade and services. We have talked about structural, operational, and execution risks associated with the outsourcing process. Outsourcing is widespread, but successful outsourcing is not easy.

Whether your organization is heavily immersed in outsourcing or just tinkering with the idea, chances are that you've already heard about the justifications, rewards, and perils associated with the process. It is pretty clear that white-collar U.S. service workers are now exposed to the buffeting winds of outsourcing, just as manufacturing workers have been for decades. The paradigm shift necessitates that each of us discover our own value proposition and our unique strengths that make us valuable in the global economy. The questions are profound, and the answers are anything but easy.

In the coming chapters, we'll look at real-life best practices for managing outsourced projects. We'll ask fundamental questions, such as what processes to follow, which toolsets to use, and how to deal with everyday challenges. Without proactive management and an appropriate governance structure, it is naive to think that outsourced projects will be automatically successful because the execution risk has been transferred to a vendor with lofty credentials. Bottom line, if you want your outsourced projects to be successful, you need to get informed and get involved. We'll show you how.

The information presented in this book is based upon extensive discussions with leading practitioners in the field—both U.S. corporations as well as overseas solution providers. These folks have rolled out many large-scale outsourced projects using the Global Delivery Model (GDM). We believe that the suggestions offered in the book, based upon industry experience and first-hand knowledge, will help you create an organizational framework for successfully executing outsourced projects.

REFERENCES

[AsiaTimes05] "The emperor strikes back with BPO sting." *Asia Times Online*, June 28, 2005. Available online on July 5, 2005, at: *http://atimes.com/atimes/South_Asia/GF28Df03.html.*

[AsiaWeek00] "Racing to Wire Asia." *TelecomAsia.Net*, December 1, 2000. Available online on July 10, 2005, at: *http://www.asiaweek.com/asiaweek/technology/2000/1201/tt.wireasia.html.*

[BostonGlobe05] "Math+Science=Innovation, but US Lags in the Equation." *The Boston Globe*, November 27, 2005.

[BostonGlobe06] "India tech firms seek US talent in offshoring twist." *The Boston Globe*, May 30, 2006.

[BusinessWeek03a] "The New Global Job Shift." *BusinessWeek*, February 3, 2003.

[BusinessWeek03b] "Corporate America's Silent Partner: India." *BusinessWeek*, December 15, 2003.

[BusinessWeek05a] "Global Aging." *BusinessWeek*, January 31, 2005.

[BusinessWeek05b] "Outsourcing Innovation." *BusinessWeek*, March 21, 2005.

[BusinessWeek05c] "The Soft Underbelly of Offshoring." *BusinessWeek*, August 25, 2005.

[BusinessWeek05d] "A New World Economy." *BusinessWeek*, August 22, 2005.

[BusinessWeek05e] "Crouching Tigers, Hidden Dragons." *BusinessWeek*, August 22, 2005.

[BusinessWeek05f] "Designing Dream Machines—in India." *BusinessWeek*, October 17, 2005.

[BusinessWorld05] "BPO Companies: Doomsday Ahead." *BusinessWorld India*, April 11, 2005.

[CNN05a] "Internet Crashes in Pakistan." *CNN International*, June 28, 2005. Available online on July 10, 2005, at: *http://edition.cnn.com/2005/WORLD/ asiapcf/06/28/pakistan.internet.reut/index.html*.

[CNN05b] "India floods toll reaches 1,000." *CNN International*, August 1, 2005. Available online on August 18, 2005, at: *http://edition.cnn.com/2005/ WORLD/asiapcf/08/01/india.flood/index.html*.

[CNN05c] "Violent Protests at Chinese Plant." *CNN International*, August 22, 2005. Available online on August 30, 2005, at: *http://edition.cnn.com/2005/ WORLD/asiapcf/08/22/china.stability.reut/index.html*

[CRN05] "2003–2004 Taulbee Survey." *Computing Research News*, May 2005. Available online on August 18, 2005, at: *http://www.cra.org/CRN/issues/ 0503.pdf*.

[Deloitte05] "Calling a Change in the Outsourcing Market." Deloitte Consulting, 2005.

[EconomicTimes05a] "Why China will Never Beat India in the BPO Space." *The Economic Times*, January 24, 2005.

[EconomicTimes05b] "IT majors shoot pay hikes at pros to kill attrition." *The Economic Times*, March 24, 2005.

[EconomicTimes05c] "KPO Leads Outsourcing Growth." *The Economic Times*, April 8, 2005.

[EconomicTimes05d] "Now, BPOs Open Way to Freelancers." *The Economic Times*, May 26, 2005.

[EconomicTimes05e] "It is shining, exports soar to $17bn." *The Economic Times*, June 3, 2005.

[EconomicTimes05f] "I want a dude for my BPO, can you get me one?" *The Economic Times*, August 4, 2005.

[EconomicTimes05g] "Oh Honey! I need a good night's sleep." *The Economic Times*, August 4, 2005.

[EconomicTimes05h] "Staff Crunch, High Cost Threat to BPO." *The Economic Times*, November 24, 2005.

[EconomicTimes05i] "IT, BPO Exports to Earn $60 billion by 2010." *The Economic Times*, December 13, 2005.

[EconomicTimes06] "Scorecard: IT Companies vs Attrition." *The Economic Times*, January 25, 2006.

[Economist05] "The Bangalore Paradox." *The Economist*, April 23, 2005.

[FBI04] Congressional Testimony of Steven M. Martinez, Deputy Assistant Director, Before the House Government Reform Committee's Subcommittee on Technology, Information Policy, Intergovernmental Relations and the Census. Federal Bureau of Investigation, September 22, 2004.

[Fortune05] "America Isn't Ready." *Fortune*, July 25, 2005.

[Frauenheim04a] Frauenheim, Ed, et al.,"Is Bangalore bigger than Silicon Valley?" *CNET News.com*, July 28, 2004. Available online on May 24, 2005, at: *http://news.com.com/Is+Bangalore+bigger+than+Silicon+Valley/2100-1022_3-5287616.htm.*

[Frauenheim04b] Frauenheim, Ed, "Report: India to host 15 percent of U.S Tech Jobs." *CNET News.com*, December 16, 2004. Available online on May 24, 2005, at: *http://news.com.com/Report+India+to+host+15+percent+of+U.S.+tech+jobs/2100-1022_3-5494147.html.*

[Frost04] "Global Offshore Outsourcing and Offshoring of IT Jobs." Frost and Sullivan, 2004.

[Gartner05] "Outsourcing Flops Blamed on Tunnel Vision." Research report by Gartner, Inc. Reported by *ZDNet.com* on June 22, 2005, at: *http://news.zdnet.com/2100-9589_22-5757832.html.*

[IHT05] "China's Building Boom Becomes a Frenzy." *International Herald Tribune*, October 18, 2005. Available online on October 25, 2005, at: *http://www.iht.com/articles/2005/10/18/news/boom.php.*

[ITAsiaOne03] "Why Buying Global Crossing Makes Sense to STT." *IT AsiaOne*, July 8, 2003. Available online on July 5, 2005, at: *http://it.asia1.com.sg/newsdaily/news003_20030708.html.*

[ITWorld05] "Pakistan begins repairs to fix Internet outage." *ITWorld.com*, July 5, 2003. Available online on July 5, 2005, at: *http://www.itworld.com/Net/2614/050705pak.*

[MSNBC04] "Study: Offshoring of U.S. jobs accelerating." *MSNBC.com*, May 18, 2004. Available online on May 25, 2005, at: *http://www.msnbc.msn.com/id/5003753.*

[MSNBC05] "South Asia a Hotbed for Earthquakes." *MSNBC.com*, October 9, 2005. Available online on October 15, 2005, at: *http://msnbc.msn.com/id/9644778.*

[Nasscom05a] "Facts and Figures." National Association of Software and Service Companies. Available online on May 25, 2005, at: *http://www.nasscom.org/artdisplay.asp?cat_id=811.*

[Nasscom05b] "Indian IT-ITES—FY05 Results and FY06 Forecast." National Association of Software and Service Companies. Available online on July 5,

2005, at: http://www.nasscom.org/download/Indian_IT_ITES_%20FY05_Results_FY06_Forecast.pdf.

[Newsweek04] "Talk is Getting Very Cheap." *Newsweek*, October, 2004. Available online on July 10, 2005, at: *http://www.msnbc.msn.com/id/6199776/site/newswee/k.*

[Newsweek05a] "Grand Theft Identity." *Newsweek*, July 4, 2005. Available online on July 10, 2005, at: *http://www.msnbc.msn.com/id/8359692/site/newsweek/.*

[Pak05] "Task to Detect Major Fault in Pakistan's Internet Cable Set Off." *Pakistan Times Online*, July 4, 2005. Available online on July 10, 2005, at: *http://pakistantimes.net/2005/07/04/top1.htm.*

[TelecomAsia05a] "The New Bandwidth Barons." *TelecomAsia.Net*, April 7, 2005. Available online on July 10, 2005, at: *http://www.telecomasia.net/telecomasia/content/printContentPopup.jsp?id=155261.*

[TelecomAsia05b] "VSNL Completes Takeover of Tyco." *TelecomAsia.Net*, July 6, 2005. Available online on July 10, 2005, at: *http://www.telecomasia.net/telecomasia/article/articleDetail.jsp?id=169055.*

[TimesofIndia04a] "Biotech Outsourcing—The Next Big Wave." *The Times of India*, July 12, 2004.

[TimesofIndia04b] "IT firms caught in attrition blues." *The Times of India*, November 17, 2004.

[TimesofIndia05a] "The World Is Your Oyster, Do You Have the Right Fork?" *The Times of India* (Mumbai edition), April 20, 2005.

[TimesofIndia05b] "Are BPOs complying with the IT Act?" *The Times of India*, April 20, 2005.

[TimesofIndia05c] "Money for Nothing and Clicks are Free." *The Times of India* (Bangalore edition), April 24, 2005.

[TimesofIndia05d] "India to Become KPO Hub: Study." *The Times of India*, May 9, 2005.

[TimesofIndia05e] "Cyber Crimes: Can the West Trust Indian BPOs?" *The Times of India*, July 1, 2005.

[TimesofIndia05f] "KPO can touch $16 b by 2010." *The Times of India*, July 4, 2005.

[TimesofIndia05g] "Airbus A380 to Rely on Indian Chip." *The Times of India*, October 23, 2005.

[UN04] *World Population Prospects, The 2004 Revision.* United Nations Department of Economic and Social Affairs, February, 2005.

[WorldBank04] *GNI per capita 2004, Atlas method and PPP.* The World Bank, July 15, 2005.

[WTO05] *World Trade Report 2005.* The World Trade Organization, June 30, 2005.

2 Development Process— What Really Works?

In This Chapter

- Introduction
- Software Development Methodologies—a Survey
- Why is Success so Elusive?
- Choosing a Methodology for Outsourced Projects
- A Proposed Model for Outsourced Projects

INTRODUCTION

Software development is a complicated business. A 2004 study by Standish Group shows that only 29 percent of projects are completed within the estimated time and budget [Standish04]. The development methodology has a significant impact on project outcome. Other important factors include executive support, project size, requirement stability, user involvement, and project management skills. The dismal overall success rate compels us to take a fresh look at the *process* of software development—whether insourced or outsourced.

Many organizations that lack experience and best-practice guidance cling to outdated practices as methodologies of choice. An approach based on dogma and unrealistic expectations creates a false sense of predictability and control—whether the project is implemented next door or across the ocean. When things don't work out as planned on paper, deadlines slip, tempers rise, and adversarial roles are taken up by the parties involved. In the end, the project is compromised even more. Sometimes a change in *attitude*—away from a command-and-control mindset to more of a discovery-and-adaptation approach—is needed in order to deliver results in the software business. Many managers attempt to define precise project goals too early and too obsessively, creating reams of paper containing detailed tasks, time-lines, and resource allocations. These important-looking activities take up time and energy, only to be junked as soon as reality hits. The early stages of novel projects are characterized by creative exploration, experimentation, and examination of op-tions—unless, of course, similar projects in the same problem domain and with the same implementation technology have been completed a few times already. It re-quires judgment calls, innovative ideas, leadership, and luck to guide a project through the patches of chaos until effective solutions emerge—activities that can hardly be planned on paper in advance.

In this chapter, we look at various development methodologies, and analyze their comparative strengths and weaknesses. We also provide pointers on how you can synthesize a strategy that can be customized for your organization.

SOFTWARE DEVELOPMENT METHODOLOGIES—A SURVEY

There are many competing methodologies being advocated today—Test Driven Development (TDD), Extreme Programming (XP), Scrum, Waterfall, Rational Unified Process (RUP), Feature-Driven Development (FDD), Aspect-Oriented Programming (AOP), Microsoft Solutions Framework (MSF), and so forth. Figure 2.1 shows when various processes came about. However, we focus on the life-cycle models at a higher level. We divide various development approaches into three overarching categories:

- Conventional
- Iterative
- Agile

While some people classify agile processes as a subset of iterative processes, we find it instructive to look at them independently, given their differences in terms of requirement definitions, architectural considerations, documentation needs, and planning activities. In the following sections, we'll study the assumptions, impli-cations, and applicability of various models in local as well as outsourced projects.

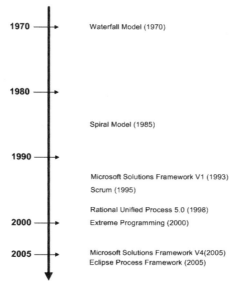

FIGURE 2.1   Life-cycle models and their timelines.

Conventional Model

Among conventional methodologies, the "waterfall" model has dominated the world of software engineering for over three decades. This process was first presented by Dr. Winston Royce in his 1970 seminal paper, Managing the Development of Large Scale Software Systems [Royce70]. In his paper, Dr. Royce dealt with the same fundamental problem that bedevils us today—how to minimize execution risk and create reliable software.

His core thesis was that if you follow an 'invisible' software development process—where implementation ideas reside only in the minds of programmers, and progress is visible only to those people who create the code—then large-scale software development projects will frequently fail. Consequently, document what's in your mind so that others can review, comment, and validate, as well as build their own interfacing systems.

In addition to extensive documentation, Dr. Royce suggested breaking down the software development life cycle into a series of distinct sequential phases (see Figure 2.2). That way, clear milestones can be established and deliverables reviewed. In many ways, this was the first attempt to introduce an organized methodology to an infant field that had hitherto been growing based on a 'code and fix' approach.

In order to undertake large projects successfully, the ad-hoc approach needed to be replaced by a standardized and predictable process.

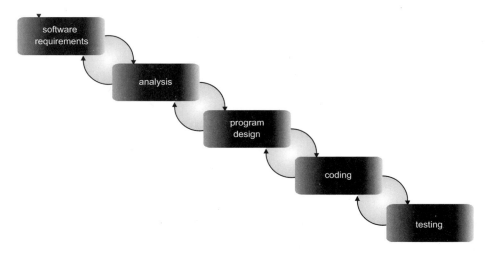

FIGURE 2.2 Phases of the waterfall model.

Although many proponents of the waterfall methodology later overlooked it, Dr. Royce was not entirely comfortable with a single-pass, document-driven approach. He suggested following at least two iterative cycles before delivering the final product to the customer [Royce70].

The waterfall model was adopted by the Department of Defense (DoD) in 1985 as the software development standard DoD-Std-2167. The official blessing of the Pentagon as well as ease of contract administration established the waterfall model as the methodology of choice in government, academic, commercial, and consulting circles. Many organizations loved it because it seemed to give them a sense of control and certainty. If you could establish a plan and make people stick to it—the way business is done in many other engineering disciplines—then you would be able to deliver software projects on time and on budget. The 'plan the work and work the plan' approach seemed to make sense. You *need* predictability of execution when your company's business plans and revenue projections are based on timely completion of software projects.

The waterfall model is used more widely in the industry than many people realize. A recent study showed that more than one-third of the respondents still use this methodology [Neill03], albeit with modifications, such as prototyping. The modified waterfall model is also widely used in offshore software development. Given its phased deliverables, which can be mapped to contractual payment schedules, the waterfall model provides perhaps the most natural way to manage long-distance vendor-client relationships.

Core Features

The waterfall model introduces a degree of engineering discipline to a field whose products are largely intangible to the users until the very end. How do you measure progress if you can't 'see' what's being done? Dr. Royce's answer was to require a set of "overhead" documentation to be produced at each stage, and then to monitor the documentation artifacts as the project moves forward. It is sort of like saying that we can't see what's going on inside a star, but by analyzing the light that's coming out, we can tell the kind of nuclear reaction taking place in its core.

However, unlike the laws of physics, there is no inviolable law that constrains the code and the artifacts to automatically reflect each other's true status. This goal has been the Holy Grail for tool vendors for many years. However, such a perfect tool has not yet been found. And therein lies the core weakness of the waterfall method—you can solve any problem on paper, but that doesn't mean the solution will work in reality. Software is not mathematics!

The core ideas of the waterfall model, as practiced currently, can be summarized as follows:

- Implement the project using clearly demarcated phases: The steps include requirements gathering (determine the top-level use cases as well as functional specifications), design (create high-level and low-level design documents to meet the user requirements), implementation (coding and unit testing), and quality assurance (system and acceptance testing).
- Create documented artifacts at each phase: Produce appropriate documents (requirements document, functional specifications, design documents, test cases, etc.) at each stage and pass them 'over the wall' to successive teams.
- Learn from the best practices in other engineering disciplines: The general approach has been used successfully in other engineering fields, such as civil and mechanical engineering.
- Mitigate risk and provide predictability: Establish a detailed plan with key milestones; on a regular basis, review the artifacts and measure progress.
- Manage contractual relationships efficiently: Vendors can perform detailed requirement analysis, get it approved by the client, go off and build the software, and finally come back to deliver it. Allows fixed-price, fixed-time projects to be contracted out; project management is simplified because of fixed milestones.

Problems

The main problem with the waterfall method is that the actual programming comes too late in the life cycle. By the time coding starts, a tremendous amount of time has already been spent in theoretical exercises—refining requirements, creating voluminous documents, writing pseudo-code, and so on. In short, you have done everything except the most important thing!

Unless the application scope is relatively limited, and the project team is exceptionally well versed with the problem domain and implementing technologies, unlike mathematics or theoretical physics, it is impossible to design a perfect software system on paper. In reality, there are the unpredictable constraints of performance, scalability, security, usability, availability, interoperability, accessibility, and extensibility. Delaying the point in time when the 'rubber hits the road' significantly increases execution risk. Additional drawbacks of the waterfall model that need to be kept in mind are as follows:

- The process is resistant to evolving requirements. In the requirements-gathering phase, the client is expected to visualize and verbalize all of his needs. However, quite often, it is not humanly possible for a person to think through and articulate everything he needs until he *sees* a partially working software. It is difficult for the human mind to imagine a perfect final solution with rich details such as behaviors, logical relationships, and look and feel. On top of that, the imagery has to be immutable, since the requirements will be frozen and signed off.
- The waterfall approach usually does not distinguish between critical and trivial requirements; it gives equal importance to all of them. This kind of static and 'methodical' thinking might work when you are designing a building, but it rarely works in real-life software engineering. You should always try to solve the riskiest problems first and deal with the relatively minor ones later. Out of 100 requirements, 20 might be most important in terms of functional value as well as execution risk. Shouldn't these 20 high-priority features be implemented first?
- In the outsourcing context, you should insist on receiving early versions containing the 'critical success factors.' It is astonishing to see how many companies do not take this common-sense approach.
- Heavy pressure occurs in the later stages of the life cycle. Integrating the subsystems and getting the whole thing to work in the production environment is often a nontrivial problem. You may need to go back to the drawing board a few times. On top of that, if testing reveals major problems in production, you could be forced to consider major schedule-killing rework. These things happen.

Iterative and Incremental Model

As mentioned earlier in the chapter, the fundamental concept of iterative development was suggested by none other than the father of the waterfall method. In his 1970 paper, Dr. Royce recommended iterating twice within the software life cycle. Larman and Basili have stated that the first known conceptual description of iterative and incremental development is found in an article by Walter Shewhart, a quality expert in the Bell Labs [Larman03]. Shewhart proposed a series of "plan-do-study-act" cycles for improving quality.

In the 1970s and 1980s, although the waterfall model remained as the government-mandated, dominant software-engineering process, several large-scale successful projects were executed at IBM and TRW using iterative methods. These projects included the Navy's Trident submarine command-and-control software (more than 1 million lines of code), NASA's avionics software for the Space Shuttle (about half a million of lines of code), and the Air Force's Command Center Processing and Display System Replacement software (more than 1 million lines of code) [Larman03 and Royce98].

In the 1990s, the IT industry went through a phase of massive expansion worldwide. New processors, machines, network infrastructures, operating systems, programming languages, and design patterns emerged and transformed the technology landscape. Along with increasing processing power, hardware costs decreased, connectivity improved, and the global Internet became a business reality. Computing became 'democratic.' The conventional 'one-size-fits-all' prescriptive mentality no longer worked.

On top of the fast-paced technological changes, and in many respects driven by them, the business world underwent rapid seismic changes. The economy became global, and 24/7 operations became commonplace. Business was characterized by faster time-to-market requirements, ability to respond to fast-changing global events, relentless pressure from venture capitalists and investors to demonstrate quick return on investments (dotcom IPOs!), and so on. The new reality was dynamic and unpredictable, necessitating a fundamental reevaluation of how software ought to be developed. In many cases, software was outdated by the time it was completed.

Research data pointed out this trend. A 1994 study by the Standish Group found that 31 percent of projects got cancelled before completion, and companies wasted $140 billion ($81 billion on cancelled projects and $59 billion on delayed projects) out of a total spending of $250 billion [Standish94]. Clearly, conventional models were failing in the brave new world.

In response to the changing business and technology environments, people came up with new ideas on how best to develop software. In the mid-1990s the folks at Rational Corporation came up with RUP, which underscored iterative development within an overarching framework composed of four distinct phases (see Figure 2.3). Microsoft published MSF, a collection of best practices based upon its vast software development experience. MSF combined elements from the waterfall as well as spiral models, and suggested a versioned release strategy—iteratively enriching a set of core functionalities and prioritizing features based upon risk (see Figure 2.4).

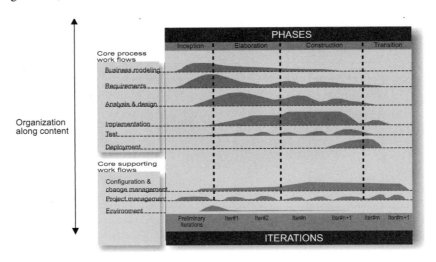

FIGURE 2.3 The Rational Unified Process.

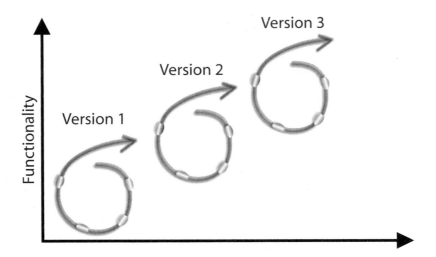

FIGURE 2.4 Microsoft Solutions Framework's *versioned release strategy.*

Although these methodologies had tactical differences, the underlying message was the same. Develop software iteratively and incrementally. Research soon validated that the new paradigm produced better results. After analyzing 50,000 projects over 10 years, a 2004 study by Standish Group found that project failure rates declined to 18 percent (from 31 percent in 1994). Project waste dropped to $55 billion (from $140 billion in 1994) out of total spending of $255 billion ($250 billion in 1994). Major drivers for this improvement included adoption of iterative development practices and reduction in project size [SoftwareMag04 and Standish04].

Core Features

The basic idea of Iterative and Incremental Development (IID) is to do a little development, then quickly integrate, test, deploy, and show whatever you've got to the customer. Make course corrections based upon customer feedback. Repeat the development, testing, and demonstration cycle until the project is completed. Intuitively and practically, this common-sense strategy works wonders in minimizing execution risk and improving project success rates. Real-life statistics mentioned previously bear this out.

IID is not devoid of planning. A coarse-grained project plan allows stakeholders to assign resources, approve budgets, and monitor progress. A fine-grained iteration plan governs short-range tactical objectives. Each iteration can be viewed as a self-contained mini-waterfall.

In order to prepare any kind of plan, you obviously need to know the requirements. IID methodologies try to nail down most of the requirements in the early phases and hope that the specifications remain largely stable in the later phases. You might argue that waterfall takes the same approach. However, the key difference is that in IID, the requirements are derived from iterative construction of working prototypes, not from abstract visualizations of an imaginary product. In IID models, the end users get to play with working prototypes and progressively refine their needs. The empirical 'feedback adaptation' based iterative process produces a vastly more realistic requirement set than the 'virtual' counterpart created in the waterfall model.

The features of 'plan-based' IIDs can be summarized as follows:

- Break up the project life cycle into phases (e.g., RUP phases are inception, elaboration, construction, and transition). Each phase contains multiple iterations. Various 'artifacts' are produced at each phase to record the work done; for example, in RUP, use cases are generated mostly during the inception and elaboration phases.
- Deal with the technically risky as well as functionally critical aspects first.
- Create working prototypes in the early phases (e.g., during the elaboration phase in RUP) to clarify and refine the requirements. These prototypes should

not be 'throw away' code, but an architecturally significant subset of the final system. This approach helps the end users to better define their needs; it also enables the programmers to create a working architectural baseline.

■ Create a coarse-grained project plan for the entire scope of work. At the beginning of each iteration, create a detailed iteration plan containing work breakdown structure and iteration-specific milestones.

■ In each iteration, go through the typical mini-waterfall-like life cycle. Refine requirements, develop, test, integrate, test again, deploy, and demonstrate.

■ Vary the length of each iteration between two to six weeks, based upon project size. The output of each iteration can be used for internal check-ins as well as for customer review, depending upon how the engagement is set up.

■ Within each iteration, create frequent builds (some organizations emphasize daily builds) to ensure regular integration and system-level testing.

Problems

Some iterative processes are considered too 'heavy' for routine projects, given the artifacts, models, and tools needed to implement them. Another conceptual problem arises from the way activities are structured in the preconstruction phases. Some IIDs (such as RUP) suggest that at the conclusion of the earlier phases (e.g., after the inception and elaboration phases in RUP), the requirements are largely stabilized and the architectural risks resolved via iterative construction of working models. Is it practical to try to achieve these dual goals at the same time? Are these goals consistent with each other?

One of the tenets of IID is to select and implement an architecturally significant subset of the user requirements (maybe 5 percent to 10 percent of all use cases) so that the technical risks are identified and addressed early [Booch99]. What if this subset does not contain the use cases that the customer would consider necessary to refine his requirements? If this happens, the suggested approach would drain resources and lose focus when trying to meet disparate goals.

For example, in a typical three-tier Web application, the user interface work is normally done using languages like HTML, JSP, or ASP.NET in the Web tier. Although there might be architectural risks to resolve in the Web tier, many of the critical architectural issues fall in the application and data tiers. If we need to evolve the Web tier (for clients to articulate their requirements) as well as the application and data tiers (to resolve technical risks), it could become a tall order, indeed.

Another problem has to do with the stability of requirements. Although requirements are stabilized in the preconstruction phases in IID, they are allowed to evolve throughout the life cycle. Furthermore, proponents argue that after each iteration, requirements can be modified via the feedback-adaptation cycle [Larman01]. Admittedly, requirements will change less during construction and subsequent phases, but what if those 'small' changes introduce architectural discontinuities? Per the golden 80–20 rule, 20 percent of the requirement changes cause 80 percent of the rework. If some of these destabilizing requirement changes come up during the latter stages, the project schedule could run into serious trouble.

Agile Model

If ever there was a proverbial 'pendulum' in the world of software development methodology, in the latter half of the 1990s, it swung hard toward the prewaterfall days of ad-hoc programming. Although proponents argue that agile models are not really a return to the old days of 'plan-less' programming (and they would largely be right), the agile rebellion against 'too much process' has nevertheless taken us back more toward the world of 'just do it' programming than many care to admit.

In the late 1990s, process rebels like Kent Beck challenged the notion of the exponential cost curve in the project life cycle and proposed a model that flattened the cost curve (see Figure 2.5) [Beck04]. They achieved this seemingly impossible feat by creating a test harness, evolving the system using short iterative cycles, and validating the changes via automated regression testing. By doing so, they were able to 'embrace' changing requirements and had little trouble abandoning the grand planning and requirement analysis phases.

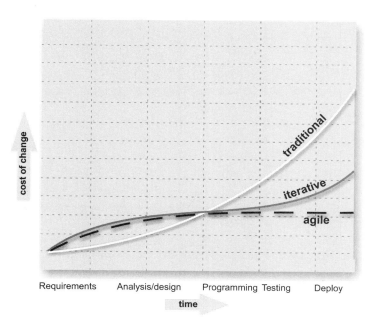

FIGURE 2.5   Cost of change curve for various methodologies.
(Reprinted with permission by Scott W. Ambler.)

In 2001, the proponents of various 'lightweight' iterative methodologies, such as XP, Scrum, Crystal, FDD, Dynamic Systems Development Method (DSDM), etc., got together and established a common platform called the Agile Foundation. They adopted a common 'manifesto' emphasizing human interactions, low documentation overhead, and evolutionary requirements [Agile01a]. Martin Fowler, one of the 17 people who participated in the creation of the agile movement in Snowbird, Utah, describes the new methodology as a balance between having too much process and no process at all [Fowler03] (see Figure 2.6).

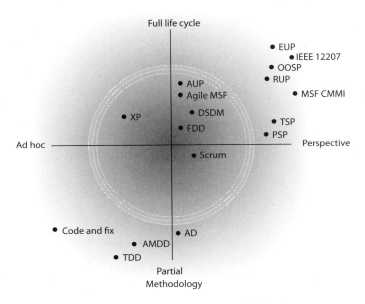

FIGURE 2.6   Classification of iterative methodologies. (Reprinted with permission by Scott W. Ambler.)

The general idea promoted by agile models is to put the development team and the customer in close physical proximity, and to forget about formal planning, ambitious architecture, or voluminous documentation. The goal is to focus on collective, iterative, needs-based programming, with an emphasis on working software rather than impressive documentation as evidence of progress. Heavy unit testing is recommended throughout the life cycle. Collaborative development is encouraged; in some methodologies, pair programming is required. For example, in extreme programming, all code is owned and maintained collectively.

In terms of vendor-client relationships, since the core strategy is to evolve the system in small steps based upon direct customer feedback, traditional fixed-bid contracts are not feasible. Time and material contracts, or variable-scope contracts need to be executed. Given the strong operational coupling required, a high degree of trust and alignment of practices between the parties are essential for friction-free execution of agile projects.

Core Features

- Select a few requirements, develop, test, deploy, and get customer feedback using short time-boxed iteration cycles. Based on the feedback, figure out what to do next.
- Customer requirements are allowed to evolve throughout the project life cycle. The customer reviews each iteration output and has the freedom to alter his requirements.
- People are not just 'resources,' to be switched at will. Individual talents, skills, and knowledge matter. If you have good people, the project is likely to succeed even if the process is bad. If you do not have good people, the project is likely to fail no matter how good the process is [Cockburn01].
- Face-to-face interactions are most effective for hi-fidelity communication.
- Documentation should be 'just enough,' and is not the primary measure of progress. Source code is the best documentation.
- Do not over-plan. Do not over-design. Do not over-engineer. Remove architectural features not needed for the current iteration.
- Write unit-level test cases before writing method code.
- Refactor constantly and massively, if needed. The extensive set of unit tests provide a safety net for catching bugs that arise out of the refactoring process.
- Consider short, time-boxed iteration lengths of one to two weeks. Drop features from the current iteration if you are running out of time.

Problems

To many practitioners, some of the agile programming practices look like 'cowboy programming'—no detailed plans, no documentation, no up-front design—just 'code and fix.' (Although many agile practitioners would disagree with this simplistic characterization, it helps to illustrate the counterpoint.) A few years ago, such an approach would surely have ended a developer's career, but nowadays the agile movement is growing and is impossible to ignore. Nevertheless, dissenting voices exist because of the following general issues:

- Much of the 'agility' of agile methods come from having a team of 'good people'—people who get along with each other, don't mind other people changing their code, and have embedded 'tacit knowledge' regarding the project's intricacies (as opposed to relying on 'external knowledge') [Cockburn02]. That's often asking a lot. What happens if such a cohesive team can't be created due to differences in personality, availability, or geography?

- Without documentation, how can non-colocated stakeholders review, validate, and monitor progress? In the offshore scenario, how will the requirements be communicated overseas? If the offshore team is intimately familiar with the problem domain and has been working with you for a long time, it is possible that you'll be able to execute simple projects based on telephone conversations only. However, the process breaks down when trying to scale up or implement novel features. In such cases, it is often more efficient to explicitly specify your needs in advance via adequate documentation, as opposed to reviewing the delivery and then going through 'scrap and rework' iterations.

- What if the tacit knowledge is wrong? Unless the customer has the resources and the management structure to closely scrutinize the output of every iteration, costly errors could creep in, especially in large projects and under boundary conditions. Should human memory be trusted as complexity increases? How will non-colocated Software Quality Assurance (SQA) teams validate the functionalities? How many people in multiple locations are expected to possess identical tacit knowledge? What happens if those people leave the company?

- Unit testing is not a panacea. Although extremely useful, even a comprehensive set of unit tests cannot guarantee that the code is absolutely foolproof. Think about changes in code behavior due to data dependencies—variations in input data as well as data retrieved from local databases and third-party services. Furthermore, think about how the same code might function differently depending upon load, multithreaded concurrent access, security credentials, network speed, and so on. For example, many popular unit-testing frameworks have difficulty dealing with asynchronous operations.

    Given the limitations of unit testing, refactoring tested code frequently might introduce subtle but grave problems that could show up later in production environment. Moreover, if refactoring involves interface changes, it could potentially impact a large number of calling methods as well as corresponding unit tests [Stephens03]. All these unplanned and sometimes expensive efforts might again become obsolete during the next cycle of refactorings.

- Is architecture really useless? Should you fire all architects? What happens to the design patterns empirically constructed over the past 10 years of software engineering? If you focus only on the requirements of the current iteration and eliminate all 'extra' code that deals with anticipated requirements, are you really designing for change? What about the idea of writing flexible code so as to promote code reuse?

- There is a fundamental disconnect between pattern-oriented architecture and agile programming that cannot easily be explained away (although many people try). Good architectural practice requires thinking about known and emerging requirements in advance (nobody said this was easy), and creating an infrastructure that is reusable, flexible, and extensible. Yes, it takes more time and investment initially, but is it really wise to say that we are not going to design for anticipated or even known requirements that are planned for later iterations? Agile methods insist on dealing with immediate, local, and tactical issues as the methodology of choice. It is hard to reconcile the two world views.

As a possible compromise, some XP practitioners have suggested starting with the simplest solution and then introducing patterns as needed [Rasmusson03]. However, this approach does not fully address the core issue. If you know (admittedly, with different degrees of confidence) that additional requirements are coming down the road, then why not plan for them in advance (at least for the ones with higher probability) by designing a flexible architecture? How many special cases need to come up before deciding to adopt a generic pattern?

■ Experience has shown that a series of local tactical changes can lead to inflexible code. The agile team needs to have the talent and the time to continually refactor so that the appropriate level of abstraction is achieved as the project moves forward. In a large system, cumulative effects of 'Band-Aid' fixes lead to more bugs, less flexibility, and longer development cycles.

■ What about enhancement and maintenance issues? After all, life doesn't stop the moment a project is completed. If it is a successful project, requirements will continue to evolve, the business will (we hope) continue to grow, and new feature requests will pile up. Soon enough, a new project will start to create the next version.

What if the original team is no longer there? Given the dearth of specifications, documentation, and modeling artifacts in an agile project, you are left with only one option—to reverse-engineer the code and try to figure out what was done and why. The "why" questions usually end up causing the most grief. Often the answers border on pure speculation, especially in complex projects. You aren't quite sure what will get broken while attempting to make a 'simple' change, or whether your Band-Aid fixes should instead have been made by extending an existing (but undocumented) framework or feature. Reverse-engineering somebody else's undocumented code is no easy task, as any programmer will tell you; programmers, in general, tend to scrap the whole thing and start from scratch.

WHY IS SUCCESS SO ELUSIVE?

As discussed earlier, per the latest Standish Group study, fewer than one in three projects succeed. The success rate seems to have stagnated since 1996 (although some incremental improvements have taken place). Why has the overall success rate not improved significantly despite the introduction of so many methodologies and despite the lessons learned? Why do we still see big-name companies with decades of experience struggle with release dates, and quality and security problems?

The reason has to do with rising software complexity and pushing the expanding technology envelopes. Realization of Moore's law (the number of transistors in a given space doubles every two years) has meant that computing power has gone up tremendously while the associated costs have gone down (current research in nanotechnology might even accelerate this trend in the future). As hardware and network technology leapfrogged, software systems evolved to keep pace. Today we create software with power and complexity unimagined a decade ago. Software technology has advanced to include breakneck developments in areas such as Web services, mobile computing, real-time collaboration, n-tier distributed systems, grid computing, bioinformatics, data mining, semantic search, information visualization, interactive entertainment, biomedical systems, integrated defense systems, embedded computing, and so on. The 24/7, always-on, globally interconnected, geographically independent world that we live in today did not exist a decade ago. To meet the needs of a fast-changing world, we are not only writing more-complex software, but we're trying to do it faster.

CHOOSING A METHODOLOGY FOR OUTSOURCED PROJECTS

Given the plethora of options that exist out there, which one should you choose for outsourced projects? The question is of more than academic interest, since unless you are somehow miraculously or continuously lucky, chances are that your organization is facing significant challenges with implementation of outsourced projects. A recent survey of 116 global organizations found that 66 percent of the participants thought business benefits were either partially realized or not achieved at all [Deloitte05]. A separate study of 25 world-class organizations (half of them part of Fortune 500) found that 70 percent of the participants had negative outsourcing experiences [Deloitte05]. Clearly, the problem is widespread, and a better way needs to be found.

An important fact to keep in mind is that none of the currently popular software development methodologies were developed in the context of offshore projects or globally distributed teams. While it may be possible to extend some existing models to fit the outsourcing scenario, other methodologies may not be suitable in the offshore context. Sooner or later, as you execute more and more offshore projects, you'll want to construct a life-cycle model that works for your situation. In the following sections, we discuss some of the issues that are likely to come up in your search for an effective offshore development strategy.

Current Outsourcing Process

The most common contractual arrangement when outsourcing is the fixed-bid contract (i.e., fixed price, fixed features, fixed time), and the dominant process followed is the modified waterfall model. The phases involved in the outsourcing context are similar to the classic waterfall model, but modified to accommodate geographically separated entities. They can be broadly categorized as follows:

- **Requirements gathering:** A small team from the offshore vendor organization, usually composed of business analysts and technical architects, visits the client site and collects business requirements. If the intended application is brand new (as opposed to legacy conversion), a 'clickable' prototype is created to help the client visualize and define requirements. The high-level requirements are then expanded into a set of functional requirements. Nonfunctional requirements, like security, performance, and availability, are also determined at this stage, along with acceptance criteria for the end product.

    The set of requirements, specifications, and acceptance criteria are signed off by the client. Estimation and scheduling activities follow, and culminate in a mutually agreed project plan with high-level milestones. The team members return to the offshore location, leaving a small team or an engagement manager on site for coordination purposes.

- **Design:** Offshore team members create high-level design documents containing top-level components and system-level interactions. They also create low-level design documents containing database schemas, component interactions, class structure, pseudo-code of key functions, and unit test cases. The offshore project manager typically creates a 'traceability matrix' that ties together top-level requirements, functional specifications, high-level design elements, specific class modules, and test cases. The traceability matrix serves as a snapshot of how various project components are woven together to meet end-user requirements. It also comes in handy when performing impact analysis and when estimating the effort associated with change requests.

- **Development:** The process followed during the implementation phase varies depending upon the client and the nature of the project. Generally, builds are released to the client based upon project milestones. Some companies follow an incremental development strategy where the features are delivered iteratively. In some cases, the principle of "continuous integration" is followed—globally distributed teams work from a single source code repository, and a build is made from it every day (or as soon as a set of source files are checked in), integrating all pending changes from multisite teams. In many cases, the operational code repository resides in the offshore location, and customers are frequently not interested in monitoring granular changes to the codebase.

Many clients do not have the resources to perform regular code review or closely monitor progress. They rely on the vendor organization to ensure code quality and deliver according to schedule.

As discussed, the source code check-in and the build process varies depending upon the client, the delivery organization, and the size of the project. Some projects have elaborate check-in policies; an authorization 'ticket' has to be obtained prior to checking in the changes. In case of global multivendor projects, often the client's source code repository is different from the vendor's source code management system, and some kind of synchronization (manual or automated) take places between the two. In order to ensure system integrity, unit tests are run prior to check-in, and build verification tests are run after the creation of public builds.

■ **Testing and deployment:** Software quality assurance usually happens in two steps. Unit, regression as well as first-level system testing take place in the offshore location. Second-level system and business testing are conducted at the client location after deployment. Since the cost of fixing a bug is less if caught early in the process, strong emphasis is given in the offshore location to ensuring compliance with the system requirements. Elaborate test plans are created with appropriate test cases and sample input/output values. In some cases, customers insist on achieving a certain percentage of code coverage (via automated testing) prior to delivery and deployment.

Improving the Current Process

Although a great many outsourced projects are being successfully executed every day, there is much room for improvement, as reported in various surveys mentioned previously. Of course, the development methodology is not the only reason for dissatisfaction. Neverthelesss, it does not do anybody any good to adopt a process that has been discarded in the U.S. However, the core problem is that given current organizational practices and insistence on fixed-bid contracts, there is little else that outsourcing vendor organizations can do. Risk mitigation has to be a two-way street.

The basic problem is that the current outsourcing model is handicapped by fundamental structural constraints. Fixed-bid contracts and the resulting adherence to the waterfall model limit flexibility. Yet, many organizations are not sure what to do about it and what adjustments to make in order to improve the process and the outcome. We feel that changes in thought, attitude, and approach are called for. The status quo prevents many organizations from maximizing the potential benefits of outsourcing.

Where Do We Go from Here?

As discussed earlier, there is no silver bullet, no one-size-fits-all prescription when it comes to managing outsourced projects. Each project is unique in terms of operational requirements, business environment, mission criticality, technology choices, and vendor relationships. Our aim is to provide you with an *understanding* of the key issues surrounding various approaches. Once you are aware of the underlying assumptions, motivations, and driving forces behind the methodologies—and their interplay with myriad real-life factors inherent in long-distance interactions—you'll be able to synthesize a strategy to suit your own objectives and circumstances.

Review Requirements and Technology Choices

The first thing to do is to review the business requirements for the project. Are the requirements stable and predictable, as in a legacy conversion project? Or are they tentative and evolving? Requirements, along with resources and schedule constraints (quality is often included as another dimension), constitute the often-cited "project triangle" (see Figure 2.7); varying one dimension causes changes in other aspects, as well.

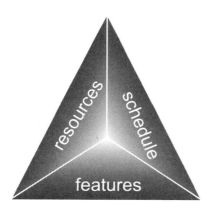 

FIGURE 2.7   The project triangle.

Once you have an idea regarding the volatility of requirements, think about the implementing technology. Is the technology mature and in widespread use? Has the vendor completed similar-size and similar-featured projects successfully using the same technology? Based upon requirement and technology considerations, use the grid in Figure 2.8 to classify your project.

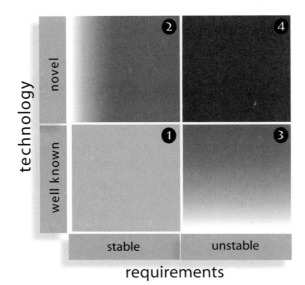

FIGURE 2.8 Classification of projects in terms of requirements stability and technology.

Analysis of Project Types

Having determined the project classification, let's drill down each project type and analyze their characteristics.

Project Type 1 (Stable Requirements, Well-Known Technology)

This category includes legacy software conversion, short-range projects in mature markets, enhancements to existing software, etc. In these projects, you anticipate few surprises in terms of requirement stability and implementing technology.

Suggested contractual model: A small time and material contract followed by a larger fixed-bid contract. The initial contract is for discovery and analysis of requirements and architectural models. The second contract is for implementation and testing.

The first contract covers the following:

- Requirement documentation.
- Creation of a clickable prototype if the user interface is being redesigned.
- Functional and nonfunctional specifications.
- Creation of a working model (not a throw-away prototype) with key features implemented; features to be selected based upon architectural risks and business value.

The underlying goal of the first contract is to ensure that the vendor actually 'got it' in terms of what needs to be done, and that everybody is on the same page regarding the implementation strategy.

The second contract is for construction of the rest of the software. Delivery is to be made iteratively, and prioritized by technical risk and business value.

Suggested development model: Plan-based iterative model.

Project Type 2 (Stable Requirements, New Technology)

Projects in this category face undefined execution risks. Consequently, the strategy is to experiment and resolve technical risks prior to full commitment.

Suggested contractual model: An initial time and material contract followed by a fixed-bid contract. The first contract covers the following:

- Requirement documentation.
- Creation of a clickable prototype if the user interface is being redesigned.
- Functional and nonfunctional specifications.
- Creation of a pilot application using the new technology.

The pilot implements features with the highest technical risks. The goal is to 'get your feet wet' with the technology—to discover the eddies and undercurrents, so to speak, before jumping in the water. Depending upon the project size and technology complexity, multiple pilots may be created to cover the range of critical requirements.

The second contract is for full-fledged development of the rest of the software. The technology risks have been identified and addressed in the preceding phases, so the remaining work should be fairly predictable.

Suggested development model: Agile model for technology risk-resolution phase; plan-based iterative model for implementation phase.

Project Type 3 (Unstable Requirements, Well-Known Technology)

This category includes long-range projects in mature companies or greenfield projects in start-up companies.

Suggested contractual model: Time and material.

When requirements are 'soft,' getting into a fixed-bid contract is a recipe for disaster. If the requirements are predicted to evolve for a while and then stabilize, you might consider a time-and-material contract for the first part and a fixed-bid contract for the latter part.

Suggested development model: Consider agile-leaning, iterative processes with short iteration cycles until requirements come into focus. You can switch to plan-based iterative practices once requirements stabilize. In order to execute an agile model offshore, you'll need to put in place appropriate IT infrastructure, toolsets, and management structure. You'll need to have the capability to rapidly transmit requirements offshore, keep explaining and elucidating the fine points until the offshore developers understand the specifications, and get back a deployed working version with the requested changes.

For larger projects, create a mix of onsite and offshore programmers working together as a team (remember the 80–20 golden rule; 20 percent onsite, 80 percent offshore). The two teams need to leverage all available tools to overcome the information loss that inevitably takes place in non-face-to-face communications. Consider sending a domain expert offshore to ensure that the shifting requirements are communicated effectively and accurately.

It may be impossible to implement some of the agile methodologies in their entirety. For example, you may not be able to co-locate the customer and the offshore teams, as suggested by XP. In general, documentation and modeling needs go up in the offshore scenario to facilitate hi-fidelity communication between geographically separated parties. The trick is to strike a balance so that the effort associated with creating the artifacts don't choke off productivity and slow the project down too much. It is a dynamic act requiring transparency, trust, and course corrections.

Project Type 4 (Unstable Requirements, New Technology)

This category includes research and development work, as well as potentially some of the most important game-changing projects in your organization. However, these projects are also among the most difficult to manage and outsource.

Suggested contractual model: Time and material.

You need a solid vendor relationship, proven management skills, and competent technical management to successfully offshore this kind of project. These projects require trust, very high 'signal-to-noise-ratio' in communications, and close coordination between multiple parties. Not only will you be trying to figure out the emerging business requirements, but you will simultaneously try to discover the capabilities of an unproven platform. The learning curve for technology adoption might be steep and necessitate frequent, sometimes face-to-face, interaction with the technology vendor organization.

Our experience suggests that it is possible to outsource high-risk projects if you are working with a trusted and skilled vendor organization. You also need to have an appropriate number of highly competent technical staff onsite to help out with technology R&D issues, and to fine-tune offshore deliveries. (Once again, consider applying the 80–20 rule; 20 percent of staff onsite for R&D and 80 percent staff offshore for R&D and implementation.) One strategy is to create pilot applications onsite, incorporating critical design and implementation decisions, and then send the sample solution offshore to apply the techniques across the requirements spectrum. The offshore team will likely encounter additional issues during implementation. Dead-end questions will need to be resolved by discovering workarounds, doing additional R&D, or by abandoning the current approach altogether and going back to the drawing board. Improvise, innovate, and adapt.

Ideally, you'll want to keep the iterations short, but given the uncertainties associated with novel technology, be prepared for significant and unexpected delays, and many dead-end efforts. This is where the trust factor comes in. You need to be able to trust that the vendor is not fleecing you with seemingly endless technical wild-goose chases. You'll also need capable in-house staff to help out the offshore team and liaise with the technology provider.

Suggested development model: Agile-leaning methodologies with short iterations until technical risks are resolved and requirements are stabilized (if ever); you can switch to iterative plan-based methodologies once requirements and technology are stabilized.

General Suggestions for All Project Types

In the preceding section, we classified outsourced projects into four general categories and suggested approaches to deal with their fundamentally different risk profiles. In this section, we present some general recommendations that are applicable regardless of the project type.

- Iterate as frequently as possible without incurring too much overhead in terms of delivery and deployment efforts. Sometimes you may find even a one-week iteration length to be too long. When under severe time pressure, you might want to monitor progress *daily* and make sure the work is coming along exactly as you want. However, delivery and deployment on a daily basis may not be feasible given the overhead involved. In such cases, consider viewing the work-in-progress software directly in the remote developer's machine (using a number of commercially available tools, such as PCAnyWhere or RAdmin).

- Do not underestimate the importance of code review by in-house technical staff who are familiar with the business logic. Every code drop should be reviewed randomly (e.g., 10-percent random code coverage) as well as selectively (focus on changes in core modules). Many a times, code review catches subtle but critical bugs that might have evaded the SQA process, especially if the scenarios are complex and time-consuming to set up. Moreover, the code review process helps maintain high programming standards and adherence to agreed-upon coding conventions. We believe that on-site code review is an essential component of success, although it is frequently not performed in outsourced projects.

- Integrate code from distributed teams frequently. Some organizations do it daily. Some practice *continous integration*. As a matter of practice, we suggest at least once a week. The exact frequency will depend upon the project size and complexity.

■ Adopt and create reusable frameworks. For example, Microsoft offers a number of 'application blocks,' such as Data Access Application Block, User Interface Process Application Block, Smart Client Offline Application Block etc. These nuggets of infrastructure code have been optimized, debugged, and tested in a variety of real-life applications. They are royalty-free and should be used to reduce, streamline, and simplify your application code.

■ If you have created any custom frameworks that have been successfully used in past projects, they should be reused even if the vendor is new to them. Using proven frameworks (custom or third-party) reduces the amount of custom code that needs to be written, decreases development and SQA time, and makes your codebase maintainable.

■ Don't be afraid to use standard design patterns. A few years ago, design patterns were the rage. Today, with the advent of agile methodologies, they seem to have fallen a bit out of style. However, patterns remain essential if you want to convey design ideas and explain implementations across oceans. Furthermore, by implementing a common approach, patterns make it easier to maintain and evolve the body of code, possibly by different vendors. Patterns are important today for the same reason they were important a decade ago—they promote reusability, flexibility, and clarity. In outsourced projects (or in any project for that matter) the goal is not just to create working software, but also to create *maintainable* software. Vendor organizations might change, vendor staff might change. A different vendor in another country might need to understand and modify the code. You should use a design that is proven, widely known, and not unique to a vendor. Design patterns fit the bill.

■ Figure out a way to manage turnover of vendor staff. No matter how much we try to treat people as replaceable resources, unless you are outsourcing low-value commodity functions only, your project needs people who have the domain knowledge. These people are familiar with the application's key algorithms, overall cause-and-effect relationships, special cases, and boundary conditions. For complex applications, this knowledge comes at a price (i.e., training as well as on-the-job experience) and is not easily replaceable. Get to know the people working on your project. Your contract with the vendor should contain clauses designed to minimize staff turnover (e.g., consider arrangements where you can pay incentive bonuses directly to key offshore team members). Given the relatively high attrition rates in major outsourcing destinations, be prepared for personnel changes; but at the same time, try your best to protect your investment in a remote developer's productivity and competency.

■ To measure quality and progress, set up useful metrics. Traditional service-level agreements contain measures that are often difficult to interpret and impossible to verify independently. Make sure you are monitoring project health by looking at meaningful data, such as defect density, bug re-open rate, code churn, code coverage, project velocity, and so on.

■ Do not ignore the importance of meaningful hi-fidelity communications between the onsite management team and the offshore development team. If there isn't an onsite engagement manager (dedicated or shared) who acts as the bridge between the client and the solution provider, the overall execution risk and level of friction go up significantly, especially if the project needs rich domain knowledge. In such cases, you need to redouble your efforts to establish and sustain open communications. During critical phases of time-sensitive projects, you may need to have multiple daily contacts with the offshore team via phone, chat, or application-sharing—once at the beginning of their day to communicate objectives and once at the end of their day to review progress. Yes, it is tough, but that's the way it has to be done sometimes.

■ No matter how frequently you hold virtual meetings and conduct teleconferences, consider sending 'ambassadors' (as Fowler calls them) to offshore locations periodically [Fowler04a]. To the offshore team, ambassadors represent a flesh-and-blood embodiment of the client. Their presence helps to inspire, motivate, focus, and validate the remote team's work.

A PROPOSED MODEL FOR OUTSOURCED PROJECTS

While we do not wish to introduce yet another paradigm in the over-crowded world of development methodologies, we would like to present a strategy that has worked for us in many large outsourced projects. The proposed model is by no means a full-fledged methodology—although it embodies key ideas from many different practices. We call it the "multi-pass" model.

The multi-pass model works best when requirements are relatively stable. The idea is similar to the way a painter draws a picture (see Figure 2.9). First, look at the broad requirement set and try to come up with a base architecture for the solution. Iteratively refine the core working models, which evolve into the system's backbone. Once the base architecture is established, incrementally enrich the functionalities via multiple passes through the requirements gamut until the feature-set is complete.

The proposed model does not replace IID or agile methodologies. It delineates a 'meta process' whereby instead of perfecting a few features in each iteration, you sweep through the selected requirements spectrum and improve *all* of them to some extent (albeit to different degrees, based upon priority). Instead of digging deep in a limited area, select the significant areas and then dig in *all* of them—as deeply as the iteration plan allows.

The multi-pass model does not force you to treat all requirements evenly or deal with every requirement in a given pass. Select mission-critical features first and

FIGURE 2.9   The multi-pass model.

progressively 'polish' them. The key idea is that since we are implementing *a number of* significant features simultaneously, we are more likely to spot potential problems with architecture, performance, interoperability, security, and availability than if we had focused on a few features intensely. If we drill down in one area but leave the other areas unexplored, in our experience, there is a greater chance of encountering architectural discontinuities, and unforeseen logical, operational, and interface problems. Dealing with unexpected surprises sooner rather than later is an essential goal of the multi-pass model.

You could argue that the multi-pass model does not result in useful software until a number of iterations have been completed, whereas if we had perfectly implemented a few features, then the customer would have gotten a partially working piece of software in case the project got cancelled. This argument certainly has merit, but it depends on the definition of what constitutes 'working software.' A few highly developed features may or may not be sufficient to deliver any business value. An *integrated* set of features may be needed in order for the software to be useful (imagine perfecting a reporting module without creating a corresponding data entry module). In any case, the multi-pass model does not prevent you from refining a subset of the requirements. It all depends on how conservatively or ambitiously you select the features for co-development.

CONCLUSION

In this chapter, we studied various development methodologies, and presented their core ideas and implications. Given the fact that over half of the projects (whether onsite or offshore) are over budget or past deadlines, we feel that it would be more effective to take a pragmatic, rather than dogmatic, approach. Given the separation of space and time, offshore projects carry higher execution risks. Consequently, outsourced projects require greater understanding of the underlying risk factors, better project governance capabilities, greater management involvement (usually much greater than initially anticipated), close monitoring of project health-related metrics, and a collaborative working relationship with the vendor organization based upon earned trust and mutual respect.

In the next chapters, we'll look at a specific collaboration platform—Microsoft Visual Studio 2005 Team System (VSTS)™—and learn about its capabilities in terms of facilitating execution of outsourced projects. We are excited about this new product and feel that its rich, built-in feature set, as well as its extensibility points, will help better manage geographically separated teams. We'll take an in-depth look at how VSTS can be leveraged and extended to provide a 'friction-free,' distributed, collaborative environment.

REFERENCES

[Agile01a] Beck, Kent, et al., The Agile Manifesto, 2001. Available online on May 24, 2005, at: *http://www.agilemanifesto.org.*

[Beck04] Beck, Kent and Cynthia Andres, *Extreme Programming Explained: Embrace Change,* Addison-Wesley, ISBN: 0321278658, 2004.

[Booch99] Booch, Grady, et al., "The Unified Process." *IEEE Software*, May/June 1999.

[Cockburn01] Cockburn, Alistair, "Agile Software Development 2: The People Factor." *IEEE Computer*, November 2001.

[Cockburn02] Cockburn, Alistair, "Agile Software Development Joins the 'Would-Be' Crowd." *Cutter IT Journal*, 2002: vol. 15, no. 1, pp. 6–12.

[Deloitte05] "Calling a Change in the Outsourcing Market." Deloitte Consulting, 2005.

[Fowler03] Fowler, Martin, "The New Methodology." ThoughtWorks, April 2003. Available online on May 24, 2005, at: *http://www.martinfowler.com/articles/newMethodology.html.*

[Fowler04a] Fowler, Martin, "Using an Agile Software Process with Offshore Development." ThoughtWorks, April 2004. Available online on May 24, 2005, at: *http://www.martinfowler.com/articles/agileOffshore.html.*

[Larman01] Larman, Craig, et al., "How to Fail with the Rational Unified Process: Seven Steps to Pain and Suffering." Valtech Technologies and Rational Software, 2001.

[Larman03] Larman, Craig and Victor Basili, "Iterative and Incremental Development: A Brief History." *IEEE Computer*, June 2003.

[Neill03] Neill, Colin and Phillip Laplante, "Requirements Engineering: The State of the Practice." *IEEE Software*, November/December 2003.

[Rasmusson03] Rasmusson, Jonathan, "Introducing XP into Greenfield Projects:Lessons Learned." *IEEE Software*, May/June 2003.

[Royce70] Royce, Winston, "Managing the Development of Large Scale Software Systems." *Proceedings of IEEE WESCON*, August 1970, pp.1–9.

[Royce98] Royce, Walker, *Software Project Management, A Unified Framework.* Addison-Wesley, ISBN: 81-7808-013-3, 1998.

[SoftwareMag04] "Standish: Project Success Rates Improved Over 10 Years." *SoftwareMag.com,* January 15, 2004. Available online on July 2, 2005, at: *http://www.softwaremag.com/L.cfm?Doc=newsletter/2004-01-15/Standish.*

[Standish94] "The CHAOS Report." The Standish Group International, Inc., 1994. Available online on July 2, 2005, at: *http://www.standishgroup.com/sample_research/PDFpages/chaos1994.pdf.*

[Standish04] "2004 Third Quarter Research Report." The Standish Group International, Inc., 2004. Available online on July 2, 2005, at: *http://www.standishgroup.com/sample_research/PDFpages/q3-spotlight.pdf.*

[Stephens03] Stephens, Walker and Doug Rosenberg, *Extreme Programming Refactored: The Case Against XP.* Apress, ISBN: 1-59059-096-1, 2003.

3 Leveraging VSTS and Customizing MSF Agile

In This Chapter

- Introduction
- VSTS for Offshore Software Development
- Overview of MSF
- MSF Agile
- Designing a Process for Outsourcing
- An Agile Process for Outsourcing
- Traceability Matrix
- Technical Review: Customizing Process Template
- Technical Review: Creating a Traceability Matrix

INTRODUCTION

Few topics in software development arouse as emotional a response as the issue of following the right 'process.' As we saw in Chapter 2, "Development Process—What Really Works," the topic is still a matter of ongoing debate, depending on your philosophy, team size, experience, mission criticality, and organizational culture. However, it makes little sense to insist on following a universal process for all situations, ignoring ground realities. A safety-critical organization like NASA and a teen-focused music Web site company do not follow identical software development practices. After all, projects vary in terms of scope, complexity, underlying technology, importance, time-to-market considerations, resource allocations, tolerance for errors, performance requirements, and so on.

Consequently, it makes more sense to talk about creating a generic framework that can be extended based upon each delivery organization's needs. MSF provides a process-creation framework that you can use to create custom processes templates to meet your specific needs. VSTS contains an integrated set of tools to 'enact' processes that are created using MSF. (You are not limited to only Microsoft-supplied process templates, you can define your own custom processes or use existing processes, like RUP or Scrum). The VSTS platform offers powerful capabilities to define and implement your preferred process throughout the enterprise.

A process devoid of an implementation mechanism often ends up being purely an academic exercise. The friction associated with switching between multiple tools for managing documents, work items, source code, test cases, and reports is one of the reasons why many lofty processes fall by the wayside. An MSF-VSTS combination enables you to not only create abstract process models, but also to roll them out in your organization via an integrated product suite.

In the following sections, we look at the architecture of VSTS and MSF. We also create a simple process for managing offshore projects. After necessary customizations, the modified process template is imported into VSTS and made available to the entire project team. Project managers, architects, developers, SQA professionals, and other stakeholders work together as per the workflow defined in the process. Thanks to VSTS, the overhead associated with ensuring compliance with the process methodology is substantially reduced, and people can focus on getting the actual work done.

INTRODUCING VISUAL STUDIO TEAM SYSTEM

VSTS offers a suite of products and technologies for end-to-end software life-cycle management. It brings together various stakeholders in a common platform so that they can work better, faster, and with less friction (see Figure 3.1). Although there are various disparate tools in the market for project management, requirements gathering, modeling, development, unit testing, system testing, process management, and issue management, VSTS offers an *integrated* solution. Furthermore, the system provides extensibility points for customization as well as integration with compatible products from third-party partners. By providing an integrated underlying framework, VSTS offers interoperability between domain-specific tools—for example, between software architecture, development, and testing tools. It also facilitates better communication and coordination between distributed team members.

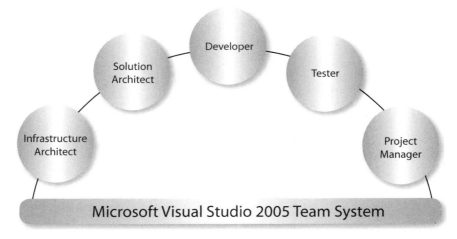

FIGURE 3.1   VSTS provides an integrated suite of project management tools.

VSTS and Offshore Software Development

We feel that VSTS is uniquely equipped to help with the inherent challenges of off-shore software development. During VSTS development, the under-development product was used internally at Microsoft (a practice called "dog-fooding") to coordinate the activities of far-flung development teams. The following VSTS features are important in the offshore scenario:

Better communication and coordination: VSTS provides a powerful platform for managing work items (e.g., tasks, bugs, enhancement requests) as well as source code. The underlying architecture is optimized for operating over the Internet. The framework offers custom notification features associated with key events to help improve communication with offshore team members.

Better status reporting: VSTS enables you to collect status information from offshore team members and automatically disseminate the data to different parties at various levels of granularity. This capability significantly reduces the frustration, effort, and expense associated with gathering information manually, especially when the teams are not interacting face to face. VSTS automatically creates a project portal site for every team project. The Web site provides insight into critical metrics regarding bug counts, task status, project health, and so on.

Better code quality: VSTS offers a unit-testing framework that allows you to automatically run selected tests during check-ins, after builds, or at any other time. The testing and source code management modules generate code coverage, code analysis, and code churn data, enabling you to gain better visibility into what's happening offshore. Check-in policies allow you to ensure code quality and compliance with corporate standards. You can leverage the toolset to ascertain as well as manage the quality and stability of the code being delivered by the offshore team.

Overview of Visual Studio Team System

VSTS is packaged as three separate product suites with different goals (see Figure 3.2):

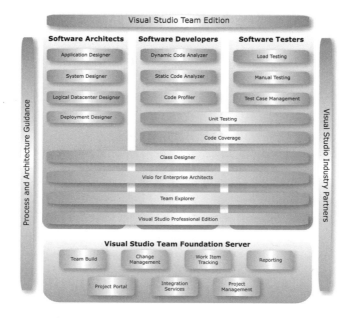

FIGURE 3.2   VSTS is packaged as three different products with an underlying server platform.

Visual Studio Team Architect: Facilitates creation of software and deployment architecture; consists of modeling tools such as Application Connection Designer, Logical Datacenter Designer, System Designer, and Deployment Designer.

Visual Studio Team Developer: Geared toward development and unit testing; contains Code Analyzer (static and dynamic), Profiler, and Unit Test Tool.

Visual Studio Team Test: Focused on software quality assurance; consists of Test Manager, Unit Test Tool, Web Test Tool, and Load Test Tool.

If you want the full range of functionalities, you can purchase Visual Studio Team Suite, which has all the features contained in the three products categories.

Underpinning the individual modules is the server component—the Team Foundation Server (TFS). TFS binds together the entire project team and is the core engine for enabling team capabilities. Without it, VSTS would be a standalone product, much like the previous versions of Visual Studio. TFS provides a shared central platform with the following features:

Work Item Management: Manages and tracks standard and custom work item types, such as scenarios, defects, and enhancement request tasks; allows customization of workflow, state transition, and queries.

Version Control: Provides branch/merge, shelving, check-in policies, work item associations, and so forth.

Build Management: Creates public builds in a dedicated build machine, runs build verification tests, and allows customization of build-related steps.

Status Reporting: Contains built-in reports related to bugs, tasks, tests, builds, and various quality indicators; additional reports can be created using SQL Server 2005 Reporting Services™.

Project Portal: Provides a Windows SharePoint Services™ (WSS) based Web site containing reports, alerts, shared documents, and threaded discussions.

Integration with Microsoft Office™: Offers out-of-the-box integration with Microsoft Office Excel 2003™ and Microsoft Office Project 2003™; additional integration is possible with other Microsoft products as well as third-party software.

Process Guidance: Provides customizable process-management framework; two built-in process templates provided—MSF for Agile Software Development (a flexible process for rapid development) and MSF for CMMI Process Improvement (contains features needed for CMMI Level 3 compliance). Additional process templates can be created from scratch, derived from the built-in templates, or imported from third-party sources.

The only major tool missing from the above list is software for capturing requirements and creating linked work breakdown structures. Third-party tools (e.g., Borland CaliberRM™) are available to fill the gap.

Team Foundation Server Architecture

TFS is designed as a three-tier system (see Figure 3.3). You can deploy TFS in single-server mode (application tier and data tier in the same machine) or dual-server mode (application tier and data tier in separate machines).

Data Tier: The data tier contains relational databases as well as an analytical database hosted by SQL Server 2005™. The databases store persistent information related to projects, users, work items, builds, tests, events, source files, and so on. The data warehouse captures key metrics from the relational tables and stores them in an Online Analytical Processing (OLAP) cube. The cube contains aggregated data for various measures; the information can be sliced along various dimensions using predefined and custom reports.

Application Tier: The application tier consists of VSTS-specific Web services, Windows services, SQL Server 2005 Reporting Services, and Windows Share-Point Services. The application tier communicates with the back-end data tier using a trusted subsystem security model (as opposed to delegation or impersonation); a selected service account is used to talk to the data tier. The application tier also contains various adapters, which are responsible for retrieving data from the operational databases and inserting them into the analytical data warehouse.

Client Tier: The client tier contains Team Explorer, and various client tools, plug-ins, and utilities. Although you can directly access the Web services running in the application tier, it is recommended that you normally go through the well-defined object model.

Team Foundation Server Integration Services

Notice in Figure 3.3 that the application tier contains Integration Services. These services are as follows (see Figure 3.4):

Registration Service: Used for adding new tools, events, artifacts, and so forth.

Notification Service: Publish-subscribe (pub-sub) event service that supports predefined as well as custom events. Notifications include emails as well as Web service calls.

Linking Service: Maintains loosely coupled relationships between various artifacts; provides benefits of a 'virtual repository.'

User Groups Service: Manages non-Active Directory groups in VSTS.

Common Structure Service: Manages project classifications and structures.

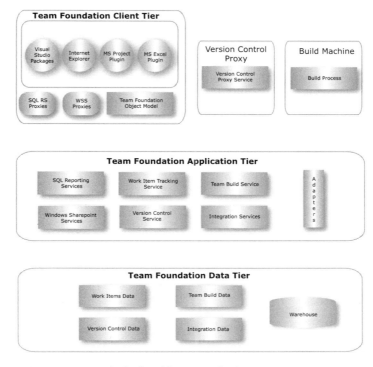

FIGURE 3.3   Technical architecture of VSTS.

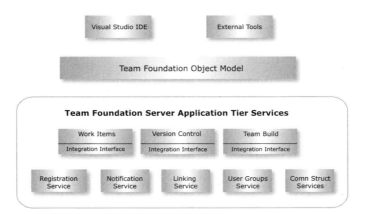

FIGURE 3.4   TFS application tier services.

Team Foundation Server Warehouse Adapters

TFS warehouse adapters collect information from the operational databases, apply necessary transformations, and insert the data in a relational database. A Web service is invoked on a scheduled basis to run the TFS warehouse adapters and refresh the OLAP cubes once the adapters have finished pushing data to the relational store (see Figure 3.5). The database schema is extensible; it can accommodate changing work item types. Custom adapters can be created to populate the data warehouse from external or custom data sources. You can analyze the stored data using built-in or custom reports created with SQL Server 2005 Reporting Services. You can also browse the databases using Microsoft Excel.

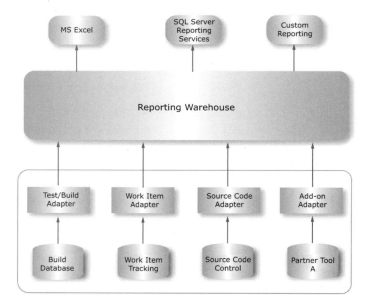

FIGURE 3.5   Adapters populate the TFS data warehouse from operational data stores.

INTRODUCING MICROSOFT SOLUTIONS FRAMEWORK

MSF is a process methodology that has been used internally at Microsoft since 1991. Currently in version four, MSF is essentially a framework for creating software development processes. In addition to a generic, extensible meta-model, MSF contains instantiations of two methodologies—MSF for Agile Software Development (MSF Agile) and MSF for CMMI Process Improvement (MSF Formal) (see

Figure 3.6). Third-party extensions include RUP, XP, and Scrum. In this chapter, we focus on MSF Agile and illustrate how it can be customized for offshore software development.

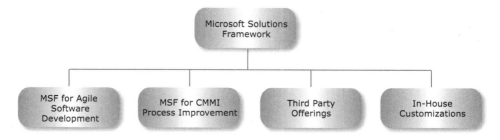

FIGURE 3.6   MSF family of processes.

INTRODUCING MSF AGILE

MSF Agile is a low-ceremony methodology that emphasizes scenario-based, iterative, test-driven, metric-focused, and result-oriented approaches to software development (see Figure 3.7). MSF Agile takes a minimalist approach, leaving it to each organization to add additional roles, rules, constraints, reports, and views.

FIGURE 3.7   MSF Agile contains extensive process guidance. (Source: MSF Agile Process Guidance).

MSF Agile embodies the following core concepts:

Iterative Development

MSF Agile advocates an iterative and incremental software development process (see Figure 3.8). Without being too prescriptive regarding the nature of iterations or lumping various iterations into distinct higher-level 'phases,' MSF Agile simply states that each iteration should contain planning, development, and testing activities, with the aim of creating a working subset of the entire feature list.

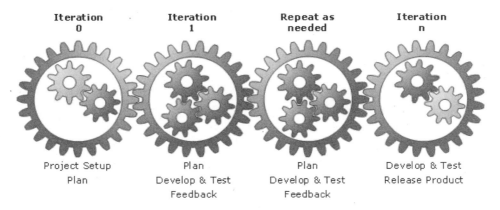

FIGURE 3.8   Iterative development is a key focus in MSF Agile (source: MSF Agile Process Guidance).

Roles

Roles are 'hats' worn by people when taking part in software development activities. In smaller teams, a single person often plays multiple roles. Roles help organize the activities of various stakeholders and manage interactions between various parties. MSF Agile defines six nonhierarchical peer-based roles (see Figure 3.9). The lack of hierarchy in the role model is deliberate, the idea being that leadership will emerge organically from within the team as opposed to being imposed from above, often without stakeholder buy-in. Although the idea might sound somewhat optimistic in real life, MSF Agile does not *preclude* a hierarchical configuration for the team structure, if you so choose.

Personas

Personas represent groups of fictional users. The goals and concerns of personas help the development team understand the different manners in which the software

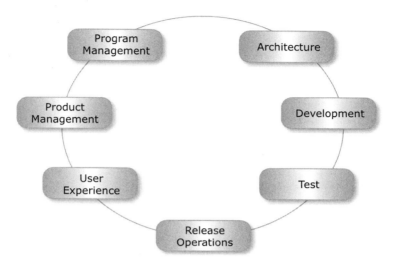

FIGURE 3.9   Roles in MSF Agile are peer-based.

could be used by the end customer. A persona represents a *specific* entity (e.g., production manger, marketing manager, quality assurance manager, etc.) that uses the system. In the absence of on-site customers guiding development efforts, personas enable the team to understand usability, functional, interoperability, and performance requirements.

Scenarios

A scenario depicts a specific path taken by the persona to achieve one of his goals. Since there could be potentially a large number scenarios in a complex product, only the significant ones need to be specified. Scenarios allow various parties to visualize key aspects of the system and their interplay in terms of achieving functional objectives. Since they often cut across various components, modules, and service boundaries, scenarios force people to think holistically about the entire application and help work out integration issues early on.

Work Streams and Activities

Work streams and activities describe routine actions performed by various team members. Work streams are collections of related activities. MSF Agile contains 14 work streams, and each of them is performed by a single role. Table 3.1 lists various work streams and their corresponding roles.

TABLE 3.1 Work Streams and Roles in MSF Agile (Source: Microsoft)

Work Stream	Roles
Create Solution Architecture	Architect
Capture Project Vision	Business Analyst
Create a Quality-of-Service Requirement	Business Analyst
Create a Scenario	Business Analyst
Build a Product	Developer
Fix a Bug	Developer
Implement a Development Task	Developer
Guide Iteration	Project Manager
Guide Project	Project Manager
Plan an Iteration	Project Manager
Release a Product	Release Manager
Close a Bug	Tester
Test a Quality-of-Service Requirement	Tester
Test a Scenario	Tester

Figure 3.10 depicts how various entities, activities, and artifacts are interrelated in MSF Agile.

Reports

MSF Agile contains an extensive set of reports that provide information regarding project status, health, and progress (see Figure 3.11 for a sample). Reports constitute an integral part of the development process, because they enable you to take a metric-based, factual approach, as opposed to an ideologically motivated, dogmatic approach toward project management. When stakeholders can easily view critical project metrics—for instance, remaining tasks, bug fix rates, regressed bugs, velocity, passed and failed tests, and so forth—they can make informed decisions about necessary course corrections. Access to near-time reports (there is a configurable delay associated with updating the data warehouse from operational data stores) enables the team to be proactive, objective, and responsive in the middle of the 'fog' of project execution.

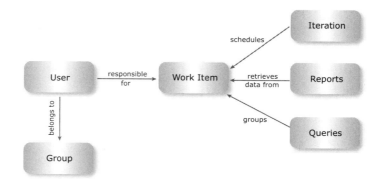

FIGURE 3.10   Relationship between entities, activities, and artifacts in MSF Agile.

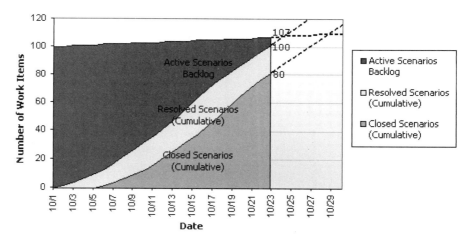

FIGURE 3.11   Reports provide near-time information on project status.

DESIGNING A PROCESS FOR OUTSOURCING

In terms of designing a process for offshore development, as discussed earlier, we believe that there is no universally perfect solution. The following factors need to be considered when designing the nuts and bolts of a workflow:

Relationship between onsite and offshore organizations: Is the offshore organization a captive branch office or a vendor? Organizational arrangements affect operational workflow issues. For example, a common question is whether a single information repository (e.g., for source code and issue management) will be used by both offshore and on-site teams, or whether various parties will maintain their own separate systems.

Project governance model: How are the on-site and offshore project management, development, and SQA teams configured and managed? What is the communication plan? Who interacts with whom across the ocean? Organizations sometimes prefer a single point of contact for the offshore team. However, this approach is often neither feasible nor desirable in larger projects if you want to avoid bottlenecks. There are pros and cons associated with each choice; you need to decide how they apply in your own scenario.

Engagement management and delivery: How are the requirements conveyed overseas, and how are the deliveries deployed? Is there an on-site engagement manager (in a vendor-client relationship) or a local project manager/tech lead (in a captive scenario) who manages communications with the offshore team? Is the offshore team responsible for deployment in test, pre-production, and production environments, or is that work performed by the on-site team?

Contractual arrangements: The contractual arrangement between offshore and on-site entities is relevant because it impacts the nature of interaction between the teams. For example, some organizations are interested in reviewing the final product (or intermediate versions at various milestones) and do not care much about what happens 'under the hood.' Other clients insist on reviewing progress weekly. For critical projects, progress may be monitored *daily*. For complex projects, there may be multiple vendor organizations involved. The interaction model needs to be clearly defined and consistently followed in order to avoid the frustrations and inefficiencies inherent in long-distance, multi-organizational coordination. In general, we suggest taking a "trust but verify" approach.

AN AGILE PROCESS FOR OUTSOURCING

In this section, we present a relatively simple process that we have successfully used in numerous real-life offshore projects. Instead of creating a brand new process from scratch, we use MSF Agile as the base and tweak it to support offshore software development (see Figure 3.12). We call the new process the "Agile Outsourcing" process.

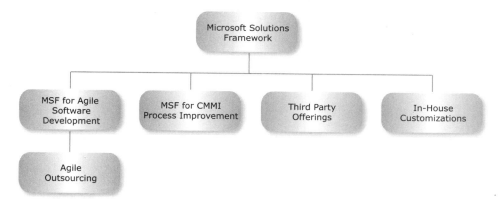

FIGURE 3.12 The Agile Outsourcing process is derived from MSF Agile.

We make the following modifications to MSF Agile:

New fields: Custom fields, like "Responsibility," are added to better track whether a task or bug is being addressed offshore or on-site (see Figure 3.13). Additional fields, such as "Actual Start Date" and "Actual End Date," are used to capture performance information so that we can get a sense of the reliability of estimates.

New workflow: Since all or a significant part of the work is done offshore, the workflow is modified to support improved productivity and efficient interaction between distributed teams. For example, we insist that all tasks and bug fixes are tested at the offshore location before a build is delivered on site.

New work items: In addition to scenarios, offshore projects usually need written requirements and functional specifications for all but trivial endeavors. Although the level of detail associated with these new artifacts varies from case to case, in our experience, not creating these documents with at least the essential details is usually asking for trouble. Face-to-face communication is difficult to replace anyway; if the offshore programmers are asked to develop code based upon oral directives or scanty emails, there is a high chance that things will go wrong.

Let's start by looking at task execution and bug-fixing workflow, and analyze how we can incorporate the presence of an offshore team working at mostly non-overlapping time periods. We assume the following:

■   Both on-site and offshore teams exist and collaborate in software development (typically, the offshore team would be much larger in size than the on-site team).

- A single source code and issue-management repository is used by all parties.
- Offshore and on-site organizations are separate but operationally interconnected.

Task Implementation Workflow

Tasks are usually generated from scenarios, as well as from functional and non-functional specifications. They represent new features or enhancement of existing functions. The modified task-management workflow is depicted in Figure 3.13.

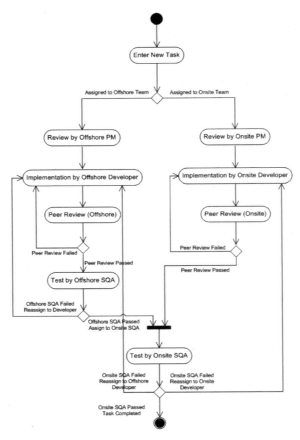

FIGURE 3.13 Task-implementation workflow.

The following steps describe the workflow:

- New tasks are imported from an external system (e.g., tasks can be imported from Microsoft Office Word 2003™ documents using custom programming) or created within VSTS.

■ After creation, a task is assigned either to the on-site team or the offshore team. Usually, this decision is based upon the relevant class ownership structure. If the task is not immediately actionable, it is placed in an inactive state (deferred, cut, obsolete, etc.). If there are additional questions that need to be resolved before a task can be executed, the task is marked as an issue.

At this point, the workflow branches, depending upon which team is responsible for task implementation.

Offshore Track

■ The offshore project manager is responsible for reviewing all assigned tasks and making sure that he clearly understands what needs to be done. This is often a nontrivial step, since he does not have the luxury of face-to-face communication with on-site domain experts. Investing time and effort to clarify specifications, as well as to resolve outstanding questions at this stage, pays rich dividends later. Your strategy for communicating requirements will depend upon the nature of the problem. For example, when creating reporting applications, we typically suggest constructing a reference input dataset and corresponding output tables for each report (often using simple tools like Microsoft Excel) before embarking upon actual implementation. The input and output datasets allow the customer and offshore team to iron out gaps in understanding prior to starting the actual work. On a related note, the communications associated with clarifications and elaborations need to captured and stored for future reference; VSTS makes this easy, since you can attach documents to work items.

■ After review by the offshore project manager, the task is assigned to an offshore developer for implementation. Unit tests are created and executed to ensure accuracy.

■ Peer review is conducted following implementation. VSTS facilitates code review via the use of *shelvesets* (more on this in Chapter 7, "Version Control and Team Build"). The reviewer makes sure that the code not only satisfies the business goals, but is also consistent with the agreed-upon standards of readability, efficiency, consistency, and reusability. Source code check-in policies can be tailored to ensure that code can't be uploaded to a shared repository without code review.

■ A local build is made, and automated Build Verification Tests (BVTs) are executed. The offshore SQA team validates the implementation in an independent environment.

■ Source code is checked into a shared repository once the local build is approved by the offshore SQA team.

On-Site Track

The initial activities of the on-site track mirror those of the off-site track, except for the obvious fact that they are performed by on-site resources. Tasks assigned to the on-site team are reviewed by the on-site project manager and implemented by on-site developers.

The on-site team creates public builds in an independent machine, integrating changes from distributed teams. Appropriate BVTs are run to ensure build quality. The on-site SQA team performs system as well as business-level tests to ensure compliance with the specifications.

The on-site SQA team (often consisting of business domain experts) is the final gatekeeper before the software is rolled out. As such, its role is critical for success. The on-site SQA team is responsible for testing *all* changes, whether they were made offshore or on site. In addition to checking specific fixes, the on-site SQA team runs a battery of manual and automated regression tests on the public build to determine the software's eligibility for release. If a task implementation does not pass the on-site SQA review, it is assigned back to the original developer (offshore or on site). The on-site SQA team consists of people who may be physically resident on site or are capable of remotely accessing on-site machines from offshore. Typically, a new build is tested in a variety of test environments—system integration testing, business integration testing, pre-production, and so forth (depending upon organizational practice and project complexity)—prior to production deployment.

Bug-Management Workflow

The bug-management workflow is similar to that of task management. A bug is reproduced, fixed, reviewed, tested offshore, and then tested again on site (see Figure 3.14).

Let's walk through the various steps:

- A new bug is entered in VSTS. Bugs may be entered by end users, internal SQA teams, developers, or other stakeholders.
- Bugs are reviewed by the on-site project manager or by a review team. Each bug goes through a 'triage' process to determine whether it needs to be acted upon or should be placed in an inactive state (e.g., obsolete, as designed, deferred, or duplicate). A priority is also assigned to each bug. A designated team member (often the project manager) further reviews the bug description and its attachments to ensure that the description is complete, and that the bug entry contains necessary supporting artifacts, such as log files or screenshots. The bug is then assigned to the offshore or on-site team. Depending on available time, the on-site project manager may or may not attempt to reproduce the bug. If the bug needs additional clarification, it is marked as an issue.

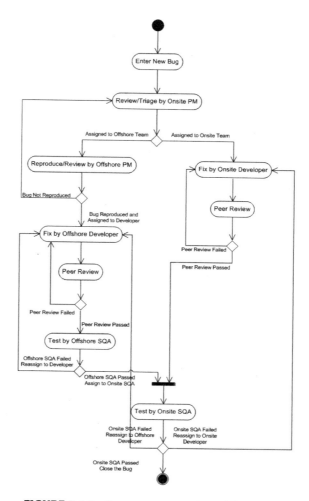

FIGURE 3.14   Bug-management workflow.

At this point, the process workflow bifurcates, depending upon which team handles bug resolution.

Offshore Track

■   When the offshore project manager receives a bug, he (or a designated team member) first attempts to reproduce it. This is usually a required step; typically, we do not want the bug to proceed further down the pipeline unless it can be reproduced in the offshore environment. If the bug can't be reproduced at the offshore location, the offshore project manager might want to interact with the originator of the bug and/or with the on-site project manager to determine whether this is a valid bug, and how to replicate it. Depending upon the nature of the bug, it may be necessary to recreate the environment where the bug occurs (e.g., hardware setup, software configuration, database content, etc.). Trying to reproduce an elusive bug in a different environment is often a time-consuming step, but an essential one, prior to assigning it to a developer for resolution.

- Once the bug is reproduced, it is assigned to an offshore developer for necessary code changes. Unit tests are written (unless they exist already) and executed as part of the fix. It is a good practice to make sure that every bug fix has a corresponding unit test.
- After the fix is made, the changes are peer-reviewed. Although this step often seems redundant (especially under deadline pressure), we strongly recommend it for nontrivial bugs. Catching a potential problem at this stage often saves untold misery later.
- A local build is made, and the offshore SQA team verifies the fix on an independent machine.
- The source code is checked into the shared repository after receiving approval from the offshore SQA team.

On-Site Track

- When the on-site tech lead or developer receives the bug, he first attempts to reproduce it. In this respect, his activities are similar to those of the offshore project manager, as described earlier. He creates units tests (unless they exist already), fixes the bug, and verifies his work.
- Whether the bug was fixed locally or offshore, it is assigned to the on-site SQA team for final verification. A public build is created, and the on-site SQA team verifies the fix in a controlled setting. The process is similar to the verification process for task implementation, as discussed in the previous section.

The steps involved in customizing the MSF Agile process template to support Agile Outsourcing are discussed later in the chapter.

TRACEABILITY MATRIX

A 'traceability matrix' ties together requirements, functional specifications, tasks, test cases, source code, and other artifacts. Creating such an inter-linked view of the system is a recommended practice in software development in general, and in offshore development in particular (since communications between distributed teams tend to be more constrained). A traceability matrix helps the team to visualize the relationships between various elements of the software and the requirements.

Furthermore, it enables them to study the impact of proposed new changes on the system. The matrix also comes in handy during the software maintenance phase; it suggests where to focus efforts in order to solve particular problems. By providing insight into the context, relationships, and motivations, the traceability matrix facilitates development, conversion, and maintenance activities.

VSTS does not contain a built-in tool for creating traceability matrices. However, in addition to using various third-party products, you can create a simple traceability matrix by leveraging the programmability features of TFS and Microsoft Excel (see Figure 3.15). The technical implementation of the utility is described later in the chapter.

	Requirement ID	Requirement Title	Functional Spec ID	Functional Spec Title	Task ID	Task Title
1	**Requirement ID**	**Requirement Title**	**Functional Spec ID**	**Functional Spec Title**	**Task ID**	**Task Title**
2	101	Requirement 1				
3	101	Requirement 1	201	Functional Spec 1		
4	101	Requirement 1	201	Functional Spec 1	301	Task 1
5	101	Requirement 1	201	Functional Spec 1	302	Task 2
6	102	Requirement 2				
7	102	Requirement 2	202	Functional Spec 2		
8	102	Requirement 2	202	Functional Spec 2	303	Task 3
9	102	Requirement 2	202	Functional Spec 2	304	Task 4
10	103	Requirement 3				
11	103	Requirement 3	203	Functional Spec 3		
12	103	Requirement 3	203	Functional Spec 3	305	Task 5
13	103	Requirement 3	204	Functional Spec 4		
14	103	Requirement 3	204	Functional Spec 4	306	Task 6
15	103	Requirement 3	204	Functional Spec 4	307	Task 7

FIGURE 3.15   An Excel-based traceability matrix.

TECHNICAL REVIEW: CUSTOMIZING THE PROCESS TEMPLATE

One of the advantages of the MSF-VSTS combination is being able to *implement* a new process. It is one thing to create a great-looking process on paper. To be able to put that process in practice throughout the development organization requires an underlying infrastructure that most people find prohibitively time-consuming and expensive to build. VSTS enables you to enact the custom process easily. We use MSF Agile as the base process and tweak it to create a custom process named Agile Outsourcing. The full source code of the process template is available on the CD-ROM.

ON THE CD

Export the Process Template

The first step in customizing MSF Agile involves exporting the process template as a set of editable XML files. On the Team menu, point to Team Foundation Server Settings, and click Process Template Manager. In the Process Template Manager dialog box, select MSF for Agile Software Development - v4.0 from the list of process templates, and click Download (see Figure 3.16).

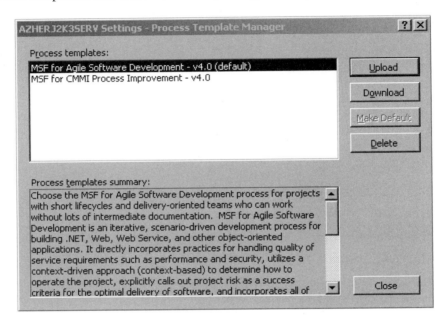

FIGURE 3.16 Exporting the MSF Agile process template from VSTS.

Once exported, the files associated with the process template are placed in the specified folder (see Figure 3.17).

Modify the Process Template

Once the process template is decomposed into a set of XML files, you can start modifying them to meet your needs.

Change the Process Name

Open ProcessTemplate.xml. Change the name of the process to "Agile Outsourcing" and also modify the description (see Listing 3.1)

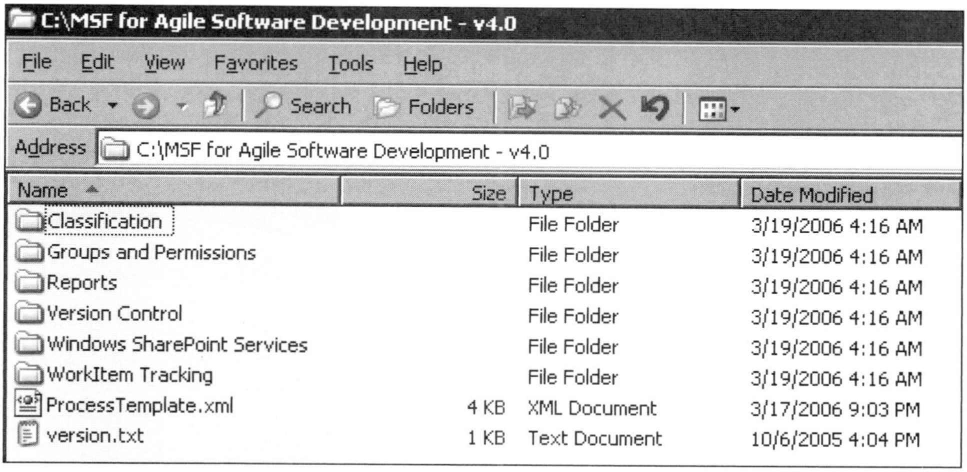

FIGURE 3.17 After exporting, the process template is serialized into XML files.

LISTING 3.1 Change the Name of the Process to Agile Outsourcing

```
<!— *************** Process Template Name & Description
    **************** —>
<name>Agile Outsourcing</name>
<description>
    Choose Agile Outsourcing process for small and
    medium-sized offshore projects where speed of execution is a
    critical success factor. This process is based upon an
    iterative, incremental, and result-oriented approach where
    working software is the primary measure of success. It
    suggests a metric-based and self-correcting strategy where
    execution risk is minimized by incremental builds, and
    productivity is enhanced through open communication.
</description>
```

Add Task-Related Fields

Open Task.xml (located in WorkItem Tracking\TypeDefinitions folder) and add the fields shown in Listing 3.2. The custom fields are added under the `Fields` node.

LISTING 3.2 Task-Related Custom Fields Added to Process Template

```
<!— *************** Agile Outsourcing >>>
    *************************************  —>
<FIELD name="Estimated Duration"
```

```
            refname= "CRM.Outsourcing.Scheduling.EstimatedDuration"
            type="Double" reportable="measure">
        <HELPTEXT>Estimated hours for this task</HELPTEXT>
    </FIELD>
    <FIELD name="Actual Duration"
            refname= "CRM.Outsourcing.Scheduling.ActualDuration"
            type="Double" reportable="measure">
        <HELPTEXT>Actual hours it took to complete the task</HELPTEXT>
    </FIELD>
    <FIELD name="Actual Start Date"
            refname= "Microsoft.VSTS.Scheduling.ActualStartDate"
            type="DateTime" reportable="dimension">
        <HELPTEXT>Actual Start Date for this task</HELPTEXT>
    </FIELD>
    <FIELD name="Actual Finish Date"
            refname= "Microsoft.VSTS.Scheduling.ActualFinishDate"
            type="DateTime" reportable="dimension">
        <HELPTEXT>Actual Finish date for this task</HELPTEXT>
    </FIELD>
    <FIELD name="Deadline Date"
            refname= "Microsoft.VSTS.Scheduling.DeadlineDate"
            type="DateTime" reportable="dimension">
        <HELPTEXT>Deadline for this task</HELPTEXT>
    </FIELD>
    <FIELD name="Percent Completed"
            refname= "CRM.Outsourcing.Scheduling.PercentCompleted"
            type="Double" reportable="measure">
        <HELPTEXT>Percent of work completed</HELPTEXT>
    </FIELD>
    <FIELD name="Predecessors"
            refname= "CRM.Outsourcing.Scheduling.Predecessors"
            type="String">
        <HELPTEXT>Predecessor tasks</HELPTEXT>
    </FIELD>
    <FIELD name="ExternalId"
            refname="CRM.Outsourcing.ExternalId" type="String">
        <HELPTEXT>
            External ID used for referencing imported work items
        </HELPTEXT>
    </FIELD>
    <FIELD name="Responsibility"
            refname="CRM.Outsourcing.Responsibility"
            type="String" reportable="dimension">
        <HELPTEXT>The team responsible for this task</HELPTEXT>
        <ALLOWEDVALUES>
            <LISTITEM value="Offshore"/>
            <LISTITEM value="Onsite"/>
```

```
  </ALLOWEDVALUES>
  <DEFAULT from="value" value="Offshore"/>
</FIELD>
<FIELD name="Test Status"
    refname="CRM.Outsourcing.TestStatus"
    type="String" reportable="dimension">
  <HELPTEXT>The UAT of the requirement.</HELPTEXT>
  <ALLOWEDVALUES>
    <LISTITEM value="Not Tested"/>
    <LISTITEM value="Offshore SQA Passed"/>
    <LISTITEM value="Offshore SQA Failed"/>
    <LISTITEM value="Onsite SQA Passed"/>
    <LISTITEM value="Onsite SQA Failed"/>
  </ALLOWEDVALUES>
  <DEFAULT from="value" value="Not Tested"/>
</FIELD>
<FIELD name="Resolved Date"
    refname="Microsoft.VSTS.Common.ResolvedDate" type="DateTime">
  <HELPTEXT>The date and time the task was resolved</HELPTEXT>
  <WHENNOTCHANGED field="System.State">
    <READONLY/>
  </WHENNOTCHANGED>
</FIELD>
<FIELD name="Resolved By"
    refname="Microsoft.VSTS.Common.ResolvedBy"
    type="String" reportable="dimension">
  <HELPTEXT>The person who closed the task</HELPTEXT>
  <WHENNOTCHANGED field="System.State">
    <READONLY/>
  </WHENNOTCHANGED>
</FIELD>
<FIELD name="Priority"
    refname="Microsoft.VSTS.Common.Priority"
    type="Integer" reportable="dimension">
  <HELPTEXT>Priority of the task</HELPTEXT>
  <ALLOWEDVALUES>
    <LISTITEM value="1"/>
    <LISTITEM value="2"/>
    <LISTITEM value="3"/>
    <LISTITEM value="4"/>
    <LISTITEM value="5"/>
    <LISTITEM value="6"/>
  </ALLOWEDVALUES>
  <DEFAULT from="value" value="2"/>
</FIELD>
```

Add Task-Related Controls

Add corresponding field controls in the Layout node in order to make the fields visible on the form. Listing 3.3 shows the XML representation of the Details tab. The CD-ROM contains the full source code of the modified process template. Figure 3.18 shows the modified task screen.

LISTING 3.3   XML Representation of the Details Tab for Tasks

```
<Tab Label="Details">
<!- *************** Agile Outsourcing >>>
    ****************************************  ->
<Group>
 <Column PercentWidth="50">
  <Group Label="General">
   <Column PercentWidth="100">
    <Control Type="FieldControl"
        FieldName="Microsoft.VSTS.Common.Issue"
        Label="Iss&amp;ue:" LabelPosition="Left"/>
    <Control Type="FieldControl"
        FieldName="Microsoft.VSTS.Common.ExitCriteria"
        Label="E&amp;xit criteria:" LabelPosition="Left"/>
    <Control Type="FieldControl"
        FieldName="Microsoft.VSTS.Build.IntegrationBuild"
        Label="Integration &amp;build:" LabelPosition="Left"/>
    <Control Type="FieldControl"
        FieldName="Microsoft.VSTS.Scheduling.TaskHierarchy"
        Label="Task C&amp;ontext:" LabelPosition="Left"
        ReadOnly="True"/>
    <Control Type="FieldControl"
        FieldName= "Microsoft.VSTS.Scheduling.RemainingWork"
        Label= "Remaining &amp;work (hours):"
        LabelPosition="Left" NumberFormat="WholeNumbers"
        MaxLength="10"/>
    <Control Type="FieldControl"
        FieldName="Microsoft.VSTS.Scheduling.CompletedWork"
        Label="Com&amp;pleted work (hours):"
        LabelPosition="Left" NumberFormat="WholeNumbers"
        MaxLength="10"/>
    <Control Type="FieldControl"
        FieldName="CRM.Outsourcing.TestStatus"
        Label="Test Status:" LabelPosition="Left"/>
    <Control Type="FieldControl"
        FieldName="CRM.Outsourcing.ExternalId"
        Label="External Id:" LabelPosition="Left"/>
   </Column>
  </Group>
 </Column>
 <Column PercentWidth="50">
```

```
<Group Label="Schedule">
 <Column PercentWidth="100">
  <Control Type="FieldControl"
      FieldName= "CRM.Outsourcing.Scheduling.EstimatedDuration"
      Label="Estimated Duration (hours):"
      LabelPosition="Left"/>
  <Control Type="FieldControl"
      FieldName= "CRM.Outsourcing.Scheduling.PercentCompleted"
      Label="Percent Completed:" LabelPosition="Left"/>
  <Control Type="FieldControl"
      FieldName="Microsoft.VSTS.Scheduling.StartDate"
      Label="Scheduled Start Date:" LabelPosition="Left"/>
  <Control Type="FieldControl"
      FieldName="Microsoft.VSTS.Scheduling.FinishDate"
      Label="Scheduled Finish Date:" LabelPosition="Left"/>
  <Control Type="FieldControl"
      FieldName="Microsoft.VSTS.Scheduling.DeadlineDate"
      Label="Deadline:" LabelPosition="Left"/>
  <Control Type="FieldControl"
      FieldName="CRM.Outsourcing.Scheduling.ActualDuration"
      Label="Actual Duration (hours):" LabelPosition="Left"/>
  <Control Type="FieldControl"
      FieldName="Microsoft.VSTS.Scheduling.ActualStartDate"
      Label="Actual Start Date:" LabelPosition="Left"/>
  <Control Type="FieldControl"
      FieldName="Microsoft.VSTS.Scheduling.ActualFinishDate"
      Label="Actual Finish Date:" LabelPosition="Left"/>
  <Control Type="FieldControl"
      FieldName="CRM.Outsourcing.Scheduling.Predecessors"
      Label="Predecessors:" LabelPosition="Left"/>
  </Column>
  </Group>
 </Column>
</Group>
<!- **************** Agile Outsourcing <<<
    **************************************   ->
</Tab>
```

The custom fields enable better progress-tracking and enhanced integration with Microsoft Project. For more information, please refer to Chapter 4, "Integrating MS Project 2003."

Change Task State Transitions

MSF Agile contains two task states by default—Active and Closed. We add another state named "Resolved" (see Figure 3.19). Since tasks are often coarse-grained work items, they need to be reviewed by business analysts or product managers (de-

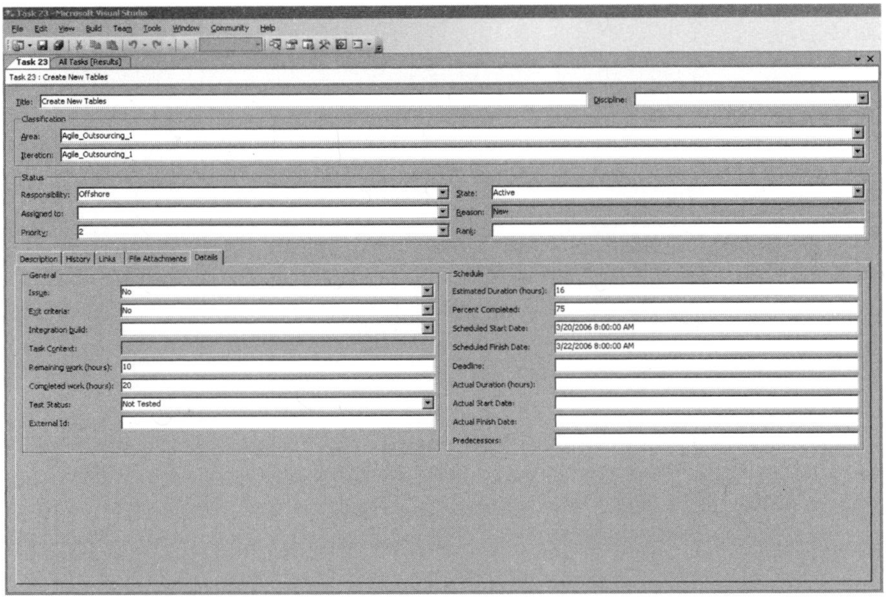

FIGURE 3.18   Modified user interface for tasks.

pending upon importance and size) before they can be marked as Closed. The Resolved state indicates that the task has been implemented by programmers, but is awaiting validation by domain experts. Listing 3.4 shows the modified workflow.

LISTING 3.4   Modified State Transitions for Tasks

```
<WORKFLOW>
 <STATES>
  <STATE value="Active">
   <FIELDS>
    <FIELD refname="Microsoft.VSTS.Common.ClosedDate">
      <EMPTY/></FIELD>
    <FIELD refname="Microsoft.VSTS.Common.ClosedBy">
      <EMPTY/></FIELD>
   </FIELDS>
  </STATE>

<!— *************** Agile Outsourcing >>>
    **************************************   —>
  <STATE value="Resolved">
   <FIELDS>
    <FIELD refname="Microsoft.VSTS.Common.ResolvedDate">
      <EMPTY/>
```

```
        </FIELD>
        <FIELD refname="Microsoft.VSTS.Common.ResolvedBy">
          <EMPTY/>
        </FIELD>
       </FIELDS>
      </STATE>
<!- **************** Agile Outsourcing <<<
     *************************************  ->

      <STATE value="Closed">
      </STATE>
     </STATES>
     <TRANSITIONS>
      <TRANSITION from="" to="Active">
       <REASONS><DEFAULTREASON value="New"/></REASONS>
       <FIELDS>
        <FIELD refname="Microsoft.VSTS.Common.ActivatedBy">
          <COPY from="currentuser"/>
          <VALIDUSER/>
          <REQUIRED/>
        </FIELD>
        <FIELD refname="Microsoft.VSTS.Common.ActivatedDate">
          <SERVERDEFAULT from="clock"/></FIELD>
        <FIELD refname="System.AssignedTo">
          <DEFAULT from="currentuser"/></FIELD>
       </FIELDS>
      </TRANSITION>

<!- **************** Agile Outsourcing >>>
     *************************************  ->
      <TRANSITION from="Active" to="Resolved">
       <REASONS>
        <DEFAULTREASON value="Completed"/>
        <REASON value="Deferred"/>
        <REASON value="Cut"/>
        <REASON value="Obsolete"/>
       </REASONS>
       <FIELDS>
        <FIELD refname="System.AssignedTo">
          <COPY from="field" field="System.CreatedBy"/></FIELD>
        <FIELD refname="Microsoft.VSTS.Common.ResolvedBy">
          <COPY from="currentuser"/></FIELD>
        <FIELD refname="Microsoft.VSTS.Common.ResolvedDate">
          <COPY from="clock"/></FIELD>
       </FIELDS>
      </TRANSITION>
```

```xml
<TRANSITION from="Resolved" to="Active">
 <REASONS>
  <DEFAULTREASON value="Resolution Denied"/>
  <REASON value="Test Failed"/>
 </REASONS>
 <FIELDS>
  <FIELD refname="Microsoft.VSTS.Common.ActivatedBy">
    <COPY from="currentuser"/></FIELD>
  <FIELD refname="Microsoft.VSTS.Common.ActivatedDate">
    <COPY from="clock"/></FIELD>
  <FIELD refname="System.AssignedTo">
    <COPY from="field"
        field="Microsoft.VSTS.Common.ResolvedBy"/>
  </FIELD>
 </FIELDS>
</TRANSITION>

<TRANSITION from="Resolved" to="Closed">
 <REASONS>
  <DEFAULTREASON value="Resolution Confirmed"/>
  <REASON value="Completed"/>
  <REASON value="Deferred"/>
  <REASON value="Cut"/>
  <REASON value="Obsolete"/>
  <REASON value="Test Passed"/>
 </REASONS>
 <FIELDS>
  <FIELD refname="Microsoft.VSTS.Common.ClosedDate">
    <COPY from="clock"/></FIELD>
  <FIELD refname="Microsoft.VSTS.Common.ClosedBy">
    <COPY from="currentuser"/></FIELD>
 </FIELDS>
</TRANSITION>

<!-       <TRANSITION from="Active" to="Closed">
 <ACTIONS>
  <ACTION value="Microsoft.VSTS.Actions.Checkin"/>
 </ACTIONS>
 <REASONS>
  <DEFAULTREASON value="Completed"/>
  <REASON value="Deferred"/>
  <REASON value="Cut"/>
  <REASON value="Obsolete"/>
 </REASONS>
 <FIELDS>
  <FIELD refname="Microsoft.VSTS.Common.ClosedDate">
    <SERVERDEFAULT from="clock"/></FIELD>
  <FIELD refname="Microsoft.VSTS.Common.ClosedBy">
```

```
        <COPY from="currentuser"/>
        <VALIDUSER/>
        <REQUIRED/>
      </FIELD>
      <FIELD refname="Microsoft.VSTS.Common.ActivatedBy">
        <READONLY/></FIELD>
      <FIELD refname="Microsoft.VSTS.Common.ActivatedDate">
        <READONLY/></FIELD>
    </FIELDS>
   </TRANSITION>
   ->
<!- *************** Agile Outsourcing <<<
    ***************************************  ->

   <TRANSITION from="Closed" to="Active">
    <REASONS>
     <DEFAULTREASON value="Reactivated"/>
    </REASONS>
    <FIELDS>
     <FIELD refname="Microsoft.VSTS.Common.ActivatedBy">
       <COPY from="currentuser"/>
       <VALIDUSER/>
       <REQUIRED/>
     </FIELD>
     <FIELD refname="Microsoft.VSTS.Common.ActivatedDate">
       <SERVERDEFAULT from="clock"/></FIELD>
     <FIELD refname="System.AssignedTo">
       <COPY from="field" field="Microsoft.VSTS.Common.ClosedBy"/>
     </FIELD>
    </FIELDS>
   </TRANSITION>
  </TRANSITIONS>
 </WORKFLOW>
```

Modify Bug Work Item Type

ON THE CD

Open Bug.xml (located in WorkItem Tracking\TypeDefinitions folder) and modify the list of fields, state transitions, and screen layout to support Agile Outsourcing. The modified definition for the bug work item can be found on the CD-ROM. Figure 3.20 shows the modified bug entry screen.

Create Requirement Work Item Type

Given the geographic separation between customers and developers, requirement documents are usually needed in offshore projects. Although MSF Agile contains scenarios—representing user interactions with the application in pursuit of business goals—requirements can play a useful role, especially in larger projects. Additionally, in a contractual relationship, requirements help define the acceptance

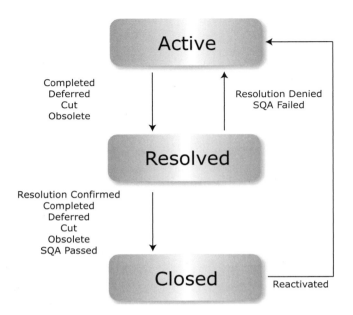

FIGURE 3.19 Modified task states and transitions.

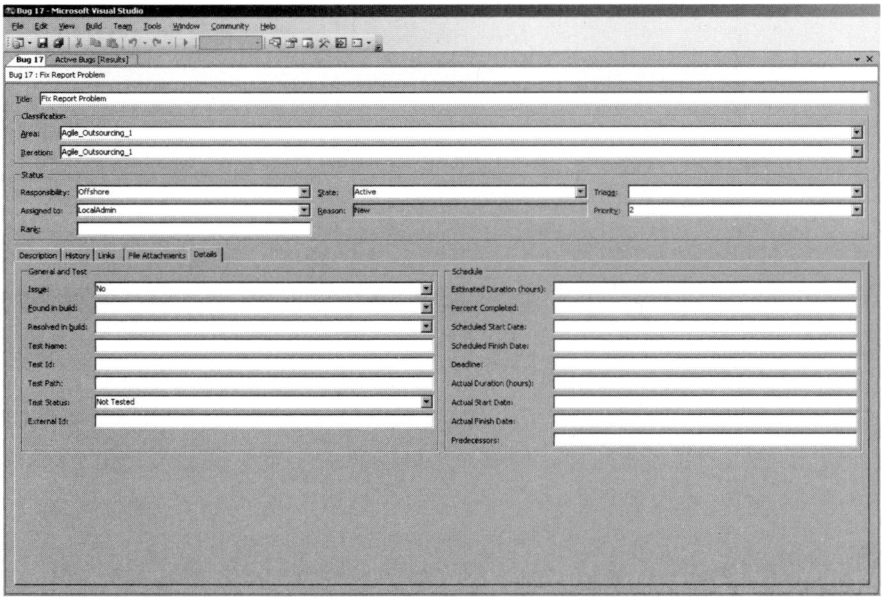

FIGURE 3.20 Modified user interface for bugs.

criteria. Payments are often tied to project milestones that satisfy certain sets of requirements.

Requirements can be functional as well as nonfunctional—for example, security and performance considerations. Typically, requirements are written from the perspective of the client and spell out customer expectations for the software.

Create a new file named "Requirement.xml," and add the necessary fields, states, transitions, and design layouts (see Figure 3.21). The CD-ROM contains full source code for the new Requirement.xml file.

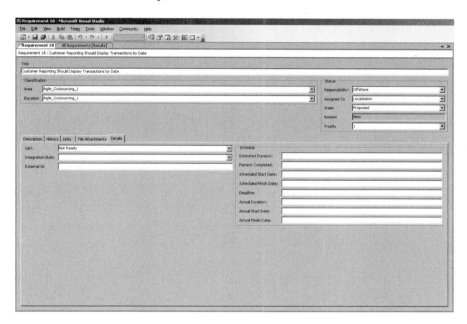

FIGURE 3.21   User interface for requirements.

Create Functional Specification Work Item Type

Functional specifications refine the requirements and provide a more fine-grained description of exactly what needs to be done to meet a certain requirement. Unlike requirements, functional specifications usually describe the implementation approach from a technical point of view. Multiple functional specifications may need to be created to satisfy a single requirement.

You may not need to create functional specifications for all work. It depends on how experienced the offshore team happens to be in your problem domain, how long you have been working with the team, and how novel the intended feature is. In general, the need for thorough specifications increases in the offshore scenario because the end user is not available for clarifications on demand. For example, consider creating a set of custom reports. Without precise specifications, offshore developers will have no actionable guidelines regarding how to calculate values for each cell.

Create a new file named "FunctionalSpecification.xml" and add the necessary fields, states, transitions, and design layouts (see Figure 3.22). The CD-ROM contains full source code for the new FunctionalSpecification.xml file.

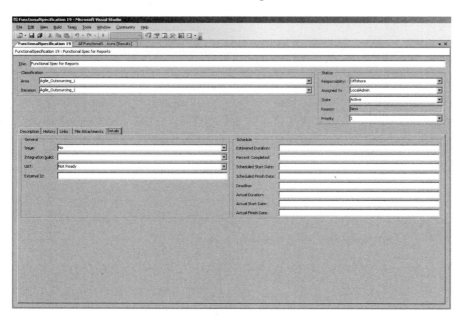

FIGURE 3.22   User interface for functional specifications.

Create New Queries

New queries are needed in order to display requirements and functional specifications in Team Explorer. Create two files named "AllRequirements.xml" and "AllFunctionalSpecifications.xml" in the WorkItem Tracking/Queries folder, as per Listings 3.5 and 3.6, respectively.

LISTING 3.5   WIQL Query for Fetching Requirements

```xml
<?xml version="1.0" encoding="utf-8"?>
<WorkItemQuery Version="1">
    <Wiql>SELECT [System.Id], [System.WorkItemType],
        [Microsoft.VSTS.Common.Discipline], [System.State],
        [System.AssignedTo], [Microsoft.VSTS.Common.Rank],
        [Microsoft.VSTS.Scheduling.CompletedWork],
```

```
            [Microsoft.VSTS.Scheduling.RemainingWork], [System.Title]
            FROM WorkItems WHERE [System.TeamProject] = @project AND
            [System.WorkItemType] = 'Requirement'
            ORDER BY [Microsoft.VSTS.Common.Rank], [System.State],
            [System.Id]
        </Wiql>
    </WorkItemQuery>
```

LISTING 3.6   WIQL Query for Fetching Functional Specifications

```
    <?xml version="1.0" encoding="utf-8"?>
    <WorkItemQuery Version="1">
        <Wiql>SELECT [System.Id], [System.WorkItemType],
            [Microsoft.VSTS.Common.Discipline], [System.State],
            [System.AssignedTo], [Microsoft.VSTS.Common.Priority],
            [System.Title] FROM WorkItems WHERE [System.TeamProject] =
            @project AND [System.WorkItemType] =
            'FunctionalSpecification' ORDER BY
            [Microsoft.VSTS.Common.Priority], [System.State],
            [System.Id]
        </Wiql>
    </WorkItemQuery>
```

Integrate New Work Item Types and Queries

Modify the file named "WorkItems.xml" (located in the WorkItem Tracking folder), and add the new types under the WORKITEMTYPES node (see Listing 3.7). The newly added work item types appear in Team Explorer (see Figure 3.23).

LISTING 3.7   Custom Work Item Types Added to the Process Template

```
    <WORKITEMTYPES>
        <WORKITEMTYPE fileName=
            "WorkItem Tracking\TypeDefinitions\Bug.xml"/>
        <WORKITEMTYPE fileName=
            "WorkItem Tracking\TypeDefinitions\Task.xml"/>
        <WORKITEMTYPE fileName=
            "WorkItem Tracking\TypeDefinitions\Qos.xml"/>
        <WORKITEMTYPE fileName=
            "WorkItem Tracking\TypeDefinitions\Scenario.xml"/>
        <WORKITEMTYPE fileName=
            "WorkItem Tracking\TypeDefinitions\Risk.xml"/>

    <!—************** CRM Outsourcing: New WorkItem Types
        ******************* —>
        <WORKITEMTYPE fileName=
            "WorkItem Tracking\TypeDefinitions\Requirement.xml"/>
        <WORKITEMTYPE fileName="WorkItem
            Tracking\TypeDefinitions\FunctionalSpecification.xml"/>
```

```
</WORKITEMTYPES>
```

Add the new queries under the QUERIES node as follows (see Listing 3.8). New queries appear in Team Explorer and allow users to fetch entries matching the new work item types (see Figure 3.24).

LISTING 3.8   New Queries Added to the Process Template

```
<QUERIES>
  <Query name="My Work Items"
      fileName="WorkItem Tracking\Queries\MyWorkItems.wiq" />
  <Query name="Project Checklist"
      fileName="WorkItem Tracking\Queries\ProjectChecklist.wiq"/>
  <Query name="All Scenarios"
      fileName="WorkItem Tracking\Queries\AllScenarios.wiq" />
  <Query name="All Quality of Service Requirements"
      fileName="WorkItem Tracking\Queries\
      AllQualityOfServiceRequirements.wiq" />
  <Query name="All Tasks"
      fileName="WorkItem Tracking\Queries\AllTasks.wiq" />
  <Query name="All Work Items"
      fileName="WorkItem Tracking\Queries\AllWorkItems.wiq" />
  <Query name="Active Bugs"
      fileName="WorkItem Tracking\Queries\ActiveBugs.wiq" />
  <Query name="Resolved Bugs"
      fileName="WorkItem Tracking\Queries\ResolvedBugs.wiq" />
  <Query name="My Work Items for All Team Projects"
      fileName="WorkItem Tracking\Queries\
      MyWorkItemsAllTeamProjects.wiq" />

  <!-************** CRM Outsourcing: Queries for New WorkItem
      Types  ****************** -->
  <Query name="All Requirements"
      fileName="WorkItem Tracking\Queries\AllRequirements.wiq" />
  <Query name="All FunctionalSpecifications" fileName="WorkItem
      Tracking\Queries\AllFunctionalSpecifications.wiq" />
</QUERIES>
```

Import the Process Template

Once the customizations are complete, import the new process information back into VSTS. This step makes the modified process template usable from VSTS. On the Team menu, point to Team Foundation Server Settings, and click Process Template Manager. In the Process Template Manager dialog box, click Upload. In the Upload Process Template dialog box, select the top-level folder associated with the newly defined process (e.g., MSF for Agile Software Development - v4.0). After the new process template is successfully imported, it appears in the list of processes, as

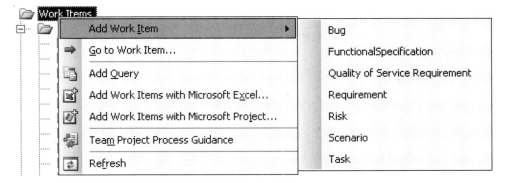

FIGURE 3.23 New work item types appear in Team Explorer.

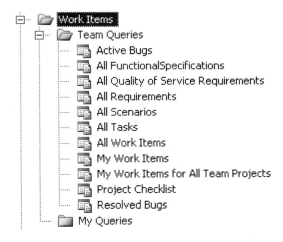

FIGURE 3.24   New queries appear in Team Explorer.

shown in Figure 3.25. You are now ready to create a new project based on the newly imported Agile Outsourcing process template.

Ad-Hoc Modification of Work Items

For the sake of completeness, we point out that work item types can be modified on an ad-hoc basis in an existing team project. VSTS provides two command line tools for this purpose: WitImport.exe and WitExport.exe. Open the command prompt window and navigate to the directory where these files are located (e.g., Program Files\Microsoft Visual Studio 8\Common7\IDE).

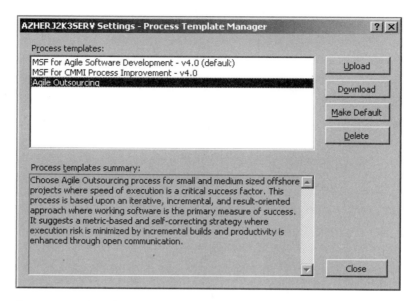

FIGURE 3.25   Agile Outsourcing process template imported in VSTS.

To export a work item definition, type the following:

```
witexport /f <your_filename> /t http://<team_server_name>
    :8080 /p <team_project_name> /n <work_item_type>
```

To upload a modified work item definition, type the following:

```
witimport /f <your_filename> /t http://<team_server_name>
    :8080 /p <team_project_name>
```

TECHNICAL REVIEW: CREATING A TRACEABILITY MATRIX

We assume that you have created the requirements, functional specifications, and tasks, as well as have set up appropriate links between them. The goal now is to create a program that will automatically generate the traceability matrix. In this example, we only correlate requirements, functional specifications, and tasks; you could extend it to associate tests cases, source code, and other artifacts. The full source code is available on the CD-ROM.

ON THE CD

Create a driver class named TMGenerator and two helper classes named Team-SystemHelper and ExcelHelper. The helper classes encapsulate the code related to TFS and Excel (see Figure 3.26). Also, create domain classes to represent Requirements, Functional Specifications, and Tasks (see Figure 3.27)

FIGURE 3.26   Class diagram for traceability matrix generator.

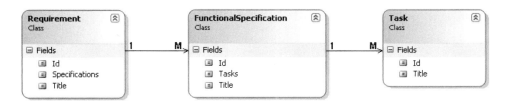

FIGURE 3.27   Work item types represented by domain classes.

The primary responsibility of the TeamSystemHelper class is to fetch the list of project-specific requirements from TFS, along with associated functional specifications and tasks (see Listing 3.9). This is performed by the GetRequirements method; the steps involved are as follows:

- Connect to the work item store, given the application server end point.
- Determine project-specific work item types. These types will be used later for identifying the kind of associated work items contained in a given work item's Links collection.

- Fetch the list of requirements using Work Item Query Language (WIQL) queries. You can modify the pGetWiql method to tailor the query and bring in a more restricted set of requirements, as needed.
- For each requirement, iterate its Links collection and fetch the list of associated functional specifications. The program inspects the linked work item's target type and picks up only linked functional specifications.
- For each functional specification, iterate its Links collection and fetch the list of associated tasks.
- Construct a fully populated collection of requirement domain objects containing embedded functional specifications and tasks.

LISTING 3.9   Source Code for the TeamSystemHelper Class

```
using System;
using System.Collections.Generic;

using Microsoft.TeamFoundation.Proxy;
using Microsoft.TeamFoundation.Client;
using Microsoft.TeamFoundation.Server;
using Microsoft.TeamFoundation.WorkItemTracking.Client;

namespace TraceabilityMatrix
{
/// <summary>
/// provides functionalities to interact with
/// TeamSystem Foundation Server
/// </summary>
class TeamSystemHelper
{
  private const string REQUIREMENT = "Requirement";
  private const string FUNC_SPEC = "FunctionalSpecification";
  private const string TASK = "Task";
  private const string TFS_USERNAME = "";
  private const string TFS_PASSWORD = "";
  private static string _serverName = "http://localhost:8080";
  private static string _teamProjectName = "Agile_Outsourcing_1";
  private static string ServerName
  {
    get { return _serverName; }
    set { _serverName = value; }
  }

  private static string TeamProjectName
  {
    get { return _teamProjectName; }
```

```csharp
        set { _teamProjectName = value; }
}

private static TeamFoundationServer _tfsServer;
private static TeamFoundationServer TfsServer
{
  get
  {
    if (_tfsServer == null)
    {
      // Connect to team server
      if (TFS_PASSWORD != string.Empty &&
          TFS_USERNAME != string.Empty)
      {
        System.Net.NetworkCredential nc =
            new System.Net.NetworkCredential(TFS_USERNAME,
            TFS_PASSWORD);

        _tfsServer = new TeamFoundationServer(ServerName, nc);
      }
      else
      {
        _tfsServer = new TeamFoundationServer(ServerName);
      }
      return _tfsServer;
    }
    else
    {
      return _tfsServer;
    }
  }
}

private static WorkItemStore _workItemStore = null;
private static WorkItemStore WorkItemStore
{
  get
  {
    if (_workItemStore == null)
    {
      // Get the WorkItemStore associated with this Team Server
      _workItemStore =
          new WorkItemStore(TeamSystemHelper.TfsServer);
      return _workItemStore;
    }
    else
    {
      return _workItemStore;
```

```csharp
        }
      }
    }

    /// <summary>
    /// returns a list of Application Server names
    /// </summary>
    /// <returns></returns>
    public static List<string> GetAppServers()
    {

      List<string> returnList = new List<string>();

      //obtain list of registered servers
      TeamFoundationServer[] colServers =
          RegisteredServers.GetServers();

      //iterate the server collection and add server name to
      //return collection
      foreach (TeamFoundationServer server in colServers)
      {
        returnList.Add (server.Name);
      }
      return returnList;
    }

    /// <summary>
    /// returns a list of Projects stored in TFS
    /// </summary>
    /// <param name="appServerName"></param>
    /// <returns></returns>
    public static List<string> GetProjects(string
        appServerUri)
    {

      List<string> returnList = new List<string>();

      TeamFoundationServer appServer =
          TeamFoundationServerFactory.GetServer(appServerUri);

      ICommonStructureService csService = (ICommonStructureService)
          appServer.GetService( typeof(ICommonStructureService));

      foreach (ProjectInfo prjInfo in csService.ListAllProjects() )
      {
          returnList.Add(prjInfo.Name);
      }
```

```
    return returnList;
}

/// <summary>
/// get list of requirements stored in the project
/// </summary>
/// <param name="projectId"></param>
/// <returns></returns>
public static List<Requirement> GetRequirements()
{

  //get Tfs Server name and Team Project Name
  //the names will be stored in private properties
  pGetTfsServerInfo();

  List<Requirement> returnList = new List<Requirement>();

  //custom objects
  Requirement requirement;
  FunctionalSpecification fs;
  Task task;

  //get ref to the project
  Project project = TeamSystemHelper.WorkItemStore.Projects[
      TeamSystemHelper.TeamProjectName];

  //get types
  WorkItemTypeCollection colWorkItemTypes =
      project.WorkItemTypes;
  WorkItemType fsType = colWorkItemTypes[FUNC_SPEC];
  WorkItemType taskType = colWorkItemTypes[TASK];

  //get Requirement collection from TFS
  string requirementWIQL =
      pGetWiql(TeamSystemHelper.TeamProjectName, REQUIREMENT);
  WorkItemCollection workItems =
      TeamSystemHelper.WorkItemStore.Query(requirementWIQL);

  //iterate the requirement collection and create output list
  foreach (WorkItem wkItem in workItems)
  {
    //create and populate the requirement object
    requirement = new Requirement();
    requirement.Title = wkItem.Title;
    requirement.Id = wkItem.Id.ToString();

    //fetch functional specifications associated
    //with this requirement
```

```
    foreach (RelatedLink lnkItemFS in wkItem.Links)
    {
      //get work item from the link
      WorkItem wkLinkedItem =
          TeamSystemHelper.WorkItemStore.GetWorkItem(
          lnkItemFS.RelatedWorkItemId);

      //check if it is a functional spec
      if (wkLinkedItem.Type == fsType)
      {
        fs = new FunctionalSpecification();
        fs.Title = wkLinkedItem.Title;
        fs.Id = wkLinkedItem.Id.ToString();

        //now check if there are tasks associated
        //with the functional spec
        foreach (RelatedLink lnkItemTask in wkLinkedItem.Links)
        {
          WorkItem wkLinkedItem2 =
              TeamSystemHelper.WorkItemStore.GetWorkItem(
              lnkItemTask.RelatedWorkItemId);

          if (wkLinkedItem2.Type == taskType)
          {
            task = new Task();
            task.Title = wkLinkedItem2.Title;
            task.Id = wkLinkedItem2.Id.ToString();

            // add the task to functional spec
            fs.Tasks.Add(task);
          }
        }

        //Add the functional spec to the
        //corresponding requirement
        requirement.Specifications.Add(fs);
      }
    }

    //add the requirement to the return list
    returnList.Add(requirement);
  }

  return returnList;
}

#region private functions
```

```csharp
/// <summary>
/// Show Domain Project Picker Dialog box and
///get App Server Name.
/// Populates ServerName and TeamProjectName properties.
///
/// </summary>
private static void pGetTfsServerInfo()
{
  DomainProjectPicker pjPicker =new DomainProjectPicker(
      DomainProjectPickerMode.AllowProjectSelect);

  pjPicker.ShowDialog();

  //get selected server info
  TeamSystemHelper.ServerName =
      pjPicker.SelectedServer.Uri.ToString();

  //get selected team project info
  TeamSystemHelper.TeamProjectName =
      pjPicker.SelectedProjects[0].Name;

}


/// <summary>
/// creates wiql string for fetching work items
/// </summary>
/// <param name="projectName"></param>
/// <param name="workItemType"></param>
/// <returns></returns>
private static string pGetWiql(string projectName,
    string workItemType)
{
  string wiql = "SELECT [System.Id], [System.Title] FROM
      WorkItems WHERE [System.TeamProject] = '{0}' AND
      [System.WorkItemType] = '{1}' ORDER BY [System.Id]";
  return string.Format(wiql, projectName, workItemType);
}


  #endregion
}
}
```

The ExcelHelper class is a wrapper class for interacting with Excel. It contains methods for creating a worksheet, writing header information, and updating a specific cell (see Listing 3.10).

LISTING 3.10   Source Code for ExcelHelper Class

```csharp
using System;
using System.Collections.Generic;
using Microsoft.Office.Interop.Excel;

namespace TraceabilityMatrix
{
class ExcelHelper
{

  #region Constants
  // Column definitions for Traceability Matrix Sheet
  public const int COL_REQUIREMENT_ID = 1;
  public const int COL_REQUIREMENT_TITLE = 2;
  public const int COL_FUNCTIONALSPEC_ID = 3;
  public const int COL_FUNCTIONALSPEC_TITLE = 4;
  public const int COL_TASK_ID = 5;
  public const int COL_TASK_TITLE = 6;
  #endregion

  private static Workbook wkBook;
  private static Worksheet wkSheet;

  /// <summary>
  /// Creates a WorkSheet in Excel for displaying
  ///the Traceability Matrix
  /// </summary>
  public static void CreateWorkSheet()
  {
    // Create Excel Worksheet
    wkBook = pCreateWorkBook();

    // Create Sheet in populate header info
    pCreateWorkSheet(wkBook, "Traceability Matrix");
    pPrepareWorkSheet();
  }
  /// <summary>
  /// Write text to specified cell
  /// </summary>
  /// <param name="row"></param>
  /// <param name="column"></param>
  /// <param name="text"></param>
  /// <param name="isBold"></param>
  public static void WriteToCell(int row,
      int column, string text, bool isBold)
  {
    wkSheet.Cells[row, column] = text;
  }
```

```csharp
#region Private Methods
/// <summary>
/// Creates a new Workbook
/// </summary>
/// <returns></returns>
private static Workbook pCreateWorkBook()
{
  // Create a new Excel Document
  Application app = new Application();
  Workbook book = app.Workbooks.Add(Type.Missing);
  app.Visible = true;

  return book;
}

/// <summary>
/// Creates a new Work Sheet
/// </summary>
/// <param name="book"></param>
/// <param name="name"></param>
/// <returns></returns>
private static void pCreateWorkSheet(Workbook book,
    string name)
{
  wkSheet = (Worksheet)book.Worksheets.Add(Type.Missing,
      Type.Missing, Type.Missing, Type.Missing);

  wkSheet.Name = name;
}

/// <summary>
/// Creates necessary column headers for Forward
/// Traceability Matrix
/// </summary>
/// <param name="workSheet"></param>
private static void pPrepareWorkSheet()
{
  // Create Columns
  WriteToCell(1, COL_REQUIREMENT_ID, "Requirement ID", true);
  WriteToCell(1, COL_REQUIREMENT_TITLE,
      "Requirement Title", true);
  WriteToCell(1, COL_FUNCTIONALSPEC_ID,
      "Functional Spec ID", true);
  WriteToCell(1, COL_FUNCTIONALSPEC_TITLE,
      "Functional Spec Title", true);
  WriteToCell(1, COL_TASK_ID, "Task ID", true);
  WriteToCell(1, COL_TASK_TITLE, "Task Title", true);
}
```

```
    #endregion
  }
}
```

The TMGenerator class is the manager class responsible for invoking the helper classes and coordinating the workflow. It obtains the set of requirements from the TeamSystemHelper class, and hierarchically traverses the embedded collections to determine the associated functional specifications and tasks (see Listing 3.11). The program then writes (to Excel) each requirement, along with related functional specifications and tasks.

LISTING 3.11   Source Code for the TMGenerator Class

```
using System;
using System.Collections.Generic;
using System.Text;
using System.Collections;

namespace TraceabilityMatrix
{
class TMGenerator
{
  private int rowPointer = 2;

  /// <summary>
  /// Creates an Excel WorkSheet containing
  /// Traceability Matrix.
  /// Depicts relationship between Requirements, Functional
  /// Specifications, and Tasks
  /// </summary>
  public void Generate()
  {

    // Get list of Requirements for the project
    List<Requirement> requirements =
        TeamSystemHelper.GetRequirements();

    //create target worksheet
    ExcelHelper.CreateWorkSheet();

    //iterate the requirements collection and write associated
    //functional specs and tasks
    foreach (Requirement req in requirements)
    {
      //write requirements
      pWriteRequirements(req.Id, req.Title);
```

```
    rowPointer++;

    // Get list of Functional Specs for the current Requirement
    List<FunctionalSpecification> specs =  req.Specifications;

    foreach (FunctionalSpecification spec in specs)
    {

      //write requirements
      pWriteRequirements(req.Id, req.Title);
      //write functional specs
      pWriteFuncSpecs(spec.Id, spec.Title);

      rowPointer++;

      // Get list of Tasks for current Functional Spec
      List<Task> tasks = spec.Tasks;

      foreach (Task task in tasks)
      {
        //write requirements
        pWriteRequirements(req.Id, req.Title);
        //write functiional specs
        pWriteFuncSpecs(spec.Id, spec.Title);
        //write tasks
        pWriteTasks(task.Id, task.Title);

        rowPointer++;
      }
    }
  }
}

#region private methods

/// <summary>
/// write Requirements in Excel worksheet
/// </summary>
/// <param name="id"></param>
/// <param name="title"></param>
private void pWriteRequirements(string id, string title)
{
  // Write reqs into Matrix sheet
  ExcelHelper.WriteToCell(rowPointer,
      ExcelHelper.COL_REQUIREMENT_ID, id, false);
  ExcelHelper.WriteToCell(rowPointer,
      ExcelHelper.COL_REQUIREMENT_TITLE, title, false);
}
```

```
/// <summary>
/// write Functional Specifications in Excel worksheet
/// </summary>
/// <param name="id"></param>
/// <param name="title"></param>
private void pWriteFuncSpecs(string id, string title)
{
  ExcelHelper.WriteToCell(rowPointer,
      ExcelHelper.COL_FUNCTIONALSPEC_ID, id, false);
  ExcelHelper.WriteToCell(rowPointer,
      ExcelHelper.COL_FUNCTIONALSPEC_TITLE, title, false);
}

/// <summary>
/// write Tasks in Excel worksheet
/// </summary>
/// <param name="id"></param>
/// <param name="title"></param>
private void pWriteTasks(string id, string title)
{
  ExcelHelper.WriteToCell(rowPointer,
      ExcelHelper.COL_TASK_ID, id, false);
  ExcelHelper.WriteToCell(rowPointer,
      ExcelHelper.COL_TASK_TITLE, title, false);
}

#endregion

}
}
```

CONCLUSION

Every organization is different in terms of skill sets, structure, culture, maturity, business domain, competitive pressure, and offshore relationships. It is unrealistic to advocate a 'one size fits all' universal process. MSF enables you to define a process that is suitable for your company, and VSTS allows you to easily implement that process throughout the enterprise. After all, defining a perfect process in the abstract does little to improve organizational efficiency; you need to be able to institute it throughout the organization via an integrated toolset.

In this chapter, we extended MSF Agile to support offshore development. We created new work item types, state transitions, queries, and work flows. Although we modified the project-specific XML files directly, third-party products are available for customizing process templates at a higher level of abstraction. You can also modify the process guidance pages (using a tool like Microsoft Infopath) to educate the team members about the custom process.

All work items are stored in TFS, and it is possible to programmatically access the work item store. You can obtain detailed information regarding work status as well as generate various metrics regarding project health. (We discuss reports in Chapter 9, "Enterprise Reporting.") Reports can be accessed via the project portal, allowing stakeholders to monitor project status from remote locations; all they need is a Web browser. In this chapter, we also leveraged TFS extensibility features to create a traceability matrix that depicts relationships between various artifacts. In the next chapters, we look at various ways TFS can be extended and integrated with other Microsoft products. The goal is to create an ecosystem of complementary technologies to maximize your efficiency in managing distributed projects.

4 Integrating Microsoft Project 2003

In This Chapter

- Introduction
- The Workflow
- Walk-Through: Project Integration
- Customizing Project Integration
- Walk-Through: Tracking Progress
- Sharing Information with Stakeholders
- Technical Review: Creating a Custom Add-in for Project

INTRODUCTION

When you send your mission-critical projects offshore, probably the most important question that keeps you awake at night is whether or not the work is coming along as per plan. As you know from real-life experience, realistic project planning and effective execution is a challenging task. A proactive, fact-based, and adaptive project management approach is essential for success in the face of rapidly changing realities. Project planning and progress tracking constitute two broad categories of functions performed by the project management team. Project management is as much an art as it is a science; without an integrated toolset, it becomes a 'shot in the dark.'

Outsourced projects present additional challenges in terms of information collection, processing, and distribution. The need for current and relevant information is critical during the project execution phase. For mission-critical, multi-site projects, you need an integrated process framework to detect emerging problems. You also need to be able to take corrective actions before it is too late. You need an early warning system with automatic tracking and alerting capabilities. For time-critical projects, you may need to frequently (even *daily*) track progress and compare current status with planned goals. However, traditionally it has been difficult to achieve this kind of visibility without adding significant overhead and cost. Project tracking based on stale data is useless. The key question is how to gather, process, and disseminate key performance indicators from distributed development locations to stakeholders, without burdening the project management team.

A related issue is that of granularity. Different stakeholders are interested in different aspects of the work being done. For example, offshore project managers want to look at the individual tasks (as per the work breakdown structure). Product managers are interested in the status of business requirements. Executive management often cares only about the status of key milestones. How can the diverse interests of various parties be satisfied without introducing substantial amounts of new data-processing and status-reporting work?

The realistic answer to both of these questions is that no matter what tools you use, the project management staff still needs to invest time and effort to identify problems, resolve issues, and manage conflicts. However, the right toolset can automate the routine tasks and free up time to focus on issues that actually matter. The goal is to be able to automatically flow information from the people who are actually doing the work (i.e., programmers, SQA professionals, etc.) directly to a project dashboard—with custom views for various stakeholders. Such an integrated framework eliminates the overhead, delay, and cost associated with manual processing, significantly reducing the friction associated with offshore project management.

In this chapter, we look at how VSTS and Microsoft Office Project 2003 (Project) can work together to streamline project management. We use VSTS to capture progress information from the implementation teams and use its Project integration features to automatically update the project plan. The project plan is primarily used by the project management team to monitor project execution; other parties may not even have Project installed in their machines. After review and analysis of the current project status using Project, the project management team takes appropriate actions to resolve issues, re-allocate resources, identify tasks on the critical path, and so forth. They can also export the status information to the project portal for review by interested parties. Another way for stakeholders to monitor project health in near time is to view predefined and custom reports (see Chapter 9, "Enterprise Reporting"). These reports (created using SQL Server 2005 Reporting Services) contain the latest updates from the implementation teams and enable you to examine the project status from a number of perspectives.

A combination of the two approaches is needed to increase efficiency and transparency of offshore development. Although not all manual steps can be eliminated in tracking the progress of large projects, we believe that you'll find the synergistic approach to be effective in reducing execution risks of outsourced projects.

THE WORKFLOW

VSTS provides extensible built-in support for bidirectional synchronization with Project. The synchronization tool enables you to import work items into Project, refresh task information in Project based upon updated data from VSTS, and publish changes back to VSTS (see Figure 4.1). You can also enter new tasks in Project; when published, the new work items are added to VSTS. The integration between VSTS and Project takes place based on a customizable XML mapping file. You can modify the XML file to suit your own process (customization of the mapping file is discussed later in this chapter).

Given the synchronization capability between VSTS and Project, we suggest the following high-level workflow for setting up a project plan and tracking project execution (see Figure 4.2).

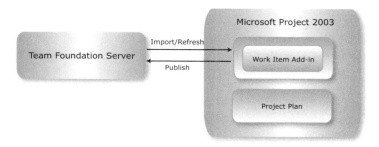

FIGURE 4.1   Project integration architecture.

1. Create a Work Breakdown Structure (WBS) from scenarios or specifications (functional as well as nonfunctional). Enter tasks derived from the WBS in VSTS.
2. Enter estimated duration of each task in VSTS.
3. Assign resources to tasks in VSTS.
4. Import task information into Project using the integration tool.
5. Add task dependencies in Project.
6. Add summary tasks and milestones in Project.
7. Level resources and schedule tasks in Project.
8. Once the project plan is finalized, use the integration tool to transfer the information back to VSTS.
9. As project execution gets underway, developers indicate their progress in VSTS every day. At regular intervals, run the synchronization tool to refresh the project plan with updated status information from VSTS.
10. Use Project to identify bottlenecks, conflicts, delayed and slipping tasks, and the like. Analyze and resolve issues as needed.

11. Create customized status reports and distribute them via the project portal site. (VSTS automatically creates a project portal site during creation of a team project.) Keep in mind that in addition to the status reports that you might create in Project, VSTS already contains several built-in reports related to task tracking and project health (refer to Chapter 9, "Enterprise Reporting," for more information). You can also create custom reports using SQL Server 2005 Reporting Services and make them available in the project portal. The portal site contains key metrics regarding the project and serves as the 'dashboard' for various stakeholders. Customize the site as needed to meet the requirements of various parties (refer to Chapter 10, "Using the Project Portal," to learn more).

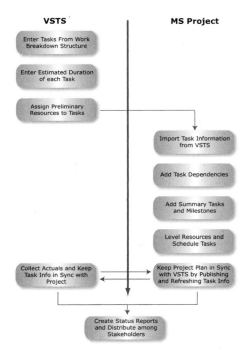

FIGURE 4.2 Suggested project management workflow.

WALK-THROUGH: PROJECT INTEGRATION

In this section, we walk through the steps involved in creating Project tasks from VSTS work items and find out how to keep the two in synch. Version one of VSTS does not support integration with Project Server (although you can integrate the two systems using custom programming). Therefore, our discussions will apply to

Microsoft Office Project 2003 only (the examples and screenshots in this chapter were created using the standard edition).

Create Work Items in VSTS

Create task work items in your team project based on scenarios and functional specifications. For each task, do the following:

■ Designate a resource for the task using the Assigned To drop-down. This is a preliminary resource assignment; resource assignment may change after resource leveling in Project. Assign resources to tasks at this stage to ensure that the resource names are available in Project. Otherwise, if you add a new resource in Project and the new resource does not exist in VSTS, synchronization will fail when you try to publish the changes from Project.

■ Click the Details tab and enter the estimated duration.

Transfer Work Items to Project

To export tasks to Project from VSTS, right-click All Tasks (under the `Team Queries` node) in Team Explorer and select Open in Microsoft Project from the drop-down menu (see Figure 4.3). This action will create a new project plan and connect it to the current team project (see Figure 4.4).

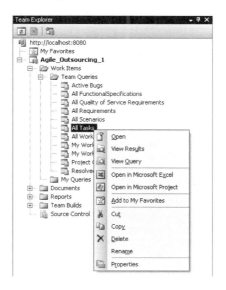

FIGURE 4.3   Work items can be exported to Project by right-clicking any team query and selecting Open in Microsoft Project.

	ⓘ	Work Item ID	Title	Duration	Jan 1, '06		Jan 8, '06	
					S M T W T F S		S M T W T F	
1		1	Setup: Set Permissions	1 day?	▨ PM1			
2		2	Setup: Migration of Source Code	2 days?	▨ PM2			
3		3	Setup: Migration of Work Items	1 day?	▨ PM1			
4		4	Setup: Set Check-in Policies	0.5 days?	▨ PM2			
5		5	Setup: Configure Build	1 day?	▨ PM1			
6		6	Setup: Send Mail to Users for Installs	0.25 days?	▨ PM2			
7		7	Create Vision Statement	1 day?	▨ PM1			
8		8	Create Personas	1 day?	▨ PM2			
9		9	Define Iteration Length	0.25 days?	▨ PM1			
10		10	Create Test Approach Worksheet in(	3 days?	▨ SQA1			
11		11	Brainstorm and Prioritize Scenarios L	3 days?	▨ PM1			
12		12	Brainstorm and Prioritize Quality of S	3 days?	▨ PM2			
13		13	Setup: Create Project Structure	1 day?	▨ PM1			
14		14	Create Iteration Plan	1 day?	▨ PM2			
15		61	Display Welcome Message	1 day?	▨ Dev1			
16		67	Add Logout Button	1 day?	▨ Dev2			
17		68	Create Unit Tests	3 days?	▨ Dev1			
18		69	Add Report Parameter Handling	1 day?	▨ Dev2			
19		70	Add User Authentication	3 days?	▨ Dev1			
20		71	Perform Integration Testing	3 days?	▨ SQA2			
21		72	Perform Regression Testing	3 days?	▨ SQA1			
22		73	Add Search Functionality	1 day?	▨ Dev1			
23		74	Add Customer Balance Report	1 day?	▨ Dev2			
24		75	Add Transaction History Report	1 day?	▨ Dev1			

FIGURE 4.4 Project integration tool creates a connected project plan from the specified team query.

You can also import VSTS work items from Project. You can use the options in the Team toolbar (see Figure 4.5) or in the Team menu to interact with VSTS. Click Choose Team Project (in the Team toolbar); in the Connect to Team Foundation Server dialog box, choose the server and the team project. Click Get Work Items (in the Team toolbar); in the Get Work Items dialog box (see Figure 4.6), select one of the queries stored in VSTS or create a simple ad-hoc query. You can further limit the tasks by individually selecting/deselecting them from the list. Click OK to import the selected tasks to Project.

FIGURE 4.5 The Team toolbar in Project.

Once a project plan is connected to a team project in VSTS, two new views and two new tables become available. The new views are: Team System Gantt and Team System Task Sheet (see Figure 4.7). The new tables are: Team Explorer Tracking and Team Explorer Full (see Figure 4.8).

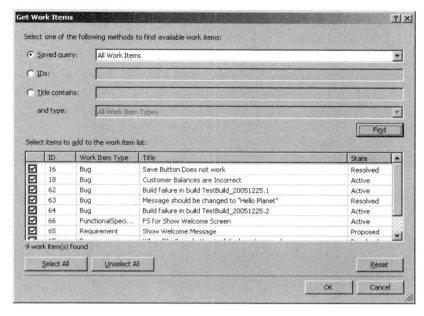

FIGURE 4.6   The Work item selection dialog in Project.

FIGURE 4.7   Connected project plans contain additional Team System-related views.

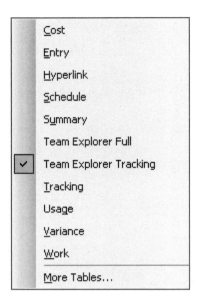

FIGURE 4.8 Connected project plans contain additional team system-related tables.

Add Summary Tasks and Milestones

Summary tasks represent important phases of the project. Think of a summary task as a 'rolled up' aggregation of a set of tasks. The duration, start date, end date, and several other attributes of summary tasks are not entered directly; these values are automatically calculated from child tasks.

Milestones represent important events in a project's lifetime. They usually have zero duration (but nonzero durations are also allowed). Milestones allow stakeholders to monitor progress at a higher level of granularity.

Enter summary tasks and milestones in the project plan as shown in Figure 4.9. Create summary tasks by indenting the child tasks under them. To designate a task as a milestone, double-click the task to bring up the Task Information dialog box. Click the Advanced tab and select Mark Task as Milestone check box (see Figure 4.10).

Notice that for summary tasks and milestones, the values in the Publish and Refresh field are set to "No." A value of "No" in this field means that these tasks are not synchronized with VSTS. Valid values in this field and their interpretations are as follows:

Yes: Indicates that the task will take part in bidirectional synchronization; changes in Project will be published to VSTS, and changes in VSTS will be transmitted to Project.

No: Indicates that the task will be local to Project and will not take part in communications with VSTS. This is the value usually set for summary tasks and milestones.

Refresh Only: Indicates that changes in Project will not be sent to VSTS, but updates from VSTS will be reflected in Project.

	Work Item ID	Title	Duration	Start	Finish	Resource Names	Work Item Type	Publish and Refresh	Jan 1, '06 S S M T W T F S S
1		⊟ Setting up Project	**3 days?**	**Sun 1/1/06**	**Wed 1/4/06**			No	
2	1	Setup: Set Permissions	1 day?	Mon 1/2/06	Mon 1/2/06	PM1	Task	Yes	PM1
3	2	Setup: Migration of Source Code	2 days?	Mon 1/2/06	Tue 1/3/06	PM2	Task	Yes	PM2
4	3	Setup: Migration of Work Items	1 day?	Mon 1/2/06	Mon 1/2/06	PM1	Task	Yes	PM1
5	4	Setup: Set Check-in Policies	0.5 days?	Mon 1/2/06	Mon 1/2/06	PM2	Task	Yes	PM2
6	5	Setup: Configure Build	1 day?	Mon 1/2/06	Mon 1/2/06	PM1	Task	Yes	PM1
7	6	Setup: Send Mail to Users for Insta	0.25 days?	Mon 1/2/06	Mon 1/2/06	PM2	Task	Yes	PM2
8	13	Setup: Create Project Structure	1 day?	Mon 1/2/06	Mon 1/2/06	PM1	Task	Yes	PM1
9	7	Create Vision Statement	1 day?	Mon 1/2/06	Mon 1/2/06	PM1	Task	Yes	PM1
10	8	Create Personas	1 day?	Mon 1/2/06	Mon 1/2/06	PM2	Task	Yes	PM2
11	9	Define Iteration Length	0.25 days?	Mon 1/2/06	Mon 1/2/06	PM1	Task	Yes	PM1
12	10	Create Test Approach Worksheet	3 days?	Mon 1/2/06	Wed 1/4/06	SQA1	Task	Yes	SQA1
13	11	Brainstorm and Prioritize Scenario	3 days?	Mon 1/2/06	Wed 1/4/06	PM1	Task	Yes	PM1
14	12	Brainstorm and Prioritize Quality o	3 days?	Mon 1/2/06	Wed 1/4/06	PM2	Task	Yes	PM2
15	14	Create Iteration Plan	1 day?	Mon 1/2/06	Mon 1/2/06	PM2	Task	Yes	PM2
16		Project Setup Completed	0 days	Sun 1/1/06	Sun 1/1/06			No	◆ 1/1
17		⊟ Developing Code	**3 days?**	**Sun 1/1/06**	**Wed 1/4/06**			No	
18	61	Display Welcome Message	1 day?	Mon 1/2/06	Mon 1/2/06	Dev1	Task	Yes	Dev1
19	67	Add Logout Button	1 day?	Mon 1/2/06	Mon 1/2/06	Dev2	Task	Yes	Dev2
20	68	Create Unit Tests	3 days?	Mon 1/2/06	Wed 1/4/06	Dev1	Task	Yes	Dev1
21	69	Add Report Parameter Handling	1 day?	Mon 1/2/06	Mon 1/2/06	Dev2	Task	Yes	Dev2
22	70	Add User Authentication	3 days?	Mon 1/2/06	Wed 1/4/06	Dev1	Task	Yes	Dev1
23	73	Add Search Functionality	1 day?	Mon 1/2/06	Mon 1/2/06	Dev1	Task	Yes	Dev1
24	74	Add Customer Balance Report	1 day?	Mon 1/2/06	Mon 1/2/06	Dev2	Task	Yes	Dev2
25	75	Add Transaction History Report	1 day?	Mon 1/2/06	Mon 1/2/06	Dev1	Task	Yes	Dev1
26		Code Development Completed	0 days	Sun 1/1/06	Sun 1/1/06			No	◆ 1/1
27		⊟ Conducting SQA	**3 days?**	**Sun 1/1/06**	**Wed 1/4/06**			No	
28	71	Perform Integraton Testing	3 days?	Mon 1/2/06	Wed 1/4/06	SQA2	Task	Yes	SQA2
29	72	Perform Regression Testing	3 days?	Mon 1/2/06	Wed 1/4/06	SQA1	Task	Yes	SQA1
30		Iteration Completed	0 days	Sun 1/1/06	Sun 1/1/06			No	◆ 1/1

FIGURE 4.9   Summary tasks and milestones added to the project plan.

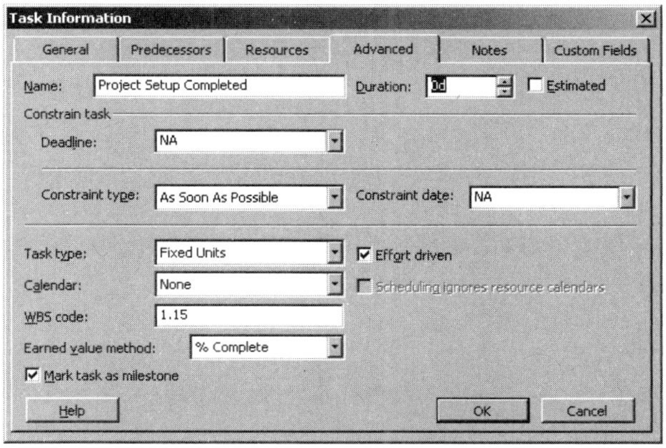

FIGURE 4.10   A task is marked as a milestone in the Advanced tab of the Task Information screen.

Summary tasks and milestones enable stakeholders to look at the project plan at different levels of detail. For example, senior management might be interested in key milestones only and might not care about additional details. To display different levels of hierarchy, click the Project menu, click Outline, click Show, and choose the level that you would like to see (see Figure 4.11 and Figure 4.12). If you would like to show only milestone information, click the Project menu and select Filtered For/Milestones.

❶	Work Item ID	Title	Duration	Start	Finish	Predecessors	Resour Name	Jan 1, '06 S S M T W T F S
1		⊞ Setting up Project	3 days?	Sun 1/1/06	Wed 1/4/06			
17		⊞ Developing Code	3 days?	Sun 1/1/06	Wed 1/4/06			
27		⊞ Conducting SQA	3 days?	Sun 1/1/06	Wed 1/4/06			

FIGURE 4.11 Project plan filtered to show summary tasks only.

❶	Work Item ID	Title	Duration	Start	Finish	Predecessors	Resour Name	Jan 1, '06 S S M T W T F S
1		⊟ Setting up Project	3 days?	Sun 1/1/06	Wed 1/4/06			
16		Project Setup Completed	0 days	Sun 1/1/06	Sun 1/1/06			◆ 1/1
17		⊟ Developing Code	3 days?	Sun 1/1/06	Wed 1/4/06			
26		Code Development Completed	0 days	Sun 1/1/06	Sun 1/1/06			◆ 1/1
27		⊟ Conducting SQA	3 days?	Sun 1/1/06	Wed 1/4/06			
30		Iteration Completed	0 days	Sun 1/1/06	Sun 1/1/06			◆ 1/1

FIGURE 4.12 Project plan filtered to show milestones only.

Schedule Tasks

Project is one of the best task scheduling tools on the market. However, the effectiveness of the scheduling process is diminished if hard-coded dates are added as task constraints. Instead, specify task dependencies, resource allocations, and so forth, and let Project do the scheduling.

To specify dependencies, select multiple tasks and click the Link Tasks icon in the Standard toolbar (or click Edit menu and select Link Tasks). The default link type is Finish-to-Start, but you can choose other link types as appropriate. You can also set up dependencies by typing the appropriate task Id in the Predecessor column.

Once the dependencies are specified, double check resource allocations and make necessary adjustments. In our suggested workflow, preliminary resource allocations take place in VSTS (so that the resource pool in Project is properly set up). Do not create any new resources in Project unless they exist in VSTS; otherwise, you'll encounter errors when you try to publish the changes. Furthermore, note that although Project allows a task to be assigned to multiple resources, VSTS allows a work item to be assigned to a single resource only. Therefore, to avoid synchronization problems, do not assign a task to more than a single resource in Project.

Perform resource leveling to make sure that resources are not over-allocated. Click the Tools menu and select Level Resources. In the Resource Leveling dialog box (see Figure 4.13) select your preferred options and click the Level Now button. You can view day-by-day task allocation for each resource by switching to the Resource Usage view (see Figure 4.14).

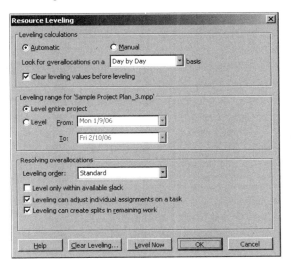

FIGURE 4.13   The Resource Leveling dialog box offers various options to fine-tune resource leveling.

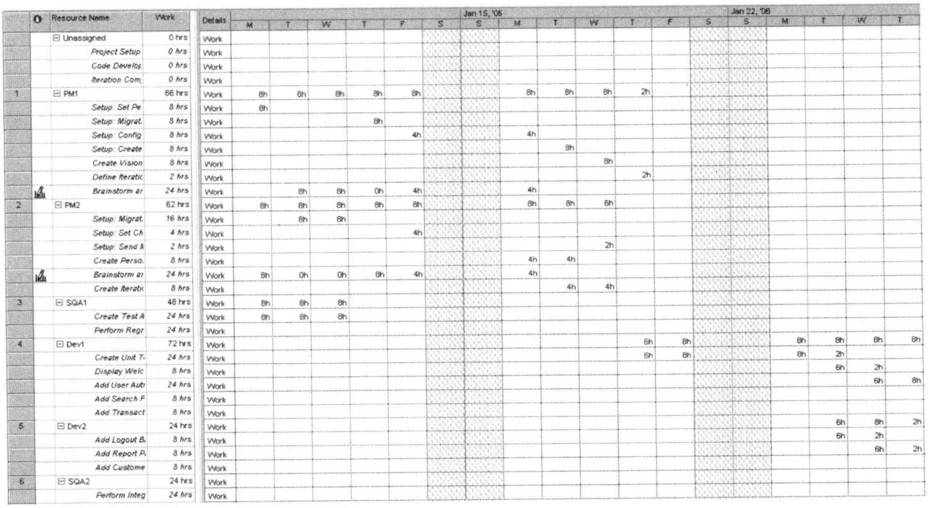

FIGURE 4.14   Resource Usage view provides detailed information regarding planned activities for each resource.

At this point, you have a project plan with task dependencies and balanced resource allocations. Feel free to further modify the project plan manually to better align the schedule with ground realities, taking into consideration issues like task-switching time, communication overhead, and efficiency of particular resources. The final project plan is shown in Figure 4.15.

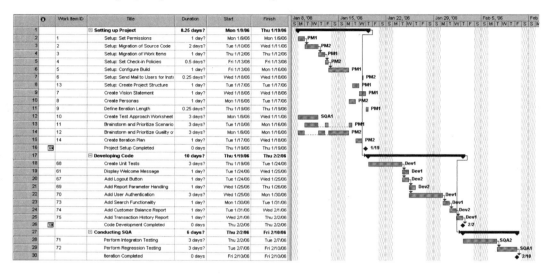

FIGURE 4.15 The final project plan contains task dependency and resource allocation information.

Publish Changes to VSTS

Synchronize the project plan with the data stored in VSTS by clicking Publish in the Team toolbar in Project. After replicating the changes in VSTS, you'll notice that various work item fields have been updated. For example, note that the Scheduled Start Date and Scheduled End Date fields have been stamped with corresponding dates from the project plan (see Figure 4.16). These values are derived from the project plan and cannot be updated from VSTS, as far as the project plan is concerned. (As discussed later in the chapter, the PublishOnly attributes of these fields are set to "true" in the VSTS/Project mapping file. Consequently, you can *not* change these dates in VSTS and update the project plan with modified values.)

Manage Data Conflicts

A conflict occurs during a publish operation if the task data in a mapped field has changed both in VSTS and the project plan since the time of last synchronization. The integration tool is smart enough to detect whether conflicting changes have been made in the two systems since the tool was last run. If a conflict is detected,

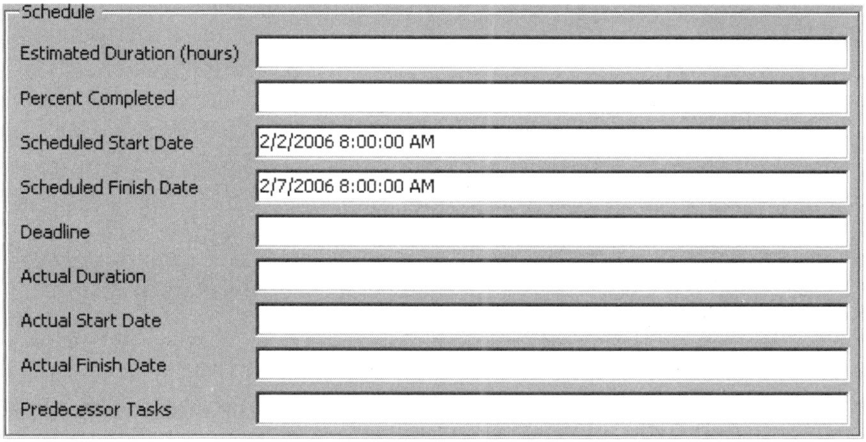

Schedule

Estimated Duration (hours)	
Percent Completed	
Scheduled Start Date	2/2/2006 8:00:00 AM
Scheduled Finish Date	2/7/2006 8:00:00 AM
Deadline	
Actual Duration	
Actual Start Date	
Actual Finish Date	
Predecessor Tasks	

FIGURE 4.16 Mapped fields in VSTS are automatically updated by the Project integration tool.

Project displays a dialog box presenting the VSTS version of the data along with the version in Project (see Figure 4.17). You can inspect the VSTS version of the work item in read-only mode by clicking the View Database Version button. Indicate your choice by selecting the appropriate check box.

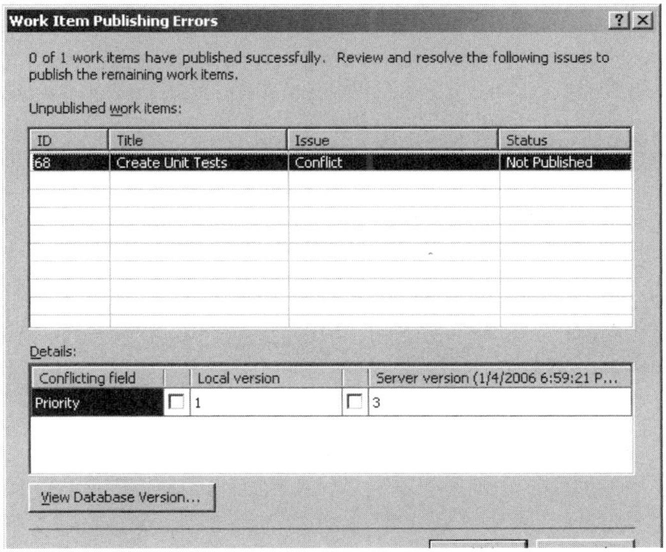

Work Item Publishing Errors   ? X

0 of 1 work items have published successfully. Review and resolve the following issues to publish the remaining work items.

Unpublished work items:

ID	Title	Issue	Status
68	Create Unit Tests	Conflict	Not Published

Details:

Conflicting field	Local version	Server version (1/4/2006 6:59:21 P...
Priority	☐ 1	☐ 3

View Database Version...

FIGURE 4.17 The Work Item Publishing Errors screen allows you to resolve conflicts.

CUSTOMIZING PROJECT INTEGRATION

The behavior of the synchronization tool can be modified to better fit your organizational needs. For example, you might want to change the way progress is tracked, as well as capture additional task-related data. In this section, we consider the following enhancements associated with the Agile Outsourcing process template (see Chapter 3, "Leveraging VSTS and Customizing MSF Agile" for more information on modifying the Agile Outsourcing process template). Figure 4.18 shows schedule-related information in the Details tab of a task work item.

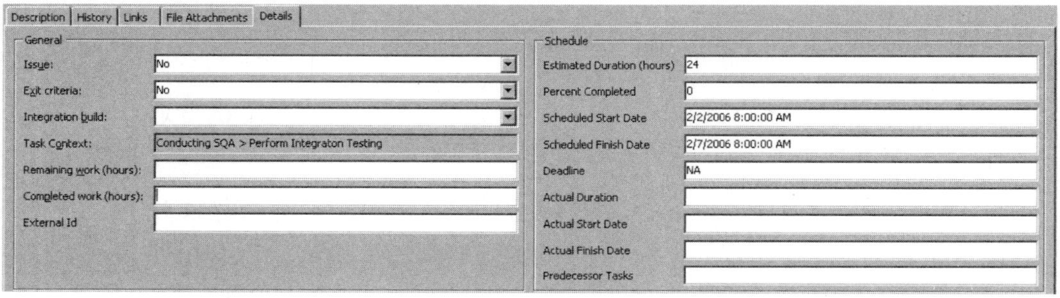

FIGURE 4.18 The Details tab in the VSTS task form contains predefined and custom fields related to scheduling.

Estimated Duration and Percent Completed: In Project, progress can be tracked in various ways (see Figure 4.19). By default, the integration tool tracks based upon the Actual Work and Remaining Work fields (in VSTS and Project). However, you may choose the simpler way of specifying progress in terms of Estimated Duration and Percent Completed, and let Project automatically calculate values for Actual Work and Remaining Work. Agile Outsourcing takes this approach and introduces two new fields—Estimated Duration and Percent Completed—for tracking progress in VSTS. You could, of course, stick to using the Actual Work and Remaining Work fields in VSTS. However, to avoid confusion, both sets of fields should *not* be used to synchronize with Project; pick one set of fields for tracking progress and use it consistently. Agile Outsourcing bidirectionally synchronizes Estimated Duration and Percent Completed fields with Project. Actual Work and Remaining Work fields are used uni-directionally to capture information from Project—changes in Project are sent to VSTS, but not vice versa.

Actual Start Date and Actual Finish Date: By default, actual start and finish dates are not synchronized between VSTS and Project. Agile Outsourcing adds two fields named Actual Start Date and Actual Finish Date for tracking progress in VSTS. These fields are bidirectionally synchronized with Project.

Deadline: If a task has a deadline, it is helpful to view the information in both VSTS and Project. Agile Outsourcing adds a field named Deadline in VSTS and bidirectionally synchronizes it with Project.

Predecessors: Since tasks frequently have dependencies, it is useful to synchronize task-dependency information between VSTS and Project. However, the challenge is that in VSTS, predecessors are indicated using VSTS-assigned work item Ids, whereas in Project, predecessors are determined using Project-assigned task Ids. Consequently, we need to translate the predecessor Ids from one system to another. The conversion is accomplished by modifying the mapping file and executing a custom add-in. When data is transferred to Project, the Predecessor Ids from VSTS are inserted in a placeholder field in Project. Subsequently, we run a custom add-in to translate the predecessor work item Ids (assigned by VSTS) to predecessor task Ids (assigned by Project). We perform the reverse process when transferring information to VSTS from Project (see "Technical Review: Creating a Custom Add-In for Project" later in this chapter).

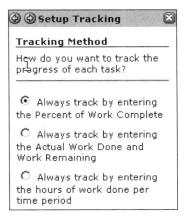

FIGURE 4.19 Tracking options available in Project.

Note that the Actual Duration field in Agile Outsourcing is *not* synchronized with Project. The meaning of this field is different in the two systems. In VSTS/Agile Outsourcing, this field represents the actual *total* time taken to complete a task. The value of the Actual Duration field is typically entered by a developer (or by an automated process) when a task is completed. The information contained in the Actual Duration field is used in custom VSTS reports that display schedule conformance and deviation. However, in Project, Actual Duration indicates the amount of work that has been done *so far;* its value is calculated according to the following formula:

$$Actual\ Duration = Duration * Percent\ Complete$$

View Field Mappings

You can view the current field mappings between VSTS and Project by clicking the Team menu and selecting View Column Mappings (the current project plan needs to be connected to VSTS to be able to see the mappings). This action brings up the Column Mapping dialog box (see Figure 4.20).

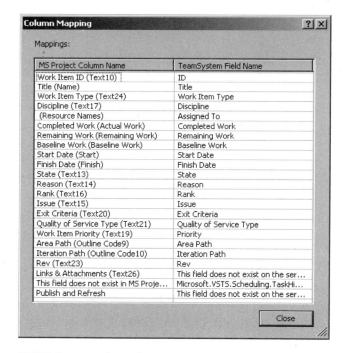

FIGURE 4.20   The Column Mapping screen in Project displays predefined mappings.

Download the Mapping File

The field mapping is based upon an XML file. You can view the contents of the XML file in one of the following ways.

Download the Agile Outsourcing process template as a set of XML files. In VSTS, on the Team menu, point to Team Foundation Server Settings and then click Process Template Manager. In the Process Template Manager dialog box, select the Agile Outsourcing process template. (Refer to Chapter 3, "Leveraging VSTS and Customizing MSF Agile," for how to create the Agile Outsourcing process template.) Click Download. The VSTS-Project mapping information is stored in a file named FileMapping.xml, which is located in the Classification directory.

Alternatively, use the TfsFieldMapping tool to download the VSTS-Project mapping information for a specific team project. Navigate to the directory containing TfsFieldMapping.exe (e.g., Program Files\Microsoft Visual Studio 8\ Common7\IDE) and type the following line in the command prompt window:

```
TfsFieldMapping download http://<your_server_name>:8080
<your_team_project_name> <path_for_file_to_download>
```

Replace "<your_server_name>" with the name of your Team Foundation Server machine, "<your_team_project_name>" with the name of your team project, and "<path_for_file_to_download>" with the location and name of the downloaded mapping file.

Whichever method is followed to fetch the mapping file, its default contents are shown in Listing 4.1:

LISTING 4.1 Contents of the Project Mapping File

```
<?xml version="1.0" encoding="utf-8"?>
<MSProject>
  <Mappings>

    <Mapping WorkItemTrackingFieldReferenceName="System.Id"
        ProjectField="pjTaskText10" ProjectName="Work Item ID"/>
    <Mapping WorkItemTrackingFieldReferenceName="System.Title"
        ProjectField="pjTaskName" />
    <Mapping WorkItemTrackingFieldReferenceName
        ="System.WorkItemType" ProjectField="pjTaskText24" />
    <Mapping WorkItemTrackingFieldReferenceName=
        "Microsoft.VSTS.Common.Discipline"
        ProjectField="pjTaskText17" />
    <Mapping WorkItemTrackingFieldReferenceName=
        "System.AssignedTo" ProjectField="pjTaskResourceNames" />
    <Mapping WorkItemTrackingFieldReferenceName=
        "Microsoft.VSTS.Scheduling.CompletedWork"
        ProjectField="pjTaskActualWork" ProjectUnits="pjHour"/>
    <Mapping WorkItemTrackingFieldReferenceName=
        "Microsoft.VSTS.Scheduling.RemainingWork" ProjectField=
        "pjTaskRemainingWork" ProjectUnits="pjHour"/>
    <Mapping WorkItemTrackingFieldReferenceName=
        "Microsoft.VSTS.Scheduling.BaselineWork"
        ProjectField="pjTaskBaselineWork" ProjectUnits="pjHour"/>
```

```
<Mapping WorkItemTrackingFieldReferenceName=
    "Microsoft.VSTS.Scheduling.StartDate"
    ProjectField="pjTaskStart" PublishOnly="true"/>
<Mapping WorkItemTrackingFieldReferenceName=
    "Microsoft.VSTS.Scheduling.FinishDate"
    ProjectField="pjTaskFinish"  PublishOnly="true"/>
<Mapping WorkItemTrackingFieldReferenceName="System.State"
    ProjectField="State" />
<Mapping WorkItemTrackingFieldReferenceName="System.Reason"
    ProjectField="pjTaskText14" />
<Mapping WorkItemTrackingFieldReferenceName=
    "Microsoft.VSTS.Common.Rank"
    ProjectField="pjTaskText16" />
<Mapping WorkItemTrackingFieldReferenceName=
    "Microsoft.VSTS.Common.Issue"
    ProjectField="pjTaskText15" />
<Mapping WorkItemTrackingFieldReferenceName=
    "Microsoft.VSTS.Common.ExitCriteria"
    ProjectField="pjTaskText20" />
<Mapping WorkItemTrackingFieldReferenceName=
    "Microsoft.VSTS.Common.QualityOfServiceType"
    ProjectField="pjTaskText21" />
<Mapping WorkItemTrackingFieldReferenceName=
    "Microsoft.VSTS.Common.RoughOrderOfMagnitude"
    ProjectField="pjTaskText22" />
<Mapping WorkItemTrackingFieldReferenceName=
    "Microsoft.VSTS.Common.Priority"
    ProjectField="pjTaskText19"
    ProjectName="Work Item Priority" />
<Mapping WorkItemTrackingFieldReferenceName=
    "System.AreaPath" ProjectField="pjTaskOutlineCode9" />
<Mapping WorkItemTrackingFieldReferenceName=
    "System.IterationPath"
    ProjectField="pjTaskOutlineCode10" />
<Mapping WorkItemTrackingFieldReferenceName="System.Rev"
    ProjectField="pjTaskText23" />
<ContextField WorkItemTrackingFieldReferenceName=
    "Microsoft.VSTS.Scheduling.TaskHierarchy"/>

<LinksField ProjectField="pjTaskText26" />
<SyncField ProjectField="pjTaskText25" />
    </Mappings>
</MSProject>
```

Notice in Listing 4.1 that the StartDate and FinishDate fields contain an attribute named PublishOnly, which is set to "true." Changes made to these dates in VSTS are not transferred to the project plan; however, updated dates from Project are sent to VSTS. As a related cautionary note, unless you are a power user and know exactly what you are doing, do *not* set the PublishOnly attributes of these fields to "false." In version one of VSTS, there are issues with the Project calculation engine, and the results are sometimes unpredictable.

Modify the Mapping File

Modify the Project mapping file to add support for the following VSTS fields:

- Percent Completed
- Estimated Duration
- Predecessors
- Actual Start Date
- Actual Finish Date
- Deadline

Add the entries shown in Listing 4.2.

LISTING 4.2   Custom Mappings Added to the Project Mapping File

```
<!— Custom fields added for Agile Outsourcing —>
<Mapping WorkItemTrackingFieldReferenceName=
    "Microsoft.VSTS.Scheduling.ActualStartDate"
    ProjectField="pjTaskText27" />
<Mapping WorkItemTrackingFieldReferenceName=
    "Microsoft.VSTS.Scheduling.ActualFinishDate"
    ProjectField=" pjTaskText28" />
<Mapping WorkItemTrackingFieldReferenceName=
    "Microsoft.VSTS.Scheduling.DeadlineDate"
    ProjectField=" pjTaskText29" />
<Mapping WorkItemTrackingFieldReferenceName=
    "CRM.Outsourcing.Scheduling.Predecessors"
    ProjectField="pjTaskText30" />
<Mapping WorkItemTrackingFieldReferenceName=
    "CRM.Outsourcing.Scheduling.PercentCompleted"
    ProjectField="pjTaskPercentComplete" />
<Mapping WorkItemTrackingFieldReferenceName=
    "CRM.Outsourcing.Scheduling.EstimatedDuration"
    ProjectField="pjTaskDuration" ProjectUnits="pjHour" />
```

Agile Outsourcing uses the fields added in Listing 4.2 to monitor progress. Since we added `EstimatedDuration` and `PercentCompleted`, we need to make the `ActualWork` and `RemainingWork` fields non-editable from VSTS by setting their `PublishOnly` attributes to "`true`" (see Listing 4.3).

To avoid confusion, we enter estimate and progress information in VSTS using the `EstimatedDuration` and `PercentCompleted` fields. If you would like to use `ActualWork` and `RemainingWork` instead, do *not* set their `PublishOnly` attributes to "`true`." Furthermore, set the `PublishOnly` attributes of `EstimatedDuration` and `PercentCompleted` to "`true`."

You need to keep in mind an important point when customizing the VSTS/ Project mapping file. The order of entries in the mapping file determines the sequence of conversion steps. This is of greater importance during the VSTS-to-Project synchronization process, since many of the fields in Project are interrelated. For example, if EstimatedDuration and PercentCompleted fields appear *after* ActualWork and RemainingWork fields in the mapping file, then during VSTS-to-Project synchronization, the values in ActualWork and RemainingWork will *always* be overwritten by the values in the EstimatedDuration and PercentCompleted fields in the project plan. That is why we set the PublishOnly attributes of ActualWork and RemainingWork fields to "true" in the mapping file, and only use EstimatedDuration and PercentCompleted fields for VSTS-Project integration purposes. We let Project automatically calculate the values of ActualWork and RemainingWork; the values in these fields are published to VSTS.

LISTING 4.3   ActualWork and RemainingWork Fields Made Read-Only in VSTS

```
<Mapping WorkItemTrackingFieldReferenceName=
    "Microsoft.VSTS.Scheduling.CompletedWork"
    ProjectField="pjTaskActualWork" ProjectUnits="pjHour"
    PublishOnly="true"/>
<Mapping  WorkItemTrackingFieldReferenceName=
    "Microsoft.VSTS.Scheduling.RemainingWork"
    ProjectField="pjTaskRemainingWork" ProjectUnits="pjHour"
    PublishOnly="true"/>
```

Upload the Mapping File

If you downloaded the Agile Outsourcing process template and made modifications to the FileMapping.xml file, use the Process Template Manager to upload the changes back to Team Foundation Server. In VSTS, on the Team menu, point to Team Foundation Server Settings and click Process Template Manager. In the Process Template Manager dialog box, select the Agile Outsourcing process template and click Upload. Subsequent team projects created using the updated process template will contain the new mappings for Project.

If you downloaded the Project mapping file using TfsFieldMapping.exe, upload the modified file to Team Foundation Server by typing the following line in the command prompt window:

```
TfsFieldMapping upload http://<your_server_name>:8080
<your_team_project_name> <path_for_file_to_upload>
```

Replace "<your_server_name>" with the name of your Team Foundation Server machine, "<your_team_project_name>" with the name of your team project, and "<path_for_file_to_upload>" with the location and name of the modified mapping file.

You can verify your changes by clicking the Team menu in Project and selecting View Column Mappings (see Figure 4.21).

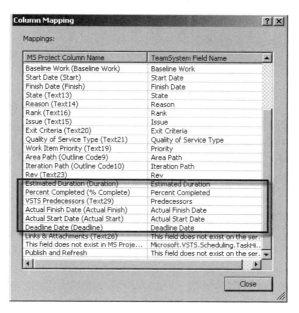

FIGURE 4.21 The Column Mapping screen in Project displays additional custom mappings.

WALK-THROUGH: TRACKING PROGRESS

After the project plan and the mapping file are set up, and project implementation begins, you'll want to monitor progress at regular intervals. Traditionally, this is where many project managers get lost, and the project plan becomes little more than a historical record of an optimistic vision. The core problem is that regularly updating the project plan with actual data is a cumbersome process. When working with remote teams, the overhead and friction associated with gathering detailed progress data often becomes prohibitive. Consequently, the original plan is abandoned, and the project is managed on an ad-hoc basis. This is one of the key pain points in offshore project management.

VSTS and its Project integration feature helps mitigate the problem of gathering work data and updating the project plan. As discussed earlier, the basic strategy is as follows:

1. Remote developers enter status information (*actuals* in Project terminology) in VSTS.
2. Actuals are automatically updated in the project plan using the Project integration feature.

3. The project manager analyses the project plan, identifies problems, and takes corrective measures.
4. Changes in the project plan are published back to VSTS.
5. Stakeholders view status information using a combination of reports created with Project and SQL Server 2005 Reporting Services.

This approach simplifies offshore project management and enhances team productivity by automating routine time-consuming tasks. Let us walk through an example.

Save a Baseline

To make effective tracking possible, save the current plan as a *baseline* before implementation begins. To save a baseline, click the Tools menu, point to Tracking, and click Save Baseline. You can save up to 10 baseline versions in the Save Baseline dialog box (see Figure 4.22). You can also update a previously saved baseline with current values.

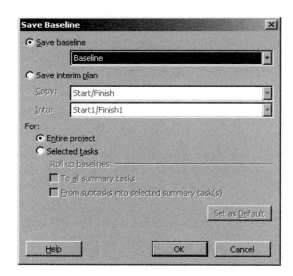

FIGURE 4.22   Use the Save Baseline dialog box to save multiple baseline versions.

Enter Actuals in VSTS

To understand the data capture and transfer process, let us look at updating a single task item. Open the Add User Authentication work item and enter actual information as follows (see Figure 4.23):

- Percent Complete: 50 (percent)
- Actual Start Date: 1/26/2006 (delayed by one day from the scheduled start date of 1/25/2006)

We'll now see how the progress information gets updated in Project.

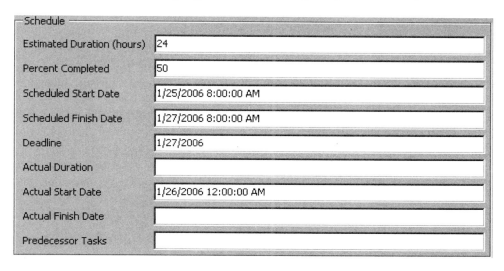

FIGURE 4.23   Progress information entered in VSTS.

Refresh the Project Plan

Launch Project and open the previously created, connected project plan. Click Refresh on the Team toolbar. The task information is updated with the corresponding values captured in VSTS (see Figure 4.24).

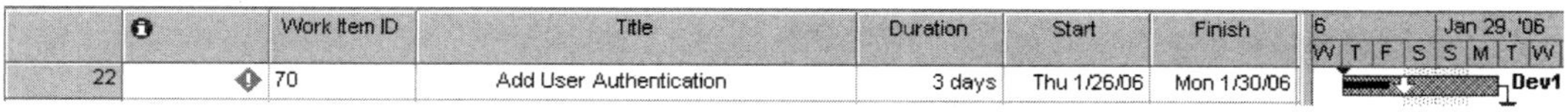

	ⓘ	Work Item ID	Title	Duration	Start	Finish	6	Jan 29, '06
22	◆	70	Add User Authentication	3 days	Thu 1/26/06	Mon 1/30/06		Dev1

FIGURE 4.24   Task updated with progress information captured in VSTS.

Note the red icon in the indicator field. Hover the mouse pointer on the icon; a message pops up stating that the task is scheduled to be completed after the deadline date.

Handle Predecessors

As discussed earlier, predecessor information is not transferred between VSTS and Project by default. However, we feel that it is important to present predecessor information in VSTS because developers typically do not use Project. Developers primarily use VSTS to look at their task assignments. VSTS/Agile Outsourcing introduces a new field called Predecessors to track task dependencies. We mapped this VSTS field to a custom field in Project in the mapping file discussed earlier.

We create an add-in in Project to process the predecessor information stored in the custom field. The add-in works as follows:

- Inserts a new button named Process Imported Tasks in the Team toolbar in Project (see Figure 4.25). When clicked, the add-in processes the predecessor information imported from VSTS and updates Project.
- The add-in automatically hooks into the event handler for the Publish button. When you click Publish, the add-in automatically processes the task dependencies and stores the information in the mapped custom field. The built-in synchronization tool then transfers the predecessor information from the custom field to VSTS.

FIGURE 4.25 Process Imported Tasks menu added to the team toolbar.

Analyze the Project Plan

Once the project plan is updated with actuals, the next order of business is to study the project plan and look for problems. Project offers a wealth of tools for examining various aspects of the plan. In this section, we look at a few simple ways to spot problems.

Study Variance Information

Open the variance table to review schedule deviations *vis-à-vis* the baseline plan. Click the View menu, point to Table, and click Variance. Add the following columns to the table to better understand deviations from the plan:

- Actual Start
- Actual Finish
- Actual Work
- Remaining Work

Figure 4.26 shows the schedule information for the Add User Authentication task. The collection of fields provides fine-grained information regarding schedule divergence.

	Task Name	Start	Finish	Baseline Start	Baseline Finish	Start Var.	Finish Var.	Actual Start	Actual Finish	Actual Work	Remaining Work
22	Add User Authentication	Thu 1/26/06	Mon 1/30/06	Wed 1/25/06	Fri 1/27/06	1 day	1 day	Thu 1/26/06	NA	12 hrs	12 hrs

FIGURE 4.26   Variance table displays information regarding schedule deviations.

Select the Tracking Gantt view to look at the schedule variance graphically. On the View menu, point to More Views, and click Tracking Gantt (see Figure 4.27). The bar at the bottom corresponds to the baseline schedule, and the bar on top represents the current schedule based upon actuals.

	ⓘ	Work Item ID	Title	Duration	Start	Finish	22, '06	Jan 29, '06
22	◈	70	Add User Authentication	3 days	Thu 1/26/06	Mon 1/30/06		50%

FIGURE 4.27   Tracking Gantt view graphically displays schedule divergence.

Filter Delayed Tasks

You can use filters to look at a specific subset of tasks. Project provides a number of predefined filters and also enables you to create custom filters. To display only the tasks that are falling behind (compared to the baseline finish date), click the Filter drop-down in the Formatting toolbar and select Slipping Tasks. The project plan displays the Add User Authentication task, since currently it is the only task projected to finish later than the planned baseline finish date.

Create a custom filter to display tasks that are projected to finish later than their deadline dates. On the Project menu, point to Filtered For and click More Filters. In the More Filters dialog box, click New to bring up the Field Definition dialog box. Enter the conditions shown in Figure 4.28; name the new filter Tasks Finishing After Deadline. Select the custom filter from the filter drop-down in the Formatting toolbar. The project plan will show only the Add User Authentication task (since currently it is the only task anticipated to go beyond its deadline).

Identify Critical Tasks

As you receive *actuals* from the offshore team and track progress, one of the key questions you'll try to answer is whether the project is slipping past its scheduled end date. In complex projects, the answer is not immediately obvious; not every delayed task jeopardizes the project deadline. Some tasks can be delayed without affecting the project end date. However, if delays in particular tasks compromise

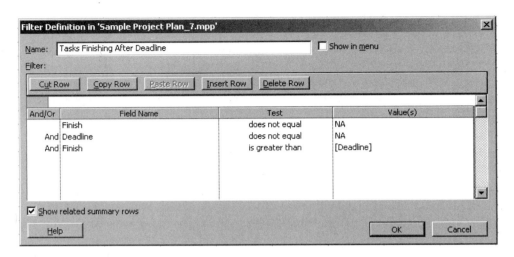

FIGURE 4.28 Create a custom filter to display tasks that are slipping beyond their deadlines.

the project completion date, you'll need to take them seriously and look for ways to resolve the problem (e.g., go for overtime hours, bring in more people, get lucky with other tasks, etc.). You could try to make up for the lost time in the next delivery, drop features, or inform stakeholders of the delay and reschedule the project completion date.

Tasks that can't be delayed without jeopardizing the project completion date are called *critical* tasks. Tasks that dictate the project end date are on the *critical path*. Note that in Project terminology, the term "critical" does not necessary mean "very important" from the perspective of the task's contribution to the overall project. "Critical" simply means that the task can't be delayed without pushing back the project end date. Furthermore, the set of tasks that are on the critical path could change as the project gets underway and schedule variances (both positive and negative) take place. Critical tasks have zero *slack* by default. To change the slack threshold, click the Tools menu and select Options. In the Options dialog box, click the Calculation tab and specify a new value for slack (choose the number of days for "Tasks are critical if slack is less than or equal to" option).

You can automatically perform critical path analysis using Project. This functionality can be invoked in various ways. For example, you can filter the project plan to show only critical tasks (see Figure 4.29). You can also use the Detail Gantt view to understand how much slack exists for various tasks; the tasks marked in red have zero slack time and represent critical tasks (see Figure 4.30).

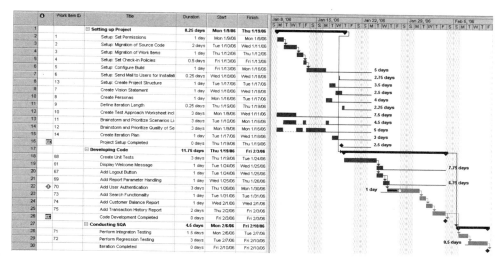

FIGURE 4.29   Filter the project plan to display critical tasks.

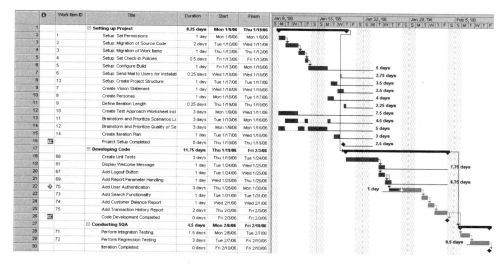

FIGURE 4.30   The Detail Gantt view displays slack times associated with tasks.

SHARING INFORMATION WITH STAKEHOLDERS

Once the project plan is updated with the latest tracking data, it is ready to be shared with various stakeholders. As discussed earlier, different parties will want to look at the status reports in different ways and at different levels of granularity. You can use built-in or custom views and reports to disseminate the information. The higher-level views and reports can be automatically derived from the fine-grained data collected from VSTS, thereby enhancing accuracy. The goal is to refresh custom views and reports with minimum manual intervention—that is, to set up a data feed from the developers' fingertips directly to management dashboards.

You can create custom documents, reports, and charts in Project, and distribute them via email or upload them to the project portal site. Moreover, stakeholders can view reports (predefined as well as custom) created using SQL Server 2005 Reporting Services from the portal site (or subscribe to them for email delivery). In this section, we look at various status-reporting options available in Project. To learn more about custom VSTS reports and the project portal, refer to Chapter 9, "Enterprise Reporting," and Chapter 10, "Using the Project Portal."

Share the Project File

If members of the target audience have Project installed on their desktops, you can simply upload the connected project plan to the SharePoint-based project portal. Distributed stakeholders can work on the plan collaboratively or simply view status information. (For more information on Web-based document sharing, refer to Chapter 10, "Using the Project Portal.") If the parties have Team Explorer installed locally and have connectivity to the TFS server, they can also refresh the project plan using the latest data in VSTS (as well as publish their local changes to VSTS). However, this option may be an overkill in some situations, and the usual requirements of stakeholders can be satisfied using a combination of Project reports and views, as well as SQL Server 2005 Reporting Services-based reports.

Share Project Views

Project offers several options to generate and share views. You can save the current view as a picture file (GIF format) by clicking the Edit menu and selecting Copy Picture (see Figure 4.31). This action takes a screen shot of the current screen.

You can also export the current view to another Office application. On the View menu, point to Toolbars and click Analysis (see Figure 4.32). On the Analysis toolbar, click Copy Picture to Office Wizard. In step three of the Wizard, choose the target Office application that you want to export the view to (see Figure 4.33). You can email the document or presentation with the view, or store it in a shared location.

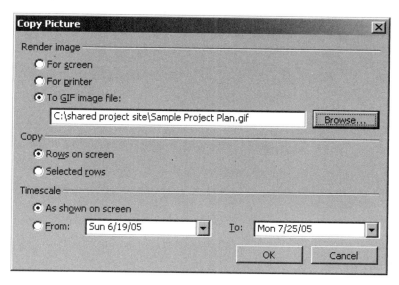

FIGURE 4.31   Copy Picture dialog box in Project.

FIGURE 4.32   The Analysis toolbar in Project.

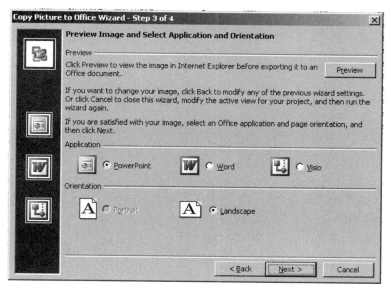

FIGURE 4.33   Select the target Office application name in Copy Picture to Office Wizard.

Share Reports

Project contains many built-in reports; you can also create custom reports. On the View menu, click Reports to display the top-level report selection dialog (see Figure 4.34). Click on each category to display predefined reports for each group.

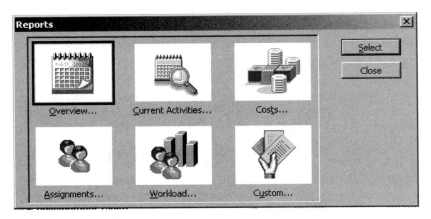

FIGURE 4.34   Top-level report categories available in Project.

However, reports in Project can not be saved; they can only be printed. If you have the Adobe PDFWriter™ printer driver (or a similar software) installed in the machine, you'll be able to create PDF files (or other files suitable for viewing reports) during printing (see Figure 4.35). You can distribute these files among the stakeholders via the project portal.

Another option is to launch the XML Reporting Wizard from the Analysis toolbar. This option saves the project plan as an XML file. (You can download the schema from *http://www.microsoft.com/downloads/details.aspx?FamilyId=FE118952-3547-420A-A412-00A2662442D9&displaylang=en.*) You can process the XML file from another application and create reports in your desired format. You can also use an XSL file to transform the XML to another format, such as HTML. Two XSL files named Crittask.xsl and Resource.xsl are included with Project. Figure 4.36 shows the HTML file produced by applying the transformation defined in Crittask.xsl. You can create custom reports in various output formats by applying different XSL transformations. The generated output files can be shared with the stakeholders via email or the project portal.

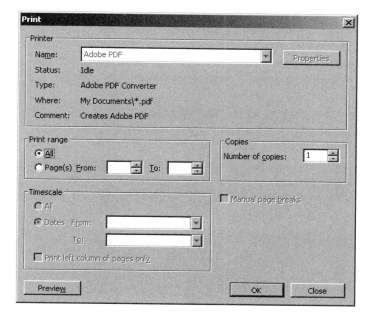

FIGURE 4.35   Print the report using Adobe PDFWriter.

Critical Tasks for Project: sample project plan.xml

ID	Name	Priority	Start	Finish
24	Brainstorm and Prioritze Scenarios List	500	2005-07-26T08:00:00	2005-07-28T17:00:00
25	Update Project Structure	500	2005-07-29T08:00:00	2005-07-29T17:00:00
26	Schedule the Iteration	500	2005-08-01T08:00:00	2005-08-01T17:00:00
27	Create Project Checklist Items for Next Iteration	500	2005-08-02T08:00:00	2005-08-02T17:00:00

FIGURE 4.36   HTML produced by applying XSL transformation to the Project XML file.

TECHNICAL REVIEW: CREATING A CUSTOM ADD-IN FOR PROJECT

As discussed earlier, the custom add-in is responsible for processing predecessor information during import as well as export. In this section, we look at the technical details of implementing the add-in. The full source code is available on the CD-ROM.

ON THE CD

Create the Add-In Project

Launch Visual Studio. In the New Project dialog box, click Extensibility under Other Project Types. Select Shared Add-in from the Visual Studio installed templates (see Figure 4.37). Enter information regarding the new project, and proceed.

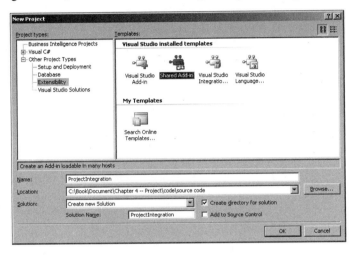

FIGURE 4.37 Select Shared Add-in template to create starter code.

In the Shared Add-in Wizard screens, fill out the routine information as requested. In the Select An Application Host screen, select Microsoft Project and uncheck everything else (see Figure 4.38). In the Choose Add-in Options screen, se-

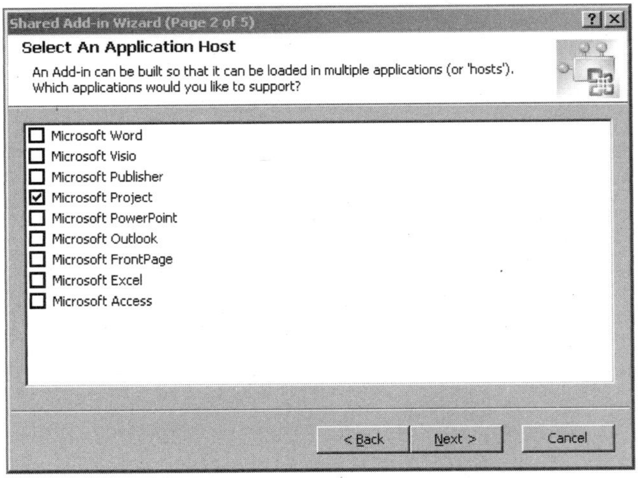

FIGURE 4.38 Select Microsoft Project as the application host.

lect the "I would like my Add-in to load when the host application loads" check box (see Figure 4.39). A project will be created containing starter code for the add-in.

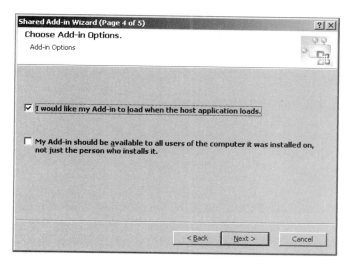

FIGURE 4.39   Select check box to load the add-in when Project starts.

Add a Reference to the Project Library

Since we'll be working with the Microsoft Office Project 2003 object model, add a reference to the Microsoft Project 11.0 Object Library. To add a reference, select Add Reference from the Project menu. Select the COM tab in the Add Reference dialog box, double-click Microsoft Project 11.0 Object Library, and click OK. These assemblies will be available if you have Project installed in the machine. If you don't see the Microsoft Project 11.0 Object Library in the list, visit *http://msdn.microsoft.com/library/default.asp?url=/library/en-us/dno2k3ta/html/OfficePrimaryInteropAssembliesFAQ.asp* to find out how to install the Primary Interop Assemblies (PIA) for Office 2003.

Modify the Starter Code

Open the file named Connect.cs (generated automatically by VSTS). This file contains a class named Connect. The Connect class implements the IDTExtensibility2 interface and is responsible for establishing communication between the host application and the add-in. The Connect class also implements the methods defined by IDTExtensibility2, such as OnBeginShutdown, OnAddInsUpdate, OnStartupComplete, OnDisconnection, and OnConnection (see Figure 4.40).

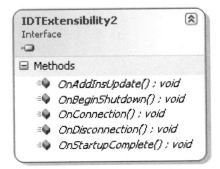

FIGURE 4.40   IDTExtensibility2 provides key methods for communication between the host application and the add-in.

Modify the OnStartupComplete method to implement the following features:

- Insert a new button named Process Imported Tasks in the Team toolbar.
- Hook into the event handler for the Publish button so that the add-in code is executed before running the default synchronization code.

The modified code for Connect.cs is shown in Listing 4.4.

LISTING 4.4   Code for Inserting Process Imported Tasks Button in the Team Toolbar and for Hooking into the Publish Event

```
namespace ProjectIntegration
{
using System;
using Extensibility;
using System.Runtime.InteropServices;
using System.Reflection;
using Microsoft.Office.Core;
using Microsoft.Office.Interop.MSProject;

/// <summary>
/// The object for implementing an Add-in.
/// </summary>
/// <seealso class='IDTExtensibility2' />
[GuidAttribute("B1C33FFF-358A-4310-A47E-F42AEE485800"),
    ProgId("ProjectIntegration.Connect")]
public class Connect : Object,
    Extensibility.IDTExtensibility2
{
  private Application applicationObject;
```

```
private object addInInstance;
private CommandBarButton _ProcessTasksButton;
private CommandBarButton _PublishButton;

/// <summary>
/// Implements the constructor for the Add-in object.
/// Place your initialization code within this method.
/// </summary>
public Connect()
{
}

/// <summary>
/// Implements the OnConnection method of the IDTExtensibility2
///interface.
/// Receives notification that the Add-in is being loaded.
/// </summary>
/// <param term='application'>
/// Root object of the host application.
/// </param>
/// <param term='connectMode'>
/// Describes how the Add-in is being loaded.
/// </param>
/// <param term='addInInst'>
/// Object representing this Add-in.
/// </param>
/// <seealso class='IDTExtensibility2' />
public void OnConnection(object application,
    Extensibility.ext_ConnectMode connectMode,
    object addInInst, ref System.Array custom)
{
  applicationObject = application as Application;
  addInInstance = addInInst;
}

/// <summary>
/// Implements the OnDisconnection method of the
///IDTExtensibility2 interface.
/// Receives notification that the Add-in is being unloaded.
/// </summary>
/// <param term='disconnectMode'>
/// Describes how the Add-in is being unloaded.
/// </param>
/// <param term='custom'>
/// Array of parameters that are host application specific.
/// </param>
/// <seealso class='IDTExtensibility2' />
public void OnDisconnection(
```

```
        Extensibility.ext_DisconnectMode disconnectMode,
        ref System.Array custom)
{
}

/// <summary>
/// Implements the OnAddInsUpdate method of the
/// IDTExtensibility2 interface.
/// Receives notification that the collection of Add-ins has
/// changed.
/// </summary>
/// <param term='custom'>
/// Array of parameters that are host application specific.
/// </param>
/// <seealso class='IDTExtensibility2' />
public void OnAddInsUpdate(ref System.Array custom)
{
}

/// <summary>
/// Implements the OnStartupComplete method of the
/// IDTExtensibility2 interface.
/// Receives notification that the host application has
/// completed loading.
/// Added custom code to show Process Imported Tasks button.
/// </summary>
/// <param term='custom'>
/// Array of parameters that are host application specific.
/// </param>
/// <seealso class='IDTExtensibility2' />
public void OnStartupComplete(ref System.Array custom)
{
   this.pHookToolbar();
}

/// <summary>
/// Implements the OnBeginShutdown method of the
///IDTExtensibility2 interface.
/// Receives notification that the host application is being
///unloaded.
/// </summary>
/// <param term='custom'>
/// Array of parameters that are host application specific.
/// </param>
/// <seealso class='IDTExtensibility2' />
public void OnBeginShutdown(ref System.Array custom)
{
}

/// <summary>
///
/// </summary>
```

```csharp
/// <summary>
///
/// </summary>
private void pHookToolbar()
{
  // Find the team system command bar
  CommandBar bar =
    applicationObject.CommandBars["Team"];

  // Exit if bar does not exist
  if (null == bar) return;

  // Add the "Process Imported Tasks" button
  _ProcessTasksButton = (CommandBarButton)
      bar.Controls.Add(MsoControlType.msoControlButton,
      Missing.Value, Missing.Value, Missing.Value, true);
  _ProcessTasksButton.Style =
      MsoButtonStyle.msoButtonCaption;
  _ProcessTasksButton.Caption = "Process Imported Tasks";
  _ProcessTasksButton.DescriptionText = "Process " +
      "TaskInformation Imported from VSTS";
  _ProcessTasksButton.TooltipText =
      _ProcessTasksButton.DescriptionText;
  _ProcessTasksButton.Click += new
      _CommandBarButtonEvents_ClickEventHandler(
      _ProcessTasksButton_Click);

  //Hook into the publish button
  _PublishButton =
      (CommandBarButton)bar.Controls["Publish"];
  if (null != _PublishButton)
  {
    _PublishButton.Click += new
        _CommandBarButtonEvents_ClickEventHandler(
        _PublishButton_Click);
  }
}


/// <summary>
/// Event handler for Process Imported Tasks button
/// </summary>
/// <param name="Ctrl"></param>
/// <param name="CancelDefault"></param>
void _ProcessTasksButton_Click(CommandBarButton Ctrl,
    ref bool CancelDefault)
{
  ProjectHelper.ProcessImportedTasks(
      this.applicationObject.ActiveProject);

  applicationObject.Message("Task Processing Completed",
      PjMessageType.pjOKOnly, Missing.Value,
      Missing.Value);
}
```

```
/// <summary>
/// Event handler for Publish button
/// </summary>
/// <param name="Ctrl"></param>
/// <param name="CancelDefault"></param>
void PublishButton_Click(CommandBarButton Ctrl,
    ref bool CancelDefault)
{
  ProjectHelper.ProcessTasksforPublish(
      this.applicationObject.ActiveProject);
}
}
}
```

Create a Helper Class

Listing 4.4 indicates that the details associated with processing task information are delegated to a class named ProjectHelper. The ProjectHelper class implements the following functionalities:

ProcessImportedTasks method: This method is invoked when the Process Imported Tasks button is clicked. The code in this method reads predecessor work item Ids (assigned by VSTS) from the custom field, looks up the corresponding task Ids (assigned by Project), and populates the task predecessor column with the correct task Ids. The code also moves Actual Start, Actual Finish, and Deadline dates from custom fields to the actual fields in the project plan.

ProcessTasksforPublish method: This method is invoked when the Publish button is clicked. In addition to moving Actual Start, Actual Finish, and Deadline dates to custom fields, the code iterates the predecessor collection of each task, looks up their VSTS-assigned work item Ids (the work item Ids are available in the Work Item ID column), and inserts them in a custom field. The VSTS-Project synchronization tool maps the custom fields to the corresponding mapped fields in VSTS.

The code is shown in Listing 4.5.

LISTING 4.5 Helper Class for Processing Imported Tasks

```
using System;
using System.Collections.Generic;
using System.Text;
using System.Runtime.InteropServices;
using System.Diagnostics;
```

```
using Microsoft.Office.Interop.MSProject;

namespace ProjectIntegration
{
/// <summary>
/// organizes and sequences tasks imported from VSTS
/// </summary>
class ProjectHelper
{
  private const string NA_VALUE = "NA" ;

  /// <summary>
  /// Process Task Information Imported from VSTS.
  /// This method performs the follows functions:
  /// 1. Translates Predecessor Information from VSTS to Project
  /// 2. Moves Actual Start Date, Actual Finish Date, and
  /// Deadline line from
  /// placeholder fields to Project fields
  /// </summary>
  /// <param name="project"></param>
  internal static void ProcessImportedTasks(Project project)
  {
    foreach (Task currentTask in project.Tasks)
    {
      // retrieve predecessor work item ids
      // from custom field
      string predecessorWorkItemIDs =
          currentTask.GetField(PjField.pjTaskText30);

      //retrieve values of Actual Start Date, Actual
      //Finish Date,and Deadline Date
      //fields from Placeholder fields
      string actualStart =
          currentTask.GetField(PjField.pjTaskText27).ToString();
      string actualFinish =
          currentTask.GetField(PjField.pjTaskText28).ToString();
      string deadline =
          currentTask.GetField(PjField.pjTaskText29).ToString();

      //populate Actual Start Date, Actual
      //Finish Date, and Deadline Date fields
      //in Project >>>
      if (actualStart != string.Empty)
          currentTask.ActualStart = actualStart;

      if (actualFinish != string.Empty)
          currentTask.ActualFinish = actualFinish;
```

```csharp
    if (deadline != string.Empty)
        currentTask.Deadline = deadline;

    //process Actual Start Date, Actual
    //Finish Date, and Deadline Date <<<

    if ((predecessorWorkItemIDs != null) &&
        (predecessorWorkItemIDs != string.Empty))
    {
      //load predecessor information in an array

      string[] workItemIDs =
          predecessorWorkItemIDs.Split(',');

      // Build an array of task IDs which
      //will be the predecessor of this task
      string[] predecessorTaskIDs =
          new string[workItemIDs.Length];

      int i = 0;
      foreach (string workItemID in workItemIDs)
      {
        // Find which task has this work item ID
        foreach (Task task in project.Tasks)
        {
          if (workItemID ==
              task.GetField(PjField.pjTaskText10))
          {
            // predecessor task identified;
            //look up its Task ID
            predecessorTaskIDs[i] = task.ID.ToString();
            i = i + 1;
            break;
          }
        }
      }

      // set the predecessors Task IDs

      currentTask.Predecessors = string.Join(", ",
          predecessorTaskIDs);

    }
  }
}

/// <summary>
```

```
/// Export Predecessor Information to Custom field.
/// Information from the Custom field will be sent to VSTS.
/// </summary>
/// <param name="project"></param>
internal static void ProcessTasksforPublish(Project project)
{
  foreach (Task currentTask in project.Tasks)
  {
    // retrieve values of Actual Start Date,
    // Actual Finish Date, and Deadline Date
    // fields from Project
    string actualStart = currentTask.ActualStart.ToString();
    string actualFinish =
        currentTask.ActualFinish.ToString();
    string deadline = currentTask.Deadline.ToString();

    // place Date values in placeholder fields
    // for transmission to VSTS
    if (actualStart.ToUpper() != NA_VALUE)
      currentTask.SetField(PjField.pjTaskText27, actualStart);
    else
      currentTask.SetField(PjField.pjTaskText27, string.Empty);

    if (actualFinish.ToUpper() != NA_VALUE)
      currentTask.SetField(PjField.pjTaskText28, actualFinish);
    else
      currentTask.SetField(PjField.pjTaskText28, string.Empty);

    if (deadline.ToUpper() != NA_VALUE)
      currentTask.SetField(PjField.pjTaskText29, deadline);
    else
      currentTask.SetField(PjField.pjTaskText29, string.Empty);

    // process Actual Start Date and Actual Finish Date <<<
    if (currentTask.PredecessorTasks.Count != 0)
    {
      // Build a string array which will hold the work
      // item ids of the predecessor tasks
      string[] workItemsIDs = new
          string[currentTask.PredecessorTasks.Count];

      int i = 0;

      // retrieve work item id of each predecessor task
      foreach (Task predTask in currentTask.PredecessorTasks)
      {
        workItemsIDs[i] =
```

```
            predTask.GetField(PjField.pjTaskText10);
        i = i + 1;
      }

      // deserialize into custom field
      string flatWorkItemIDs = string.Join(", ",
          workItemsIDs);
      currentTask.SetField(PjField.pjTaskText30,
          flatWorkItemIDs);
    }
   }
  }
 }
}
```

CONCLUSION

In this chapter, we discussed how global project management can be simplified by using VSTS with Project. Project managers no longer need to invest significant amounts of time and effort collecting, processing, and distributing status information. The project management team can instead focus on high-value functions, such as analyzing trends, spotting deviations, and making course corrections. The fundamental idea, as illustrated in this chapter, is to capture routine status information directly from the source (from developers and testers)—as a by-product of their normal activities—and to seamlessly flow the information into the project plan. Alterations to the project plan are transmitted back to the team members via VSTS, without manual intervention.

In offshore projects, given the geographic and time-zone separation between various parties, the synergistic combination of VSTS and Project creates a stream-lined information-management infrastructure. The combined toolset eliminates overhead, provides timely data, eliminates potential 'system loss' in the communications pipeline, and speeds up decision-making. Both on-site and offshore managers can communicate with greater clarity and efficiency. Clients can gain deeper visibility regarding the progress of their offshore projects. In summary, once the infrastructure is in place, you can reap significant value in terms of improved transparency, early problem detection, and resource optimization. An efficient project-management workflow improves productivity and reduces the execution risk of outsourced projects.

FURTHER READING

Chatfield, Carl, et al., *Step by Step Microsoft Project 2003.* Microsoft Press, ISBN: 0-7356-1955-7, 2004.

"Project 2003 SDK." Microsoft Corporation, 2005. Available online on July 22, 2005, at: *http://www.microsoft.com/downloads/details.aspx?FamilyID= 4D2ABC8C-8BCA-4DB9-8753-178C0D3099C5&displaylang=en.*

Stover, Teresa, *Microsoft Office Project 2003.* Microsoft Press, ISBN: 0-7356-1958-1, 2004.

5

Integrating Microsoft Outlook 2003

In This Chapter

- Organizing Emails
- Organizing Tasks
- An Add-In for Processing Emails and Tasks
- Technical Review: Creating a Custom Add-In for Outlook

INTRODUCTION

Modern life cannot be imagined without emails. Email was the handmaiden of the Internet. It has revolutionized communication—and the way we live, work, and play. The specification for the Simple Mail Transfer Protocol (SMTP) was published in 1982. (For more information about the SMTP protocol, visit the Internet Engineering Task Force Web site at *http://www.ietf.org/rfc/rfc0821.txt.*) Few people could imagine at that time that this relatively obscure technology (along with the Hypertext Transport Protocol (HTTP) created in 1989) would transform global communication. The world has become smaller, commerce has become 24/7, and communication speed has become limited only by human biological response times and the speed of light.

Microsoft Office Outlook 2003™ (Outlook) is one of the most popular email programs on the market. Beyond email-processing capabilities, Outlook incorporates powerful contact-management, scheduling, and task-management features. When it comes to offshore communications, it is probably the most frequently used application. Outlook contains a play-by-play archive of issues that were specified, discussed, and resolved. This treasure-trove of information can be organized, searched, and leveraged to add significant value in management of offshore projects.

When distributed teams collaborate on a project, they interact primarily by email and instant messaging (during overlapping work times), supplemented by phone calls. In the offshore scenario, email is the predominant mode of communication. The conversation history contains many of the assumptions, concerns, work-arounds, and compromises that go into product development. During development and maintenance phases, the email store can provide valuable insight regarding *why* something was designed in a particular way. Although detailed specifications are usually maintained in a central document repository, emails contain a great deal of *supplementary* information. They amplify, clarify, and exemplify the specifications. A tremendous amount of 'out of band' information is exchanged via emails no matter how formal the specifications are. This auxiliary information is lost over time unless it is captured and organized. In this chapter, we show you how to do this efficiently using Outlook.

By default, VSTS does not provide a mechanism to interact with Outlook. However, given the extensible nature of the VSTS framework, you can write custom code to leverage the power of both applications and make them interoperate. In this chapter, we demonstrate how to create an Outlook add-in to associate emails with VSTS work items, as well as how to import VSTS tasks into Outlook. We also discuss some key features of Outlook that will enable you to better organize your offshore correspondence. However, a detailed discussion of Outlook's features is beyond the scope of this book. You can consult the Further Reading section at the end of this chapter to learn more about Outlook. For more information, you can also visit the Microsoft Office Web site at *http://office.microsoft.com/en-us/default.aspx* (click the Outlook link under Products).

ORGANIZING EMAILS

There are many strategies that you can follow to avoid being overwhelmed by email clutter. The basic objective is to automate the classification and organization of emails so that you can minimize the time spent performing routine functions. Without meaningful organization, in the course of a few months or years, it becomes impossible to sort out who said what and why. Unless you can devise an intelligent and semi-automated way to deal with the deluge of emails, you will be overwhelmed by the massive information overload that most information workers face daily.

In this section, we demonstrate some of Outlook's built-in functionalities and programmable features for setting up an email-management process that is relatively easy to maintain. The process will also serve as a starting point for VSTS integration. Outlook offers powerful capabilities to streamline information management. We discuss ways to leverage its features to improve efficiency and productivity in offshore project management.

Create Project Folders

Like folders in Windows Explorer, folders in Outlook help organize the contents of your mailbox. To create a custom folder, on the File menu, point to New, and then click Folder. In the Create New Folder dialog box, specify the name and location of the folder (leave the default Mail and Post items as folder content). Create a root folder named Software Projects and add project-specific nodes under tit (see Figure 5.1). Later in the chapter, we'll create custom rules to automatically direct incoming emails to their respective folders. We'll also create an add-in to automatically synchronize Outlook folder contents with VSTS.

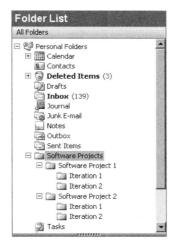

FIGURE 5.1   Create new folders to store emails.

Create New Categories

Categories make it easier to search and organize various items, such as emails and tasks. Use this feature to tag emails so that you can automatically figure out which project and iteration folders they belong to. To create a new category, on the Edit menu, click Categories. In the Categories dialog box, click Master Category List. In the Master Category List dialog box (see Figure 5.2), add the following categories:

- Software Project 1 Iteration 1
- Software Project 1 Iteration 2
- Software Project 2 Iteration 1
- Software Project 2 Iteration 2

FIGURE 5.2 Add project-specific categories to the Master Category List.

Once the new categories are created, you can associate emails with them. When creating an email, click Options on the toolbar. In the Message Options dialog box, click Categories. In the Categories dialog box, select the check box for the appropriate project-iteration category (see Figure 5.3).

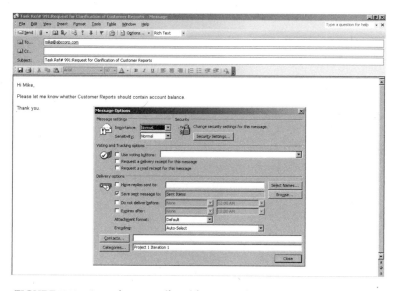

FIGURE 5.3 Associate emails with categories.

When the recipient receives the email, the category information is preserved (see Figure 5.4). Later in the chapter, we'll use the category information to automatically route incoming emails to appropriate folders. If you look at the content of the Sent Items folder, you'll find that the category information is preserved there also. To group by categories, right-click the column header and click Categories from the drop-down menu.

FIGURE 5.4   Category information is displayed in the recipient mailbox.

You can also use the category information to restrict search requests. Click Tools, point to Find, and then click Advanced Find. In the Advanced File dialog box, click the More Choices tab. Click Categories to specify the categories that you are interested in (see Figure 5.5).

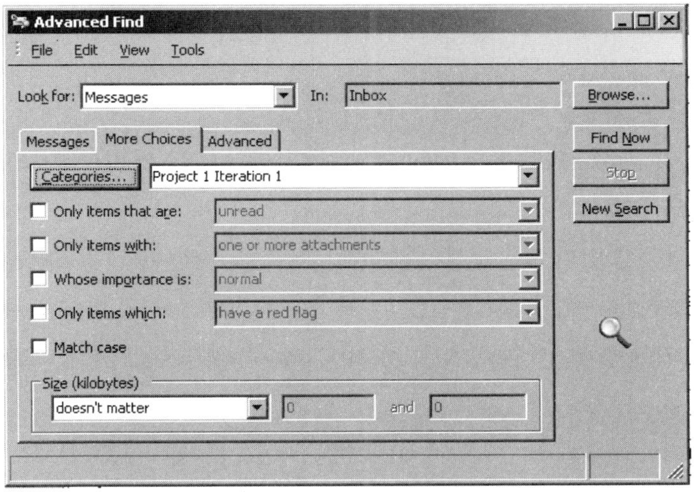

FIGURE 5.5   Use Categories to limit searches.

Create a Custom Email Form

The general-purpose email form used for everyday communication has been around for more than a decade. However, when dealing with complex offshore projects, you need a more structured way to capture and convey information.

Using Outlook, you can customize the standard email form to better suit individual project needs. One of the simplest changes that you can make is to explicitly tag each mail item with the appropriate project category. Another change is to introduce a custom field to store the VSTS task Id that the communication refers to. You could, of course, insert this information in the Subject field—and you may still have to if the Exchange Servers and the Outlook clients are not configured at both ends to support custom forms. However, a custom email form standardizes the communication format, resulting in fewer mistakes and a smoother workflow.

To design a custom email form, start with an existing email form. On the Tools menu, point to Forms, and then click Design a Form. In the Design Form dialog box, select Standard Forms Library from the drop-down menu, select Message from the list, and then click Open (see Figure 5.6). The standard email form opens up on a design surface (see Figure 5.7). Notice the Edit Compose Page and Edit Read Page options on the toolbar. The Compose Page represents the page that you see when creating an email. The Read Page corresponds to the page seen by the recipient when they open your email.

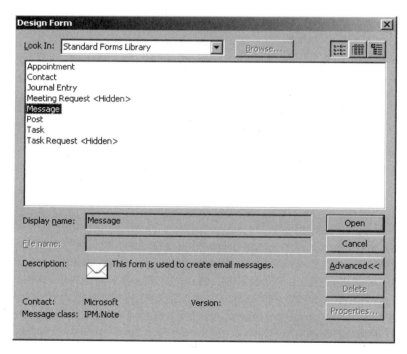

FIGURE 5.6 Select the message form for customization.

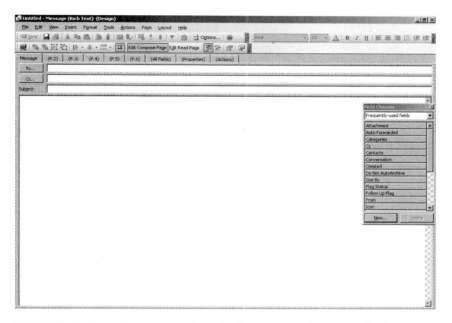

FIGURE 5.7 Open the message form in Design mode for customization.

Add the following elements to the standard form for the Compose Page:

Categories button and Categories text box: Click Edit Compose Page. Bring up the Field Chooser dialog box (click the Field Chooser icon in the toolbar if Field Chooser is not already visible). Select All Mail Fields from the dropdown list. Drag "Categories…" and "Categories" fields to the design surface. You'll see a Categories button and a Categories text box appear on the form. During email composition, you can click the Categories button to select the appropriate category (corresponding to your project and iteration); the selected category name will be displayed in the associated Categories text box. Make the Categories text box read-only (select the text box control and choose Properties from the right-click menu), since it'll be populated by clicking the Categories button.

WorkItemRef text box: This field will contain the VSTS task Id associated with the email. Since this is not a predefined Outlook field, you first need to create a custom field. Select User-defined Fields in Inbox from the drop-down list in the Field Chooser, and click New. Create a new text field named WorkItemRef (see Figure 5.8). Drag the newly created field to the form.

The completed form is shown in Figure 5.9.

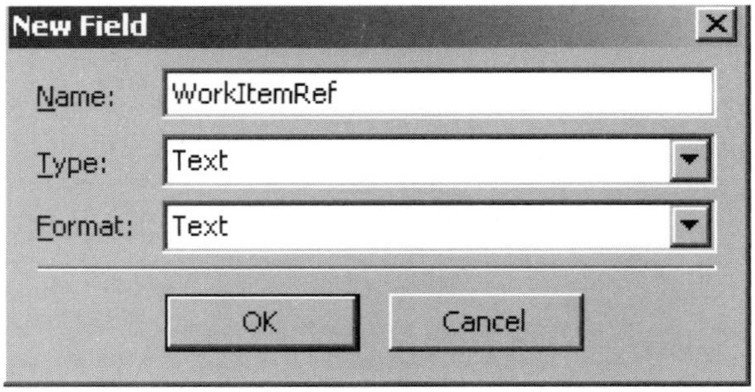

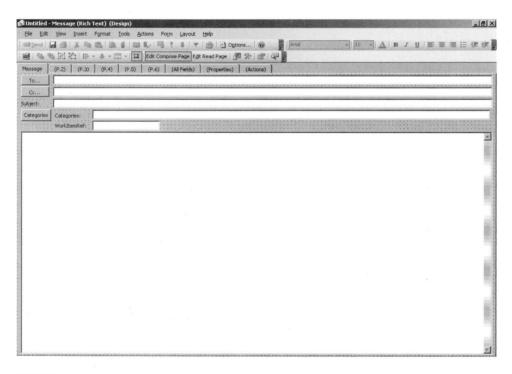

FIGURE 5.8   Create a custom form field.

FIGURE 5.9   A custom email form (Compose mode) for Project-related communications.

Create the Read view of the form in a similar way. However, do not add the Categories button. Also, make the other two custom fields read-only, since the recipient will not change this information (see Figure 5.10).

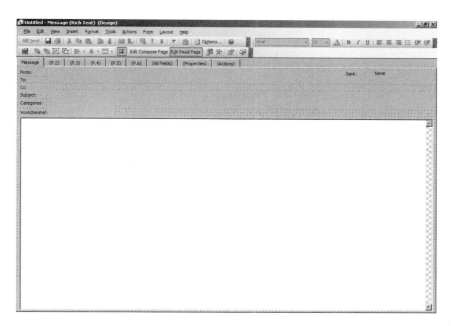

FIGURE 5.10   Custom email form (Read mode) for project-related communications.

Since the form will be used to communicate with offshore parties who probably do not have access to your company's Exchange Server, you need to send the form definition along with the email item so that the form can be displayed correctly at the recipient's end. This increases the size of the email, but is often the only way to ensure that remote parties are looking at the same email view (assuming of course, that all parties are using Outlook). Click the Properties tab and select "Send form definition with item" check box (see Figure 5.11).

Publish the Custom Email Form

Once you have created the custom form, you need to publish it before it can be used. On the Tools menu, point to Forms, and then click Publish Forms. In the Publish Form dialog box, you have three options:

Organizational Forms Library: If you would like the custom form to be available to everybody in the organization, select Organizational Forms Library from the drop-down list. Users can access this form by clicking New on the Outlook toolbar, followed by Choose Form (see Figure 5.12).

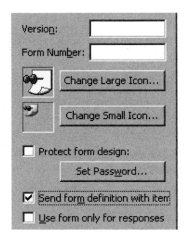

FIGURE 5.11   Embed the form definition in the email.

FIGURE 5.12   Select a custom form from the Organizational Library.

Personal Forms Library: This option makes the form available only to you. You can select these forms in the same way as the ones in the Organizational Forms Library.

Outlook Folder: If you publish the form to a specific Outlook folder, the form becomes available to everybody who has access to that folder (assuming it is a public folder). Earlier in the chapter, we created an Outlook folder named Software Projects to hold all emails related to project execution. You can publish the custom form to the Software Projects folder; call it Project Email Form. To send an email using this form, Select the Software Project folder as the current folder, and click the Actions menu. You'll see a new entry named New Project Email Form (see Figure 5.13). Use this form to send project-related emails.

Communicate Using the Custom Form

You are now ready to send emails using the custom form. On the Actions menu, click New Project Email Form. In the custom email form, specify the routine information regarding recipients, subject, and so forth. Click Categories to include category information. Specify the VSTS work item Id using the WorkItemRef text field (see Figure 5.14). When the recipient opens the email, he'll see the custom fields defined for Read mode (see Figure 5.15).

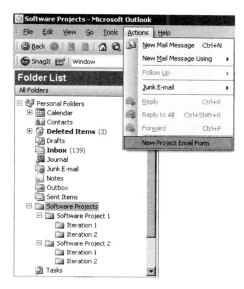

FIGURE 5.13   New menu item for sending emails using the custom form.

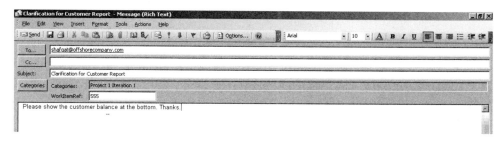

FIGURE 5.14   Send email using the custom email form.

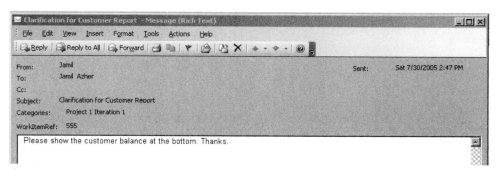

FIGURE 5.15   The custom form as viewed by the recipient.

In order to be able send and receive custom forms, you need to make sure that the Exchange Servers at both ends are configured to support messages encoded in Transport Neutral Encapsulation Format (TNEF). For more information on how to set up TNEF, refer to the Microsoft Knowledgebase article, "How e-mail message formats affect Internet e-mails in Outlook," (id# 290809) at *http://support.microsoft.com/kb/ 290809/*.

Create Custom Rules

Create custom rules to inspect incoming messages, look up category information, and automatically redirect messages to appropriate folders. For example, if an email arrives with its category set to "Project 1 Iteration 1," a custom rule will file this email in the "Software Projects\Software Project 1\Iteration 1" folder. This kind of automatic classification mechanism reduces the manual effort involved in the workflow—improving efficiency and eliminating human errors.

On the Tools menu, click Rules and Alerts to launch the Rules and Alerts dialog box. Click New Rule to display the Rules Wizard screen. Select "Start from a blank rule" option and "Check messages when they arrive" (see Figure 5.16). In the next screen, in the Step 1: Select Conditions list, select "assigned to <u>category</u> category" check box. In the Step 2: Edit the Rule Description section, click the "category" hyperlink and choose "Project 1 Iteration 1" category.

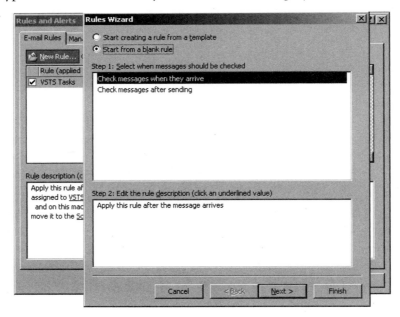

FIGURE 5.16   Assigning a custom rule for incoming emails using the Rules Wizard.

In the next screen, in the Step 1: Select Action(s) list, select "move it to the spec-ified folder" check box. In the Step 2: Edit the Rule Description section, click "specified" hyperlink and choose the "Software Projects\Software Project 1"\ Iteration 1" folder. Navigate to the Finish screen and specify the name of the rule. The last screen looks like Figure 5.17.

FIGURE 5.17   The custom rule for filing incoming emails.

Create additional rules to handle other projects and iterations as needed. You can run the newly created rule(s) on existing items (click Run Rules Now in Rules and Alerts screen) or wait for new emails to arrive.

Create Search Folders

You can use search folders to find emails and organize them in virtual folders with-out moving them from their original locations. This is useful if the emails are buried in multiple folders—maybe under different classification schemes—and you would like to group them in folder-based views using specific criteria, without having to physically move them to a new folder structure.

On the File menu, point to New, and then click Search Folder. In the New Search Folder dialog box, select Create a Custom Search Folder and click Choose. In the Custom Search Folder dialog box (see Figure 5.18), enter the name of the folder to search and click Criteria. In the Search Folder Criteria dialog box (see Fig-ure 5.19) enter filter conditions to narrow the search. Click the More Choices tab,

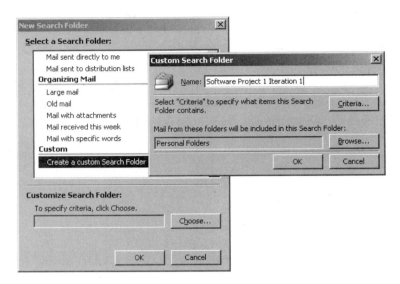

FIGURE 5.18 Custom Search Folder creation form.

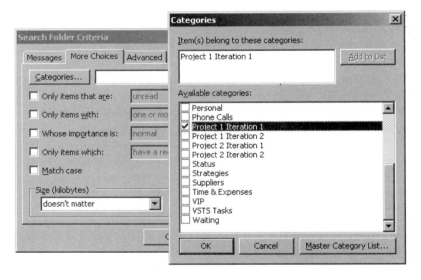

FIGURE 5.19 Create category filters to find relevant emails.

and then click Categories. Select the Project 1 Iteration 1 category. Close the forms and click Search Folders in the folder list. You'll find a new folder named Software Project 1 Iteration 1 containing the relevant emails; you can further filter the content as needed (see Figure 5.20).

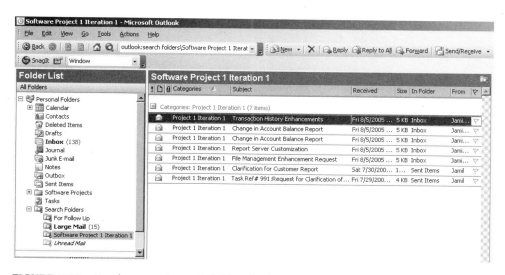

FIGURE 5.20   Newly created search folder displaying related emails.

ORGANIZING TASKS

Outlook tasks represent action items that you are interested in tracking over time. You can use Outlook to set up task reminders, enter progress information, assign tasks to other people, and to group them in various ways. Tasks can be grouped by overdue tasks, by person responsible, by category, by task timeline, and so forth (see Figure 5.21). In the next section, we create an add-in for importing significant tasks from VSTS. The add-in can also update VSTS tasks with progress information gathered in Outlook. In a typical outsourcing scenario, you'll probably not export *all* VSTS tasks to Outlook, since VSTS is the core tool for assigning tasks to distributed project members as well as for capturing progress information from them. However, you may find it useful to extract *some* critical tasks from the VSTS repository and to track them in Outlook—leveraging Outlook's powerful alerts, reminders, and calendaring capabilities.

In addition to tracking VSTS tasks, when interacting with offshore teams, you are likely to assign various 'housekeeping' tasks to various remote personnel who may not have access to VSTS. In such cases, by using Outlook's task-management features, you'll be able to make the collaborative process more streamlined and friction-free.

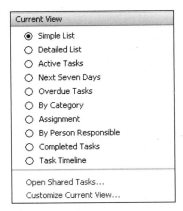

FIGURE 5.21   Default task views in Outlook.

Send Task Requests

When working with offshore teams, you'll often find it useful to send a task request via email. Click New, Task Request. In the task form, enter information related to the task, including Due Date and Start Date (see Figure 5.22). Send the task request

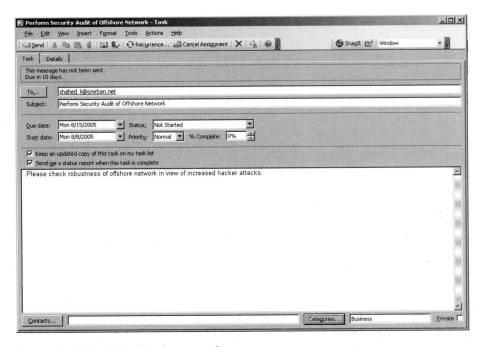

FIGURE 5.22   Outlook task request form.

to the appropriate offshore team member. The form also contains an option to keep a copy of the task locally on your machine so that you don't forget about it yourself you can also choose to receive notification when the task is completed. Keep both options turned on.

The recipient receives the task request via email, as shown in Figure 5.23. Notice that the Message Class for the task request is IPM.TaskRequest. (The Message-Class for normal emails is IPM.Note.) Also, the Subject field contains the words "Task Request:"; you could use this information to automatically route task requests to custom folders. When the recipient opens the task, he sees two buttons named Accept and Decline (see Figure 5.24) in addition to task information. (There is also a button named Assign Task that can be used to assign the task to a third party.) When the person clicks Accept or Decline, the sender of the task is notified of the action. Moreover, as the person executing the task updates task progress information, the original sender receives status notifications, as well.

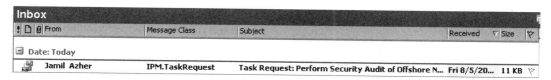

FIGURE 5.23   Task request received via email.

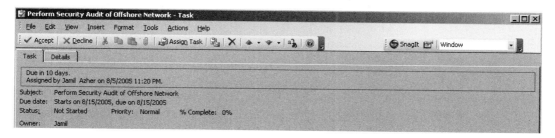

FIGURE 5.24   Accept, Decline, and Assign Task buttons enable the recipient to take appropriate actions.

AN ADD-IN FOR PROCESSING EMAILS AND TASKS

In the previous sections, we looked at exchanging emails using a custom email form, and we set up rules so that emails are automatically stored in appropriate folders. We also reviewed task management features and sent task requests across organizational boundaries. In this section, we create an add-in to associate emails with corresponding VSTS work items as well as to synchronize selected VSTS tasks with Outlook tasks. The functionalities are accessed via a custom toolbar (see Figure 5.25).

FIGURE 5.25   Custom add-in toolbar.

Attach Emails

The objective of email integration is to store emails as attachments to work items in VSTS. This capability allows the communication history to be efficiently searched, referenced, and organized. As discussed earlier, the supplemental information repository (complementing the specifications) is enormously helpful to people responsible for fixing bugs, providing enhancements, and doing legacy conversions. The communication archive helps comprehend *why* certain decisions were made, what the trade-offs were, what options were considered, and what compromises were eventually agreed upon.

In the offshore scenario—where the people doing the development work do not have the luxury of interacting with domain experts face to face—performing software maintenance often becomes akin to playing Russian roulette. You never know what's going to get broken by the latest 'fix.' Although the problem goes deeper than having access to a complete set of specifications along with supporting information, we can safely say that *not* having access to such information significantly increases the risks associated with software maintenance.

The custom add-in provides the following email-related functionalities:

Attach emails to VSTS work items: Allows you to select one or more emails and attach them to specified work items. You can also choose whether or not the emails are converted to a single document and associated with the work item as a single attachment. You can use the custom work item picker dialog box to specify the target work items. Alternatively, the add-in can look up the content of the WorkItemRef custom email field and attach emails automatically.

Synchronize Outlook folders with VSTS: Enables you to select an Outlook folder (e.g., "Software Projects\Software Project 1\Iteration 1") and automatically attach emails stored in that folder to corresponding VSTS work items. Just like attaching individual emails, you can either specify the target work items or have the add-in perform automatic associations based upon the content of WorkItemRef custom email field. Multiple emails can be joined as a single document attachment or as separate files.

The email attachment functionality is invoked by clicking the Attach Email(s) button in the add-in toolbar (see Figure 5.25).

Synchronize Tasks

The add-in also allows you to import selected VSTS tasks into Outlook. This functionality is useful if you want to assign specific tasks to people who do not have VSTS. This feature is also helpful when you want to monitor certain tasks using Outlook's calendar and notification capabilities. You can refresh Outlook tasks by fetching current information from VSTS, as well as publish changes made in Outlook back to VSTS. The add-in provides the following task-related functionalities:

Import Tasks: Creates new Outlook tasks from selected VSTS tasks.

Refresh Tasks: Updates existing Outlook tasks with current information from VSTS.

Publish Tasks: Updates VSTS tasks with current task information in Outlook.

TECHNICAL REVIEW: CREATING A CUSTOM ADD-IN FOR OUTLOOK

We use Visual Studio 2005 Tools for Office (VSTO) to create the add-in. VSTO allows you to write smart client applications for Office. With an improved security model, simplified deployment architecture (via ClickOnce), and the benefits of managed code, VSTO changes the way Office applications (such as Outlook) are customized and extended.

The Outlook Object Model

Before writing the add-in code, a quick overview of the Outlook object model would be helpful (see Figure 5.26). Just like other Office applications, Application is the top-level class in Outlook. Among its child classes, one of the most frequently used is the Explorers collection. An Explorer represents an Outlook window where folder contents are displayed. The ActiveExplorer property returns the currently active Explorer object (provided one exists).

The Inspectors collection contains Inspector objects. An Inspector represents a window where the contents of a single item are displayed. The ActiveInspector property returns the currently active Inspector object (provided one is available).

FIGURE 5.26 The Outlook object model.

The `CommandBars` property of an `Explorer` or `Inspector` object represents all menus and toolbars associated with the window. We'll add a custom `CommandBar` containing custom buttons.

The `NameSpace` class represents Outlook's MAPI profile, and contains the list of folders, such as mails, tasks, and appointments. The `Folders` property returns a collection of `MAPIFolder` objects.

Create an Add-in Project

ON THE CD

After installing VSTO, you'll see new Office templates installed in Visual Studio (see Figure 5.27). Select Outlook Add-In and create an Office project. You'll find that two projects are created—an add-in project containing skeletal code and a set-up project that builds a Microsoft Installer (MSI) file for installing the add-in in Outlook. The full source code is included on the CD-ROM.

Open the auto-generated ThisApplication.cs file. This partial class serves as the communication layer between Outlook and the custom add-in. Notice that the code contains two key methods: `ThisApplication_Startup` and `ThisApplication_Shutdown`. These two life-cycle methods are designed to contain initialization and finalization code for your add-in.

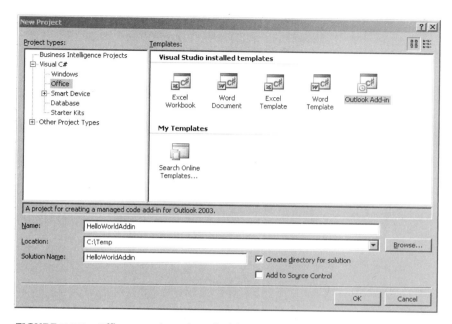

FIGURE 5.27 Office templates installed by VS 2005 Tools for Office.

Create the Work Items Toolbar

The first thing to do is to create a custom toolbar in Outlook for the add-in (see Figure 5.25). This is accomplished in `ThisApplication_Startup` method; the actual work is delegated to the following private method:

LISTING 5.1 Code for Adding a Custom Toolbar

```
/// <summary>
/// Add a new toolbar to interact with VSTS
/// </summary>
private void pSetupToolbar()
{
  // Step #1: Add a custom toolbar
  // First, get access to the CommandBars on the active explorer.
  CommandBars commandBars =
      this.ActiveExplorer().CommandBars;

  // Check if the bar is already there.
  bool commandBarExists = false;
  foreach (CommandBar bar in commandBars)
    if (bar.Name == COMMAND_BAR_NAME)
    {
```

```
      commandBarExists = true;
      this.myCommandBar = bar;
  }

// If bar is not there, then add the bar.
if (!commandBarExists)
   this.myCommandBar = commandBars.Add(COMMAND_BAR_NAME,
      MsoBarPosition.msoBarTop,
      System.Reflection.Missing.Value,
      true); // Temporary = True, means the command bar is not
             //permanent

this.myCommandBar.Visible = true;

//Step #2: Create the buttons on the toolbar

this.attachToButton = this.pCreateButton(this.myCommandBar,
   WORK_ITEM_BUTTON_NAME, WORK_ITEM_BUTTON_CAPTION,
   WORK_ITEM_BUTTON_NAME);
this.attachToButton.Click += new
   _CommandBarButtonEvents_ClickEventHandler(
   attachEmailButton_Click);
this.pSetPicture(this.attachToButton, "AttachIcon.bmp",
   "AttachIconMask.bmp");

this.attachFolderContentButton =
   this.pCreateButton(this.myCommandBar,
   ATTACH_FOLDER_CONTENT_BUTTON_NAME,
   ATTACH_FOLDER_CONTENT_BUTTON_CAPTION,
   ATTACH_FOLDER_CONTENT_BUTTON_NAME);

this.attachFolderContentButton.Click += new
   _CommandBarButtonEvents_ClickEventHandler(
   attachFolderContentButton_Click);

this.pSetPicture(this.attachFolderContentButton,
   "AttachIcon.bmp", "AttachIconMask.bmp");

this.importTasksButton = this.pCreateButton(this.myCommandBar,
   IMPORT_WORK_ITEM_BUTTON_NAME,
   IMPORT_WORK_ITEM_BUTTON_CAPTION,
   IMPORT_WORK_ITEM_BUTTON_NAME);

this.importTasksButton.Click += new
   _CommandBarButtonEvents_ClickEventHandler(
   importTasksButton_Click);
```

```
        this.pSetPicture(this.importTasksButton, "ImportTasks.bmp",
            "ImportTasksMask.bmp");

        this.publishTaskButton = this.pCreateButton(this.myCommandBar,
            PUBLISH_TASKS_BUTTON_NAME, PUBLISH_TASKS_BUTTON_TEXT,
            PUBLISH_TASKS_BUTTON_NAME);

        this.publishTaskButton.Click += new
            _CommandBarButtonEvents_ClickEventHandler(
            publishTaskButton_Click);
        this.publishTaskButton.Enabled = false;
        this.pSetPicture(this.publishTaskButton, "PublishTasks.bmp",
            "PublishTasksMask.bmp");

        this.refreshTasksButton = this.pCreateButton(this.myCommandBar,
            REFRESH_TASK_BUTTON_NAME, REFRESH_TASK_BUTTON_TEXT,
            REFRESH_TASK_BUTTON_NAME);
        this.refreshTasksButton.Click += new
            _CommandBarButtonEvents_ClickEventHandler(
            refreshTasksButton_Click);
        this.refreshTasksButton.Enabled = false;
        this.pSetPicture(this.refreshTasksButton, "RefreshTasks.bmp",
            "RefreshTasksMask.bmp");

//Step #3: Trap FolderSwitch event
    this._FolderSwitchEventHandler = new
        ExplorerEvents_10_FolderSwitchEventHandler(
        ThisApplication_FolderSwitch);
    this.ActiveExplorer().FolderSwitch +=
        this._FolderSwitchEventHandler;

//Step #4: Trap Inspector Creation event
    this.myInspectors = this.Inspectors;
    this.myInspectors.NewInspector += new
        InspectorsEvents_NewInspectorEventHandler(
        Inspectors_NewInspector);
    }
```

As you can see in Step #1 in Listing 5.1, we first access the CommandBars collection in ActiveExplorer. ActiveExplorer represents the current Outlook window where folder contents are displayed. The CommandBars.Add method allows you to add a custom toolbar.

Add Custom Buttons

Once the custom toolbar is created, the following buttons are added to the toolbar (see Step #2 in Listing 5.1). Table 5.1 lists the new buttons added to the toolbar.

TABLE 5.1   Custom Buttons Added to the Toolbar

Name of Button	Description
Attach Email(s)	Attaches email(s) to one or more VSTS work items.
Attach Folder	Attaches emails located in an Outlook folder to VSTS work items.
Import Tasks	Creates new Outlook tasks from VSTS tasks.
Refresh Tasks	Retrieves updated task information from VSTS.
Publish Tasks	Publishes updated task information to VSTS.

Trap the Folder-Switching Event

Trap the FolderSwitch event of ActiveExplorer so that appropriate buttons can be enabled and disabled based upon current folder selection (see Step #3 in Listing 5.1). Listing 5.2 shows the event-handling code.

LISTING 5.2   Code for Activating/Deactivating Custom Buttons Based upon Current Folder Selection

```
/// <summary>
/// activates/deactivates custom buttons based
/// upon current folder
/// </summary>
void ThisApplication_FolderSwitch()
{
  //activate Attach Button if current folder is Mail
  if (this.ActiveExplorer().CurrentFolder.DefaultItemType ==
      OlItemType.olMailItem)
    this.attachToButton.Enabled = true;
  else
    this.attachToButton.Enabled = false;

  //activate Import Tasks, Refresh Tasks, and Publish Tasks if
  //current folder is Task
  if (this.ActiveExplorer().CurrentFolder.DefaultItemType ==
      OlItemType.olTaskItem)
  {
    this.publishTaskButton.Enabled = true;
    this.refreshTasksButton.Enabled = true;
    this.importWorkItemButton.Enabled = true;
  }
  else
  {
    this.publishTaskButton.Enabled = false;
```

```
      this.refreshTasksButton.Enabled = false;
      this.importWorkItemButton.Enabled = false;
   }
}
```

Trap the Inspector Creation Event

An inspector represents a window created for viewing a single item. In Step #4 in Listing 5.1, we trap the NewInspector event and display a custom email attachment button in the inspector window (see Figure 5.28). Listing 5.3 shows the event-handling code.

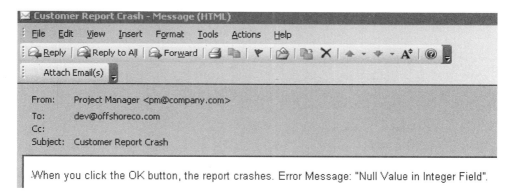

FIGURE 5.28   Attach Email(s) button added to email inspector window.

LISTING 5.3   Code for Showing Attach Email(s) Button in Email Inspector Window

```
/// <summary>
/// Adds the work item attach toolbar on new email inspectors
/// </summary>
/// <param name="inspector"></param>
private void pSetupToolbarOnInspector(Inspector inspector)
{
  // Only Email inspectors will have the attachment feature
  if (!(inspector.CurrentItem is MailItem)) return;

  // First, get access to the CommandBars on the active explorer.
  CommandBars commandBars =
      inspector.CommandBars;

  CommandBar workItemCommandBar = null;

  // Check if the bar is already there.
  bool commandBarExists = false;
```

```
    foreach (CommandBar bar in commandBars)
      if (bar.Name == COMMAND_BAR_NAME)
      {
        commandBarExists = true;
        workItemCommandBar = bar;
      }

    // If bar is not there, then add the bar.
    if (!commandBarExists)
    {
      workItemCommandBar = commandBars.Add(COMMAND_BAR_NAME,
          MsoBarPosition.msoBarTop,
          System.Reflection.Missing.Value,
          true); // Temporary = True, means the command bar
                 // is not permanent

      workItemCommandBar.Visible = true;

      // Create the buttons on the command bar
      CommandBarButton attachEmailButton =
          this.pCreateButton(workItemCommandBar,
          WORK_ITEM_BUTTON_NAME,
          WORK_ITEM_BUTTON_CAPTION, WORK_ITEM_BUTTON_NAME);
      attachEmailButton.Click += new
          _CommandBarButtonEvents_ClickEventHandler(
          attachEmailButton_Click);
    }
}
```

Implement Attach Email(s)

When you click Attach Email(s) on the custom toolbar, the add-in asks you whether you want to select the target work items manually or whether the add-in should automatically select the work items based upon the content of the custom WorkItemRef field in the email. If you decide to go for manual selection, a work item picker dialog box is displayed. Listing 5.4 shows the code associated with displaying a custom dialog box for selecting VSTS work items.

LISTING 5.4 Code Snippet for Displaying Work Item Picker Dialog Box

```
/// <summary>
/// Show custom dialog box and get list of work items
/// </summary>
/// <returns></returns>
internal static IList<WorkItem> SelectWorkItems(
    string workItemType)
{
```

```
//get Tfs server and team project info
//info will be stored in class properties
pGetTfsServerandProjectInfo();

WorkItemStore wkStore = TeamSystemHelper.WorkItemStore;
if (null == wkStore) return null;

//show work item picker dialog box and
//let user select the work item(s)
WorkItemPickerCustomDialog wkDialog =
    new WorkItemPickerCustomDialog();

//set Tfs server name
wkDialog.ServerName = TeamSystemHelper.ServerName;

//set Team Project name
wkDialog.TeamProjectName = TeamSystemHelper.TeamProjectName;

wkDialog.ShowDialog();

//fetch selected work items
ArrayList wkItems = wkDialog.SelectedWorkItems;
wkDialog.Dispose();

//determine what kind of work item to return
WorkItemType wkType = null;
if (workItemType != "All")
{
  //get work item type
  Project teamProject =
      wkStore.Projects[TeamSystemHelper.TeamProjectName];
  wkType = teamProject.WorkItemTypes[workItemType];
}

//create type-safe return collection
if (wkItems != null)
{
  IList<WorkItem> workItems = new List<WorkItem>();
  foreach (WorkItem workItem in wkItems)
  {
    if (workItemType != "All")
    {
      //insert only specified type in return collection
      if (workItem.Type.Name == wkType.Name)
      workItems.Add(workItem);
    }
    else
    {
```

```
        workItems.Add(workItem);
      }
    }

    return workItems;
  }
  else
  {
    return null;
  }
}
```

In the work item picker dialog box, select one or more VSTS work items that are relevant to the email, and click OK. The email will be attached to the specified work items in VSTS. Listing 5.5 shows the partial associated code; the full source code is included on the CD-ROM.

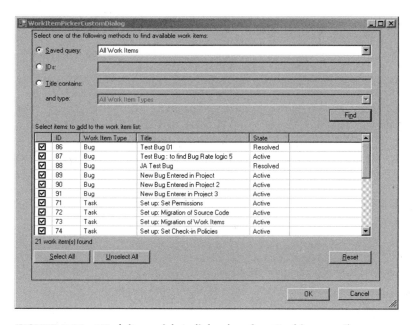

FIGURE 5.29 Work item picker dialog box for attaching emails.

LISTING 5.5 Code for Attaching One or More Emails to Specified Work Item(s)

```
/// <summary>
/// If user wants to manually specify target work items,
/// show work item picker dialog box.
```

```
/// Otherwise use the workItemRef custom field in mails
/// to get the work item
/// The specified mails are attached to the selected
/// work items. This can be one-to-one
/// attachment or can be many-to-many attachment.
/// </summary>
/// <param name="mails"></param>
internal static void AttachEmailsToWorkItem(List<MailItem> mails)
{
  // Ask user if he wants to select work item manually
  DialogResult manualSelection = MessageBox.Show(
      "Do you want to select work items manually?",
      MESSAGEBOX_CAPTION,
      MessageBoxButtons.YesNo, MessageBoxIcon.Question);

  if (manualSelection == DialogResult.Yes)
  {
    // Let user select the work item(s)
    IList<WorkItem> workItems = SelectWorkItems("All");
    if (null == workItems) return;
    pAttachMailsToWorkItem(mails, workItems);
  }
  else
  {
    // Ask for user confirmation
    DialogResult autoAttachment =
        MessageBox.Show("All selected emails will be attached to
        Work Item automatically.",
        MESSAGEBOX_CAPTION, MessageBoxButtons.OKCancel,
        MessageBoxIcon.Information);
    if (autoAttachment == DialogResult.OK)
    {
      pAttachMailsToReferredWorkItem(mails);
    }
  }
}


/// <summary>
/// Attach the specified mails to the specified work items
/// </summary>
/// <param name="mails"></param>
/// <param name="workItems"></param>
private static void pAttachMailsToWorkItem(IList<MailItem> mails,
    IList<WorkItem> workItems)
{
  if (mails.Count > 1)
  {
    DialogResult result = MessageBox.Show("Do you want to
```

```csharp
        attach each email as a separate file", "Email
        Attachment", MessageBoxButtons.YesNo,
        MessageBoxIcon.Question);

    if (result == DialogResult.Yes)
    {
      bool successful = true;
      //attach all mails as separate file
      foreach (MailItem mail in mails)
      {
        successful = pAttachMailToWorkItem(workItems, mail);
        if (!successful)
          break;
      }

      //Inform user about status
      pShowMessage(successful);
    }
    else
    {
      // Merge all file content
      StringBuilder content = new StringBuilder();
      foreach (MailItem mail in mails)
      {
        pGetMailContent(content, mail);

        content.Append(Environment.NewLine);
      }

      // Work item attachment comment
      string comment = "";

      // File name for combined mail
      string fileName = DateTime.Now.ToString("MMM dd yyyy mm-
          hh") + "_Combined" + ATTACHMENT_FILE_EXTENTION;

      // Create temporary file
      FileInfo file = pCreateTempFile(content.ToString(),
          fileName);

      bool successful = pAttachFileToWorkItems(workItems,
          comment, file);
      file.Delete();

      //Inform user about status
      pShowMessage(successful);
    }
  }
```

```csharp
    else
    {
      if (mails.Count == 1)
      {
        bool successful = pAttachMailToWorkItem(workItems,
            mails[0]);
        pShowMessage(successful);
      }
      else
        Debug.Write("No mail found in the list.");
    }
}

private static void pAttachMailsToReferredWorkItem(
    List<MailItem> mails)
{
  WorkItemStore wkStore = TeamSystemHelper.WorkItemStore;
  if (wkStore == null)
    return;

  bool successful = true;
  int attachmentCount = 0;
  foreach (MailItem mail in mails)
  {
    int workItemId = pGetWorkItemIdForMail(mail);
    if (workItemId != 0)
    {
      // increase count
      attachmentCount++;

      // Get the workItem
      WorkItem workItem = wkStore.GetWorkItem(workItemId);
      List<WorkItem> workItems = new List<WorkItem>();
      workItems.Add(workItem);

      // Attach the mail with work item
      successful = pAttachMailToWorkItem(workItems, mail);
    }
  }

  // Inform status to user
  if (successful)
  {
    MessageBox.Show(attachmentCount.ToString() + " mail(s)
        attached to work item(s)", MESSAGEBOX_CAPTION,
        MessageBoxButtons.OK, MessageBoxIcon.Information);
  }
}
```

Implement Import Tasks

When you click the Import Tasks custom button, the ImportWorkItemForm dialog box is displayed. You can add VSTS work items to Outlook tasks list as well as to Outlook Calendar (see Figure 5.30). In the Import Work Items dialog box, click Select Work Items. In the work item picker dialog box, select the work items to import—usually tasks that you would like to track in Outlook or assign to people who do not have VSTS. Click Import to add selected VSTS work items to the Outlook task list (see Figure 5.31) as well as to Outlook Calendar (see Figure 5.32). Listing 5.6 shows the code associated with adding VSTS work items to Outlook tasks. Listing 5.7 shows the code associated with adding VSTS tasks to Outlook calendar.

FIGURE 5.30 VSTS work items import form.

LISTING 5.6 Code for Creating an Outlook Task from a VSTS Work Item

```
/// <summary>
/// create Outlook task from VSTS work item
/// </summary>
/// <param name="item"></param>
/// <param name="newTask"></param>
internal static void CreateTaskFromWorkItem(WorkItem item,
    TaskItem newTask)
{
  newTask.Subject = item.Title;
  newTask.Categories = item.Project.Name;
  newTask.Body = TeamSystemHelper.BuildTaskBody(item);
```

```
newTask.StartDate = TeamSystemHelper.StartDateTime(item);
DateTime dueDate = TeamSystemHelper.EndDateTime(item);

// Due date of a task cannot occur before start date
if (dueDate > newTask.StartDate)
  newTask.DueDate = TeamSystemHelper.EndDateTime(item);
//update progress tracking fields
newTask.TotalWork = TeamSystemHelper.Duration(item);
newTask.ActualWork = TeamSystemHelper.CompletedWork(item);
newTask.PercentComplete =
    TeamSystemHelper.PercentCompleted(item);

if (item.State == "Closed")
{
  // Task closed
  if (!newTask.Complete)
    newTask.MarkComplete();
}
else
{
  if (newTask.StartDate > DateTime.Now)
  {
    // turn on reminder
    newTask.ReminderTime = newTask.StartDate.AddMinutes(-15);
    newTask.ReminderSet = true;
    newTask.ReminderOverrideDefault = true;
    newTask.ReminderPlaySound = true;
  }
  else
  {
    newTask.ReminderSet = false;
    newTask.ReminderOverrideDefault = true;
  }
}

// 3. Store the work item URI in user properties
UserProperty uriProp =
    newTask.UserProperties.Add(TeamSystemHelper.WORK_ITEM_URI,
    OlUserPropertyType.olText, Missing.Value, Missing.Value);
uriProp.Value = item.Uri.ToString();

// 4. Save the task
newTask.Save();
}
```

Notice in Listing 5.6 that the URI of each VSTS work item is stored in a custom property of the corresponding Outlook task. The work item URI is used to correlate VSTS work items with Outlook tasks.

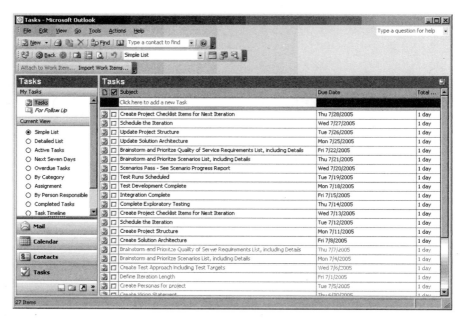

FIGURE 5.31   VSTS tasks imported as Outlook tasks.

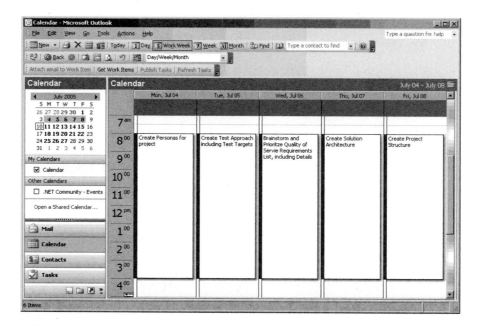

FIGURE 5.32   VSTS tasks added to Outlook calendar.

LISTING 5.7   Code for Creating an Outlook Appointment from a VSTS Work Item

```
/// <summary>
/// create a new appointment in Outlook Calendar from work item
/// </summary>
/// <param name="item"></param>
/// <param name="newAppointment"></param>
internal static void CreateAppointmentFromWorkItem(WorkItem item,
    AppointmentItem newAppointment)
{
  newAppointment.Subject = item.Title;
  newAppointment.Categories = item.Project.Name;
  newAppointment.Start = TeamSystemHelper.StartDateTime(item);

  // If there is no time part in the start date,
  // let's assume the appointment is from 8 AM
  DateTime dayStartsAt = newAppointment.Start.Date.AddHours(8);
  if (newAppointment.Start < dayStartsAt )
  {
    newAppointment.Start = dayStartsAt;
  }

  newAppointment.Duration = TeamSystemHelper.Duration(item);
  // If no duration set for appointment, then assume it will take
  //the whole working day
  if (0 == newAppointment.Duration)
    newAppointment.Duration =
        (int)TimeSpan.FromHours(8).TotalMinutes;
  newAppointment.Body = TeamSystemHelper.BuildTaskBody(item);

  if (item.State == "Closed")
  {
    // Task closed
  }
  else
  {
    if (newAppointment.Start > DateTime.Now)
    {
      // Engage reminder
      newAppointment.ReminderMinutesBeforeStart = 15;
      newAppointment.ReminderSet = true;
    }
    else
    {
      newAppointment.ReminderSet = false;
      newAppointment.ReminderOverrideDefault = true;
    }
  }
```

```
// 3. Store the work item URI in user properties
UserProperty uriProp = newAppointment.UserProperties.Add(
    TeamSystemHelper.WORK_ITEM_URI,
    OlUserPropertyType.olText, Missing.Value, Missing.Value);
uriProp.Value = item.Uri.ToString();

// 4. Save the task
newAppointment.Save();

}
```

Implement Refresh Tasks

You can click Refresh Tasks to connect to VSTS and fetch the latest status information of each task. Listing 5.8 shows the associated code.

LISTING 5.8   Code for Refreshing Outlook Tasks from VSTS Work Items

```
/// <summary>
/// Refresh task information in Outlook from VSTS
/// </summary>
/// <param name="tasks"></param>
internal static void RefreshTasks(IList<TaskItem> tasks)
{
    //get Tfs server and team project info
    //info will be stored in class properties
    pGetTfsServerInfo();

    // Connect to work item store
    WorkItemStore store = TeamSystemHelper.WorkItemStore;

    if (null == store) return;
    // for each task specified, find the work item and
    //update the task
    foreach (TaskItem task in tasks)
    {
        // Find the work item URI from the task's user
        //properties collection
        UserProperty workItemProperty = task.UserProperties.Find(
            TeamSystemHelper.WORK_ITEM_URI, Missing.Value);
        if (null != workItemProperty)
        {
            string uri = workItemProperty.Value as string;

            // Use the uri to locate the work item from work item store
            WorkItem item = store.GetWorkItem(new Uri(uri));
            if (null != item)
            {
                // Work Item found, update Task only if
                //the work item is newer
```

```
            if( item.ChangedDate > task.LastModificationTime )
              pUpdateTaskFromWorkItem(item, task);
        }
      }
    }
}

internal static String BuildTaskBody(WorkItem item)
{
  Field field = item.Fields[DESCRIPTION];
  if (null != field && null != field.Value)
  {
    string summary = (string)field.Value;
    if (null == summary)
      summary = string.Empty;

    return summary;
  }
  else
    return string.Empty;
}


/// <summary>
/// update task attributes from corresponding work item
/// </summary>
/// <param name="workItem"></param>
/// <param name="task"></param>
/// <returns></returns>
private static bool pUpdateTaskFromWorkItem(WorkItem workItem,
    TaskItem task)
{
  // Update task status
  if (workItem.State == "Closed")
  {
    task.Status = OlTaskStatus.olTaskComplete;
  }

  // Check if the description is changed
  string workItemDescription = BuildTaskBody(workItem);
  if (task.Body != null && workItemDescription != task.Body)
  {
    Field field = workItem.Fields[DESCRIPTION];
    if (null != field)
    {
      task.Body = field.Value.ToString();
    }
  }
```

```csharp
// Change the title
if (workItem.Title != task.Subject)
{
  task.Subject = workItem.Title;
}

// Update total work
int totalWork = Duration(workItem);
if (totalWork != task.TotalWork)
{
  // Update the total work of this task
  task.TotalWork = totalWork;
}

// Update actual work
int actualWork = CompletedWork(workItem);
if (actualWork != task.ActualWork)
{
  // Update the total work of this task
  task.ActualWork = actualWork;
}

// Update percent completed
int percentCompleted = PercentCompleted(workItem);
if (percentCompleted != task.PercentComplete)
{
  task.PercentComplete = percentCompleted;
}

// save the task
try
{
  task.Save();
  return true;
}
catch (System.Exception x)
{
  Debug.WriteLine(x);
  return false;
}
}
```

Implement Publish Tasks

Click Publish Tasks to transmit current task information from Outlook to VSTS. To test this feature, mark some tasks as completed in Outlook (see Figure 5.33) and click Publish Tasks. Switch to VSTS and view the tasks updated in Outlook; you'll find that the State field of each task has been marked as Closed (see Figure 5.34). Listing 5.9 shows the code associated with this functionality.

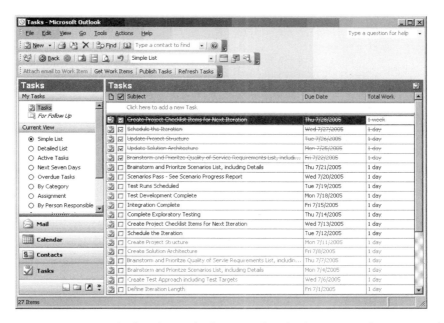

FIGURE 5.33 Outlook tasks marked as completed prior to exporting to VSTS.

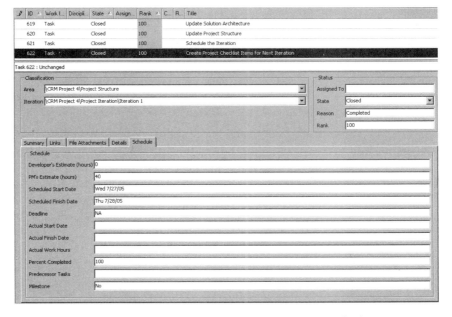

FIGURE 5.34 Tasks labeled Closed after importing from Outlook.

LISTING 5.9   Code for Updating VSTS Work Items from Outlook Tasks

```
/// <summary>
/// update VSTS work item information from Outlook
///task information
/// </summary>
/// <param name="tasks"></param>
internal static void PublishTasks(IList<TaskItem> tasks)
{
  //get Tfs server and team project info
  //info will be stored in class properties
  pGetTfsServerInfo();

  // Connect to work item store
  WorkItemStore store = TeamSystemHelper.WorkItemStore;
  if (null == store) return;

  // for each task specified, find the work item
  // and update the work item
  foreach (TaskItem task in tasks)
  {
    // If the task has been modified after creation
    if (task.LastModificationTime != task.CreationTime)
    {
      // Find the work item URI from the task's user
      //properties collection
      UserProperty workItemProperty = task.UserProperties.Find(
          TeamSystemHelper.WORK_ITEM_URI, Missing.Value);
      if (null != workItemProperty)
      {
        string uri = workItemProperty.Value as string;

        // Use the uri to locate the work item from
        //work item store
        WorkItem item = store.GetWorkItem(new Uri(uri));
        if (null != item)
        {
          // Work Item found, update only if the
          //work item is older
          if (item.ChangedDate < task.LastModificationTime)
            pUpdateWorkItemFromTask(item, task);
        }
      }
    }
  }
}

/// <summary>
/// update work item attributes from current
```

```
/// task status information
/// </summary>
/// <param name="workItem"></param>
/// <param name="task"></param>
/// <returns></returns>
private static bool pUpdateWorkItemFromTask(WorkItem workItem,
    TaskItem task)
{
  // Update work item status from outlook's task status
  if (task.Status == OlTaskStatus.olTaskComplete )
  {
    // The task is marked as completed, so it the
    //work item is still Active,
    // make is closed.
    if (workItem.State == "Active")
    {
      if (!workItem.IsOpen) workItem.Open();
      workItem.State = "Closed";
      workItem.Reason = "Completed";

      workItem.Validate();
    }
  }


  // Check description
  string workItemDescription = BuildTaskBody(workItem);
  if (task.Body != null && workItemDescription != task.Body)
  {
    Field field = workItem.Fields[DESCRIPTION];
    if (null != field)
    {
      if (!workItem.IsOpen) workItem.Open();
      field.Value = task.Body;
    }
  }

  // Check title
  if (workItem.Title != task.Subject)
  {
    if (!workItem.IsOpen) workItem.Open();
    workItem.Title = task.Subject;
  }

  // Check total work
  int totalWork = Duration(workItem);
  if (totalWork != task.TotalWork)
  {
```

```
        if (!workItem.IsOpen) workItem.Open();
        // Update the total work of this task
        totalWork = task.TotalWork;
        workItem.Fields[DURATION].Value = (double)totalWork/60.0;
      }

      // Check completed work
      int completedWork = CompletedWork(workItem);
      if (completedWork != task.ActualWork)
      {
        if (!workItem.IsOpen) workItem.Open();
        // Update the completed work of this task
        completedWork = task.ActualWork;
        workItem.Fields[COMPLETED_WORK].Value =
            (double)completedWork/60.0;
      }

      // Check percent completed
      int percentCompleted = PercentCompleted(workItem);
      if (percentCompleted != task.PercentComplete)
      {
        if (!workItem.IsOpen) workItem.Open();
        workItem.Fields[PERCENT_COMPLETE].Value =
            task.PercentComplete;
      }

      // Save the item
      try
      {
        if (workItem.IsDirty)
        {
          workItem.Save();
          return true;
        }
        else
        {
          return false;
        }
      }
      catch (System.Exception x)
      {
        Debug.WriteLine(x);
        return false;
      }
    }
```

CONCLUSION

Not many people live and work in seclusion. In a 'wired' world, we are interdependent on one other for our physical, intellectual, and professional needs. Email has become a core tool for exchanging ideas, sharing information, and coordinating actions. It is hard to imagine today how businesses operated without email systems just a decade ago. Email has revolutionized communication and made possible the 24/7 interconnected world that we live in.

Outlook provides powerful capabilities for managing email communications. In this chapter, we saw how the standard email form can be customized to streamline information interchange. We also created a custom add-in to attach emails to VSTS work items, and to synchronize task information between Outlook and VSTS. The combination of VSTS and Outlook provides a strong platform for facilitating exchange of information throughout the project life cycle. During all phases of a project, emails carry a huge of amount of 'out-of-band' information that needs to be processed, classified, and stored. Outlook and VSTS facilitate effective information management and subsequent efficient retrieval.

A recent study by IDC showed that up to 60 percent of an organization's business-critical information is locked away in its email system [DMR05]. Another IDC study indicates that about 60 billion emails are sent worldwide every day [VNU02]. Many people are overwhelmed by the information overload. They feel that processing, organizing, and storing information (sometimes to satisfy regulatory requirements) is a never-ending up-hill battle.

In this chapter, we presented a strategy to unlock the power of the information buried in your email repository and to integrate it with VSTS. This simple, yet effective approach will help you better manage your offshore projects not only during initial development, but also during subsequent maintenance phases, when the original team members are long gone.

FURTHER READING

[Boyce04] Boyce, Jim, *Microsoft Office Outlook 2003 Inside Out*. Microsoft Press, ISBN: 0-7356-1514-4, 2004.

[DMR05] *"Do You Know What is in Your Employees' Inbox?"* DMReview, May 20, 2005. Available online on August 15, 2005, at: *http://www.dmreview. com/article_sub.cfm?articleId=1028055.*

[Microsoft03] *"Developing Custom Forms Using Microsoft Outlook 2002."* Microsoft Corporation, 2003. Available online on July 30, 2005, at: *http://msdn.microsoft.com/library/default.asp?url=/library/en-us/dnout2k2/html/odc_ olcustfrm1.asp.*

[Microsoft05] *"Architecture of the Outlook Add-in Support in Visual Studio 2005 Tools for Office."* Microsoft Corporation, 2005. Available online on July 30, 2005, at: *http://msdn.microsoft.com/office/understanding/vsto/default.aspx? pull=/library/en-us/odc_vsto2005_ta/html/Office_VSTOOutlookAdd-inAr- chitecture.asp.*

[VNU02] *"You have mail: 31 billion a day."* VNUNet.com, September 30, 2002. Available online on August 15, 2005, at: *http://www.vnunet.com/vnunet/ news/2120233/mail-31-billion-day.*

6 Facilitating Real-Time Communication

In This Chapter

INTRODUCTION

Effective communication is critical for success when working with offshore teams. A friction-free, global, collaborative work environment requires new tools, processes, and attitudes. When you are working with people whom you barely know and who work when you sleep, how do you develop the trust, cordiality, and interpersonal relationships that underpin great team achievements? How do you forge the common vision and mindshare that is naturally created from coffee-machine conversations or quick sketches on a whiteboard? Can you replace eye contacts and handshakes?

We feel that face-to-face communication is not *entirely* replaceable using the technologies available today. However, although we cannot make geography completely irrelevant, we can accomplish a lot by effectively using the available tools and technologies. Furthermore, not all outsourced projects require a strong coupling between distributed teams (many development and support teams are entirely located overseas). In this chapter, we demonstrate how you can set up an integrated development environment with seamless communication and collaboration capabilities, where distributed teams can operate cohesively and efficiently. High-volume and high-fidelity interaction between distributed teams is a key enabler of success in offshore projects.

It is often argued that because on-site and offshore team members usually work in non-overlapping time zones for offshore projects, real-time communication is not important or even feasible. Our experience suggests otherwise. We strongly feel that you need to do whatever it takes and *make* real-time communication possible during parts of the work day—by adjusting your hours and family life, as well as the offshore team's office hours. Issues often come up that need immediate attention, interaction, and resolution. If these problems get postponed until the next business day, the project schedule may be jeopardized.

VSTS can be extended to provide an integrated communication platform in conjunction with Microsoft Office Communicator 2005™ (Office Communicator), Live Communications Server 2005™ (LCS), and Microsoft Office Live Meeting™ (Live Meeting). The combined toolset allows you to conduct real-time, multimodal collaboration with offshore team members via chat, audio, video, Short Message Service (SMS), application sharing, and online meetings. In this chapter, we show you how to write custom extensions to VSTS to create a presence-aware development surface.

PRESENCE DETECTION

Presence awareness facilitates effective communication. When working with people half a world away, you'll often want to know if they are available for immediate interaction. Real-time presence-detection capability allows you to find people online with minimum overhead. You can communicate with them without the expense and hassle of overseas phone calls. In our experience, real-time communication has often meant the difference between project success and failure—especially when the on-site and offshore teams are tightly coupled, and waiting another day is not an option.

The goal is to create a seamless work environment that facilitates distributed team collaboration without having to switch between tools. A unified toolset reduces learning curves, enhances user experience, and creates a more productive work environment.

We add presence-detection capabilities in VSTS by extending Team Explorer. A custom node named Contacts is created to display presence information (see

Figure 6.1). This node displays a list of team members along with their online status. It also provides a mechanism to associate conversations with work items. Ad-hoc conversations are lost if they are not stored in a manner that makes subsequent retrieval easy and intuitive. We store conversations as attachments to relevant work items.

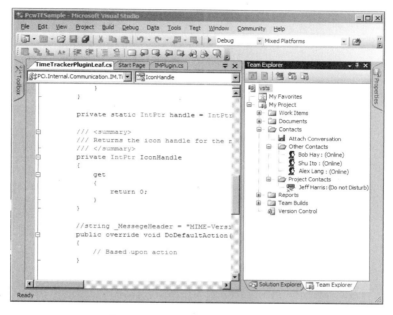

FIGURE 6.1   Integrated presence detection in VSTS.

The Contacts node contains the following child nodes:

- **Project Contacts:** Displays team users who belong to the current team project.
- **Other Contacts:** Displays other contacts from the Office Communicator contact list.
- **Attach Conversation:** Allows you to attach conversations to work items.

Behind the scenes, Office Communicator APIs are used to provide presence detection and real-time communication capabilities. Office Communicator provides a rich set of automation APIs for instant messaging, application sharing, audio/video chats, and file transfer. We leverage the presence-detection APIs to display the online status of team members. When you double-click a username, Office Communicator pops up and allows you to interact with the selected person in real time.

The Contacts node is created by writing a custom plug-in. The technical details are discussed later in the chapter.

MICROSOFT OFFICE COMMUNICATOR 2005

Office Communicator is an enterprise-class, real-time communication tool. It offers a wealth of communication capabilities, such as text chat, PC-based audio and video, file transfer, application sharing, Voice over Internet Protocol (VoIP) support, and enterprise telephony (see Figure 6.2). Office Communicator is the preferred client for Microsoft Office Live Communications Server 2005. LCS provides a standards-based, scalable server platform with enterprise-wide, real-time communication and collaboration capabilities.

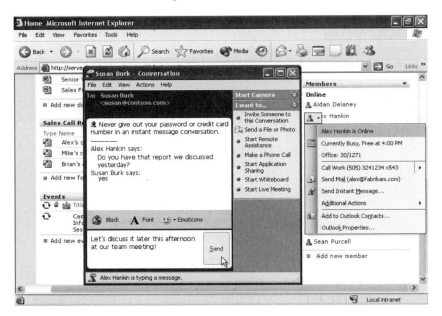

FIGURE 6.2 Office Communicator provides presence detection and real-time communication capabilities.

You can use Office Communicator to securely collaborate over the Internet using a variety of communication modes. In conjunction with LCS, Office Communicator enables you to interact with team members within your organization as well as with your offshore partners. You can also work with users from public Instant Messaging (IM) networks such as Yahoo!, America Online, and MSN. Instead of using different client software for various IM services, you can use Office Communicator to communicate with all of your contacts from a single interface.

You can conduct text chat as well as application-sharing sessions simultaneously with multiple parties (see Figure 6.3). PC-based video and audio conversations, however, can only be conducted on a one-to-one basis. For more-complex group interactions, you can use Microsoft Live Meeting, which provides a scalable online meeting infrastructure.

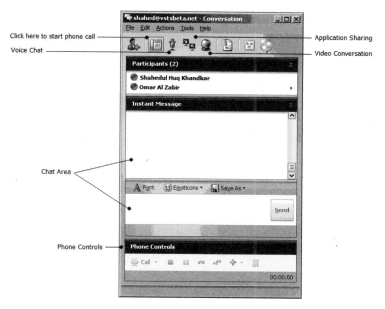

FIGURE 6.3 Office Communicator provides multimodal communication capability.

Before initiating a communication request, you can look up the person's online availability and choose the appropriate interaction mode (e.g., email, chat, phone, etc.). Office Communicator can detect a person's actions on the computer and automatically update his status. You can also manually change your online status at any time. Additionally, Office Communicator can indicate "In a Meeting" or "Out of Office" status, based upon current scheduling information in Outlook calendar. You can also ask Office Communicator to notify you when a person comes online via the "Tag Contact" feature.

Office Communicator includes powerful telephony-integration features. Desktop phones and computers are typically used as separate devices (although they are usually located right next to each other), but it is possible to control your telephone from your computer. Office Communicator accomplishes this feat by interacting with the PBX system via LCS and the Remote Call Control (RCC) gateway (see Figure 6.4). This configuration allows Office Communicator to control both incoming and outgoing calls. For example, Office Communicator can detect incoming calls and automatically forward them to your home phone or cell phone. It can also interact with an external conference provider to quickly set up multiparty conference calls. If you would like to bypass the traditional phone system and use your computer as the communication end point, Office Communicator enables you to initiate VoIP calls directly from your PC. The VoIP call can be transported to the offshore location via the Internet and connected to the specified target machine. Alternatively, the call can be routed to an overseas phone via the Public Switched Telephone Network (PSTN) network in that country, using an appropriate gateway (e.g., an SIP-PSTN gateway). Enterprise telephony integration allows Office Communicator to become a powerful 'softphone,' reducing costs and offering a plethora of voice communication options.

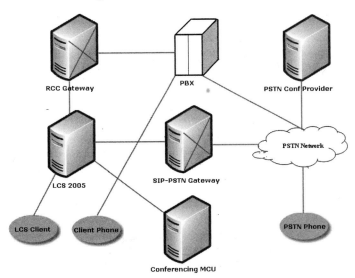

FIGURE 6.4 Enterprise telephony infrastructure provided by Office Communicator and LCS.

MICROSOFT OFFICE LIVE COMMUNICATIONS SERVER 2005

LCS provides an enterprise-class, real-time collaboration backbone. Microsoft applications such as Office, Office Communicator, and Outlook use LCS as the underlying infrastructure for presence detection and online communication. LCS provides enterprise features such as automatic encryption, logging, and archiving—

as well as Active Directory and Exchange Server integration (see Figure 6.5). You can take advantage of LCS to increase productivity and reduce the latency inherent in offline, asynchronous communication.

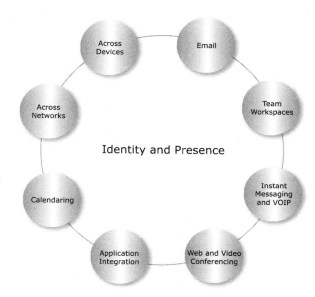

FIGURE 6.5   LCS enables rich collaboration capabilities in the organizational workflow.

One of the key features of LCS from the perspective of an offshore model is its ability to work across firewalls. Using 'federation,' trusted partner organizations can establish a secure communication channel across firewalls without requiring a Virtual Private Network (VPN) connection (see Figure 6.6). LCS federation is distinct from Active Directory federation. LCS federation uses standards-based protocols (SIP/SIMPLE) that allow heterogeneous instant messaging and presence-detection systems to interoperate using XML messages. For more information on SIP/SIMPLE see the Internet Engineering Task Force (IETF) Web site at *http://www.ietf.org/html.charters/simple-charter.html*.

The federation solves the thorny problem of having IM conversations with the offshore team members when they do not belong to the same organization. For security and privacy reasons, IT departments are usually unwilling to open up firewall ports and allow unrestricted IM interactions. Additionally, unless the two organizations set up a VPN link, they are forced to use the public IM networks, which carries all kinds of security risks, such as identity spoofing, 'man in the middle' attacks, eavesdropping, and virus attacks. LCS federation solves these problems by authenticating and encrypting all server-to-server traffic (between access proxies), and authenticating and signing all client-to-server traffic. Instant messaging, presence, and application-sharing traffic are automatically protected by transport layer security, such as Secure Sockets Layer (SSL). Audio and video streams are encrypted using Data Encryption Standard (DES). Federating servers authenticate each other using Mutual Transport Layer Security (MTLS), where both parties are required to provide security certificates.

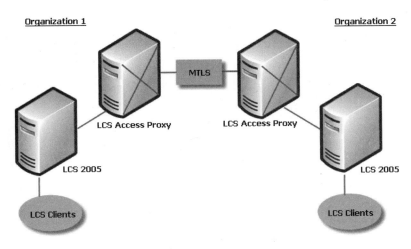

FIGURE 6.6 Live Communications Server federation.

In addition to extensive security measures, LCS allows you to control individual activities using both per-user Access Control Lists (ACLs) and group policy settings (e.g.. to prevent file transfers). For offshore partners who do not have LCS installed, you can selectively allow public IM connectivity (see Figure 6.7) while maintaining encryption (up to the public IM network's access proxy), logging, and control over unsolicited commercial messages (by setting Spam over IM (SPIM) filters). However, when using public IM clients, you can only use one-to-one IM sessions; file transfer and audio/video conferencing are not supported. For more information on IM connectivity issues, check out Microsoft Knowledgebase article #897567 at *http://support.microsoft.com/default.aspx?scid=kb;en-us;897567.*

In a nutshell, we feel that LCS provides a vital infrastructure piece for facilitating secure offshore communications. For more information on LCS, check out: Microsoft Web site at *http://office.microsoft.com/en-us/FX010908711033.aspx.*

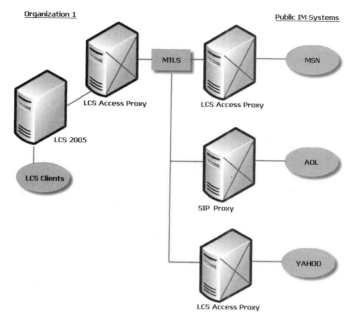

FIGURE 6.7   LCS offers public IM connectivity.

MICROSOFT OFFICE LIVE MEETING 2005

When working on outsourced projects, sooner or later you'll encounter the need to conduct virtual meetings with multiple parties. You'll need to show or view presentations and documents, look at applications running on your computer or remote computers, as well as collaboratively create and annotate documents in real time. All of these visual interactions add tremendous value when communicating with overseas teams. Simple phone conversations often do not convey the context and relevant details needed to explain complex issues or troubleshoot stubborn problems. In multi-vendor situations as well as when working with multiple teams on integration projects, you'll find that unless you bring all parties to the same 'table'—and interactively work through the problems on a reference machine—you could end up spending weeks talking and sending emails back and forth, but making no real progress.

Live Meeting is a hosted service that enables you to conduct virtual meetings globally. Although you can conduct small meetings using Office Communicator and LCS, there are times when you will need to conduct structured virtual meetings with a larger audience. Furthermore, Live Meeting is a hosted service and does not require any IT infrastructure investment. You just pay for the service on a pay-per-use or subscription basis and start using it. For smaller organizations, using the meeting service without infrastructure procurement, installation, and maintenance costs is often an attractive option.

Although you can launch Live Meeting using just the Web browser, you'll experience a richer user interface by downloading the desktop console (see Figure 6.8), which is available from the Microsoft Web site at *http://www.microsoft. com/downloads/details.aspx?FamilyId=BA25749F-CA2F-451B-A20F-205896A79E60&displaylang=en.* The console area contains several panes that allow you to view attendee and resource information, conduct one-on-one chats, share applications or portions thereof (see Figure 6.9), transfer control of documents or applications to other parties, and conduct polls. There is also a whiteboard (see Figure 6.10) where you can collaboratively enter free-form information. Meeting invitations can be sent out via email by clicking the Send E-mail Invite link and entering meeting information in the dialog box that pops up (see Figure 6.11).

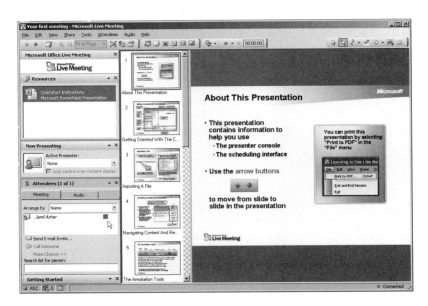

FIGURE 6.8   Live Meeting main screen.

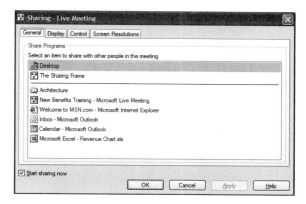

FIGURE 6.9   Share an application or document using Live Meeting.

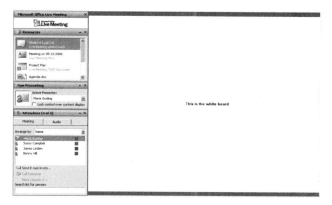

FIGURE 6.10   Free-form collaboration using the whiteboard.

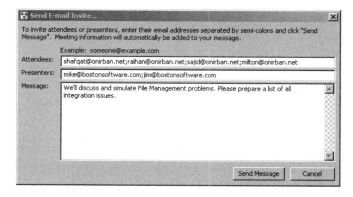

FIGURE 6.11   Invite attendees via email.

Live Meeting provides add-ins (download from Microsoft Web site at *http://www.microsoft.com/downloads/details.aspx?FamilyId=D1984810-117A-45FF-BFEC-2756C6111097&displaylang=en)* that enable integration with Office products such as Outlook, Project, PowerPoint, Excel, and Office Communicator. After installing the add-in, Office users can instantly schedule ad-hoc meetings and automatically share the document they are currently working on. Outlook users gain additional functionality in terms of being able to schedule meetings, just like regular meetings, and automatically send out invitations; the scheduled meetings appear in the Outlook calendar just like ordinary meetings (see Figure 6.12).

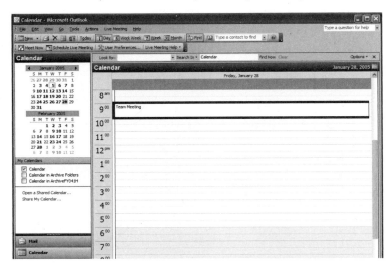

FIGURE 6.12 Scheduling collaborative virtual meetings from Outlook.

MICROSOFT OUTLOOK SMS ADD-IN

SMS is an efficient, low-cost, less-intrusive, and generally reliable mode of communication. You can use SMS to send messages to cell phones. Another advantage is that SMS supports store-and-forward delivery. If the target cell phone is turned off, the SMS messages are queued. Delivery takes place when the mobile phone is turned on. SMS messages can also be easily generated from automated systems—for example, by a build monitoring service, to provide notification of a build failure.

Given the wide adoption of cell phones in developing countries (where land lines are often difficult and expensive to get), chances are that every offshore team member carries a cell phone. You should take maximum advantage of this pervasive mobile telecom infrastructure as well as the low message-delivery costs.

You can use Microsoft Outlook 2003 SMS Add-In (MOSA) to send a message directly from Outlook using a mobile phone. You need to connect a Global Systems for Mobile Communications (GSM) compatible phone to a PC running Outlook. Connectivity with the PC can be established via a USB/serial cable and/or Bluetooth. (Make sure your cell phone supports PC connectivity.) The advantage of using MOSA is that you can save, group, search, and forward SMS messages just like normal emails. MOSA is a free add-in and can be downloaded from Microsoft Web site at *http://www.microsoft.com/downloads/details.aspx?FamilyID=240080b4-986e-4afb-ab21-3af2be63508b&displaylang=en.*

Once MOSA is installed, you'll find two new buttons on the Outlook toolbar named New SMS Message and Options. Click Options to configure your cell phone (see Figure 6.13).

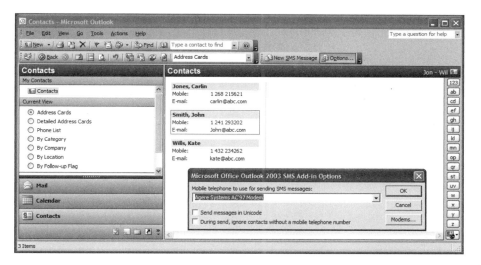

FIGURE 6.13   Configuration options for your mobile phone.

Click New SMS Message to launch the SMS message entry form. Specify the recipient information and the message text. Clicking To will bring up the Outlook contact list—you'll see a list of people who have mobile numbers (see Figure 6.14). Since you'll be sending messages overseas, the recipient's mobile number will probably be preceded by "011" and also contain the country code. To learn more about the correct format for target international cell-phone numbers and whether an international SMS feature is available with your service, check with your cell-phone carrier.

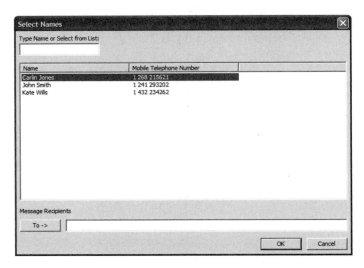

FIGURE 6.14 Select recipient(s) from the Outlook contact list.

Once you have chosen the recipient, type in a short message and click Send (see Figure 6.15). MOSA can send plain SMS messages only; Multimedia Messaging Service (MMS) is not yet supported.

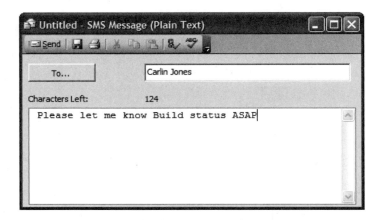

FIGURE 6.15 A populated SMS message form ready to be sent.

If cell phone carriers in the foreign country (or third-party international SMS providers) offer Web-based SMS capabilities, feel free to use it. The usefulness of MOSA comes from its being able to treat SMS messages in the same way as emails.

TECHNICAL REVIEW: CREATING A PLUG-IN FOR PRESENCE DETECTION

The plug-in creation work can be divided into the following steps:

- Create a helper class to communicate with Team Foundation Server.
- Create a helper class to call Office Communicator automation APIs.
- Create a plug-in to add custom nodes to Team Explorer.
- Create a VSIP package to host the plug-in.

ON THE CD

The full source code of the plug-in is available on the CD-ROM. Figure 6.16 shows the class diagrams for the helper classes.

FIGURE 6.16   Class diagrams for `TeamSystemHelper` and `OfficeCommunicatorHelper`.

Helper Class for the Team Foundation Server

The `TeamSystemHelper` class is responsible for interacting with Team Foundation Server. It provides information regarding work items and users that belong to a team project. This class contains the following key methods; Listing 6.1 contains the source code.

- `GetWorkItems`: Retrieves a list of work items for a team project. This method is used when the Attach Conversation node is clicked.
- `SelectWorkItems`: Displays work item selection dialog box and returns the list of selected work items. This method is invoked when the ellipses are clicked in the Attach Conversation to Work Item form.

■ `GetProjectMembers`: Fetches a list of users for a team project. This method is used to populate the list of users in the Team Explorer tree.

The functionalities of Team Foundation Server are accessed via the server object model (see Figure 6.17.

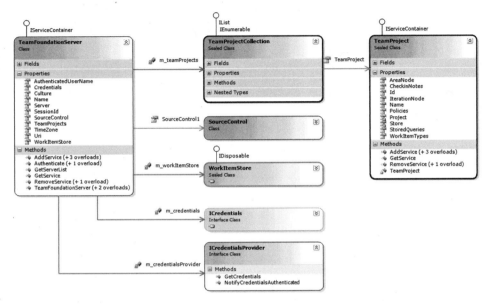

FIGURE 6.17   Top-level classes in Team Foundation Server object model.

LISTING 6.1   Source Code for `TeamSystemHelper` Class

```
using System;
using System.Collections;
using System.Collections.Generic;
using System.Text;
using System.IO;
using System.Diagnostics;

using Microsoft.TeamFoundation.Server;
using Microsoft.TeamFoundation.Proxy;
using Microsoft.TeamFoundation.Controls;
using Microsoft.TeamFoundation.Client;
using Microsoft.TeamFoundation.WorkItemTracking.Client;

namespace PresenceDetectionPlugInNS
{
public class TeamSystemHelper
{
```

```csharp
private static readonly string TFS_USERNAME = string.Empty;
private static readonly string TFS_PASSWORD = string.Empty;
private static readonly string TFS_DOMAIN = string.Empty;

private static string _serverName = "";
private static string _teamProjectName = "";

internal static string ServerName
{
  get { return _serverName; }
  set { _serverName = value; }
}

internal static string TeamProjectName
{
  get { return _teamProjectName; }
  set { _teamProjectName = value; }
}

private static TeamFoundationServer _tfsServer;
private static TeamFoundationServer TfsServer
{
  get
  {
    if (_tfsServer == null)
    {
      //connect to team server
      if (TFS_PASSWORD != string.Empty && TFS_USERNAME !=
          string.Empty)
      {
        System.Net.NetworkCredential nc =
            new System.Net.NetworkCredential(
            TFS_USERNAME, TFS_PASSWORD, TFS_DOMAIN);

        _tfsServer = new TeamFoundationServer(ServerName, nc);
      }
      else
      {
       _tfsServer = new TeamFoundationServer(ServerName);
      }
      return _tfsServer;
    }
    else
    {
      return _tfsServer;
    }
  }
}
```

```csharp
private static WorkItemStore _workItemStore = null;
private static WorkItemStore WorkItemStore
{
  get
  {
    if (_workItemStore == null)
    {
      // Get the WorkItemStore associated with this Team Server
      _workItemStore =
          new WorkItemStore(TeamSystemHelper.TfsServer);
      return _workItemStore;
    }
    else
    {
      return _workItemStore;
    }
  }
}

/// <summary>
/// fetches work items stored in the specified team project
/// </summary>
/// <param name="projectName"></param>
/// <returns></returns>
public static WorkItemCollection GetWorkItems(
    string projectName)
{
  // 1. Get list of projects in this server
  ProjectCollection oProjCollection = WorkItemStore.Projects;

  // 2. Obtain a specific project
  Project oProject = oProjCollection[projectName];

  // 3. Build a query string which fetches all
  // workItems by projectName
  string wiql = string.Format("SELECT [System.Title] FROM
      WorkItems where [System.TeamProject] = '{0}'",
      oProject.Name);

  // 4. Execute the WIQL
  WorkItemCollection col = WorkItemStore.Query(wiql);

  return col;
}

/// <summary>
/// get list of team members belonging to
/// the specified team project
```

```csharp
/// </summary>
/// <param name="projectName"></param>
/// <returns></returns>
public static List<Identity> GetProjectMembers(
    string projectName)
{
  try
  {

    ICommonStructureService css =
        TfsServer.GetService(typeof(ICommonStructureService))
        as ICommonStructureService;

    ProjectInfo[] projects = css.ListProjects();

    ProjectInfo currentProject = null;

    foreach (ProjectInfo prj in projects)
    {
      if (string.Compare(prj.Name, projectName) == 0)
      {
        currentProject = prj;
      }
    }

    // We did not find any project so lets quit processing
    if (currentProject == null)
    {
      return new List<Identity>();
    }

    // Get unioned list of users in projects
    List<Identity> projectUsers =
        pGetProjectMembers(currentProject);

    return projectUsers;
  }
  catch (Exception ex)
  {
    System.Diagnostics.Debug.WriteLine(ex);
    return null;
  }
}

/// <summary>
/// Show custom dialog box and get list of work items
/// </summary>
/// <returns></returns>
```

```csharp
internal static IList<WorkItem> SelectWorkItems(
    string workItemType)
{
  WorkItemStore wkStore = TeamSystemHelper.WorkItemStore;
  if (null == wkStore) return null;

  //show work item picker dialog box and
  //let user select the work item(s)
  WorkItemPickerCustomDialog wkDialog =
      new WorkItemPickerCustomDialog();

  //set Tfs server name
  wkDialog.ServerName = TeamSystemHelper.ServerName;

  //set Team Project name
  wkDialog.TeamProjectName = TeamSystemHelper.TeamProjectName;

  wkDialog.ShowDialog();

  //fetch selected work items
  ArrayList wkItems = wkDialog.SelectedWorkItems;
  wkDialog.Dispose();

  //determine what kind of work item to return
  WorkItemType wkType = null;
  if (workItemType != "All")
  {
    //get work item type
    Project teamProject =
        wkStore.Projects[TeamSystemHelper.TeamProjectName];
    wkType = teamProject.WorkItemTypes[workItemType];
  }

  //create type-safe return collection
  if (wkItems != null)
  {
    List<WorkItem> workItems = new List<WorkItem>();
    foreach (WorkItem workItem in wkItems)
    {
      if (workItemType != "All")
      {
        //insert only specified type in return collection
        if (workItem.Type.Name == wkType.Name)
          workItems.Add(workItem);
      }
      else
      {
        workItems.Add(workItem);
```

```
      }
    }

    return workItems;
  }
  else
  {
    return null;
  }
}

#region private methods

/// <summary>
/// get list of Windows Users for the specified project
/// </summary>
/// <param name="project"></param>
/// <param name="groupSecirityService"></param>
/// <returns></returns>
private static List<Identity> pGetProjectMembers(
    ProjectInfo project)
{
  List<Identity> listUsers = new List<Identity>();

  Hashtable htSid = new Hashtable();

  IGroupSecurityService gps =
      TfsServer.GetService(typeof(IGroupSecurityService))
      as IGroupSecurityService;

  Identity[] groups = gps.ListApplicationGroups(project.Uri);

  foreach (Identity group in groups)
  {
    //populate Members collection of the group
    Identity expandedGroup = gps.ReadIdentity(SearchFactor.Sid,
        group.Sid,QueryMembership.Expanded);

    if (expandedGroup.Members != null)
    {
      foreach (string userSid in expandedGroup.Members)
      {
        if (!htSid.ContainsKey(userSid))
        {
          Identity user = gps.ReadIdentityFromSource(
              SearchFactor.Sid, userSid);
          //add users to return collection
          htSid.Add(userSid, userSid);
```

```
                    listUsers.Add(user);
                }
            }
        }
    }
    return listUsers;
}
#endregion
}
}
```

The `GetWorkItems` method returns a `WorkItemCollection` containing work items for a given project. Work items are retrieved from `WorkItemStore`. `WorkItemStore` exposes a method named `Query`, which is used to fetch the work items based upon custom queries. We create a custom query using Work Item Query Language (WIQL).

The `SelectWorkItems` method displays a custom form for selecting work items. The work items are filtered if needed, and those matching the specified input type are returned.

The `GetProjectMembers` method returns the list of users for a particular team project. It obtains a list of team projects (using `ICommonStructureService` methods), iterates through the project collection, and acquires a reference to the specified project. The private method `pGetProjectMembers` is called to obtain the list of members for the target project; `pGetProjectMembers` obtains the list of project users by retrieving the groups associated with the team project (using `IGroupSecurity-Service` methods) and then looks up the users that belong to each group.

Helper Class for Office Communicator

`OfficeCommunicatorHelper` class encapsulates all communications with Office Communicator (see Listing 6.2). It exposes the following key methods:

- `GetUserStatusDescription`: Returns descriptive information regarding the current online status of a user.
- `ShowChatWindow`: Automatically signs in a user (if he is offline) and launches the Office Communicator chat window.
- `GetOCUserForVstsUser`: Given a VSTS user, it returns a corresponding Office Communicator user.
- `IsProjectMember`: Checks whether the specified Office Communicator user is a member of the specified team project.

LISTING 6.2   Source Code for `OfficeCommunicatorHelper` Class

```
using System.Collections;
using System.Collections.Generic;
using System.Windows.Forms;

using CommunicatorAPI;
using Microsoft.TeamFoundation.Server;

namespace PresenceDetectionPlugInNS
{
public class OfficeCommunicatorHelper
{
  private static Hashtable _htIdentity2ContactMap = null;
  private static MessengerClass _ocInstance = null;

  /// <summary>
  /// reference to the target Office Communicator instance
  /// </summary>
  public static MessengerClass Communicator
  {
    get
    {
      return _ocInstance;
    }
  }

  /// <summary>
  /// creates the instance of the current office
  ///communicator user
  /// </summary>
  public static void Initialize()
  {
    _ocInstance = new MessengerClass();
  }

  /// <summary>
  /// determine online status of the specified user
  /// </summary>
  /// <param name="contact"></param>
  /// <returns></returns>
  public static string GetUserStatusDescription(
      IMessengerContact contact)
  {
    string state = "";
    if (contact != null)
    {
      if (contact.Status  == MISTATUS.MISTATUS_ONLINE)
```

```
{
  state = "Online";
}
else if (contact.Status == MISTATUS.MISTATUS_OFFLINE)
{
  state = "Offline";
}
else if (contact.Status == MISTATUS.MISTATUS_AWAY)
{
  state = "Away";
}
else if (contact.Status == MISTATUS.MISTATUS_BE_RIGHT_BACK)
{
  state = "BeRightBack";
}
else if (contact.Status == MISTATUS.MISTATUS_BUSY)
{
  state = "Busy";
}
else if (contact.Status ==
    MISTATUS.MISTATUS_DO_NOT_DISTURB)
{
  state = "DoNotDisturb";
}
else if (contact.Status == MISTATUS.MISTATUS_IDLE)
{
  state = "Idle";
}
else if (contact.Status ==
    MISTATUS.MISTATUS_IN_A_CONFERENCE)
{
  state = "In a Conference";
}
else if (contact.Status == MISTATUS.MISTATUS_IN_A_MEETING)
{
  state = "In a Meeting";
}
else if (contact.Status == MISTATUS.MISTATUS_INVISIBLE)
{
  state = "Invisible";
}
else if (contact.Status == MISTATUS.MISTATUS_OUT_OF_OFFICE)
{
  state = "Out of Office";
}
else if (contact.Status == MISTATUS.MISTATUS_OUT_TO_LUNCH)
{
  state = "Out to Lunch";
```

```csharp
    }
    else if (contact.Status == MISTATUS.MISTATUS_ON_THE_PHONE)
    {
      state = "On the Phone";
    }
    else if (contact.Status == MISTATUS.MISTATUS_UNKNOWN)
    {
      state = "Unknown";
    }
  }
  else
  {
    state = "Not in Contact list";
  }
  return "(" + state + ")";
}

/// <summary>
/// fetches list of Contacts in Office Communicator
/// </summary>
/// <param name="mLIST"></param>
/// <returns></returns>
public static IMessengerContacts GetContactList()
{
  return (IMessengerContacts) _ocInstance.MyContacts;
}

/// <summary>
/// display the Office Communicator text chat window
/// </summary>
/// <param name="email"></param>
/// <returns></returns>
public static object ShowChatWindow(string email)
{
  if (GetUserLogOnStatus() != MISTATUS.MISTATUS_OFFLINE)
  {
    return _ocInstance.InstantMessage(email);
  }
  else
  {
    bool result = pAutoSignin();
    if (result == true)
    {
      return _ocInstance.InstantMessage(email);
    }
    else
    {
      return false;
```

```csharp
        }
      }
    }

    /// <summary>
    /// returns current user's online status
    /// </summary>
    public static MISTATUS GetUserLogOnStatus ()
    {
      return _ocInstance.MyStatus;
    }

    /// <summary>
    /// get corresponding Office Communicator Contact
    /// name for a specified
    /// Windows user
    /// </summary>
    /// <param name="vstsUser"></param>
    /// <returns></returns>
    public static IMessengerContact GetOCUserForVSTSUser(
        Identity vstsUser)
    {
      //fetch list of Office Communicator contacts
      IMessengerContacts ocContacts = GetContactList();

      //check account name
      foreach (IMessengerContact ocContact in ocContacts)
      {
        //Logon name is always like: userName@domain
        string[] tokens = ocContact.SigninName.Split('@');
        if (tokens.Length > 0)
        {
          if (tokens[0].ToLower() ==
              vstsUser.AccountName.ToLower())
          {
              return ocContact;
          }
        }
      }
      //no match found
      return null;
    }

    /// <summary>
    /// Determine if the specified OC contact is
    ///a user in the specified team project
    /// </summary>
    /// <param name="messengerContact"></param>
```

```csharp
/// <param name="projectName"></param>
/// <returns></returns>
public static bool IsProjectContact(IMessengerContact
   messengerContact, string projectName )
{
  string[] token = messengerContact.SigninName.Split('@');
  //check account name
  if (token.Length > 0)
  {
    string userName = token[0];
    List<Identity> vstsUsers =
        TeamSystemHelper.GetProjectMembers(projectName);
    foreach (Identity vstsUser in vstsUsers)
    {
      if (vstsUser.AccountName.ToLower() == userName.ToLower())
        return true;
    }
  }
  //no match found
  return false;
}

public static bool IsMySelf(IMessengerContact messengerContact)
{
  if (messengerContact.SigninName.ToLower() ==
      _ocInstance.MySigninName.ToLower())
  {
    return true;
  }
  else
  {
    return false;
  }
}

/// <summary>
/// log on to Office Communicator
/// </summary>
/// <returns></returns>
private static bool pAutoSignin()
{
  //Ask user if he wants to Sign in
  DialogResult result = MessageBox.Show(
      "Your current status is 'Offline'. You can not see any
      contact list unless you Login" +
      " Do you want to Signin ?", "Auto Signin",
      MessageBoxButtons.YesNo);
```

```
        if (result == DialogResult.Yes)
        {
          _ocInstance.AutoSignin();
          return true;
        }
        else
        {
          return false;
        }
      }
    }
  }
```

Plug-In for Showing a List of Users in Team Explorer

In the previous sections, we created two helper classes for communicating with Team Foundation Server and Office Communicator. In this section, we work on displaying the list of users and their presence status in Team Explorer.

The strategy is to create a VSIP package for hosting the plug-in in Visual Studio. When running the plug-in in debug mode on the development machine, the package will be registered in an experimental hive in the system registry, and a new instance of Visual Studio will be launched in "sandbox" mode. When development is complete, create an Microsoft Windows Installer (.msi) file containing the final registry entries and runtime assemblies. The end users will run the MSI file to install the package containing the Team Explorer plug-in in Visual Studio.

Step 1—Install VSIP Software Development Kit

Install the latest version of Visual Studio 2005 Software Development Kit (SDK), which can be downloaded from the Microsoft Web site at *http://msdn.microsoft. com/vstudio/extend/*. The SDK contains a number of utilities and assemblies for creating and registering packages.

Step 2—Create a Package

Create a class named `PresenceDetectionPackage` that inherits from `Microsoft.Team-foundation.Common.PluginHostPackage` (see Figure 6.18). The package contains a number of custom attributes that indicate the service hosted by the package, as well as registry keys and values (see Listing 6.3). The full source code is available on the CD-ROM.

ON THE CD

LISTING 6.3 Custom Attributes Used in `PresenceDetectionPackage`

```
[MSVSIP.DefaultRegistryRoot("Software\\Microsoft\\VisualStudio
    \\8.0")]
[MSVSIP.InstalledProductRegistration(false, "#100", "#102",
```

```
        "1.0", IconResourceID = 400)]
[MSVSIP.ProvideLoadKey("Standard", "1.0", "Package Name",
    "Company", 1)]
[ProvideService(typeof(PresenceDetectionPlugin))]
[PluginRegistration(Catalogs.TeamProject,
    "PresenceDetectionPlugIn", typeof(PresenceDetectionPlugin))]
[Guid("8d87d091-1fc5-4b78-9116-6e7584b267bb")]
```

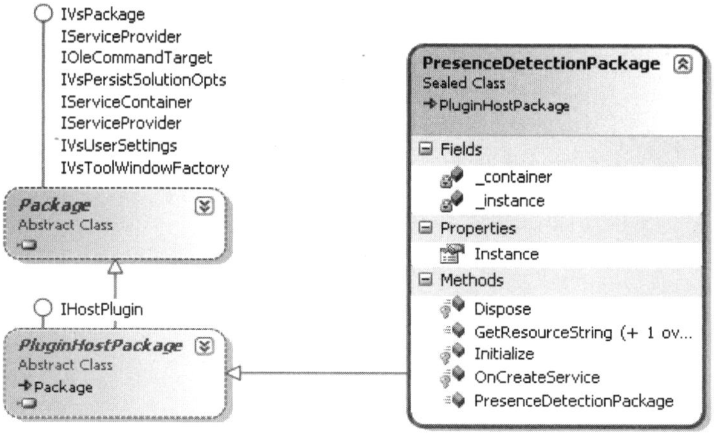

FIGURE 6.18 Class diagram for PresenceDetectionPackage.

Step 3—Override OnCreateService Method in Package Class

Microsoft.Teamfoundation.Common.PluginHostPackage contains an abstract method named OnCreateService, which we override in inherited class PresenceDetection-Package (see Listing 6.4). In this method, return an instance of the actual plug-in worker class named PresenceDetectionPlugin. The OnCreateService method is called when the Contacts node is rendered in Team Explorer tree.

LISTING 6.4 Overriding OnCreateService Abstract Method

```
protected override object OnCreateService(
    IServiceContainer container, Type serviceType)
{
  if (serviceType == typeof(PresenceDetectionPlugin))
  {
    return new PresenceDetectionPlugin();
  }
  _container = container;
  throw new ApplicationException(serviceType.ToString());
}
```

Step 4—Create Plug-in Worker Class

Create the main worker class named `PresenceDetectionPlugin`. `PresenceDetectionPlugin` inherits from `Microsoft.Teamfoundation.Common.BasicAsyncPlugin` (see Figure 6.19) and performs the following tasks:

- Creates the Project Contacts, Other Contacts, and Attach Conversation nodes.
- Retrieves a list of users from Team Foundation Server (via the `TeamSystemHelper` class) as well as Office Communicator (using the `OfficeCommunicatorHelper` class).
- Subscribes to events raised by Office Communicator.

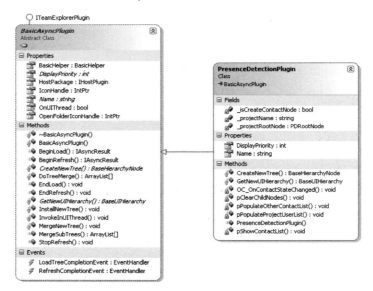

FIGURE 6.19 Class diagram for `PresenceDetectionPlugin`.

- In the `PresenceDetectionPlugin` class constructor (see Listing 6.5), call the `OfficeCommunicatorHelper` class to initialize Office Communicator and subscribe to the `OnContactStatusChange` event. The `OnContactStatusChange` event is raised when the online status of an Office Communicator user changes. We trap this event and refresh the Project Contacts and Other Contacts nodes in Team Explorer.

LISTING 6.5 Code for Handling Communicator Events

```
public PresenceDetectionPlugin():
```

```
      base(PresenceDetectionPackage.Instance)
{
  try
  {
    // Initialize the helper class
    OfficeCommunicatorHelper.Initialize();

    // Subscribe to Office Communicator contact's
    // status change event
    OfficeCommunicatorHelper.Communicator.OnContactStatusChange
        +=new DMessengerEvents_OnContactStatusChangeEventHandler(
        OC_OnContactStateChanged);

  }
  catch (Exception ex)
  {
    MessageBox.Show(ex.ToString());
  }
}
```

Step 5—Create Custom Nodes in Team Explorer

Hook into the Team Explorer tree hierarchy by overriding the abstract method `Cre-ateNewTree` in the `PresenceDetectionPlugin` class (see Listing 6.6). This method is inherited from `Microsoft.Teamfoundation.Common.BasicAsyncPlugin`. Override `CreateNewTree` and create the Contacts subtree containing the Project Contacts, Other Contacts, and Attach Conversation nodes (see Figure 6.20).

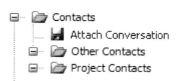

FIGURE 6.20   Contact nodes created in Team Explorer.

LISTING 6.6   Code for Creating Contacts Subtree

```
/// <summary>
/// Create the Contact sub-tree
/// </summary>
/// <param name="hierarchy"></param>
/// <returns></returns>
protected override BaseHierarchyNode
    CreateNewTree(BaseUIHierarchy hierarchy)
{
```

```
//TeamSystemHelper will using this server
//name to connect to TFS server
TeamSystemHelper.ServerName = hierarchy.ServerName;
_projectName = hierarchy.ProjectName;

try
{
  //acquire reference to the project root node
  _projectRootNode =
      new PDRootNode(hierarchy.ServerName + '/' +
      hierarchy.ProjectName);

  if (_isCreateContactNode == true)
  {
    _isCreateContactNode = false;
    // show contact list under the project
    pShowContactList(_projectRootNode);
  }
}
catch (Exception ex)
{
  // Trap all exceptions.
  Debug.WriteLine("ERROR: " + ex.Message);
}

return _projectRootNode;
}

#region private functions
private void pShowContactList(BaseHierarchyNode teNode)
{
  try
  {
    // Clear child nodes below the specified root node
    this.pClearChildNodes(teNode);

    //create Project Contacts node
    PDFolderNode projectContactNode =
        new PDFolderNode(teNode.CanonicalName +
        "/Contacts/ProjectContacts", "Project Contacts");

    //create Other Contacts node
    PDFolderNode otherContactNode =
        new PDFolderNode(teNode.CanonicalName +
        "/Contacts/OtherContacts", "Other Contacts");

    //create Save Conversation leaf node
    PDLeafACNode attachConversationLeafNode =
        new PDLeafACNode(teNode.CanonicalName +
        "/Contacts/AttachConv", "Attach Conversation",
```

```
        _projectName);

      //Add Project Contacts node to TE tree
      teNode.AddChild(projectContactNode);

      //Add Other Contacts node to TE tree
      teNode.AddChild(otherContactNode);

      //Add Save Conversation node to TE tree
      teNode.AddChild(attachConversationLeafNode);

      //populate Nodes with users
      pPopulateProjectUserList(projectContactNode);
      pPopulateOtherContactList(otherContactNode);
    }
    catch (Exception ex)
    {
      Debug.WriteLine(ex);
    }
  }
```

The private method `pShowContactList` creates the child folder nodes Project Contacts, Other Contacts, and a leaf node named Attach Conversation. This method receives a reference to the plug-in's root node and creates custom child nodes using the `AddChild` method exposed by `BaseHierarchyNode`.

As shown in method `pShowContactList` in Listing 6.6, Project Contacts and Other Contacts folder nodes are created using the `PDFolderNode` class. User names are shown using `PDLeafNode` class. The Attach Conversation leaf node is created using the `PDLeafACNode` class. The node classes inherit from `BaseHierarchyNode` (see Figure 6.21). `BaseHierarchyNode` is the abstract superclass for all Team Explorer nodes and provides a wealth of virtual methods and properties. Override the `DoDe-faultAction` method in the `PDLeafACNode` class to show a custom form when the user double-clicks the Attach Conversation node. Override the `DoDefaultAction` method in the `PDLeafNode` class to launch Office Communicator when the user double-clicks a contact name.

Step 6–Populate the Project Contacts Custom Node

The `pPopulateProjectUserList` method in the `PresenceDetectionPlugin` class is used to insert the names of project users under the Project Contacts node (see Listing 6.7). Obtain a list of project users by calling the `GetProjectMembers` method of the `TeamSystemHelper` class. The corresponding Office Communicator user name is then obtained by calling the `GetOCUserForVSTSUser` method of the `OfficeCommunicatorHelper` class. The username is displayed as in the Team Explorer tree along with his online status information (see Figure 6.22).

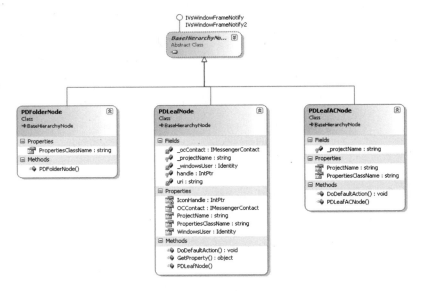

FIGURE 6.21 Class diagrams for folders and leaf nodes.

LISTING 6.7 Code for Adding Users Under the Project Contacts Node

```
/// <summary>
/// populate Project Contacts node with users in team project
/// </summary>
/// <param name="teNode"></param>
private void pPopulateProjectUserList(BaseHierarchyNode teNode)
{
  // Clear child nodes below the specified node
  this.pClearChildNodes(teNode);

  List<Identity> projectUsers =
      TeamSystemHelper.GetProjectMembers(_projectName);

  foreach (Identity user in projectUsers)
  {
    IMessengerContact messengerContact =
        OfficeCommunicatorHelper.GetOCUserForVSTSUser(user);
    if {messengerContact != null)
    {
      if (!OfficeCommunicatorHelper.IsMySelf(messengerContact))
      {
        PDLeafNode leaf = new PDLeafNode(teNode.CanonicalName +
            "/" + user.AccountName, user.AccountName + " : " +
            OfficeCommunicatorHelper.GetUserStatusDescription(
```

```
                messengerContact), user.AccountName, _projectName);

            leaf.OCContact = messengerContact;
            leaf.WindowsUser = user;
            teNode.AddChild(leaf);
            CommandID commandID = leaf.ContextMenu;
        }
      }
    }
  }
```

FIGURE 6.22   Populated contacts nodes showing online status of users.

Step 7–Populate the Other Contacts Custom Node

The pPopulateOtherUserList method in PresenceDetectionPlugin is used to insert the names of contacts that are not in the team project user list. For example, if you and your vendor organization are using separate copies of Team Foundation Server, then a remote user will not belong to your local project user list. In that case, you can add him as a contact in Office Communicator. His name and online status will be displayed in the Team Explorer tree under the Other Contacts node (see Figure 6.22).

In the pPopulateOtherUserList method, obtain a list of Office Communicator contacts from the OfficeCommunicatorHelper class (see Listing 6.8).

LISTING 6.8   Code for Adding Users Under the Other Contacts Node

```
/// <summary>
/// populate Other Contacts node with users
/// in Office Communicator
/// </summary>
/// <param name="teNode"></param>
private void pPopulateOtherContactList(BaseHierarchyNode teNode)
{
```

```
// Clear child nodes below the specified node
this.pClearChildNodes(teNode);
// Get current users from Office Communicator contact list
IMessengerContacts ocContacts =
    OfficeCommunicatorHelper.GetContactList();
foreach (IMessengerContact ocContact in ocContacts)
{
  if (!OfficeCommunicatorHelper.IsProjectContact(ocContact,
     _projectName))
  {
    if (!OfficeCommunicatorHelper.IsMySelf(ocContact))
    {
      //Create a new leaf and add in the tree
      PDLeafNode leaf = new PDLeafNode(
          teNode.CanonicalName + "/" + ocContact.FriendlyName,
          ocContact.FriendlyName + " : "
          + OfficeCommunicatorHelper.GetUserStatusDescription(
          ocContact), ocContact.FriendlyName, _projectName);
      leaf.OCContact = ocContact;
      leaf.WindowsUser = null;
      teNode.AddChild(leaf);
    }
  }
 }
}
```

Step 8–Launch Office Communicator

Office Communicator is launched when the user double-clicks a contact name (see Figure 6.23). As discussed earlier in the chapter, Office Communicator offers the capability to conduct multimodal, real-time communication (e.g., chat, audio, video, application-sharing, etc.) sessions with remote parties.

To launch Office Communicator, override the DoDefaultAction method of the PDLeafNode class (see Listing 6.9). DoDefaultAction is inherited from Microsoft.Team-foundation.Common.BaseHierarchyNode. BaseHierarchyNode contains a virtual implementation of DoDefaultAction and leaves it up to the subclass to provide custom behavior.

LISTING 6.9 Code for Adding Users Under Other Contacts

```
public override void DoDefaultAction()
{
  if (_occontact != null)
```

```
{
  OfficeCommunicatorHelper.ShowChatWindow(
      _ocContact.SigninName);
}
else
{
  MessageBox.Show("This user does not have LCS account");
}
}
```

FIGURE 6.23   Office Communicator launched from VSTS.

Step 9-Activate the Attach Conversation Node

Activate the Attach Conversation leaf node to launch the Attach Conversation to Work Item form (see Figure 6.24). You can use this form to associate Instant Messenger conversation files (or any conversation text, including emails) with a work item. You can copy the chat text from Office Communicator and paste it in the Content text area of the form. Alternatively, you can save the communication text from Office Communicator in a file and click the Attach File button on the form. The objective is to save the communication as an attachment to a work item so that it can be retrieved later.

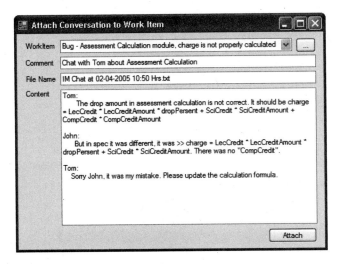

FIGURE 6.24   The Attach Conversation to Work Item form allows you to save the conversation as an attachment.

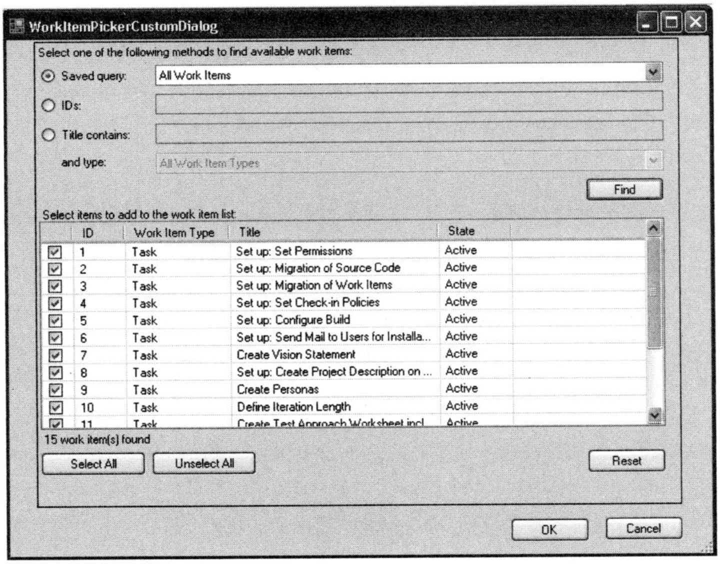

FIGURE 6.25   WorkItemPickerCustomDialog screen for selecting associated work items.

The Attach Conversation to Work Item form is launched when you double-click the Attach Conversation node. Similar to the approach in the previous step, we override the DoDefaultAction method of PDLeafACNode class to display the form (see Listing 6.10).

LISTING 6.10   Code for Launching the Attach Conversation Form

```
public override void DoDefaultAction()
{
    AddAttachmentToWorkItem addAttachmentToWorkItemForm =
        new AddAttachmentToWorkItem(base.ProjectName);
    addAttachmentToWorkItemForm.Show();
}
```

As you can see from Listing 6.10, the DoDefaultAction method launches the AddAttachmentToWorkItem form. When the form is loaded, the work item drop-down is populated with the list of work items. You can select a work item from the drop-down list. Alternatively, click the ellipsis button to launch the WorkItem-PickerCustomDialog box (see Figure 6.25). The SelectWorkItems method of the TeamSystemHelper class contains the code to display the custom form and returns a list of selected work items.

To populate the work item drop-down, we call the GetWorkItems method of the TeamSystemHelper class. This method connects to the Team Foundation Server and fetches a list of work items for the specified project (see Listing 6.1).

Click Select File to choose the conversation file you would like to attach. The content of the file is displayed in the Content area. Click Attach to add the file to the selected work item as an attachment (see Listing 6.11).

LISTING 6.11   Code for Attaching Conversation to a Work Item

```
private void pAttachContent()
{
  //Get the workItem user has selected
  ArrayList workItems = pGetSelectedWorkItem();
  if (workItems.Count > 0)
  {
    //get file path
    string filePath = pGetFilePath();

    if (filePath.Length != 0)
    {
      if (filePath.Length > 0)
      {
        foreach (WorkItem selectedWorkItem in workItems)
        {
          //Open work Item to edit
          selectedWorkItem.Open();
```

```
            //Save this file as attachment with the
            //selected workItem
            Attachment attachment = new Attachment(filePath,
                "PresenceDetection Conversation");

            //attach the file with selected workItem
            selectedWorkItem.Attachments.Add(attachment);

            //Save the workItem
            selectedWorkItem.Save();
          }
          if (_RemoveTmpFile)
          {
            pRemoveFile(filePath);
          }

          //Close the current form
          this.Close();
        }
      }
      else
      {
        MessageBox.Show("Please Set FileName.");
      }
    }
    else
    {
      MessageBox.Show("Please Select any WorkItem.");
    }
  }
  private string pGetFilePath()
  {
    /* Note: User can select an existing file using the file
     * Browser and attach it with the work item or, User can write
     * his desired text file name and write the content in 'file
     * Content' text box
     */

    //check if file already exists
    FileInfo file = new FileInfo(txtAttachmentFileName.Text);
    if (file.Exists)
    {
      if (file.Extension.ToLower() == "txt")
      {
        //Create a tmp file in default folder
        return pCreateFile(file.Name, txtAttachmentFileName.Text);
      }
      else
```

```
      {
        //a non-text file selected. User cannot edit.
        //so return the source file path.
        return file.FullName;
      }
    }
    else
    {
      //no file found, create a tmp file using the txtConversation
      return pCreateFile(txtAttachmentFileName.Text,
          txtConversation.Text);
    }
  }
```

USING THE PLUG-IN FOR REAL-TIME COMMUNICATION

In the preceding section, we created a plug-in for presence detection and hosted it in Team Explorer. As mentioned earlier, the plug-in provides the online status of your contacts, both VSTS project users as well as Office Communicator contacts, without leaving the Integrated Development Environment (IDE). When you click a contact, the plug-in launches Office Communicator and enables you to interact with the team member in real time. Instead of 're-inventing the wheel,' we use Office Communicator to provide powerful real-time communication and collaboration capabilities.

CONCLUSION

As you work with people halfway across the planet, you realize how small the world has become, thanks to recent revolutionary advances in technology. We live in an interconnected, 24/7 world. The more you work with offshore partners on mission-critical projects, the more you'll find that the traditional concepts of efficiency and work habits become obsolete. When you go to sleep, your offshore team members are waking up. When you work, they rest. You have a 24/7 delivery chain that never stops. For you to be able to stay on top of the situation, you have to redefine what normal office hours are, and find a new balance between work and family life that is sustainable. You must anticipate the needs of people whom you have never met. To be able to work efficiently, sometimes you'll need to interact with your offshore partners on demand—many times at odd hours and at odd locations—and they need to be able to do the same. Welcome to the twenty-first century workplace.

Given the challenges associated with managing distributed teams, we need to get maximum leverage out of available technology and eliminate friction as much as possible. In this chapter, we have discussed how the VSTS IDE (Integrated Development Environment)—where programmers spend most of their waking hours—can be enhanced with presence detection and real-time communication capabilities. We have also studied the capabilities offered by Office Communicator, Live Communications Server, and Live Meeting in terms of facilitating offshore communication. The suite of communication technologies discussed—email, phone, text chat, audio, video, and SMS—provide you with flexible options.

No matter how competent the team members are, many business problems are too complex, case-specific, and interdependent to develop software in isolation. Even if such an application could theoretically be developed, the vagaries of hardware, software, and third-party integration requirements would render the application less than optimal in real life. Modern software development is a collaborative activity. However, long distance collaboration without effective tool support is a pipe dream. To maximize the value of offshore outsourcing, put in place an infrastructure that facilitates transparency of implementation, promotes exchange of ideas, and forges a sense of shared mission. We believe the tools and technologies discussed in this chapter will help you achieve that goal.

7 Version Control and Team Build

INTRODUCTION

A critical requirement of global software development is the ability to effectively share code among distributed teams. Gone are the days when source code had to be transferred between locations using the venerable File Transfer Protocol (FTP) (although this method is still used by more teams than would care to publicly admit). A modern version-control system enables distributed team members to work with private copies of the code and check in their changes to a central repository. A good version-control software detects conflicts caused by concurrent changes, maintains change histories of shared files, allows rollback of defective changes, provides the capability to branch the source tree and merge changes back, facilitates association of work items with changes, offers the ability to label versions, supports automated builds, and provides seamless integration with the IDE. When it comes to distributed development, you need to consider additional issues, such as security and access control over the Internet, potential loss of connectivity, performance over low-bandwidth connections, granularity as well as frequency of check-ins, and so forth.

In addition to the underlying infrastructure, you need to think about instituting check-in policies to ensure a consistent code quality, regardless of where a piece of software is created. Since you can not remain physically present in the offshore location to ensure compliance with the coding standards, the tool should be able to enforce policies and detect violations. Policies are usually specified with regard to the need for code review, successful execution of specified test cases prior to check-ins as well as after builds, percentage of code coverage via automated tests, adherence to coding conventions, and so forth. After all, source code is the primary asset in any software development effort; the version-control system should help ensure quality, accuracy, and consistency of the codebase. Of course, check-in policies and the actual process of checking in code will vary depending upon a project's size, complexity, and team structure. When working with multiple distributed teams or working on large projects, more-stringent code check-in policies and processes need to be set up, given the potential for breaking a public build and affecting a large number of people. In some large organizations, programmers upload source code to an intermediate system, which performs intermediate builds and validates the changes before submitting the verified code to the shared version-control repository.

You need a version-control system that can work seamlessly with your build system. There should be an automated process for checking out code from the version-control repository, creating a build on an independent machine, running build verification tests, and rejecting the offending changes in case of a build failure. The version-control system should also interface with your issue-management system so that you can figure out which issues were addressed in a given check-in or build.

VSTS provides an integrated framework for version control, build management, and work item tracking. As a whole, the value of Team Foundation Version Control (TFVC) is greater than the sum of its parts. The smooth interaction of the underlying components enables you to customize and implement an effective development process throughout the enterprise. A version-control system sitting in isolation is of limited value. When you can combine it with other integral systems that underpin your development process, only then can you achieve hitherto impossible results and see new possibilities emerge. In this chapter, we explore how TFVC can be leveraged to reduce friction and mitigate execution risks associated with distributed development.

WALK-THROUGH: USING VERSION CONTROL

Before diving into the details of various features, it would be instructive to take a high-level look at the steps involved in adding a simple solution to the version-control repository. Let us walk through a concrete example.

Create a Team Project

Before you can add any code to the repository, you need to create a team project. A team project hosts not only the source code but also work items (e.g., requirements, functional specifications, tasks, bugs, etc.), reports, documents, portal site, and so forth. You can use the same team project to host multiple Visual Studio projects. Think about what makes sense given your project's administrative boundaries, team size, and organizational structure. To create a new team project, on the File menu, point to New, and then click Team Project.

Create a Visual Studio Solution

Once the appropriate team project is set up, create a simple Windows application to display a "Hello World" message when a button is clicked (see Listing 7.1).

LISTING 7.1   Source Code of Sample Application for Testing Version-Control Features

```
// … using directives omitted …
namespace VersionControlTestProj
{
public partial class Form1 : Form
{
    public Form1()
    {
        InitializeComponent();
    }

    /// <summary>
    /// Click Event Handler for Button
    /// </summary>
    /// <param name="sender"></param>
    /// <param name="e"></param>
    private void btnShowMsg_Click(object sender, EventArgs e)
    {
        lblMessage.Text = "Hello World";
    }

    private void Form1_Load(object sender, EventArgs e)
    {
    }
}
}
```

Right-click the project name in Solution Explorer and select Add Project to Source Control (see Figure 7.1) from the drop-down menu. In the Add Solution to Source Control dialog box, select the team project where you would like to host the source code, and click OK (see Figure 7.2).

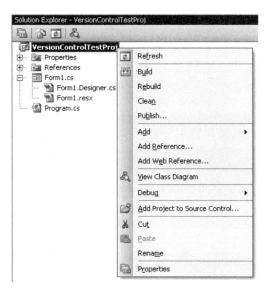

FIGURE 7.1 Right-click the project name and choose Add Project to Source Control to add the solution to version control.

FIGURE 7.2 Select a team project to host the source code.

Add Source Files to the Repository

Bring up the Pending Changes window (see Figure 7.3). On the View menu, point to Other Windows, and then click Pending Changes. Click the Check In icon (located on the toolbar of the Pending Changes window) to upload the files to the server.

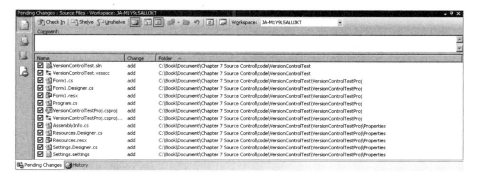

FIGURE 7.3   Pending Changes window shows the files to be uploaded to the server.

Launch Source Control Explorer

Open the Source Control Explorer. On the View menu, point to Other Windows, and then click Source Control Explorer. Click the Check In icon (in the Pending Changes window). Expand the team project node (in the Folders pane of the Source Control Explorer) and you'll see the files that were checked in (see Figure 7.4)

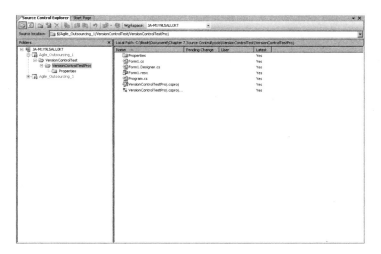

FIGURE 7.4   Source Control Explorer showing the list of files in the current workspace.

Check Out and Modify a Source File

Right-click a file (e.g., Form1.cs) in the Source Control Explorer, and select Check Out for Edit from the drop-down menu. In the Check Out dialog box, accept the default lock type (None - Allow Shared Checkout), and click Check Out (see Figure 7.5). The pending change status for the file will be marked as "edit." Double-click the file to open it in the editor and make changes as per Listing 7.2.

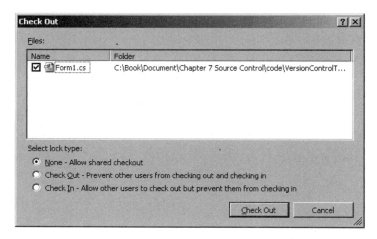

FIGURE 7.5   You can specify the lock type in the Check Out dialog box.

LISTING 7.2 Change the Button Click Event Handler to Show a Different Message

```
/// <summary>
/// Click Event Handler for Button
/// </summary>
/// <param name="sender"></param>
/// <param name="e"></param>
private void btnShowMsg_Click(object sender, EventArgs e)
{
    //message changed to "Hello Universe"
    //lblMessage.Text = "Hello World";
    lblMessage.Text = "Hello Universe";
}
```

Check In the Modified File

Bring up the Pending Changes window. You'll find that the modified file is listed with its change status marked as "edit" (see Figure 7.6). If we had additional files with modifications, they would be listed in this screen, as well. The set of files being checked in is called a *changeset*. Each changeset is assigned a unique number and is checked in as an atomic unit. If any file cannot be checked in, all other files in the changeset are rolled back to avoid leaving the repository in an unknown state (e.g., you could be checking in a set of interdependent files).

FIGURE 7.6   Pending Changes Windows displays changes made in the local workspace.

Before checking in the files, click the Work Items channel (in the left-hand panel of the Pending Changes window; this panel is called the channel bar). This action brings up a window containing the list of work items in the current team project (see Figure 7.7). You can select one or more work items associated with the current modification; use the drop-down in the Check-in Action column to specify whether the work item has been resolved or just impacted by the changes. Additional information about the changeset can be specified by clicking the Check-In Notes channel (see Figure 7.8). The Policy Warnings channel allows you to determine whether the current modifications conform to your specified check-in policies (more on this in later sections). Finally, click the Check-In button (located on the toolbar of the Pending Changes window) to commit your changes to the repository. Double-click and open the file (Form1.cs) to verify that the changes have been applied.

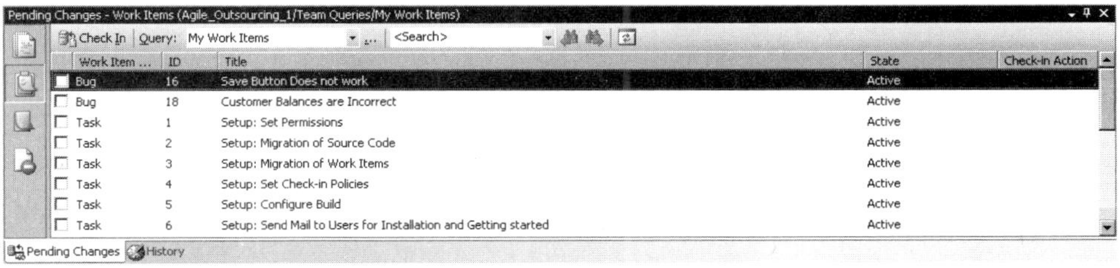

FIGURE 7.7   Source code modifications can be associated with work items during check in.

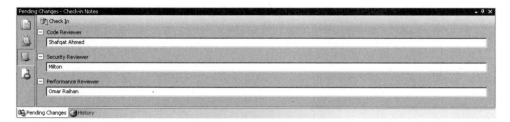

FIGURE 7.8 Additional information about modifications can be captured during check in.

TECHNICAL ARCHITECTURE

TFS is based on a three-tier architecture. TFVC follows a similar pattern (see Figure 7.9). The various tiers are organized as follows:

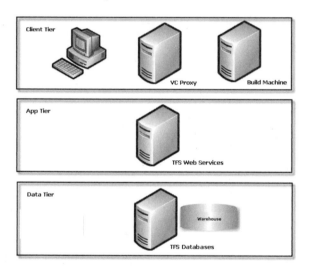

FIGURE 7.9 Team foundation version control is based upon a three-tier architecture.

Client tier: The client tier contains the Source Control Explorer as well as the command line tool. This tier also hosts the build tool. The client tier provides a programmable object model for invoking functionalities available in the application tier.

Application tier: The application tier consists of a number of ASP.NET Web services. For source code management purposes, the main Web service is called

Repository.asmx. Repository.asmx, as well as other version control-related Web services, are located in the VersionControl virtual directory under the Team Foundation Server Web site on the application tier machine. You can review various methods (and their request and response parameters) that belong to Repository.asmx by browsing the .ASMX page (see Figure 7.10). Click any method name to inspect the associated Simple Object Access Protocol (SOAP) message structure; click the service description to view the Web Service Description Language (WSDL) file.

Data tier: The data tier contains SQL Server 2005 databases. Checked-in items are stored in binary fields. Information regarding versions, workspace mappings, branches, merges, policies, and labels are also persisted in the data tier. The databases can be backed up and managed using standard SQL Server 2005 database administration procedures.

FIGURE 7.10   Browse Repository.asmx to inspect its Web methods.

DISTRIBUTED DEVELOPMENT ISSUES

When you have globally distributed development teams, you need a version-control system that is designed and optimized for distributed development. Treating remote developers the same way as local developers (except for the fact that remote developers are probably connecting over a VPN) will provide suboptimal results, no matter how reliable and 'fat' your Internet connectivity is. Keep in mind the following issues when considering a version-control system for offshore development:

1. Will local and remote teams use the same master repository? This question merits detailed examination, depending on your organizational structure (e.g., branch office, captive, or vendor), number of remote teams involved, size of the project, code churn, Internet speed, project-governance model, and the like.

2. If there are multiple master repositories (and they may not even be the same version-control software), how will you handle synchronization and conflict resolution? Will you implement an agreed-upon policy (manually or automatically)? In other words, what is the process associated with checking source code out of one system and into another system, and vice versa?

3. When working with an offshore organization, do you want them to check in work-in-progress code or only stable versions? If they are to check in only stable versions, will they maintain a separate local repository for local file sharing? How will code synchronization take place between their local repository and the master repository?

4. Where is the build machine located? Who maintains the build environment? How frequently are the builds made? Are builds created manually or automatically?

5. What is the process associated with running build-verification tests? What happens if the tests fail? (Some companies require programmers to remain in the office until the tests pass.) What is the process associated with rolling back changes? Will you roll back *all* changes or just some? If you roll back only some changes, then how will you determine which changes to roll back?

6. How will the code be shared (often, between distributed teams) for code review purposes? Do you need to create a private branch to store the code under review, or does your version-control system allow you to share code without requiring formal check-ins? Can you indicate to the reviewer which work items are addressed by the modified code? How are comments and changes made by the reviewer communicated to the original developer?

7. Can you enforce unit testing, code coverage, and code-review policies prior to check-ins?

8. What happens if there is loss of connectivity between the remote team and the master repository? In addition to network failure, connectivity could be lost because of virus attacks, hacking, or something as mundane as system outage due to scheduled maintenance. (For example, due to differences in time zones, scheduled downtime in one location could be a peak working time in another location.) How are the changes reconciled when connectivity is restored?

While it may be impossible to find a version-control system that provides *all* the functionalities you are looking for, you need to at least make sure that your most important requirements are satisfied by the chosen system. This is particularly important given some of the unique (and often unfamiliar) challenges associated with offshore development.

VSTS AND DISTRIBUTED DEVELOPMENT

Microsoft states that TFVC is optimized for low-bandwidth operations. TFVC was used internally at Microsoft to support distributed development of VSTS. The VSTS development team was located in multiple continents. They accessed a single master version-control repository and performed nightly builds.

TFVC optimizations to support distributed development include

- Web service-based architecture operating over HTTP and HTTPS.
- Simplified port requirements for connection through a firewall: Team Foundation Server uses the following ports: 80 (http), 443 (https), 8080 (used by TFS Web services), and 8081 (client-to-proxy server). However, in version one of TFS and TFVC, only Integrated Windows Authentication is supported for accessing application-tier Web services. As a result, remote clients are not able to connect via Internet proxy servers that do not maintain a persistent connection with the Web server. Support for basic authentication is expected in TFS Service Pack 1 from Microsoft (via a new ISAPI filter). In the meantime, remote clients need to connect via VPN.
- File compression before transmission: Files are compressed before transmission between the client and the server machines, unless compression results in a larger file size (which could happen with encrypted or precompressed files).
- Compression of SOAP response messages.
- Proxy server for storing local copies of downloaded files: When files are downloaded for the first time, the proxy server stores them in the local cache. Subsequent requests are satisfied from the local cache, unless a newer version of the file has been checked in to TFVC. File uploads go directly to the Team Foundation Server, bypassing the proxy. To use the proxy server from client machines, click the Tools menu and then click Options. In the Options dialog box, expand the Source Control node in the tree, select the Visual Studio Team Foundation Server node, and specify the proxy server settings in the right hand pane (see Fig 7.11). The proxy server is usually installed in a standalone machine in the remote location and connected to the client machines via a high-speed LAN (Local Area Network) connection. Connection between the proxy server and the Team Foundation Server is usually over a WAN (Wide Area

Network) link, since the proxy server is situated in a remote location. The proxy server and the Team Foundation Server can be in different domains, as long as there is a trust relationship between them. However, in Version one of TFS, the requirement for a trusted connection means that the proxy server needs to be linked to TFS via a VPN connection.

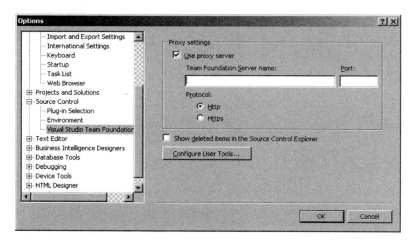

FIGURE 7.11 Create a proxy server to speed up file downloads.

In the following sections, we review selected issues in distributed development and how they are handled by TFVC.

Scheduled Download

As discussed earlier, TFVC can be configured to use a proxy server to reduce the overhead associated with remote access. However, the proxy server can cache a file only after first-time access. If you are downloading a new file, you'll encounter a performance hit when accessing the file over a slow connection for the first time. To avoid the performance penalty associated with first-time access, configure TFVC to download the latest files from the server at scheduled intervals. This operation can be performed at the beginning of the workday in the offshore location. The Team Foundation command line tool tf.exe can be used to perform an automatic download, as follows.

Create a batch file in the workspace folder. The file should contain the following line:

```
tf get /noprompt > results.txt
```

The get operation takes various parameters, which you can look up in the TFVC documentation and customize per your requirements. The /noprompt option suppresses dialog boxes that might pop up (e.g., to resolve conflicts). The `> re-sults.txt` portion of the command redirects the output to a text file. When creating the batch file, make sure to specify the appropriate path for tf.exe—for example, Program Files\Microsoft Visual Studio 8\Common7\IDE.

Use the Windows scheduler to run the batch file at specified intervals. Click Start, point to Control Panel, Scheduled Tasks, and then click Add Scheduled Tasks. In the Scheduled Tasks Wizard, specify appropriate options to run the batch file periodically.

Disconnected Mode Operation

To be usable for offshore development, a version-control system must to be able to support disconnected operations. If connectivity is lost between the offshore team and the on-site source-control repository, developers need to be able to continue to work offline and check in changes when communication is restored. Although TFVC does not directly support this functionality, you can get the job done using the Team Foundation Power Toy (tfpt.exe) tool. As of this writing, the Power Toy is included in the Visual Studio 2005 SDK; the SDK can be downloaded from *http://msdn.microsoft.com/vstudio/extend/*. However, the Power Toy is expected to be moved to the Team Foundation Server downloads page at *http://msdn.microsoft.com/vstudio/teamsystem/downloads*.

Let's look at how the Power Toy can be used in the following disconnected scenarios:

Edit: If you need to edit a file that has not been checked out, remove its read-only attribute (right-click the file from Windows Explorer, choose Properties from the drop-down menu, and uncheck the read-only attribute). Make changes to the file as needed. Do not re-apply the read-only attribute.

Add: If you need to add a new file, add it to the local workspace. Do not mark the file read-only.

Delete: If you need to delete a file, remove its read-only attribute and delete it.

Rename: Do not rename a file; the Rename operation is currently not supported.

When connectivity is restored, type the following line in the command prompt window:

```
tfpt online
```

If files have been deleted (by default, the tool does not detect deleted files), type:

```
tfpt online /delete
```

The Power Toy will display a window containing changes in the local work-space (see Figure 7.12). You can choose the modified files to be uploaded by se-lecting the appropriate check boxes and clicking Pend Changes. This action will cause the selected files to appear in the Pending Changes window. You can check in the modified files from the Pending Changes window, just like any other files that have been checked out and edited. If a file in the server has been modified during the time when connectivity was lost, TFVC will detect a conflict during check-in and display the Resolve Conflicts dialog box. You can tell TFVC to try to automat-ically merge changes, or you can use the options in the Resolve Version Conflict di-alog box (see Figure 7.13) to reconcile the changes.

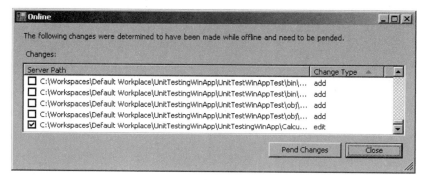

FIGURE 7.12 The Power Toy detects local changes and allows them to be uploaded to the Version Control repository.

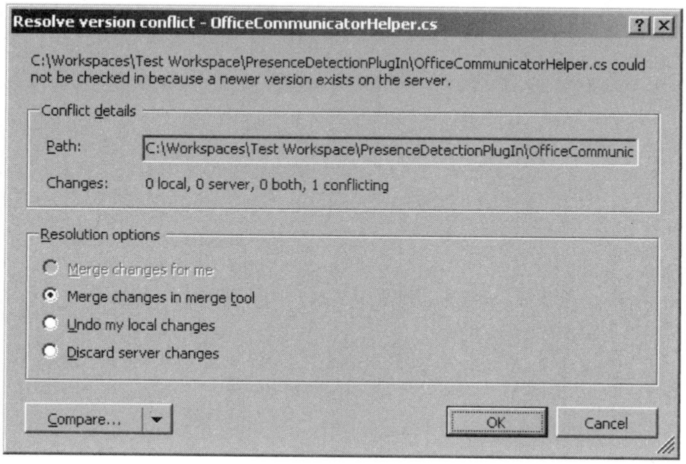

FIGURE 7.13 The Resolve version conflict screen presents various options for merging changes.

UTC Time Support

Timestamps are stored in Coordinated Universal Time (UTC) format in Team Foundation Server. The client tools (e.g., Source Control Explorer, command line tools, etc.) convert UTC time to local time while displaying the file timestamp. This feature is of prime importance in offshore development, as teams are located in multiple time zones. Distributed teams need to get information regarding source code check-in time, build time, work item creation time, and work item resolution time, based on their own locales.

Check-In Policies

You can use check-in policies to control the quality of the code checked into the repository as well as to capture metadata about the changes. Offshore project managers spend a lot of time worrying about the quality of work done—since they cannot walk over and take a quick peek at what's being done. Is the code well structured, well commented, reasonably efficient, peer reviewed, and unit tested? Are multiple teams overwriting each others' code (which tends to happen more often than people care to admit)? Does each check-in contain appropriate notes describing the changes, so that when you look at the change history you don't have to guess? Check-in policies allow you to specify what criteria must be fulfilled before developers are able to upload code. From an operational standpoint, this capability helps reduce the friction and uncertainty associated with offshore development.

Check-in policies are configured on a per-team-project basis. Right-click the project name in Team Explorer, point to Team Project Settings, and click Source Control. In the Source Control Settings dialog box, click the Check-In Policy tab. Click Add to specify appropriate check-in policy requirements for the project (see Figure 7.14). VSTS contains three predefined policies, as follows:

Code Analysis: Specifies that the code must pass static analysis related to performance, security, interoperability, and maintainability. You can select detailed analysis options from the Code Analysis Policy Editor screen (see Figure 7.15). Click the entries in the Status column to toggle between Warning and Error flags; the flag will be displayed if the corresponding condition is not met.

Testing Policy: Selects unit tests to be successfully executed prior to a successful check-in.

Work Items: Requires developers to associate code changes with work items before check-ins. This feature provides visibility into the underlying reasons for code changes and facilitates traceability. This policy also prevents unnecessary or unauthorized code churn (of special importance in a mature codebase).

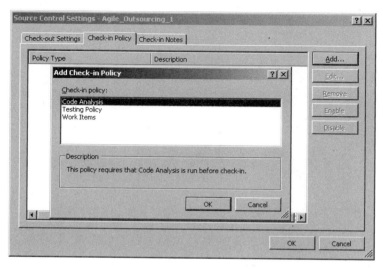

FIGURE 7.14 Built-in check-in policies defined in VSTS.

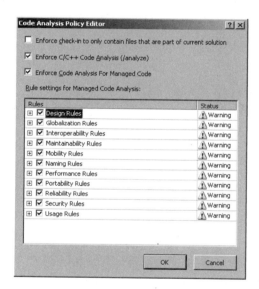

FIGURE 7.15 Specify static code analysis options for check-in.

Once the check-in policies are set up, TFVC will check for policy exceptions every time a file is checked in. Developers can view policy exceptions by clicking the Policy Warnings channel in the channel bar associated with the Pending Changes window (see Figure 7.16). If a developer ignores the policy warnings and attempts to check in the code, TFVC will display a warning screen (see Figure 7.17) alerting the developer that the attempted check-in does not meet established change-control policies. However, the developer is allowed to override the policy warnings by providing a reason. If a check-in takes place overriding a policy, the email associated with the check-in event will have a line in it ("Policy Override Reason") containing the reason specified by the developer.

FIGURE 7.16   Check-ins are evaluated for policy compliance, and appropriate warnings are displayed.

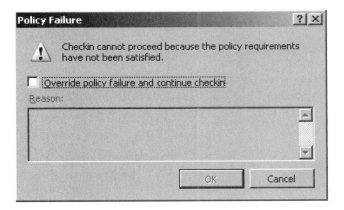

FIGURE 7.17   TFVC displays a warning if an attempted check-in violates change-control policies.

During a typical check-in, if alerted to policy violations due to missing work item associations, you can click the Work Items channel in the channel bar and correlate one or more work items with the current changeset (see Figure 7.18). Use the drop-down in Check-in Action column to specify the kind of action. The available options are as follows:

Associate: Choose this option to create a link between the work item and the changeset being checked in. To view the link, open the work item and click its

Links tab; the link to the changeset is displayed in the list box. Select the link and click the Open button to view additional details (see Figure 7.19).

Resolve: This option may or may not be available, depending on the type of work item. In addition to creating a link between the work item and the changeset being checked in, selecting this option will transition the work item to a "Resolved" state. The default reason associated with the transition to the Resolved state (as specified in the process template) will be indicated in the Reason field.

FIGURE 7.18 Check-ins can be correlated with work items by using the Work Item channel.

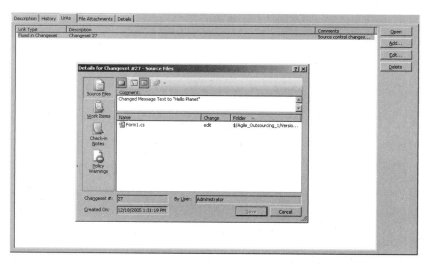

FIGURE 7.19 A link is automatically created between the selected work items(s) and the changeset.

In addition to the three predefined policies, you can create additional custom policies via programming. (Create a class that implements `IPolicyDefinition` and `IPolicyEvaluation`; these interfaces are defined in Microsoft.TeamFoundation. VersionControl.Client.dll.) Figure 7.20 shows the properties and methods of selected interfaces and classes that you'll need to work with. (Refer to Visual Studio 2005 Team System Extensibility Kit for additional information regarding how to create custom policies.)

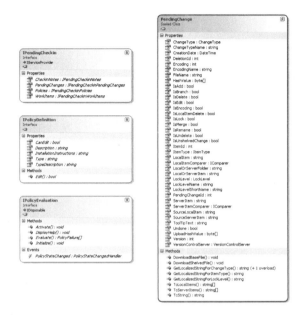

FIGURE 7.20 Selected interfaces and classes involved in creating a custom check-in policy.

Check-In Notifications

VSTS provides out-of-the-box capability to provide notifications when certain activities, such as code check-ins, take place. In the offshore scenario, where you are working with remote teams in non-overlapping time zones, being able to receive real-time code check-in and build notifications (via email, SMS, instant messenger message, or pager) helps improve team communications and coordination.

Select a team project in Team Explorer. On the Team menu, click Project Alerts. In the Project Alerts dialog box, specify the events you are interested in subscribing. Event subscribers will receive notifications via email (see Figure 7.21). Select the "Anything is Checked in" alert to be notified of check-ins to the Version Control Repository.

Although the VSTS user interface provides subscription options for a limited number of events, you can create subscriptions for additional events. Event notification formats include email (HTML or plain text) as well as SOAP Web service call. You can receive Team Foundation Server events via a custom Web service and generate your own alerts using SMS, instant messenger alerts, RSS feeds, and so forth.

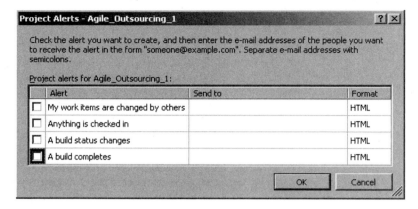

FIGURE 7.21   Recipients can subscribe to email notifications for certain team system events.

Team Foundation Server includes an extensible event-management framework exposed via the `IEventService` interface (see Figure 7.22). A command line utility named `BisSubscribe.exe` is also available to hook into events, apply necessary filtering, and set up subscriptions. Refer to Visual Studio 2005 Team System Extensibility Kit for additional information regarding custom subscription and notification options.

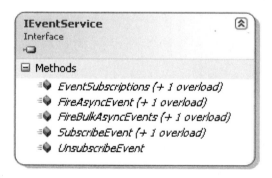

FIGURE 7.22   `IEventService` contains key event-management methods.

Shelvesets and Code Review

A frequent requirement in distributed development is the need to share source code for things like code review or proof-of-concept demos, without having to formally check in the code in the source-control repository. Checking code into the main production branch for purely review purposes is not recommended. It causes the following potential confusions:

Updated version numbers: Every time a file is checked in, its version number is updated in the server. (In TFVC the file version number is marked with the corresponding changeset number.) You don't want to add unnecessary complexity in the version space because of check-ins associated with code review. If the code review process involves multiple back and forth exchanges, the version space becomes even more convoluted.

Unstable builds and checkouts: While the code is waiting to be reviewed, a potentially unstable build could get created (especially if the team follows a practice of *continuous integration* or nightly builds). Even if a new build is not made, other people could check out the tentative code and make changes. It is desirable to have a stable (i.e., reviewed and tested) version exist in the production branch at all times.

Additions to change history: The change history gets complicated by uncontrolled check-ins to the repository. Instead of containing a historical audit of 'real' changes, the change history is littered with tentative and unconfirmed changes.

Rollbacks in case of code review failure: If the code review process fails and the changes need to be rolled back, complications could arise, and the system could end up in an indeterminate state, especially if other people have already made changes on top of your changes.

As a result of these problems, when it comes to long-distance code-sharing, developers frequently resort to email or FTP. In some organizations, programmers create private branches, but the process is often cumbersome and sometimes impossible due to access restrictions.

TFVC offers a feature called *shelvesets,* which allows you to upload your code to the server without a formal check-in. In addition to long-distance code review, you can use shelvesets to back up the current state of your workspace. Once the work-in-progress code is saved in a shelveset, you can proceed to work on something else. When you are finished with the new work, you can check in your new changes, unshelve the original code, and simply pick up where you left off. In addition to source files, shelvesets contain check-in notes and associated work items, facilitating code review and subsequent check-in. Other developers get read-only access to shelvesets created by you.

You can only shelve files that have pending changes. For a quick walk-through, check out one or more files from TFVC for editing. Create a shelveset by clicking the Shelve icon in the Pending Changes window. (You can also right-click the project from Solution Explorer and choose Shelve Pending Changes from the drop-down menu.) From the Shelve - Source Files dialog box, select the files to shelve (see Figure 7.23). You can also specify the check-in notes as well as work item associations by clicking the icons in the left-hand channel bar. The two check boxes in the bottom of the screen are used to indicate the following:

- If the Preserve Pending Changes Locally check box is selected, the pending changes in your local workspace will be retained. If this check box is cleared, TFVC will undo the check-outs for the files being shelved.
- If the Evaluate Policies and Check-in Notes before Shelving check box is selected, the configured check-in policies will be executed before shelving.

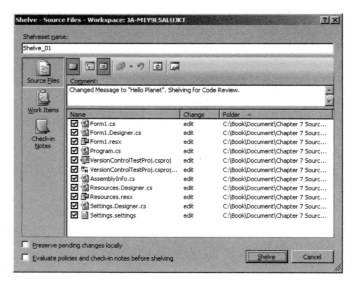

FIGURE 7.23 Shelve–Source Files window captures information necessary for creating a shelveset.

You can retrieve the changes from a shelveset by clicking the Unshelve button in the Pending Changes window. (You can also right-click the project from Solution Explorer and choose Unshelve Pending Changes from the drop-down menu.) In the Unshelve dialog box (see Figure 7.24), specify the shelveset you are interested in; you can select your own shelvesets as well as shelvesets created by others (you only have read-only access to other people's shelvesets). Select a shelveset and click the Details button. In the Shelveset Details dialog box (see Figure 7.25), select which files to unshelve. Additionally, use the two check boxes to specify the following:

- Whether you would like to restore the work item associations and check-in notes (i.e., select or clear the Restore work items and check-in notes check box).

■   Whether you would like delete the shelveset from the server after restoring it in your local workspace (i.e., select or clear the Preserve shelveset on server check box).

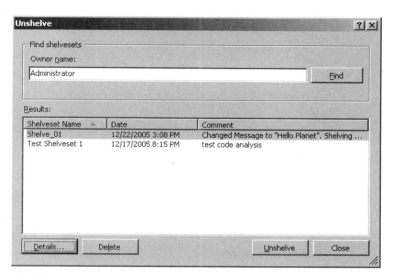

FIGURE 7.24   All shelvesets stored in TFVC are available for download.

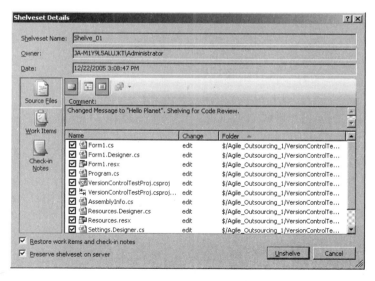

FIGURE 7.25   Available options for unshelving can be specified in the Shelveset Details screen.

A conflict occurs if your workspace already contains files with pending changes, and you try to unshelve one or more of these modified files from a shelveset. Under these circumstances, TFVC displays an error screen. At this time, TFVC does not offer a mechanism to resolve the conflict. However, you can use the Team Foundation Power Toy (tftp.exe) mentioned earlier to do conflict resolution via merge operations. From the command prompt, type the following command:

```
tfpt unshelve
```

The tool presents options to resolve conflicts manually or automatically. The Unshelve/Merge Shelveset screen is displayed if a conflict is detected (see Figure 7.26). If an Edit-Edit conflict is detected, the three-way merge screen (Figure 7.27)—displaying server, local, and shelved versions—helps to identify and resolve the conflicting changes.

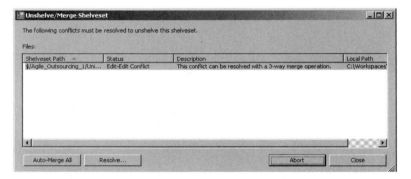

FIGURE 7.26   The Unshelve/Merge Shelveset details screen shows detected conflicts.

SELECTED FEATURES

Some operational aspects of TFVC need special emphasis. If you have worked with other version-control systems, you are probably curious to know how certain routine operations are performed in TFVC. You need to be aware of some of these basic characteristics in order to avoid confusion.

A fundamental feature to keep in mind is that TFVC maintains intimate knowledge of what is supposed to exist in your local workspace. TFVC knows about the folder structure, lists of files, file versions, file contents, and so forth. The information is stored in the TfsVersionControl database on the Team Foundation Server data tier machine. This architecture significantly improves performance during get operations, since TFVC does not have to compare the server version of

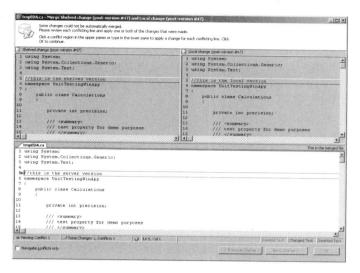

FIGURE 7.27   The Merged Shelved change screen shows the shelved, local, and server versions of the file.

each file with its local version. For large projects with thousands of files, the performance improvement is considerable, especially when accessing over low-bandwidth connections.

However, this technical approach means that if changes are made directly in the local file system, bypassing TFVC, synchronization with the server will be lost. Your local ad-hoc changes will not be recorded in TFVC.

Understanding Workspaces

A workspace represents a private copy of files. When you make changes, the modifications are not instantly available to all users; your changes are persisted in the local workspace until you check in the modified files to the TFVC repository. To create a new workspace, on the File menu, point to Source Control, and then click Workspaces. In the Manage Workspaces dialog box, click Add. In the Add Workspace dialog box (see Figure 7.28), type the name of the workspace, specify folder mappings, and click OK.

Notice in Figure 7.28 that a new workspace is associated with an owner and a computer. This is a vital piece of information to keep in mind as you work with TFVC. The workspace and folder-mapping data are maintained in the version-control server database, along with owner and computer information. If another user logs into your computer and attempts to map the same working folder in another workspace, the operation will fail. TFVC will detect that the local folder is already mapped in a different workspace owned by another user. A working folder can only belong to a single workspace—therefore, to a single user in a particular machine.

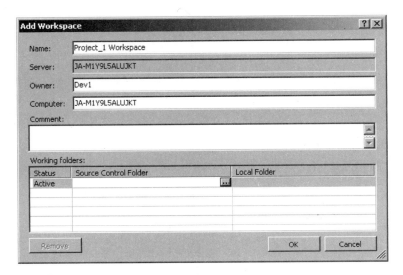

FIGURE 7.28 Create a new workspace using the Add Workspace dialog box.

There is a related quirk that you need to be aware of. If you change the folder mappings of an existing workspace and check out a file without performing a Get Latest operation (right-click the file and select Check Out for Edit from the drop-down menu), the file becomes writable in the old location. It does not get copied over to the new location. This behavior is confusing, since Source Control Explorer displays the new local path on screen, leading you to believe that that you are working with files in the new location. To avoid this problem, when you change folder mappings, always perform a Get Latest operation (right-click the file or folder and select Get Latest Version from the drop-down menu) before editing a file.

Adding Files and Folders

If you add any files or folders to your project using Windows Explorer, those files or folders will not be visible in the Source Control Explorer (the Pending Changes window will not display the newly added files or folders, either). The recommended way to add files or folders is via the Solution Explorer; right-click the newly added file and select Check In from the drop-down menu (see Figure 7.29). You can also add files or folders by clicking the Add Files icon in the Source Control Explorer (see Figure 7.30). Select the files and folders to be added in the Add to Source Control dialog box.

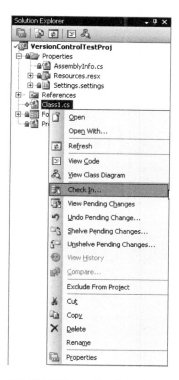

FIGURE 7.29 Check in changes from Solution Explorer after adding files or folders.

FIGURE 7.30 Files or folders can be added from the Source Control Explorer.

Deleting Files and Folders

If you delete a file from TFVC server, it is deleted locally as well. To some users, this behavior comes as a surprise. However, based upon our earlier discussion, when you delete a file from the server, TFVC has no choice but to remove it from the local workspace also, in order to maintain consistency between the server repository and the local file system.

To test this behavior, right-click a file from Source Control Explorer and select Delete from the drop-down menu. In the Pending Changes window, the file will show up with its status as "delete." (In Source Control Explorer, the file will be displayed with a red "X" mark next to it; see Figure 7.31). The file is not actually deleted at this stage; it will be physically deleted when the changeset is checked in. Click the Check-In icon in the Pending Changes window. The file will be removed both from the server repository as well as the local workspace.

Name ▲	Pending Change	User	Latest
✖ 📄 Class1.cs	delete	Administrator	Yes

FIGURE 7.31   TFVC marks the status as "delete" before actually deleting a file.

TFVC behaves in a similar manner when deleting folders. When you delete a folder, its contents (including subfolders and files) are marked for deletion, as well. However, if the folder (or any of its subfolders) contains files that have not been checked in to TFVC, then those folders will not be deleted. On a related note, only folders that are mapped to your local workspace can be deleted from TFVC.

You can undelete files and folders if they have been mistakenly deleted. To test this feature, on the Tools menu, click Options. In the Options dialog box, expand the Source Control node and select Visual Studio Team Foundation Server. In the right pane, select Show Deleted Items in the Source Control Explorer check box. Turning on this option will cause Source Control Explorer to display the deleted file. Right-click the deleted file and select Undelete from the drop-down menu. Check-in the pending undelete from Pending Changes window (or from the right-click drop-down menu), and the file will be restored both in the server repository as well as in the local workspace.

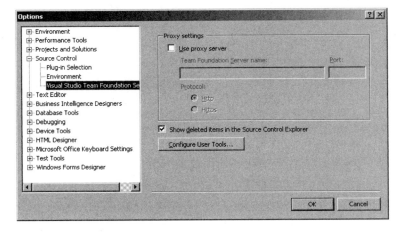

FIGURE 7.32   You can choose to view deleted files in Source Control Explorer by enabling the Show Deleted Items in the Source Control Explorer check box.

Get Latest Version

Performing a Get Latest operation on a file or folder does not always retrieve the latest version. Unless you are aware of the underlying reason, this behavior can be confusing and could result in costly mistakes. If you make changes to a file and bypass TFVC—maybe you edited the file without first checking it out or copied it from a separate working folder—TFVC does not have a way to learn about the local modifications. Consequently, it continues to believe that the local workspace already possesses the latest version. Therefore, when you click Get Latest Version, it does nothing at all!

To test this behavior, remove the read-only attribute from a local file and edit it using Notepad or an external editor. Save your changes. Launch Source Control Explorer, right-click the edited file, and choose Get Latest Version from the drop-down menu. Double-click and open the file. You'll find that your local changes are still there, and the version from the server did not get downloaded.

If you want to force a download from the server, right-click the file and select Get Specific Version from the drop-down menu. In the Get pop-up screen, turn on the Force get of file versions already in workspace option (see Figure 7.33). Click the Get button. If there is a mismatch, TFVC will display the Resolve Conflicts screen (see Figure 7.34). Click Resolve. On the Resolve Writable File Conflict screen, you can look at the differences by clicking Compare (see Figure 7.35). After you inspect the differences, select the appropriate option to resolve the conflict.

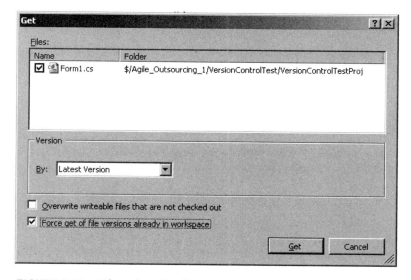

FIGURE 7.33 When downloading a specific version you can specify a force get.

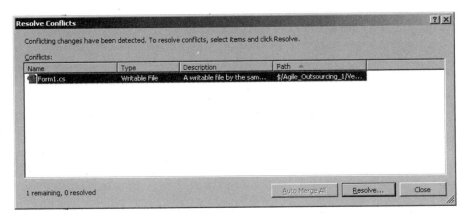

FIGURE 7.34 The Resolve Conflicts screen displays files that have discrepancies between server and local versions.

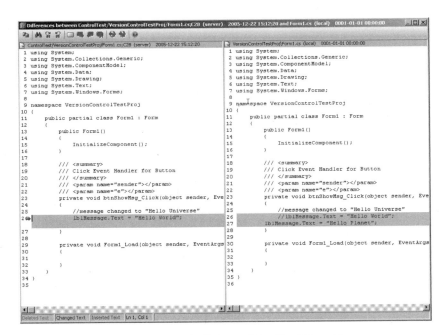

FIGURE 7.35 TFVC contains a built-in tool for file differencing.

A similar problem occurs if you rename or delete a folder in the local workspace and then perform a Get Latest Version from the Source Control Explorer. The folder and its contents do not get downloaded from the server; TFVC thinks that the latest version is already present in the local workspace.

Another point to note is that, unlike some other source code management systems, the version number of a file in TFVC is not unique to the file and is not incremented by one each time the file is modified. The file version number is derived from the corresponding changeset number. Therefore, the current version number of a file is based on the number of the changeset in which the file was last checked in. A few corollaries to keep in mind:

- If multiple files are checked in during a single changeset, all of them will be stamped with the same version number.
- The version numbers of a file may not be consecutive (e.g., there may have been intermediate changesets in the system in which a particular file was not modified). Consequently, when you look at the version history (right-click the file and choose View History from the drop-down menu) do not be confused if you see discontinuous changeset numbers.

If you are interested in downloading a specific version of the file, right-click the file and select Get Specific Version from the drop-down menu. In the Get pop-up screen, select Changeset from the Version By drop-down. Note that when you retrieve a specific version of the file, the latest version of the file in the server does *not* change. The specific version of the file is copied only to the local workspace. If you now double-click the file for editing, TFVC will prompt you to choose whether you want to edit the server version or the local version.

Rolling Back a Changeset

You might want to roll back a changeset for many reasons—to undo a destabilizing check-in, revert to a last 'known good state,' and so on. TFVC does not contain a built-in feature to roll back a changeset. However, you can use the Team Foundation Power Toy utility (tfpt.exe) to accomplish this task. Prior to running the tool, commit or undo all pending changes in the local workspace. In the command prompt window, type

```
tfpt rollback
```

The utility displays the Find Changeset screen, where you can select the changeset to be rolled back (see Figure 7.36). The Rollback Changeset dialog box lists the files and the compensating changes that will be applied to perform the rollback. In the next screens, you'll have the option to automatically or manually merge the changes and resolve conflicts if needed. Finally, the rollback operation will pend appropriate changes to the local workspace. Return to Source Control Explorer, review the list of source files and corresponding changes in the Pending Changes window, and check in the files.

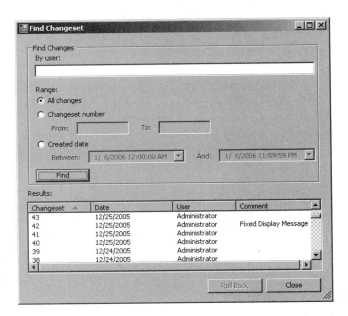

FIGURE 7.36 Specify the changeset to be rolled back in the Find Changeset screen.

If the changeset being rolled back is not the latest changeset, a rollback operation could require manual conflict resolution, depending upon the nature of changes involved. Let's look at a simple example to understand how the process works.

Create a file with just three lines and add it to TFVC. Make additional modifications and check them in to TFVC. After each check-in, the file should look as follows:

Changeset #1
```
line 1: nothing
line 2: nothing
line 3: nothing
```

Changeset #2
```
line 1: Hello World (modified)
line 2: nothing
line 3: nothing
```

Changeset #3
```
line 1: Hello World
line 2: Hello Planet (modified)
line 3: nothing
```

Changeset #4
```
line 1: Hello World
line 2: Hello Earth (modified)
line 3: Hello Universe (modified)
```

If you try to roll back Changeset #3 at this stage, the Power Toy will detect problems in `line 2` and `line 3`. To resolve the conflicts, the tool displays a merge window where you can manually merge changes (see Figure 7.37). On the other hand, if you try to roll back the last changeset (Changeset #4), the tool does it automatically without any manual intervention.

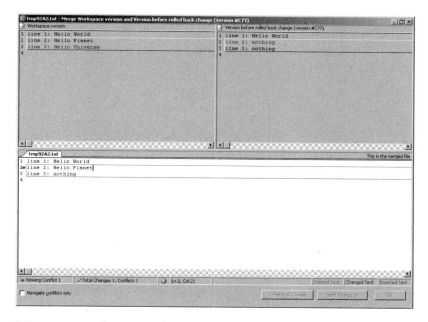

FIGURE 7.37   The merge dialog box facilitates conflict resolutions.

Specifying Additional Check-In Notes

Out of the box, TFVC allows you to specify the names of the Code Reviewer, Security Reviewer, and Performance Reviewer during check-in (see Figure 7.38). You might want to customize the check-in notes and add additional metadata associated with check-ins. For example, you might want to add set-up or testing instructions during check-ins. In the offshore scenario, the additional information helps create a smoother workflow between development, SQA, and release-management teams.

In version one of TFVC, check-in notes can be specified only at the changeset level; they cannot be specified at the file level.

Check-in notes can be customized either from the user interface or by editing the process template associated with the team project. If the custom check-in notes will be used in all of your new team projects, edit the process template. Otherwise, for a single team project, use the user interface to specify additional check-in notes.

To modify the process template, export it (refer to Chapter 3, "Leveraging VSTS and Customizing MSF Agile," for additional information) and open the VersionControl.xml file. The default content of this file for the MSF Agile process is shown in Listing 7.3.

LISTING 7.3 Contents of VersionControl.xml file Exported from the MSF Agile Process Template

```xml
<?xml version="1.0" encoding="utf-8" ?>
<tasks>
  <task id="VersionControlTask"
      name="Create Version Control area"
      plugin="Microsoft.ProjectCreationWizard.VersionControl"
      completionMessage="Version control Task completed.">
    <dependencies/>
    <taskXml>
      <permission allow="Read, PendChange, Checkin, Label, Lock,
          ReviseOther, UnlockOther, UndoOther, LabelOther,
          AdminProjectRights, CheckinOther"
          identity="[$$PROJECTNAME$$]\Project Administrators"/>
      <permission allow="Read, PendChange, Checkin, Label, Lock"
          identity="[$$PROJECTNAME$$]\Contributors"/>
      <permission allow="Read"
          identity="[$$PROJECTNAME$$]\Readers"/>
      <permission allow="Read, PendChange, Checkin, Label, Lock"
          identity="[$$PROJECTNAME$$]\Build Services"/>

      <checkin_note label="Code Reviewer"
          required="false" order="1"/>
      <checkin_note label="Security Reviewer"
          required="false" order="2"/>
      <checkin_note label="Performance Reviewer"
          required="false" order="3"/>

      <exclusive_checkout required="false"/>
    </taskXml>
  </task>
</tasks>
```

Note the nodes named `checkin_note`. You can modify the existing nodes or add additional nodes to customize the check-in notes for your team project.

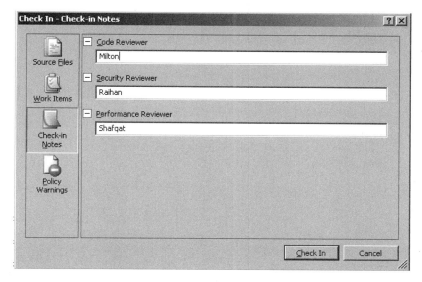

FIGURE 7.38   The Check-in Notes screen allows custom metadata to be associated with changesets.

To customize the check-in notes using the user interface, right-click the project name in Team Explorer, point to Team Project Settings, and click Source Control. In the Source Control Settings dialog box, click the Check-in Notes tab. Click Add to specify additional check-in notes (see Figure 7.39). In the same screen, you can also specify whether or not check-in notes are required for the current team project.

In addition to check-in notes, you can capture additional information regarding source code modifications in the changeset comment field (select the Source Files channel in the Pending Changes window). Since TFVC does not allow you to specify comments on a per-file basis, we suggest including the change description for each modified file in the changeset comment field. Recording the change history of each file is useful for code maintenance. You can, of course, add additional, higher-level descriptive information regarding the changeset in this field.

Differencing Files

You can compare the contents of two versions of a single file, as follows:

- Right-click the file in Source Control Explorer and select View History from the drop-down menu.

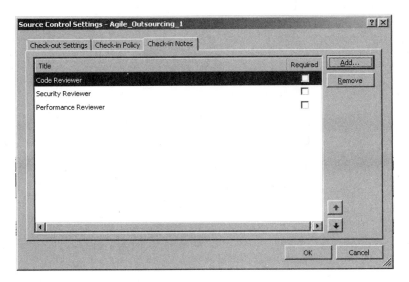

FIGURE 7.39 Check-in notes may be marked as required on a per-project basis.

- In the History window, highlight the two versions you would like to compare, and select Compare from the right-click, drop-down menu.

You can compare the contents of multiple files in a folder and its subfolders by running the tf.exe tool from the command prompt. To compare changes in all files between the version on a particular date and the latest version, open the command prompt window and type

```
tf diff $/<source_control_folder_name> /r
    /version:D<date_spec>~T
```

Replace `<source_control_folder_name>` with the name of your source control folder (you can look it up from the Source Location drop-down in Source Control Explorer) and `<date_spec>` with a comparison date (e.g., 01/01/2006). The `tf diff` command supports many other options, which you can find at *http://msdn2.microsoft.com/en-us/library/6fd7dc73.aspx.*

WORKING WITH TEAM BUILD

Once the team members have checked in their source code in to TFVC, the next step in the development process is to make a public build. A team build allows you to integrate and validate changes from all team members. In large projects with distributed offshore teams, integrating changes and resolving code conflicts is a challenge (especially if multiple people in multiple locations modify the same files). The frequency of builds depends upon your process methodology, team size, project complexity, and so on. Agile methods recommend short iterations with frequent builds. Many organizations go for weekly builds. Others perform nightly builds. Some companies practice *continuous integration*, where a build is made as soon a check-in takes place.

In the offshore scenario, a team build becomes especially important because of the following reasons:

A single set of build binaries and supporting files reduces friction: In offshore projects, a frequent source of friction stems from differences in runtime versions and execution environments in offshore and on-site locations. As a result, often a program that runs fine in one location crashes in another, bugs that occur in one computer can't be reproduced on another—and a host of frustrating problems crop up. The root cause frequently turns out to be inconsistencies in runtime assemblies, configuration files, back-end databases, Operating Systems, and the like. If a public build is made on a 'clean' machine with the latest source code checked out from TFVC, and if a reference machine is set up with the latest build binaries, configuration files, and databases, then it would go a long way toward resolving friction between globally distributed teams.

Conflict resolution and integration of changes committed by global teams: When working with people you hardly know and hardly meet (and therefore, can't conduct ad-hoc face-to-face conversations with), it is particularly important to continually ensure that your assumptions, interfaces, and expectations are still valid in terms of component or service interactions. Of course, this is easier said than done. The only practical way to make sure the system is still functioning as expected is to create a public build and execute appropriate build-verification tests.

Team Build Architecture

Team Build is based upon a distributed architecture similar to the rest of VSTS (see Figure 7.40). The flexible architecture enables you to deploy the services and components on a single physical machine or on multiple machines.

The various components of the team build are as follows:

Build Machine: Typically, you'll set up a dedicated 'clean' machine as the build machine where source code is downloaded from TFVC and compiled. In addition to the build binaries, this machine should contain configuration files, supporting databases, and third-party assemblies needed by your application at runtime. The build machine also contains the MSBuild.exe program and associated task files for creating the actual build. (The tasks are executed in a script file named Microsoft.TeamFoundation.Build.targets located in the Program Files\MSBuild\Microsoft\VisualStudio\v8.0\TeamBuild directory.) Under the covers, Team Build uses MSBuild to create the build. After a build is made, the binaries are placed in a specified drop location (usually a network share).

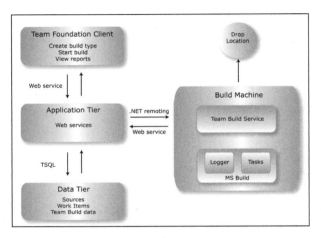

FIGURE 7.40 The Team Build architecture facilitates flexible deployment and customization.

Client Tier: The client tier is hosted in Team Explorer under the Team Builds node and allows you to create build types (see Figure 7.41). Each build type specifies the solutions to build, the verification tests to perform, the name of the build machine, the location of working files, the path to the final drop location, and so forth. You can kick off build runs from the client and view comprehensive build reports.

FIGURE 7.41 The Team Builds node in Team Explorer provides build creation and execution functionalities.

Application Tier: The application tier consists of team build-related Web services (Figure 7.42 shows the methods of the BuildController.asmx web service). The application tier receives build-related requests from the client and coordinates the workflow between the build machine and the data tier. Using .NET remoting, the application tier communicates with a Windows service named Team Build Service running on the build machine. The Team Build Service is responsible for launching the MSBuild program on the build machine. During execution of the build, the application tier receives various Web service-based requests from MSBuild tasks (e.g., get source files from TFVC) and talks to the data tier as needed to satisfy those requests. When the build is completed, the application tier receives the build results from the Team Build Logger (running on the build machine) and sends the information to the data tier for storage.

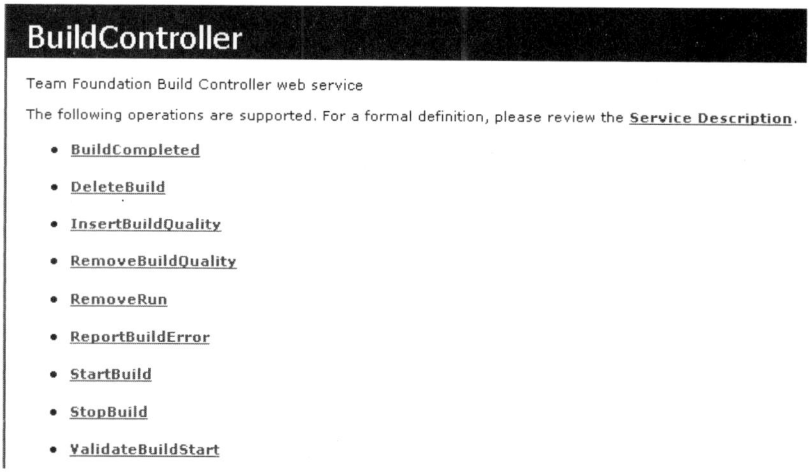

BuildController

Team Foundation Build Controller web service

The following operations are supported. For a formal definition, please review the **Service Description**.

- **BuildCompleted**
- **DeleteBuild**
- **InsertBuildQuality**
- **RemoveBuildQuality**
- **RemoveRun**
- **ReportBuildError**
- **StartBuild**
- **StopBuild**
- **ValidateBuildStart**

FIGURE 7.42   The BuildController Web service offers several build-related methods.

Data Tier: The data tier provides the source code files, associated work items, and other persisted information required by the Team Build. Additionally, it stores build execution-related data that can be used for creating comprehensive build reports (using SQL Server 2005 Reporting Services or other tools). The build-related information is stored in the relational database (see Figure 7.43) and is also available for reporting via the analytical data warehouse (see Figure 7.44).

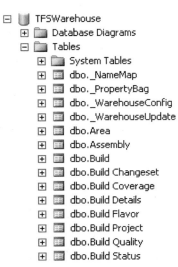

FIGURE 7.43 The TFSWarehouse relational database contains several tables to store build-related information.

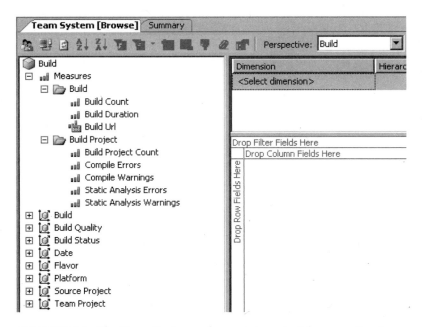

FIGURE 7.44 The Team System cube contains a build perspective for organizing build-related, aggregate information.

Team Build Workflow

Team Build provides integrated build-management functionality. Instead of just compiling the source code and creating binary assemblies, it performs a whole suite of functions. Here is a summary of the steps performed by Team Build:

1. Checks out the latest source code from TFVC into the build machine. You can write a custom task or modify the behavior of the Get task to fetch a specific labeled version instead of the latest version. Note that all solutions in a specified workspace are downloaded to the build machine from TFVC, even if you are building a single solution. However, only the specified solution(s) are actually compiled.
2. Performs static analysis to determine code quality.
3. Creates the actual build using MSBuild.
4. Executes specified build-verification tests and gathers code coverage data.
5. Fetches associated work items and stamps their "Resolved In Build" fields with the current build number. If the build fails, it automatically creates a new bug work item, indicating build failure.

Team Build Walk-Through

Let us walk through the basic steps involved in setting up and running a build. Assuming that you have permission to create builds, you can run builds on the build machine from any client machine on the network. Start by creating a new build type. Right-click the Team Builds node of your selected team project and select New Team Build Type from the drop-down menu. The New Team Build Type Creation Wizard pops up to collect build-related information (see Figure 7.45).

Run the wizard and enter build configuration information, as follows:

Welcome screen: Type the name of the new build type and provide other descriptive information.

Selections screen: Select the solutions you would like to build and the order in which they should be built. You can filter the list of solutions by using the workspace drop-down. Selecting a particular workspace in the drop-down causes the solution list to display only the solutions that are mapped to the specified workspace. Select "All Solutions Under Team Project" in the drop-down if you want to view all available solutions under the current team project.

Configurations screen: Specify whether you would like to create a Debug or Release build, or both. You can also choose whether the build should be optimized for a specific processor type.

Location screen: Specify the name of the build server, the directory where the source code will be downloaded and compiled, and the final drop location where the build binaries will be placed.

Options screen: Select the unit tests that should be executed to validate the build. You can also choose whether static code analysis should be conducted as part of the build process.

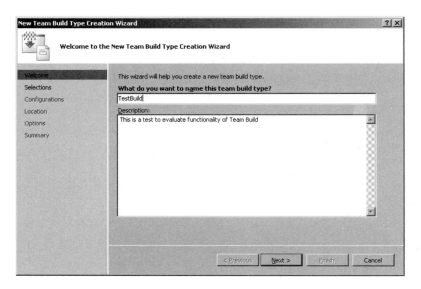

FIGURE 7.45 New Team Build Type Creation Wizard captures build configuration data.

When the wizard is completed, the new build type shows up under the Team Builds node (see Figure 7.46). The output of the wizard is stored in a file name Tfs-Build.proj. You can view the build configuration file by right-clicking the new build type in Team Explorer and selecting View Team Build Type from the drop-down menu.

The build configuration file and other associated files are automatically checked in to TFVC. Launch Source Control Explorer and select the team project for which the new build type was created. You'll find a new node named Team-BuildTypes; this is the parent node for all build types that you have created. Select the name of the build type that you previously created and you'll see the files associated with the build configuration (see Figure 7.47). You can map the Team-BuildTypes node to a local workspace and check out the TfsBuild.proj file for editing.

FIGURE 7.46   Newly created build type is added under the Team Builds node in Team Explorer.

FIGURE 7.47   Team Build configuration files are automatically added to TFVC.

To execute the build, right-click the build type in Team Explorer and choose Build Team Project (YourProjectName) from the drop-down list. Team Build will perform a series of build steps and finally present a comprehensive build report (see Figure 7.48). The report contains detailed information regarding the build steps performed (click on the BuildLog file), changesets incorporated (click on the changeset Id to view additional details), work items addressed (click on a work item Id and inspect the "Resolved in Build" field; you'll find that the field has been automatically stamped, as shown in Figure 7.49). Click on the hyperlinked entry for the build name to open the drop location and to view the build binaries.

Deploying Satellite Files

In order to run properly, your application may need third-party assemblies, configuration files, or databases. These files often need to be placed in the drop location by the offshore development team so that the on-site SQA team has a self-contained set of files to work with. To avoid confusion, it is important for all parties to work with a single set of build binaries as well as supporting files.

FIGURE 7.48   The Team Build report provides detailed information regarding the build process and outcome.

FIGURE 7.49   Resolved work items are automatically stamped with the build number.

If a supporting file is checked in to TFVC, right-click the file in Solution Explorer and select Properties from the drop-down menu. Choose the Copy to Output Directory option and set it to Copy Always or Copy if Newer .

If the file is not available in TFVC, you need to take a different approach. Edit the TfsBuild.proj file, override the AfterDropBuild target, and execute the Copy task (i.e., add the code shown in Listing 7.4 to the TfsBuild.proj file). Targets defined in TfsBuild.proj override the ones defined in Microsoft.TeamFoundation.Build.targets.

LISTING 7.4   Override AfterDropBuild Target in TfsBuild.proj file, and Add a Custom Copy Action

```
<Target Name="AfterDropBuild">

  <!-- Copy Third Party dll File -->
  <CreateItem Include="C:\PrivateAssemblies\ThirdParty.dll" >
    <Output ItemName="FileToCopy" TaskParameter="Include" />
  </CreateItem>
  <Copy
    SourceFiles="@(FileToCopy)" DestinationFolder=
    "@(FileToCopy ->'$(DropLocation)\$(BuildNumber)')"
    ContinueOnError="true" />
</Target>
```

Generating Build Notifications

Project managers responsible for managing offshore projects are typically interested to know when a new build takes place. Instead of calling the offshore team every so often to learn about build completion status, or relying upon their memory and effort to call you, you can subscribe to Team Build events and receive automatic notifications. Select a team project in Team Explorer and click the Team menu; select Project Alerts. Subscribe to build events listed in the Project Alerts dialog box (see Figure 7.50). The email you receive will be marked with build success or failure flags.

Viewing Build Results

You can access detailed information regarding an offshore build by using nothing more than a Web browser. You can view results of build verification tests, code coverage information, code churn data, associated changesets, resolved work items, and so forth (see Figure 7.51). The build report can be launched by typing the following in your browser: http:/<your_tfs_server_name>/ReportServer/Pages/ReportViewer.aspx?%2f<your_team_project_name>%2fBuilds&rs:Command=Render; replace "<your_tfs_server_name>" with the name of your application tier machine and "<your_team_project_name>" with the name of your team project.

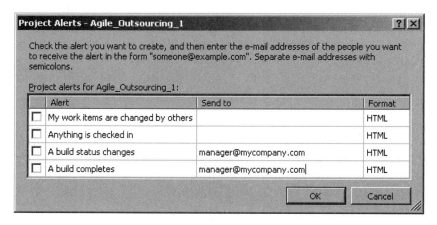

FIGURE 7.50 The Project Alerts dialog box allows subscription of build events.

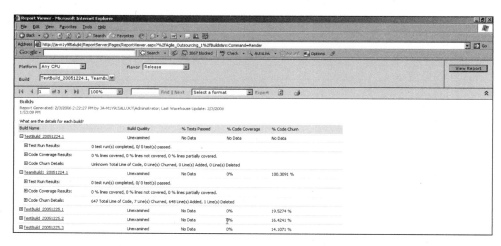

FIGURE 7.51 The build report provides detailed information regarding team builds.

CONCLUSION

In this chapter, we learned how the VSTS infrastructure can be leveraged to provide powerful source code and build-management functionalities. We have seen that in addition to standard version-control features, you can use VSTS to perform atomic check-ins, undertake parallel development via branching and merging, associate changes with work items, define and enforce check-in policies, conduct static code analysis, run unit tests, generate reports, create public builds, send out notifications, and provide build information via the project portal. Since all information is stored in SQL Server 2005 databases, backing up data for disaster-recovery purposes is easy. We have also seen that the architecture of TFVC and Team Build are optimized for efficient operation in a distributed environment.

TFVC can be used with Microsoft IDEs such as Visual Studio 2005, Visual Studio .NET 2003, Visual Basic 6, Visual C++ 6, etc. (IDEs other than VS 2005 are supported via TFS MSSCCI provider). Third-party products are available for accessing TFVC from the UNIX and Macintosh platforms. Various toolkits simplify code migration from other version-control systems. Both TFVC and Team Build provide flexible extensibility points for customizing the tools to suit your development process. We believe that this enterprise-class toolset will enhance your ability to effectively execute outsourced projects and improve their outcome.

8 Unit Testing with Team Test

INTRODUCTION

No matter how small or large your outsourced projects happen to be, quality is always a top concern. However, as obvious as it may sound, how do you define software quality? Is it something that can it be agreed upon and measured objectively? Can it be quantified, predicted, and improved?

In real life, the answers are not as straightforward as many of us would like them to be. A lot of times, we tend to focus on immediately observable numbers (such as bug counts), but ignore more-subtle and harder to quantify aspects, such as architecture, efficiency, clarity, security, and maintainability. A low bug count throughout the project life cycle might even indicate a lack of ambition, complexity, or technological advancement. Many highly successful software titles had buggy first versions (e.g., Windows 3.0). Sometimes, insisting on low bug counts too early in path-breaking projects turns out to be counterproductive. Be careful what you wish for.

Nevertheless, when used in the proper context, standard metrics are an important component of overall quality measurement, along with other less-quantifiable aspects. At the end of the day, software needs to perform as per its stated goals. When development is done halfway around the world by people you have never met—who have not had a chance to discuss and clarify the requirements face to face—you need even greater verifiable assurance that the system is doing what it is supposed to, at all levels of abstraction. Since user-level test cases may not cover all possible usage scenarios and exercise all possible code paths, you need visibility and run-time reliability at various levels to ensure well-functioning software. Creating a test harness (as automated as possible) at unit, system, and business levels enables the software to adapt and evolve with significantly reduced execution risk. This is why Test Driven Development (TDD) methodologies have gained such widespread popularity. The waterfall model (see Chapter 2, "Development Process—What Really Works?") advocated testing software *after* writing production code. In terms of process methodology, TDD suggests creating test cases *before* writing implementation code.

VSTS makes it easy to create unit, Web, and load tests. One of the arguments against TDD has been the difficulty associated with writing and debugging sometimes voluminous test code in order to effectively test implementation code. In complex projects, you could end up generating more test code than production code. Maintaining, organizing, and efficiently executing the body of test code often becomes a challenge in itself. By integrating test creation and management facilities into the framework, VSTS eliminates a lot of routine work, allowing you to focus on validating the real logic. The platform also provides code coverage information, enabling objective determination of test completeness.

You can review the tests conducted offshore at various levels of granularity. VSTS provides a set of built-in as well as customizable reports (see Chapter 9, "Enterprise Reporting," for additional information) that allow you to review the test results at critical points—for example, during build verification. Like all VSTS reports, the reports containing the test results can be viewed on demand from the project portal; they can also be delivered automatically via email at scheduled intervals using the report subscription feature. These capabilities are particularly useful in the offshore scenario. VSTS provides the necessary infrastructure tools to ensure implementation of your quality plan. It facilitates generation and management of test cases. The platform enables Internet-based distribution of test results to globally distributed stakeholders. When you put it all together, VSTS offers a compelling value proposition for ensuring software quality.

TYPES OF TESTS

In this chapter, we focus on various aspects of creating and executing unit tests. VSTS allows you to create different types of tests for various application types and testing strategies. Available test types are as follows (see Figure 8.1):

Unit Test: For testing individual methods in your application, you can create unit tests from existing code or from scratch. Windows as well as Web applications can be unit tested.

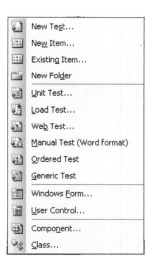

FIGURE 8.1   Types of tests available in VSTS.

Web Test: A series of HTTP requests for testing Web sites can be recorded from browser sessions via the Web Test Recorder (see Figure 8.2) or created from scratch. You can specify various input parameters and view corresponding responses from the Web site. Recorded Web tests can be converted to source code for additional customizations.

Load Test: For stress-testing Web applications, you can specify various load settings, network type, and browser configurations, and monitor various performance counters under different load conditions.

Manual Test: These are used for test cases that are not automated and need to be conducted manually. A manual test is typically created based on a Microsoft Word 2003 template and contains the sequence of steps to perform. At end of the test run, you can manually indicate whether the test passed or not.

FIGURE 8.2 Web Test Recorder creates Web tests from browser sessions.

Generic Test: Use these tests to invoke third-party testing tools. You can specify the environment settings and command line parameters to use when calling an external testing program; a zero return value indicates success.

Ordered Test: Used to run a collection of tests in a specified order. You can include any test type (except a load test) in the ordered test set. You can also specify whether the testing process should stop if an individual test fails or continue running the remaining tests.

WALK-THROUGH: CREATING AND RUNNING UNIT TESTS

Unit tests allow you to test the source code at an atomic level. They are typically created and executed by programmers, and not by SQA professionals. You can write unit tests to test class constructors, methods, and properties. The underlying idea is to create software in small pieces at a time, to test each piece independently, and to build complex logical structures using those simple, easily testable building blocks. The fundamental notion is simple, but extremely powerful. It works.

Unit tests can be created from existing code or from scratch. There is debate in the industry regarding how isolated a unit-testable target method ought to be from external dependencies—such as from third-party services, databases, message queues, and so on. We believe that this is a judgment call on the part of an experienced developer, since the strategy will vary based upon the specific problem in question. Although not a panacea—a target method could behave differently depending upon load, security context, data, or multithreaded calls—unit tests are of key importance in Agile projects. You should insist on creating them for all outsourced projects.

In the offshore scenario, since the implementation team is physically situated on the other side of the planet, you can't look at the test results from the VSTS IDE. You can remotely view the test results via SharePoint-hosted reports. In addition to the built-in reports, you can create custom reports as needed.

Creating a Unit Test from Scratch

To construct a new unit test from scratch, create a test project (see Figure 8.3). VSTS automatically generates an empty unit test class named UnitTest1.cs. This class contains skeletal code with various test-related attributes (these attributes are discussed in detail later in the chapter). If you follow a TDD approach, create a unit test for a non-existent target method. Of course, the test class will not compile at this time since the target method does not exist. That's fine. In the unit test, you have specified the input parameters and the expected output value(s) from the proposed method. Create an assembly containing the implementation code for the target method. Add a reference to the target assembly and run the unit test class. In a nutshell, this is the development approach recommended by TDD.

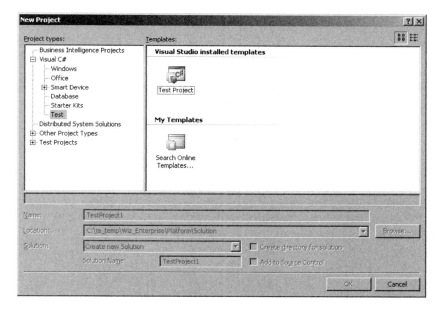

FIGURE 8.3   Creating a test project in VSTS.

Creating Unit Tests from Existing Code

ON THE CD

If you are creating unit tests for an existing codebase, VSTS takes care of a lot of the routine work. Let's walk through an example. Create a simple class library project as shown in Listing 8.1. The full source code is available on the CD-ROM.

LISTING 8.1   Sample Class Containing Source Code for Unit Testing

```
using System;
using System.Collections.Generic;
```

```csharp
using System.Text;

namespace UnitTestingWinApp
{
public class Calculations
{
    private int precision;

    /// <summary>
    /// test property for demo purposes
    /// </summary>
    public int Precision
    {
        get
        {
            return precision;
        }
        set
        {
            precision = value;
        }
    }

    /// <summary>
    /// divide two numbers given the numerator and denominator
    /// </summary>
    /// <param name="numerator"></param>
    /// <param name="denominator"></param>
    /// <returns></returns>
    public decimal Divide(decimal numerator, decimal denominator)
    {
        if (!pIsZero(denominator))
        {
            return numerator / denominator;
        }
        else
        {
            throw new DivideByZeroException();
        }
    }

    /// <summary>
    /// check if the denominator is zero
    /// </summary>
    /// <param name="denominator"></param>
    /// <returns></returns>
    private bool pIsZero (decimal denominator)
    {
```

```
        if (denominator == 0)
            return true;
        else
            return false;
    }
}
}
```

Right-click anywhere in the code and select Create Unit Tests from the drop-down menu (see Figure 8.4). In the Create Unit Tests dialog box (see Figure 8.5), specify the methods and properties to be included in tests. The class members are autoselected depending on where you clicked in the source code.

You can control the visibility of private methods for testing purposes. There is debate in the development community whether private methods should be directly tested or not. Some people feel that constructing unit tests for private methods makes the test code too susceptible to change, since private methods are generally allowed to evolve freely. Others feel that if the codebase is somewhat mature, it makes sense to explicitly test *all* methods. In any case, VSTS gives you the option to decide either way. If you do not want to create tests for private methods, click Filter and unselect the Display Non-Public Items option. Click Settings to

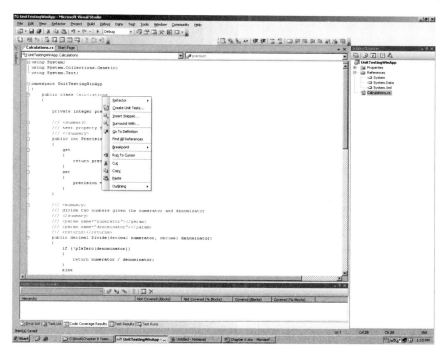

FIGURE 8.4   Unit tests can be created from anywhere in source code.

specify additional options regarding naming style, nature of assertion, documentation, and so forth. In the Output Project drop-down, specify Create a New Visual C# Test Project. For maintenance purposes, keep test and implementation codebases in separate assemblies. Click OK to generate the test project.

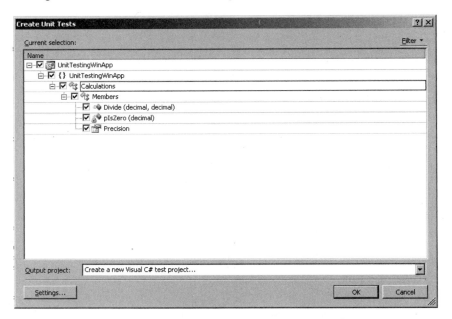

FIGURE 8.5 Create Unit Tests screen contains test customization options.

Modifying Autogenerated Code

Open the autogenerated test class and modify the code as follows:

- Specify the input parameters for target methods that require parameters. VSTS initializes them to their default values, since it does not know how to populate them.
- Change `Assert` statements to `Assert.AreEqual`, `Assert.AreNotEqual`, and so forth, as appropriate for the test case. In addition to a default `Assert.AreEqual` statement, VSTS inserts an `Assert.Inconclusive` statement in all unit tests, indicating the need to specify an appropriate check. (To turn off automatic inclusion of `Assert.Inconclusive` statements, click Settings in the Create Unit Tests dialog box. In the Test Generation Settings dialog box, clear Mark All Test Results Inconclusive by Default check box.)

Listing 8.2 shows the source code for the modified test class.

LISTING 8.2   Autogenerated Test Class Modified to Test Calculations Class

```csharp
// The following code was generated by Microsoft Visual
// Studio 2005.
// The test owner should check each test for validity.
using Microsoft.VisualStudio.TestTools.UnitTesting;
using System;
using System.Text;
using System.Collections.Generic;
using UnitTestingWinApp;

namespace UnitTestWinAppTest
{
/// <summary>
///This is a test class for UnitTestingWinApp.Calculations
///and is intended
///to contain all UnitTestingWinApp.Calculations Unit Tests
///</summary>
[TestClass()]
public class CalculationsTest
{
  private TestContext testContextInstance;

  /// <summary>
  ///Gets or sets the test context which provides
  ///information about and functionality for
  ///the current test run.
  ///</summary>
  public TestContext TestContext
  {
    get
    {
      return testContextInstance;
    }
    set
    {
      testContextInstance = value;
    }
  }

  #region Additional test attributes
  //
  //You can use the following additional attributes
  //as you write your tests:
  //
  //Use ClassInitialize to run code before running
  //the first test in the class
  //
```

```
//[ClassInitialize()]
//public static void MyClassInitialize(TestContext testContext)
//{
//}
//
//Use ClassCleanup to run code after all tests
//in a class have run
//
//[ClassCleanup()]
//public static void MyClassCleanup()
//{
//}
//
//Use TestInitialize to run code before running each test
//
//[TestInitialize()]
//public void MyTestInitialize()
//{
//}
//
//Use TestCleanup to run code after each test has run
//
//[TestCleanup()]
//public void MyTestCleanup()
//{
//}
//
#endregion

/// <summary>
///A test for Divide (decimal, decimal)
///</summary>
[TestMethod()]
public void DivideTest()
{
  Calculations target = new Calculations();

  decimal numerator = 10;
  decimal denominator = 2;
  decimal expected = 5;
  decimal actual;
  actual = target.Divide(numerator, denominator);

  Assert.AreEqual(expected, actual,
      "UnitTestingWinApp.Calculations.Divide did not return the
      expected value.");
}
```

```
/// <summary>
///A test for pIsZero (decimal)
///</summary>
[DeploymentItem("UnitTestingWinApp.dll")]
[TestMethod()]
public void pIsZeroTest()
{
  Calculations target = new Calculations();

  UnitTestWinAppTest.UnitTestingWinApp_CalculationsAccessor
      accessor = new UnitTestWinAppTest
      .UnitTestingWinApp_CalculationsAccessor(target);

  decimal denominator = 0;
  bool expected = true;
  bool actual;
  actual = accessor.pIsZero(denominator);

  Assert.AreEqual(expected, actual,
      "UnitTestingWinApp.Calculations.pIsZero did not
      return the expected value.");
}

/// <summary>
/// A test for Precision
/// </summary>
[TestMethod()]
public void PrecisionTest()
{
  Calculations target = new Calculations();

  int val = 3;
  target.Precision = val;

  Assert.AreEqual(val, target.Precision,
      "UnitTestingWinApp.Calculations.Precision was
      not set correctly.");
}
}
}
```

Running Unit Tests

The newly created tests can be run in multiple ways. For example, you can run all unit tests in a given project by clicking Start Selected Test Project with Debugger or Start Selected Test Project without Debugger on the Test Tools toolbar. Additionally, you can run unit tests from the Test Manager. The Test Manager provides an organized test management console and enables you to run tests selectively. Click Test Manager on the Test Tools toolbar. Alternatively, on the Test menu, point to Windows, and click Test Manager (see Figure 8.6). Select the tests you want to run by selecting the corresponding check boxes. After making your selections, click Run Checked Tests on the Test Manager toolbar. The execution results are displayed in Test Results window (see Figure 8.7). Notice that during test execution, the test results cycle through Pending, In Progress, and Passed/Failed states.

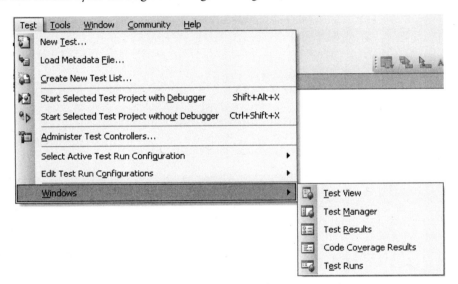

FIGURE 8.6   The Test Manager provides a unified test-management console.

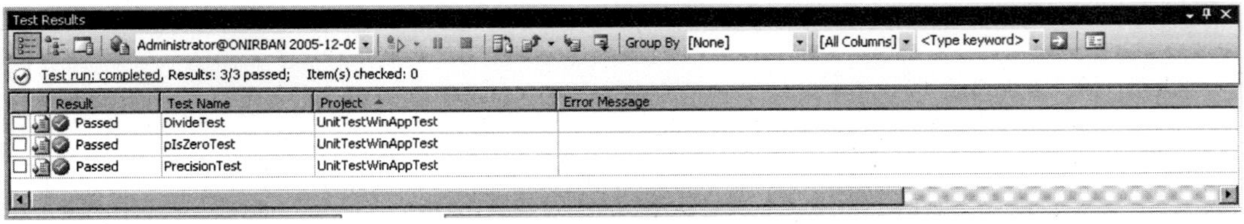

FIGURE 8.7   The Test Results window provides the status of tests executed.

VIEWING CODE COVERAGE INFORMATION

Code coverage is a key metric that provides insight into the effectiveness of your unit-testing strategy. For offshore projects, insist on receiving code coverage information for every build. Otherwise, you'll have no factual idea about the reliability of the delivery. Some companies require a minimum code coverage percentage before source code can be checked into the shared repository. VSTS provides line and block coverage information. Other coverage types, such as statement coverage, branch coverage, and decision coverage, are not supported in version one.

To turn on code coverage, click the Test menu, point to Edit Test Run Configurations, and click the appropriate test configuration. In the test configuration dialog box, click Code Coverage from the list box and select the target assembly to instrument (see Figure 8.8); click Apply. Go back to Test Manager and click Run Checked Tests (the tests need to be run without the debug option). Code coverage results are visible in the Code Coverage Results window (see Figure 8.9). You can also open the source file, click Show Code Coverage Coloring option on the Test Tools toolbar, and visually examine the lines of code that were covered or missed by the tests.

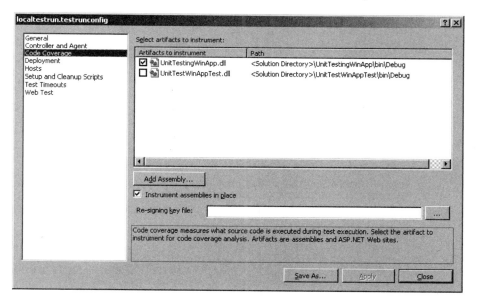

FIGURE 8.8   Instrument the target assembly for code coverage.

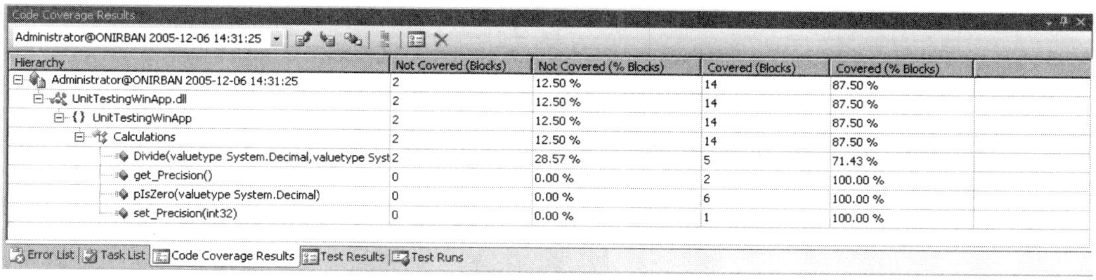

Hierarchy	Not Covered (Blocks)	Not Covered (% Blocks)	Covered (Blocks)	Covered (% Blocks)	
Administrator@ONIRBAN 2005-12-06 14:31:25	2	12.50 %	14	87.50 %	
UnitTestingWinApp.dll	2	12.50 %	14	87.50 %	
UnitTestingWinApp	2	12.50 %	14	87.50 %	
Calculations	2	12.50 %	14	87.50 %	
Divide(valuetype System.Decimal,valuetype Syst	2	28.57 %	5	71.43 %	
get_Precision()	0	0.00 %	2	100.00 %	
pIsZero(valuetype System.Decimal)	0	0.00 %	6	100.00 %	
set_Precision(int32)	0	0.00 %	1	100.00 %	

FIGURE 8.9   Code Coverage Results window.

AN IN-DEPTH LOOK AT THE AUTOGENERATED TEST PROJECT

The autogenerated test project contains necessary code to invoke the specified methods and properties in the `Calculations` class (see Figure 8.10). The test project contains a reference to the `Microsoft.VisualStudio.QualityTools.UnitTestFramework` assembly; this assembly contains the classes belonging to `Microsoft.VisualStudio.TestTools.UnitTesting` and `Microsoft.VisualStudio.TestTools.UnitTesting.Web` namespaces, as well as other classes related to test-authoring and execution.

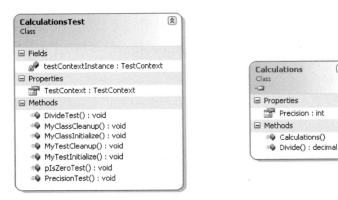

FIGURE 8.10 Test project class diagram.

Test Attributes

The `UnitTestWinAppTest` class is marked with an attribute named `TestClassAttribute`. (In source code, you'll find the attribute specified as `[TestClass()]`; by convention, we add the suffix "Attribute" when referring to an attribute class. We follow the same approach when referring to all attributes in this chapter.) The test methods are annotated with `TestMethodAttribute`. Only methods marked with `TestMethodAttribute` are run by Test Manager; other methods (such as additional helper methods in the class) will not be considered as unit test methods. Expand the Additional Test Attributes node in the `UnitTestWinAppTest` class and notice the following new attributes:

ClassInitializeAttribute: A method marked with this attribute is executed before any test method is run; typically used to set up resources like database connections. The method should be marked static, since it is called before the test class is instantiated. The method takes `TestContext` as a parameter.

ClassCleanupAttribute: A method marked with this attribute is executed after all tests are run; it can be used to release resources. The method should be marked static.

TestInitializeAttribute: A method marked with this attribute is executed before each test is run.

TestCleanupAttribute: A method marked with this attribute is executed after each test is run.

The Test Life Cycle

It is important to know that the test class is *re-instantiated* before each unit test (you can easily verify this behavior by inserting debugging code inside the class constructor). This kind of 'stateless' behavior has to do with support for test controller and agent architecture. If a large number of tests are submitted to a controller, the controller divides the tests among available agents. The agents run the tests in parallel.

Therefore, you cannot use nonstatic class members to persist values—for example, to pass values from one test method to another. Nonstatic variables get wiped clean and re-initialized before running each test, since the class itself gets recreated.

Although the class constructor is invoked multiple times during test class execution (once for each test), methods marked with ClassInitializeAttribute and ClassCleanupAttribute are executed just once. The method marked ClassInitializeAttribute is run before the first unit test, and the method marked ClassCleanupAttribute is run after the last unit test. The life cycle of the test class is shown in Figure 8.11.

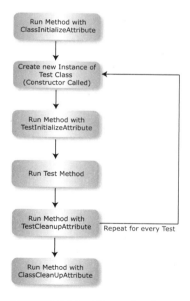

FIGURE 8.11   Life cycle of a test class.

The TestContext Class

The TestContext class (see Figure 8.12) contains various useful pieces of information about the current test execution. This test class contains a public property that returns the associated TestContext class (refer to Listing 8.2). Among other uses, you could use the TestContext class for the following purposes:

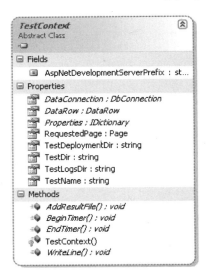

FIGURE 8.12 Methods and properties of the TestContext class.

- To determine the name of the currently running test (use the TestName property). You could use this information to selectively initialize instance members (with test-specific values) from a method marked with the TestInitializeAttribute.
- To run data-driven tests (use the DataConnection and DataRow properties; refer to the next section for more information).
- To figure out various directories associated with test execution and logging (use the TestDir, TestLogsDir, and TestDeploymentDir properties).
- To pass information from the test initialization method to actual test methods (add custom properties to the Properties collection). However, you need to be aware of the pitfalls associated with this technique. In fact, if you add custom properties to the TestContext.Properties collection from a method marked with ClassInitializeAttribute, the custom property will be available to the *first* test method only; subsequent test methods will not be able to retrieve the custom properties (see Listing 8.3). Microsoft will probably fix this behavior in the next version of VSTS. For now, since the TestContest class is not accessible from the test class constructor (i.e., its reference set to null), your only option

is to add custom TestContext properties from a class marked with TestInitializeAttribute if you wish to pass custom properties to test methods via TestContext. Also, you *cannot* add custom properties in one test method and access them in another method.

LISTING 8.3 Custom Properties Added in the Class Initialization Method and Available Only to the First Unit Test Method

```
[ClassInitialize()]
public static void MyClassInitialize(TestContext testContext)
{
  //add custom properties to TestContext class for test purposes
  testContext.Properties["custom_property_1"] = "test_value_1";
  testContext.Properties["custom_property_2"] = "test_value_2";
}
[TestMethod()]
public void DivideTest()
{
  #region TestContext related tests
  //since this is the first test method run, custom properties
  //are available in TestContext
  //retrieve custom properties from TestContext
  string value1 =
      (string)this.TestContext.Properties["custom_property_1"];
  System.Diagnostics.Debug.WriteLine("value 1:" + value1);
  string value2 =
      (string)this.TestContext.Properties["custom_property_2"];
  System.Diagnostics.Debug.WriteLine("value 2:" + value1);
  #endregion
  //......
  //other code omitted
}


[DeploymentItem("UnitTestingWinApp.dll")]
[TestMethod()]
public void pIsZeroTest()
{
  #region TestContext related tests

  //since this is NOT the first test method run, custom
  //properties are NOT available in TestContext
  //the following code does NOT retrieve custom properties
  //string value1 =
      (string)this.TestContext.Properties["custom_property_1"];
  //System.Diagnostics.Debug.WriteLine("value 1:" + value1);
  //string value2 =
      (string)this.TestContext.Properties["custom_property_2"];
```

```
//System.Diagnostics.Debug.WriteLine("value 2:" + value1);

#endregion
//......
//other code omitted
}
```

Assert Classes

The `Microsoft.VisualStudio.TestTools.UnitTesting` namespace contains a number of assert classes (see Figure 8.13) that are extensively used in unit tests to determine whether a target method call succeeded or failed. If an assertion fails, an exception of type `AssertFailedException` is raised (the `Assert.Inconclusive` method raises an `AssertInconclusiveException`).

The basic idea, of course, is to compare the return value of a method with an expected value. Given the wide variety of potential return types and values from method calls, it is frequently more efficient to use the assert classes instead of writing plain `if`/`else` statements with conditional operators, and throwing exceptions to indicate test failure.

The `Assert` class is used to compare strings, numbers, object references, and the like. It contains a large number of overloaded static methods to determine things like equality, inequality, and null value.

If you need to compare a collection of values, as opposed to a single value, consider using the `CollectionAssert` class. The `CollectionAssert` class enables you to perform item-by-item comparisons between two collections, figure out whether a collection contains a subset of items in another collection, as well as determine the presence of an item in a collection.

If your tests call for sophisticated string-based comparisons—using regular expressions, for example—use the `StringAssert` class. The `StringAssert` class contains methods to search for the presence of a substring within another string, as well as methods with powerful regular expression-based pattern-matching capability.

Exception Handling

Exceptions play a deciding role in evaluating the success or failure of a test method. If an exception is thrown during the execution of a test method, the test is reported to have failed. As discussed earlier, an `AssertFailedException` is raised by an assert method if an assertion fails. Do not trap this exception (or its base classes `UnitTestAssertException` and `Exception`) in your test code by using a `try`/`catch` block. For example, the code in Listing 8.4 should *not* be used, as it will cause the test method to *always* pass, regardless of errors in assertion and target method execution.

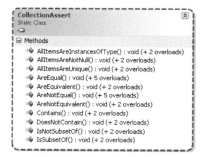

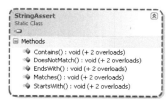

FIGURE 8.13   Assert classes contains methods to determine equality and inequality.

LISTING 8.4   This Test Will Always Pass Because the Catch Block Traps All Exceptions

```
try
{
  Calculations target = new Calculations();

  decimal numerator = 10;
  decimal denominator = 2;

  /// expected result
  decimal expected = 3;
  decimal actual;
  actual = Decimal.Round(target.Divide(
      numerator, denominator), 2);

  Assert.AreEqual(expected, actual,
      "UnitTestingWinApp.Calculations.Divide did not
      return the expected value.");
}
catch (Exception ex)
{
  System.Diagnostics.Debug.WriteLine(ex);
}
```

Of course, many kinds of exceptions can be thrown by the test method and the target method, in addition to `AssertFailedException`. Any untrapped exception will cause the unit test to fail. If you expect a certain exception to be raised by the target method (perhaps you are conducting negative testing), you would want the test to pass if the intended exception is thrown by the target method. You can achieve this by trapping the exception using a `try`/`catch` block in the test method—or better yet, mark the test method with `ExpectedExceptionAttribute`, as shown in Listing 8.5. The test fails if the target method does *not* raise the expected exception.

LISTING 8.5 This Test Will Pass If the Target Method Raises a DivideByZeroException

```
[ExpectedException (typeof(DivideByZeroException))]
[TestMethod]
public void DivideTest()
{
    Calculations target = new Calculations();
    decimal numerator = 10;
    decimal denominator = 0;
    decimal actual;
    actual = Decimal.Round(target.Divide(
        numerator, denominator), 2);
}
```

Invoking Private Methods

Notice in Listing 8.2 that the test class contains a unit test named `pIsZeroTest`, which invokes a private method `pIsZero` in the `Calculations` class. Since the target method is private, it cannot be invoked directly from an external class. The test class uses a private accessor method to call the target private method. The private accessor (named `pIsZero`, as well) is located in a class named `App_CalculationsAccessor` in the VSCodeGenAccessors.cs file. Listing 8.6 shows the autogenerated code associated with the accessor class and method.

LISTING 8.6 Private Accessor Class and Methods

```
using Microsoft.VisualStudio.TestTools.UnitTesting;
namespace UnitTestWinAppTest
{
[System.Diagnostics.DebuggerStepThrough()]
[System.CodeDom.Compiler.GeneratedCodeAttribute("Microsoft.Visual
    Studio.TestTools.UnitTestGeneration", "1.0.0.0")]
internal class BaseAccessor
{
  protected Microsoft.VisualStudio.TestTools.UnitTesting
      .PrivateObject m_privateObject;
```

```
    protected BaseAccessor(object target,
        Microsoft.VisualStudio.TestTools.UnitTesting.PrivateType
        type)
    {
      _privateObject = new Microsoft.VisualStudio
          .TestTools.UnitTesting.PrivateObject(target, type);
    }
    protected BaseAccessor(
        Microsoft.VisualStudio.TestTools.UnitTesting.PrivateType
        type) : this(null, type)
    {
    }

    internal virtual object Target
    {
      get
      {
        return m_privateObject.Target;
      }
    }

    public override string ToString()
    {
      return this.Target.ToString();
    }

    public override bool Equals(object obj)
    {
      if (typeof(BaseAccessor).IsInstanceOfType(obj))
      {
        obj = ((BaseAccessor)(obj)).Target;
      }
      return this.Target.Equals(obj);
    }

    public override int GetHashCode()
    {
      return this.Target.GetHashCode();
    }
}
[System.Diagnostics.DebuggerStepThrough()]
[System.CodeDom.Compiler.GeneratedCodeAttribute("Microsoft.Visual
    Studio.TestTools.UnitTestGeneration", "1.0.0.0")]

internal class UnitTestingWinApp_CalculationsAccessor :
    BaseAccessor
{
  protected static
```

```
            Microsoft.VisualStudio.TestTools.UnitTesting.PrivateType
            m_privateType = new
            Microsoft.VisualStudio.TestTools.UnitTesting.PrivateType(
            typeof(global::UnitTestingWinApp.Calculations));

        internal UnitTestingWinApp_CalculationsAccessor(
            global::UnitTestingWinApp.Calculations target) :
            base(target, m_privateType)
        {
        }
        internal int precision
        {
          get
          {
            int ret = ((int)(m_privateObject.GetField("precision")));
            return ret;
          }
          set
          {
            m_privateObject.SetField("precision", value);
          }
        }

        internal bool pIsZero(decimal denominator)
        {
          object[] args = new object[] {denominator};
          bool ret = ((bool)(m_privateObject.Invoke("pIsZero",
            new System.Type[] {typeof(decimal)}, args)));
          return ret;
        }
    }
}
```

UnitTestingWinApp_CalculationsAccessor inherits from BaseAccessor, defined in the same file (see Figure 8.14). If there are multiple private accessors, they all inherit from the same BaseAccessor superclass. One of the constructors for the BaseAccessor class takes an object instance and a Microsoft.VisualStudio.Test-Tools.UnitTesting.PrivateType name (the other constructor simply delegates to this primary constructor). Using the two input parameters, the constructor creates an instance of Microsoft.VisualStudio.TestTools.UnitTesting.PrivateObject, wrapping the specified object. PrivateObject is a wrapper class designed to invoke nonpublic methods via reflection. The private accessor method uses the PrivateObject instance (created by BaseAccessor constructor) to invoke the target private method pIsZero.

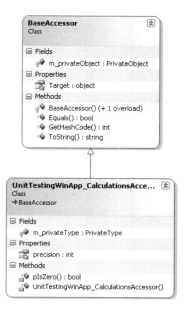

FIGURE 8.14 Class diagram of the private accessor class.

Data-Driven Tests

There are times when you'll need to read test data from an external file, such as a database, and pass the information as input to the test methods. Using the Calculations class as an example, suppose you would like to test the Divide method by invoking it with a variety of parameters. Instead of hardcoding the values in the test class, it would be more efficient and flexible to be able to read the values from a database. To create a data-driven test, follow these steps:

■ Create a database in SQL Server 2005, containing a table with input as well as expected output values (see Figure 8.15).
■ Open Test Manager and select the unit test that will read from the database (DivideTest, in this case); right-click the test name and select Properties from the drop-down menu.
■ Click the ellipsis (...) in the Data Connection String property. Specify connection information, and select the database containing test data.
■ Return to the Properties window and fill in the Data Table Name property; select the table name from the drop-down. Figure 8.16 shows the Properties window at this stage.

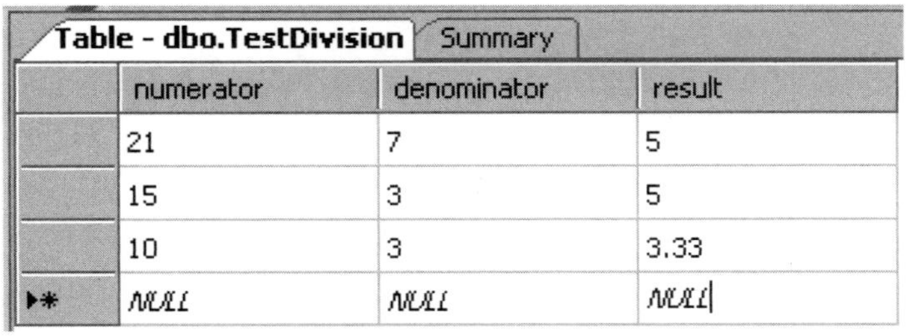

FIGURE 8.15 Table dbo.TestDivision is used as a data source for the unit test.

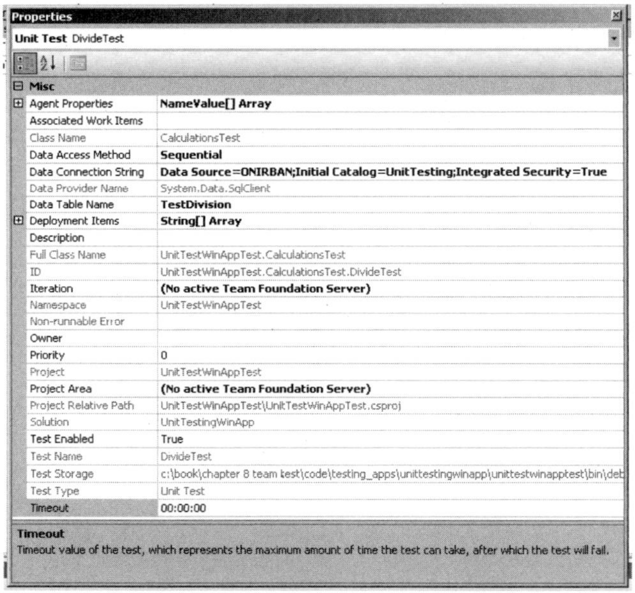

FIGURE 8.16 Unit Test configured to use a table as data source.

If you take a look at the source code of the unit test method, you'll notice that an attribute named `DataSourceAttribute` has been added to the method; this attribute specifies the connection information to the data store.

When the test is executed, VSTS fetches each row from the data table and calls the test method. The information from the data source is contained in the `DataRow` property of the `TestContext` class. We extract the numerator, denominator, and expected result from `DataRow`, and use the data to call the target method and evaluate its return value (see Listing 8.7). The `DataRow` property has several overloaded versions that allow you to retrieve data by specifying the column name, index, or corresponding System.Data.DataColumn type.

LISTING 8.7   Test Class Modified to Execute Data-Driven Tests

```
/// <summary>
/// A test for Divide (decimal, decimal)
/// </summary>
[DataSource("System.Data.SqlClient", "Data Source=(local);Initial
    Catalog=UnitTesting;Integrated Security=True",
    "TestDivision", DataAccessMethod.Sequential), TestMethod()]
public void DivideTest()
{
  #region TestContext related tests
  //……
  //code omitted
  #endregion

  Calculations target = new Calculations();
  //read numerator from table
  decimal numerator = Convert.ToDecimal(
      (double)TestContext.DataRow["numerator"]) ;

  ///read denominator from table
  decimal denominator = Convert.ToDecimal(
      (double)TestContext.DataRow["denominator"]);

  ///read expected result from table
  decimal expected = Convert.ToDecimal(
      (double)TestContext.DataRow["result"]);

  decimal actual;
  actual = Decimal.Round (target.Divide(numerator,
      denominator),2);

  Assert.AreEqual(expected, actual,
      "UnitTestingWinApp.Calculations.Divide did not return the
      expected value.");
}
```

It is important to remember the following facts regarding data-driven tests:

- The test class is *re-instantiated* for each row of data. Therefore, you can't pass information from one invocation of the test method to the next without using static variables.

- The data is read from the database at the *beginning* of the test execution. Therefore, if you update the database while a test is running, the changes will not be visible during that test run.
- You can specify tables as well as views as SQL Server data sources. Sometimes you might want to apply filters or aggregate test data from multiple tables; views come in handy in such cases.
- The constructor for `DataSourceAttribute` has an overloaded version (the one used in Listing 8.7), where you can specify via the `DataAccessMethod` parameter how you would like to access the data source—in sequence or at random. Valid values are `DataAccessMethod.Sequential` and `DataAccessMethod.Random`.

Reading the Data Source from the Configuration File

Instead of hardcoding the connection string inside your test class, you might want store it in an external configuration file for greater flexibility. Follow these steps:

- Right-click the test project in Solution Explorer and select Add, New Item. From the predefined templates, select Application Configuration File (see Figure 8.17).

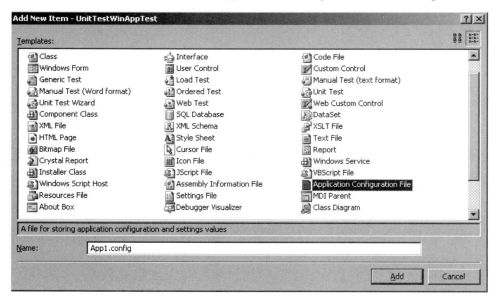

FIGURE 8.17 Add the Application Configuration File to the test project.

- Modify the newly created App.Config file as per Listing 8.8. Notice that we create a SQL Server connection named `SQLConnection` and a data source called `MyTestDataSource`. Change the `connectionString` attribute of `SQLConnection` as needed to point to your SQL Server database. Change the `dataTableName` attribute of `MyTestDataSource` to point to your test data table.

■ Modify the attribute named `DataSourceAttribute` associated with the test method, as shown in Listing 8.9. In the attribute's constructor, specify the name of the data source created in the App1.Config file.

LISTING 8.8   Data Source Specified in the Application Configuration File

```
<?xml version="1.0" encoding="utf-8" ?>
<configuration>
 <configSections>
  <section name="microsoft.visualstudio.testtools"
      type="Microsoft.VisualStudio.TestTools.UnitTesting
      .TestConfigurationSection, Microsoft.VisualStudio
      .QualityTools.UnitTestFramework, Version=8.0.0.0,
      Culture=neutral, PublicKeyToken=b03f5f7f11d50a3a"/>
 </configSections>
 <connectionStrings>
  <add name="SqlConnection" connectionString="Data Source=
      (local);Initial Catalog=UnitTesting;Integrated Security
      =True;" providerName="System.Data.SqlClient" />
 </connectionStrings>
 <microsoft.visualstudio.testtools>
  <dataSources>
   <add name="MyTestDataSource"
      connectionString="SqlConnection"
      dataTableName="TestDivision"
      dataAccessMethod="Sequential"/>
  </dataSources>
 </microsoft.visualstudio.testtools>
</configuration>
```

LISTING 8.9   Test Method Modified to Read the Data Source from the Application
Configuration File

```
/// <summary>
///A test for Divide (decimal, decimal)
///</summary>
[DataSource("MyTestDataSource")]
[TestMethod]
public void DivideTest()
{
  #region TestContext related tests
  //......
  //code omitted
  #endregion

  Calculations target = new Calculations();
```

```
//read numerator from table
decimal numerator = Convert.ToDecimal(
    (double)TestContext.DataRow["numerator"]) ;

///read denominator from table
decimal denominator = Convert.ToDecimal(
    (double)TestContext.DataRow["denominator"]);

///read expected result from table
decimal expected = Convert.ToDecimal(
    (double)TestContext.DataRow["result"]);

decimal actual;
actual = Decimal.Round (target.Divide(
    numerator, denominator),2);

Assert.AreEqual(expected, actual,
    "UnitTestingWinApp.Calculations.Divide did not
    return the expected value.");
}
```

UNIT-TESTING WEB APPLICATIONS

Creating unit tests for ASP.NET applications has traditionally been difficult. Although there are third-party tools available for testing Web applications, the *integrated* set of test tools offered by VSTS provides unmatched benefits in terms of interoperability, management, reporting, execution, and usability. Although you could factor out and independently test some code that belongs to a typical Web application, you still need the ability to test the application code (especially the user interface-related code) inside the native ASP.NET environment. Since the UI (User Interface) code uses Web controls and sometimes built-in classes like HttpContext, Request, and Response (these classes are often also used by UI helper classes), you'll find it difficult to effectively test your code outside the ASP.NET worker process.

Although VSTS can create unit tests for code files located in the App_Code directory, it lacks the ability to automatically generate unit tests for aspx pages. Later in the chapter, we present a workaround for testing aspx pages. We feel that the ability to test aspx pages is an important need that you'll encounter in your development process.

Creating Unit Tests for Class Files

Start by creating a simple Web application. The sample IIS Web application (see Figure 8.18) accepts two numbers and displays the result of dividing the first number by the second (see Figure 8.19). The code-behind class is shown in Listing 8.10.

The helper class that does the actual work is identical to the one used earlier for unit testing Windows applications (see Listing 8.1). The helper class is located in the App_Code subdirectory under the root folder.

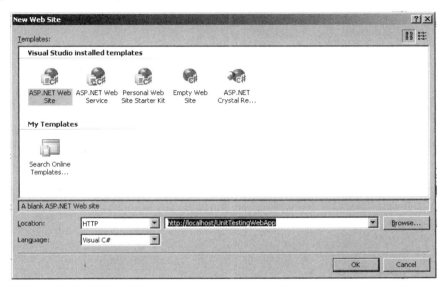

FIGURE 8.18   Create an ASP.NET Web Site under IIS to test unit-testing functionality.

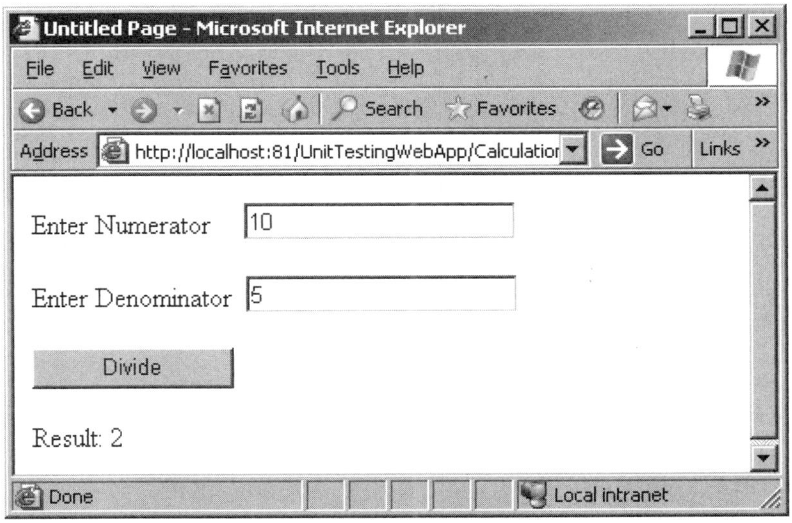

FIGURE 8.19   User interface for test application.

LISTING 8.10 Source Code for the Code-Behind Class

```
using System;
using System.Data;
using System.Configuration;
using System.Collections;
using System.Web;
using System.Web.Security;
using System.Web.UI;
using System.Web.UI.WebControls;
using System.Web.UI.WebControls.WebParts;
using System.Web.UI.HtmlControls;
using UnitTestingWebApp;

public partial class Default2 : System.Web.UI.Page
{
  protected void Page_Load(object sender, EventArgs e)
  {
  }
  protected void btnDivide_Click(object sender, EventArgs e)
  {
    //extract numerator and denominator values
    decimal numerator = Decimal.Parse(txtNumerator.Text);
    decimal denominator = Decimal.Parse(txtDenominator.Text);

    //call Helper class to perform division
    Calculations calculations = new Calculations();
    decimal result = calculations.Divide(numerator, denominator);

    //show result
    lblResult.Text = "Result: " + result.ToString();
  }
}
```

Open the Calculations class, right-click the class name, and choose Create Unit Tests from the drop-down menu. In the Create Unit Tests dialog box, make sure all target methods are checked. Only the class files resident in the App_Code directory are available for unit testing. VSTS automatically generates a unit test class, as shown in Listing 8.11.

LISTING 8.11 Source Code of Autogenerated Class for Testing Web Applications

```
using Microsoft.VisualStudio.TestTools.UnitTesting;
using System;
using System.Text;
using System.Collections.Generic;
using Microsoft.VisualStudio.TestTools.UnitTesting.Web;
namespace UnitTestingWebAppTest
```

```
{
/// <summary>
///This is a test class for UnitTestingWebApp.Calculations
///and is intended
///to contain all UnitTestingWebApp.Calculations Unit Tests
///</summary>
[TestClass()]
public class CalculationsTest
{
  private TestContext testContextInstance;

  /// <summary>
  /// Gets or sets the test context which provides
  /// information about and functionality for
  /// the current test run.
  ///</summary>
  public TestContext TestContext
  {
    get
    {
      return testContextInstance;
    }
    set
    {
      testContextInstance = value;
    }
  }
  #region Additional test attributes
  #endregion

  /// <summary>
  /// A test for Divide (decimal, decimal)
  /// </summary>
  [TestMethod()]
  [HostType("ASP.NET")]
  [UrlToTest("http://localhost/UnitTestingWebApp/
      Calculations.aspx")]
  public void DivideTest()
  {
    object target = UnitTestingWebAppTest
        .UnitTestingWebApp_CalculationsAccessor.CreatePrivate();
    UnitTestingWebAppTest.UnitTestingWebApp_CalculationsAccessor
        accessor = new UnitTestingWebAppTest
        .UnitTestingWebApp_CalculationsAccessor(target);

    decimal numerator = 0; // TODO: Initialize to
                           //an appropriate value
```

```csharp
    decimal denominator = 0; // TODO: Initialize to an
                             // appropriate value

    decimal expected = 0;
    decimal actual;

    actual = accessor.Divide(numerator, denominator);

    Assert.AreEqual(expected, actual,
        "UnitTestingWebApp.Calculations.Divide did not
        return the expected value.");
    Assert.Inconclusive("Verify the correctness of
        this test method.");
}

/// <summary>
/// A test for pIsZero (decimal)
/// </summary>
[TestMethod()]
[HostType("ASP.NET")]
[UrlToTest("http://localhost/UnitTestingWebApp/
    Calculations.aspx")]
public void pIsZeroTest()
{
  object target = UnitTestingWebAppTest
      .UnitTestingWebApp_CalculationsAccessor.CreatePrivate();

  UnitTestingWebAppTest.UnitTestingWebApp_CalculationsAccessor
      accessor = new UnitTestingWebAppTest
      .UnitTestingWebApp_CalculationsAccessor(target);

  decimal denominator = 0; // TODO: Initialize to an
                           // appropriate value

  bool expected = false;
  bool actual;

  actual = accessor.pIsZero(denominator);

  Assert.AreEqual(expected, actual,
      "UnitTestingWebApp.Calculations.pIsZero did not
      return the expected value.");
  Assert.Inconclusive("Verify the correctness of
      this test method.");
}

/// <summary>
/// A test for Precision
```

```
/// </summary>
[TestMethod()]
[HostType("ASP.NET")]
[UrlToTest("http://localhost/UnitTestingWebApp/
    Calculations.aspx")]
public void PrecisionTest()
{
  object target = UnitTestingWebAppTest
      .UnitTestingWebApp_CalculationsAccessor.CreatePrivate();

  int val = 0; // TODO: Assign to an appropriate
               // value for the property
  UnitTestingWebAppTest.UnitTestingWebApp_CalculationsAccessor
      accessor = new UnitTestingWebAppTest
      .UnitTestingWebApp_CalculationsAccessor(target);

  accessor.Precision = val;
  Assert.AreEqual(val, accessor.Precision, "UnitTestingWebApp
      .Calculations.Precision was not set correctly.");
  Assert.Inconclusive("Verify the correctness of
      this test method.");

  }
 }
 }
```

The autogenerated test class contains the necessary attributes for testing the target Web application. However, as in the case of the autogenerated test class for Windows applications, you need to make a few changes:

■ Change the values of input parameters for targets methods as appropriate; VSTS initializes all variables to their default values.
■ Insert appropriate Assert statements to compare the actual output with expected output.
■ Make sure UrlToTestAttribute points to a valid page; if this attribute is not set correctly, you'll encounter all sorts of errors.

Once the above changes are made, run the tests from Test Manager or Test View. You can also obtain code coverage information in a manner similar to that of Windows applications.

Creating Unit Tests for ASPX Pages

By default, VSTS does not allow you to unit-test methods in an ASP.NET page. However, you can get around this limitation by using custom programming. The workaround is based on the RequestedPage property of the TestContext class. The RequestedPage property provides a reference to the target page specified in Url-ToTestAttribute. Once you obtain a reference to the current page, you can look up the Web controls on that page, set their property values, and invoke event handlers. Event handlers can be called by wrapping the page class in a Microsoft.VisualStudio.TestTools.UnitTesting.PrivateObject class and calling the Invoke method provided by PrivateObject. We used the same technique earlier (using a different overloaded constructor for Invoke) for executing private target methods. The technique is demonstrated in Listing 8.12.

LISTING 8.12   Test Method for Unit-Testing ASP.NET Web Pages

```
[TestMethod()]
[HostType("ASP.NET")]
[UrlToTest("http://localhost:81/UnitTestingWebApp
    /Calculations.aspx")]
public void TestWebPage()
{
  Page page = TestContext.RequestedPage;
  TextBox txtNumerator =
      (TextBox)page.FindControl("txtNumerator");
  TextBox txtDenominator =
      (TextBox)page.FindControl("txtDenominator");
  Label lblResult = (Label)page.FindControl("lblResult");

  Button btnDivide = (Button)page.FindControl("btnDivide");

  txtNumerator.Text = "10";
  txtDenominator.Text = "2";
  PrivateObject po = new PrivateObject(page);
  po.Invoke("btnDivide_Click", btnDivide, EventArgs.Empty);
  Assert.AreEqual("Result: 5", lblResult.Text ,"Division Error");
}
```

Running Unit Tests in ASP.NET Development Server

When testing a Web site that is running under ASP.NET Development Server, mark the test method with an additional attribute named AspNetDevelopmentServerHostAttribute. The modified attribute section of the test method is shown in Listing 8.13.

LISTING 8.13   Attributes Required for Test Methods Targeting Web Applications Running Under ASP.NET Development Server

```
[TestMethod()]
[HostType("ASP.NET")]
[UrlToTest("http://localhost/UnitTestingWebApp/
    Calculations.aspx")]
[AspNetDevelopmentServerHost(
    "%PathToWebRoot%\\UnitTestingWebApp",
    "/UnitTestingWebApp")]
```

For information on how VSTS interprets the `%PathToWebRoot%` variable, visit *http://msdn2.microsoft.com/en-us/library/ms243136.aspx#SettingPathToWebApp*.

Debugging ASP.NET Unit Tests

Sooner or later, you'll need to debug the test code. However, unlike the test code for Windows applications, the test code for ASP.NET projects can't be debugged by simply inserting a breakpoint in the test class and executing the test project with the Debug option enabled. Since the code is executed in a separate process, the breakpoint will not be hit. In order to debug the test code, attach the debugger to the remote process. On the Debug menu, click Attach to Process. In the Attach to Process dialog box, select the appropriate process (either IIS worker process or the correct ASP.NET Development Server instance), and click Attach (see Figure 8.20).

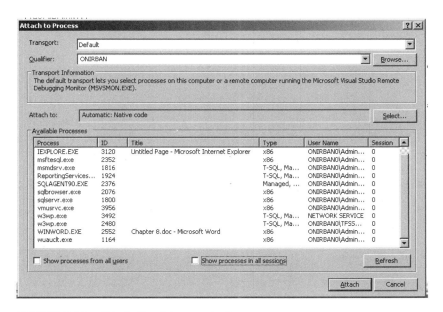

FIGURE 8.20   Attach the debugger to the process.

Since the ASP.NET project could be running under IIS or ASP.NET Development Server, do one of the following:

1. If the target project is running under IIS, attach the debugger to the correct worker process.
2. If the target project is running under ASP.NET Development Server, the process is slightly more involved. Since ASP.NET Development Server instances are dynamically created and destroyed for each test run, you can't attach the debugger to a process before launching the test. Consequently, start the test run (with Debug on of course), and pause it as soon as you see the ASP.NET Development Server instantiated (it'll show up on the taskbar). The pause option is available in the Debug toolbar. Once ASP.NET Development Server is launched and the debugger is paused, you can attach the debugger to the correct ASP.NET Development Server instance. It is a bit circuitous, perhaps, but it works.

UNIT-TESTING WEB SERVICES

Creating unit tests for Web services is straightforward. To review the steps involved, create a simple Web service under ASP.NET Development Server for performing divisions over the Web, as shown in Listing 8.14.

LISTING 8.14   A Simple Web Service Created for Examining Unit-Testing Functionality

```
using System;
using System.Web;
using System.Web.Services;
using System.Web.Services.Protocols;

[WebService(Namespace = "http://CRM.Outsourcing.Chapter8")]
[WebServiceBinding(ConformsTo = WsiProfiles.BasicProfile1_1)]
public class CalculationService : System.Web.Services.WebService
{
  public CalculationService ()
  {
    //Uncomment the following line if using designed components
    //InitializeComponent();
  }
  [WebMethod]
  public decimal Calculate(decimal numerator,
      decimal denominator)
  {
```

```
    //create Helper class and delegate work
    Calculations calculations = new Calculations();
    decimal result = calculations.Divide(numerator, denominator);
    return result;
  }
}
```

Right-click anywhere in the code window and select Create Unit Tests from the drop-down menu. VSTS will generate the test class shown in Listing 8.15.

LISTING 8.15   Autogenerated Test Class for Testing a Web Service

```
// The following code was generated by Microsoft
// Visual Studio 2005.
// The test owner should check each test for validity.
using Microsoft.VisualStudio.TestTools.UnitTesting;
using System;
using System.Text;
using System.Collections.Generic;
using Microsoft.VisualStudio.TestTools.UnitTesting.Web;
using UnitTestingWebService_Local_Test.localhost;

namespace UnitTestingWebService_Local_Test
{
/// <summary>
/// This is a test class for UnitTestingWebService_Local_Test
///.localhost.CalculationService and is intended
/// to contain all UnitTestingWebService_Local_Test
///.localhost.CalculationService Unit Tests
/// </summary>
[TestClass()]
public class CalculationServiceTest
{

  /// ... routine code omitted ...

  /// <summary>
  /// A test for Calculate (decimal, decimal)
  /// </summary>
  [TestMethod()]
  public void CalculateTest()
  {
    CalculationService target = new CalculationService();
    // TODO: Use [AspNetDevelopmentServer] and
    // TryUrlRedirection() to auto launch and bind web service.

    decimal numerator = 0;
    // TODO: Initialize to an appropriate value
```

```
            decimal denominator = 0;
            // TODO: Initialize to an appropriate value
            decimal expected = 0;
            decimal actual;
            actual = target.Calculate(numerator, denominator);
            Assert.AreEqual(expected, actual,
                "UnitTestingWebService_Local_Test.localhost
                .CalculationService.Calculate did not " +
                "return the expected value.");
            Assert.Inconclusive("Verify the correctness
                of this test method.");
        }
    }
}
```

Modifying Autogenerated Test Classes

Make the following changes to the test class:

- Specify values for input parameters (as well as expected value), and change Assert classes as appropriate.
- If running the web service in ASP.NET Development Server, mark the test method with AspNetDevelopmentServerAttribute. This attribute is used to automatically launch the ASP.NET Development Server.
- If running the web service in ASP.NET Development Server, call the TryUrlRedirection method (offered by the WebServiceHelper class) from the test method. The method call enables the Web service to dynamically point to the specified URL. If this method is not invoked, the Web service will point to the URL specified in the Web reference.

When invoked from the command line (via MSTest.exe), specifying AspNet-DevelopmentServerAttribute and calling the TryUrlRedirection method are essential. Otherwise, the tests do not run from the command line, such as during an automated build process. However, if the target Web service is running under IIS or on a remote machine, it is not necessary to add AspNetDevelopmentServer-Attribute or to call the TryUrlRedirection method.

The modified code for testing a Web service under ASP.NET Development Server is shown in Listing 8.16.

LISTING 8.16   Modified Autogenerated Test Class for Testing a Web Service

```
/// <summary>
/// A test for Calculate (decimal, decimal)
```

```
/// </summary>
[TestMethod()]
[AspNetDevelopmentServer("CalculationServer",
    "%PathToWebRoot%\\UnitTestingWebService")]
public void CalculateTest()
{
  CalculationService target = new CalculationService();
  // TODO: Use [AspNetDevelopmentServer] and TryUrlRedirection()
  //to auto launch and bind web service.
  WebServiceHelper.TryUrlRedirection (target, this.TestContext,
      "CalculationServer");

  decimal numerator = 10;
  decimal denominator = 2;
  decimal expected = 5;
  decimal actual;
  actual = target.Calculate(numerator, denominator);
  Assert.AreEqual(expected, actual,
      "UnitTestingWebService_Local_Test
      .localhost.CalculationService.Calculate did not " +
      "return the expected value.");
}
```

CONCLUSION

An effective testing strategy reduces execution risk. Functional as well as nonfunctional requirements need to be verified early, continually, and comprehensively. Unit testing, despite its shortcomings, has become a core component of agile and iterative development methodologies. Creating unit-test cases is no longer an afterthought, but is integrated into the process of writing source code. Of course, passing unit tests is a necessary task, but it is not a sufficient condition for success. The software still has to be tested from functional, nonfunctional, system, integration, and business standpoints. That's why SQA teams are engaged in the project from inception, and the data generated from their efforts drives release decisions at every iteration.

When it comes to offshore development, creation and execution of effective test cases becomes doubly important, given the physical separation between end users and development teams. Properly constructed test cases help clarify requirements, eliminate confusion, and simplify communication between distributed stakeholders. Yes, it requires up-front effort to create and maintain meaningful test cases, but this exercise helps reduce friction and wasted efforts, especially when you don't have the luxury of high-fidelity face-to-face communication. Test cases should become part of the specification.

From a project management standpoint, it is necessary for the tests to be run at offshore as well as on-site locations. The results of test execution need to be communicated to various stakeholders at appropriate levels of granularity, and decisions need to be made based upon meaningful analysis of the data. Of course, everything can be achieved if you invest enough time and resources; but in real life—where we operate under resource constraints and deadline pressures—the key question is whether the quality metrics can be generated, processed, and disseminated with minimal overhead.

VSTS provides a testing framework that simplifies creation, management, and execution of test cases. The test results are captured in the data warehouse and become available for analysis using SQL Server 2005 Reporting Services reports. The project portal provides access to all custom and built-in reports. Distributed stakeholders can view current and historical metrics and trends using nothing more than a Web browser. We feel that the VSTS infrastructure offers the capability to dramatically streamline the way you run offshore projects.

9 Enterprise Reporting

In This Chapter

- Overview of TFS Data Warehouse
- Using Excel for Ad-hoc Reporting
- Exploring Selected Built-In Reports
- Customizing Reports
- Exploring Selected Custom Reports
- Delivering Reports
- Overview of Team System Cube Design
- Examining Cube Structure in Detail
- Refreshing Cube Data

INTRODUCTION

Reports enable you to keep your finger on the pulse of outsourced projects. In globally sourced projects—where you do not have the luxury of walking over and asking team members how everything is going—meaningful reports allow you to understand what's going on, identify choke points, and forecast outcomes. Useful reports reveal trends and provide insight into underlying causes—patterns often missed by people who are busy with day-to-day operations. Despite the importance of analyzing key metrics regarding project health, traditionally it has been difficult to collect and process this data without incurring significant overhead. In many organizations, the project management staff spends a huge amount of time gathering, evaluating, formatting, and disseminating status information. A lot of this work is repetitive and recurring. As stakeholders demand more and more custom-tailored information in their attempt to gain visibility, the project management staff quickly becomes bogged down. Performing routine, time-consuming, high-overhead reporting work often prevents the project management team from identifying the *real* problems and bottlenecks.

In offshore projects, the friction associated with long-distance status reporting often prevents stakeholders from receiving timely information and making necessary course corrections. One of the key frustrations associated with outsourced projects is lack of visibility. The effort and expense associated with obtaining detailed visibility on a sustained basis (sometimes on a daily basis) are just too high. Furthermore, since data collection and reporting are often done manually, the information is prone to human errors. Asking programmers, "What have you done this week?" is not the best way to collect factual data.

VSTS provides powerful data analysis and reporting capabilities. The project data is stored in relational and analytical databases, and is available for analysis in a variety of ways. You can analyze the information using a front-end tool like Excel, or leverage the enterprise-class reporting infrastructure offered by SQL Server 2005 Reporting Services (referred to simply as "Reporting Services"). In additional to running predefined standard reports, you can create custom reports using Visual Studio 2005. Custom reports can be used to identify trends, to drill down specific areas, or to create different views and levels of aggregations for various stakeholders. Reports are the primary mechanism to regularly disseminate project health metrics without manual intervention. Although in reality there are always critical exceptions and problematic boundary conditions that need to be resolved via human intervention, you'll be able to focus on the important problems while VSTS takes care of the routine status-reporting activities. Now *that* is progress.

OVERVIEW OF THE TFS DATA WAREHOUSE

Team Foundation Server captures project-related information via service-specific adapters and stores them in back-end databases (see Figure 9.1). The primary relational database is named TFSWarehouse. Although there are other relational databases, such as TFSWorkItemTracking, TFSVersionControl, TFSBuild, and so forth, they are not meant for public access at this time. The main analytical database is also called TFSWarehouse and contains pre-aggregated measures and dimensions.

At regular intervals, an application tier Web service named WarehouseController.asmx runs the adapters and refreshes the relational and Online Analytical Processing (OLAP) databases with current data. The Web service also makes necessary schema changes in the databases, if needed, to incorporate work item customizations in the process template.

Most of the time, you'll be accessing the OLAP database for your reporting needs. However, for advanced requirements, you may need to access the relational database, as well.

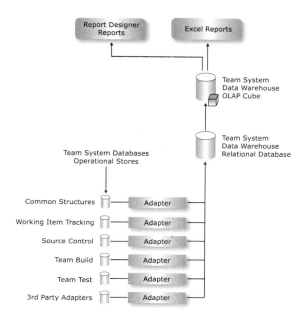

FIGURE 9.1   Project information is captured via adapters, and stored in a relational database and in an OLAP data warehouse.

To view the data stores, launch SQL Server Management Studio. Connect to Database Engine to see the relational databases. Connect to Analysis Services to view the OLAP databases (see Figure 9.2 and Figure 9.3).

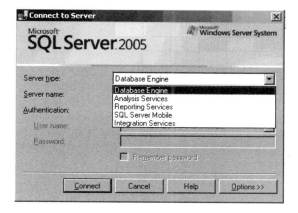

FIGURE 9.2   Connect Object Explorer to the appropriate server type to view relational and OLAP databases.

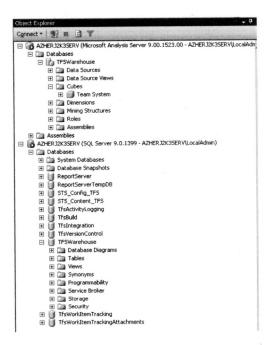

FIGURE 9.3 Both relational and OLAP databases can be viewed in Object Explorer.

USING EXCEL FOR AD-HOC REPORTING

The project-related information stored in relational and analytical databases can be viewed using front-end tools, such as Microsoft Excel. For quick, ad-hoc reporting, this approach provides a simple but effective solution, since you don't need any specialized skills, such as knowledge of how to write MDX queries. Let's walk through an example.

In Excel, on the Data menu, point to Import External Data and click New Database Query. Click OLAP Cubes tab and create a new data source (see Figure 9.4). Specify the connection information in the Multidimensional Connection 9.0 dialog box. The perspectives defined in the Team System cube appear as distinct cubes in Excel (more on this later in the chapter). In the Create New Data Source dialog box, choose a cube (actually a perspective defined in SQL Server 2005 Analysis Services), depending on what aspect of the project data you plan to analyze. Excel creates a pivot table based on the selected cube (see Figure 9.5).

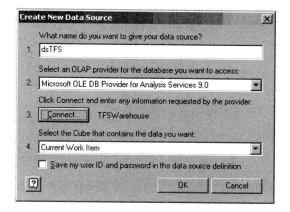

FIGURE 9.4   Create a new data source to connect to TFSWarehouse cube.

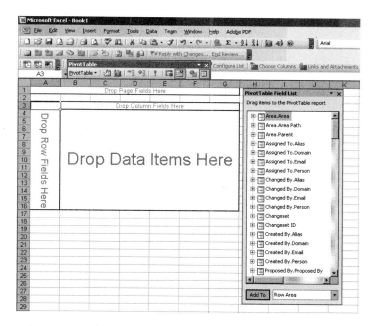

FIGURE 9.5   The Team System cube is available for analysis in Excel.

Once the data is available in Excel, you can analyze the information using Excel's native pivot table capabilities. Drag-and-drop fields from the PivotTable Field List to create a custom pivot table (see Figure 9.6). You can also generate charts (see Figure 9.7) by clicking the Chart Wizard button in the PivotTable toolbar.

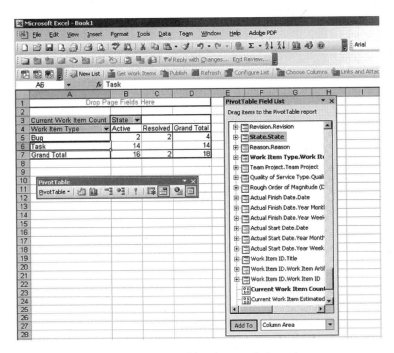

FIGURE 9.6 Pivot table created by drag-and-dropping measures and dimensions from the Team System cube.

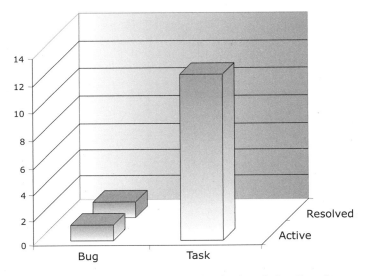

FIGURE 9.7 Pivot table data can be displayed visually using the Chart Wizard.

EXPLORING SELECTED BUILT-IN REPORTS

In this section, we explore some of the predefined reports available out-of-the-box in the MSF for Agile Software Development - v4.0 process template. These reports provide summary as well as detailed information regarding the health of your project. You can learn about the status of various tasks, allocation of resources, number of open and resolved bugs, outcome of various tests, build results, and so on. Since the reports can also be viewed from the project portal, stakeholders and goal-donors can monitor the execution of outsourced projects over the Web from anywhere in the world. We find this capability very exciting.

Bug Rates

One of the most closely tracked metrics is the number of bugs in the software. Perhaps more than anything else, this key number drives resource allocation, release planning, and customer satisfaction. The Bug Rates report shows the count of total number of active bugs, newly activated bugs, and resolved fixed bugs (see Figure 9.8).

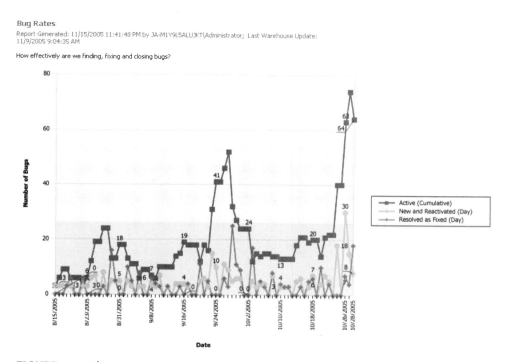

FIGURE 9.8   The Bug Rates report shows bug discovery and resolution information.

How it Works

■ To determine the total number of active bugs, the report sums up the [Cumulative Count] measure.

■ To determine the count for new and reactivated bugs on a particular day, the report aggregates the [State Change Count] measure for currently active bugs. Bugs can be active because they are newly discovered, or reactivated from resolved or closed states. The [State Change Count] measure is incremented each time the state of the bug changes.

■ To determine the count for resolved (fixed) bugs, the report aggregates the [State Change Count] measure for those bugs.

Figure 9.9 shows the structure of the underlying dataset for this report (row variables are Date, State, and Reason).

			Work Item Count	State Change Count
8/15/2005	Active	Accepted	(null)	(null)
8/15/2005	Active	Closed in Error	(null)	(null)
8/15/2005	Active	New	3	3
8/15/2005	Active	Regression	(null)	(null)
8/15/2005	Resolved	Fixed	(null)	(null)
8/16/2005	Active	Accepted	(null)	(null)
8/16/2005	Active	Closed in Error	(null)	(null)
8/16/2005	Active	New	6	3
8/16/2005	Active	Regression	(null)	(null)
8/16/2005	Resolved	Fixed	(null)	(null)
8/17/2005	Active	Accepted	(null)	(null)
8/17/2005	Active	Closed in Error	(null)	(null)
8/17/2005	Active	New	9	3
8/17/2005	Active	Regression	(null)	(null)
8/17/2005	Resolved	Fixed	(null)	(null)
8/18/2005	Active	Accepted	(null)	(null)
8/18/2005	Active	Closed in Error	(null)	(null)
8/18/2005	Active	New	9	3
8/18/2005	Active	Regression	(null)	(null)
8/18/2005	Resolved	Fixed	3	3

FIGURE 9.9 Underlying data structure for the Bug Rates report.

Bugs by Priority

Once you have a general idea about bug counts from the Bug Rates report, you'll want to drill down and get a better idea about the importance of the outstanding bugs. If the bugs are mostly trivial, you'll be less concerned about the quality of the software than if the bugs are of high importance. The Bugs by Priority report breaks down the number of total, newly activated, and resolved bugs by priority, and displays the numbers for each day (see Figure 9.10).

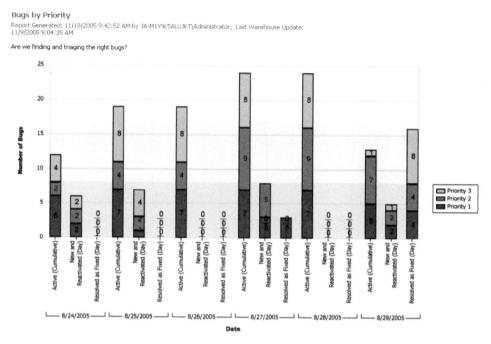

Bugs by Priority
Report Generated: 11/18/2005 9:42:52 AM by JA-M1Y9L5ALUJKT\Administrator; Last Warehouse Update: 11/9/2005 9:04:35 AM

Are we finding and triaging the right bugs?

FIGURE 9.10   The Bugs by Priority report shows bug discovery and resolution information.

How it Works

Behind the scenes, the MDX operations are similar to the Bug Rates report, with the addition of priority as a row dimension. Figure 9.11 shows the structure of the underlying dataset for this report (row variables are Date, State, Reason, and Priority).

Project Velocity

The Project Velocity report shows how fast work items are being fixed by developers and closed by SQA professionals (see Figure 9.12). This report gives you a sense of how fast work is being done. You can filter the data to show specific work item types, such as bugs, tasks, and requirements. You can also change the granularity of the time dimension by selecting daily, weekly, or monthly views of the data. The report also shows the average number of bugs resolved within a given time span. You can use this metric to determine productivity of the development team as well as to predict how long it might take to resolve the currently active work items.

				Work Item Count	State Change Count
8/24/2005	Active	Accepted	1	(null)	(null)
8/24/2005	Active	Accepted	2	(null)	(null)
8/24/2005	Active	Accepted	3	(null)	(null)
8/24/2005	Active	Closed in Error	1	(null)	(null)
8/24/2005	Active	Closed in Error	2	(null)	(null)
8/24/2005	Active	Closed in Error	3	(null)	(null)
8/24/2005	Active	New	1	5	1
8/24/2005	Active	New	2	2	2
8/24/2005	Active	New	3	4	2
8/24/2005	Active	Regression	1	1	1
8/24/2005	Active	Regression	2	(null)	(null)
8/24/2005	Active	Regression	3	(null)	(null)
8/24/2005	Resolved	Fixed	1	2	(null)
8/24/2005	Resolved	Fixed	2	2	(null)
8/24/2005	Resolved	Fixed	3	2	(null)
8/25/2005	Active	Accepted	1	(null)	(null)
8/25/2005	Active	Accepted	2	(null)	(null)
8/25/2005	Active	Accepted	3	(null)	(null)
8/25/2005	Active	Closed in Error	1	(null)	(null)
8/25/2005	Active	Closed in Error	2	(null)	(null)

FIGURE 9.11 Underlying data structure for the Bugs by Priority report.

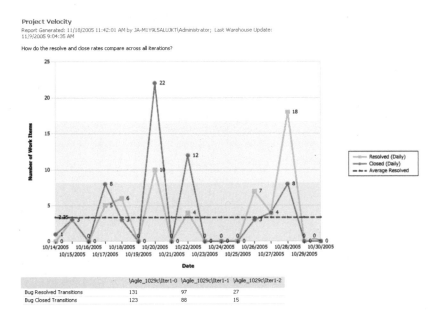

Project Velocity

Report Generated: 11/18/2005 11:42:01 AM by JA-M1Y9L5ALUJKT\Administrator; Last Warehouse Update: 11/9/2005 9:04:35 AM

How do the resolve and close rates compare across all iterations?

	\Agile_1029c\Iter1-0	\Agile_1029c\Iter1-1	\Agile_1029c\Iter1-2
Bug Resolved Transitions	131	97	27
Bug Closed Transitions	123	88	15

FIGURE 9.12 The Project Velocity Report shows how fast the project is moving forward.

How it Works

This report works by using the [State Change Count] measure for resolved and closed bugs. To calculate the averages, the [State Change Count] measure is divided by the number of days, weeks, or months. The structure of the Date dimension makes this calculation easy, since it contains separate hierarchies for Year/Month and Year/Week (see Figure 9.13).

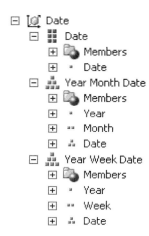

FIGURE 9.13 Hierarchies in the Date dimension.

Figure 9.14 shows the structure of the underlying dataset for this report (row variables are Date, Week, Month, and State).

				DailyAverageTransitionCount	WeeklyAverageTransitionCount	MonthlyAverageTransitionCount	State Change Count
10/14/2005	Week of 10/9/2005	October, 2005	Resolved	3.35294117647059	16.75	102	(null)
10/14/2005	Week of 10/9/2005	October, 2005	Closed	3.76470588235294	20.75	161	1
10/15/2005	Week of 10/9/2005	October, 2005	Resolved	3.35294117647059	16.75	102	3
10/15/2005	Week of 10/9/2005	October, 2005	Closed	3.76470588235294	20.75	161	3
10/16/2005	Week of 10/16/2005	October, 2005	Resolved	3.35294117647059	16.75	102	(null)
10/16/2005	Week of 10/16/2005	October, 2005	Closed	3.76470588235294	20.75	161	(null)
10/17/2005	Week of 10/16/2005	October, 2005	Resolved	3.35294117647059	16.75	102	5
10/17/2005	Week of 10/16/2005	October, 2005	Closed	3.76470588235294	20.75	161	8
10/18/2005	Week of 10/16/2005	October, 2005	Resolved	3.35294117647059	16.75	102	6
10/18/2005	Week of 10/16/2005	October, 2005	Closed	3.76470588235294	20.75	161	3
10/19/2005	Week of 10/16/2005	October, 2005	Resolved	3.35294117647059	16.75	102	(null)
10/19/2005	Week of 10/16/2005	October, 2005	Closed	3.76470588235294	20.75	161	(null)
10/20/2005	Week of 10/16/2005	October, 2005	Resolved	3.35294117647059	16.75	102	10
10/20/2005	Week of 10/16/2005	October, 2005	Closed	3.76470588235294	20.75	161	22
10/21/2005	Week of 10/16/2005	October, 2005	Resolved	3.35294117647059	16.75	102	0
10/21/2005	Week of 10/16/2005	October, 2005	Closed	3.76470588235294	20.75	161	0
10/22/2005	Week of 10/16/2005	October, 2005	Resolved	3.35294117647059	16.75	102	4
10/22/2005	Week of 10/16/2005	October, 2005	Closed	3.76470588235294	20.75	161	12
10/23/2005	Week of 10/23/2005	October, 2005	Resolved	3.35294117647059	16.75	102	(null)
10/23/2005	Week of 10/23/2005	October, 2005	Closed	3.76470588235294	20.75	161	(null)

FIGURE 9.14 Underlying data structure for the Project Velocity report.

Work Items

The Work Items report is a workhorse report that you'll probably use many times (see Figure 9.15). It provides a listing of all work items recorded in the system, subject to various filter conditions (see Figure 9.16). You can filter by state, person the item is assigned to, reason, priority, and so forth, and customize the report to your needs. The entries in the Id column are hyperlinked; clicking on a work item Id opens up an Internet Explorer window containing additional details.

Work Items

Report Generated: 11/18/2005 3:08:11 PM by JA-M1Y9L5ALUJKT\Administrator; Last Warehouse Update: 11/9/2005 9:04:35 AM

What are our current work items?

ID	Assigned To	State	Reason	Rem. Hrs.	WI Type	Priority	Title
82	robot_dev_1_10	Active	Regression	0	Bug	1	Bug66, Filed day 1
83	robot_test_1_7	Active	Regression	0	Bug	3	Bug67, Filed day 1
85	robot_test_1_6	Resolved	Fixed	0	Bug	2	Bug69, Filed day 2
86	robot_dev_1_6	Active	Regression	0	Bug	2	Bug70, Filed day 2
87	robot_test_1_3	Active	Regression	0	Bug	3	Bug71, Filed day 2
89	robot_dev_1_9	Active	Regression	0	Bug	1	Bug73, Filed day 3
90	robot_test_1_7	Resolved	Fixed	0	Bug	2	Bug74, Filed day 3
91	robot_dev_1_9	Active	Regression	0	Bug	2	Bug75, Filed day 4
93	robot_dev_1_8	Resolved	Fixed	0	Bug	2	Bug77, Filed day 4
97	robot_dev_1_12	Active	Regression	0	Bug	1	Bug81, Filed day 8
102	robot_test_1_7	Active	Regression	0	Bug	1	Bug86, Filed day 9
103	robot_dev_1_11	Resolved	Fixed	0	Bug	3	Bug87, Filed day 10
105	robot_dev_1_9	Active	Regression	0	Bug	2	Bug89, Filed day 10
107	robot_dev_1_11	Active	Regression	0	Bug	3	Bug91, Filed day 10
109	robot_dev_1_6	Resolved	Fixed	0	Bug	3	Bug93, Filed day 11
110	robot_test_1_6	Active	Regression	0	Bug	3	Bug94, Filed day 11
111	robot_test_1_6	Resolved	Fixed	0	Bug	2	Bug95, Filed day 11
117	robot_test_1_5	Active	Regression	0	Bug	1	Bug101, Filed day 13
118	Tom Patton	Active	New	0	Bug	2	TestMethod1: Bug created for the test
119	Tom Patton	Active	New	0	Bug	2	TestMethod3: Bug created for the test
120	Tom Patton	Active	New	0	Bug	2	TestMethod4: Bug created for the test
125	robot_test_1_6	Active	Regression	0	Bug	1	Bug106, Filed day 15
129	robot_dev_1_2	Active	Regression	0	Bug	2	Bug110, Filed day 16
133	robot_dev_1_6	Active	Regression	0	Bug	1	Bug114, Filed day 17
136	robot_dev_1_7	Resolved	Fixed	0	Bug	3	Bug117, Filed day 19
138	robot_pm_1_2	Active	Regression	0	Bug	1	Bug119, Filed day 19
140	robot_dev_1_1	Active	Regression	0	Bug	2	Bug121, Filed day 19

FIGURE 9.15 The Work Items report.

ExplicitProject	Agile_1029c	Iteration	Agile_1029c
Area	Client	Work Item Type	All (No Filter)
Assigned To	All (No Filter)	State	Active, Resolved
Reason	All (No Filter)	Priority	All (No Filter)
Issue	All (No Filter)	Exit Criteria	All (No Filter)
Found In Build	All (No Filter)	Fixed In Build	All (No Filter)

FIGURE 9.16 Filter criteria for the Work Items report.

However, in version one of VSTS, although the Work Items report is available in the Report Server, it is not visible in Team Explorer. To make this report (as well as some other reports) available in Team Explorer, export the process template and open the ReportTasks.xml file (located in the Reports folder). Remove the `Hidden` property associated with the Work Items report. Upload the modified process template back to VSTS. You should now be able to see the Work Item report in Team Explorer for new team projects.

How it Works

This report fetches `[Work Item Url]`, `[Completed Work]`, and `[Remaining Work]` measures from Team System cube and slices the data based upon various filter conditions. Figure 9.17 shows the structure of the underlying dataset for this report (row variables are Id, Title, Assigned To, State, Reason, Priority, and Work Item Type).

							Work Item URL	Completed Work	Remaining Work
90	Bug74, Filed day 3	robot_test_1_7	Resolved	Fixed	2	Bug	http://tompat3:8080/WorkIte...	0	0
91	Bug75, Filed day 4	robot_dev_1_9	Active	Regression	2	Bug	http://tompat3:8080/WorkIte...	0	0
93	Bug77, Filed day 4	robot_dev_1_8	Resolved	Fixed	2	Bug	http://tompat3:8080/WorkIte...	0	0
97	Bug81, Filed day 8	robot_dev_1_12	Active	Regression	1	Bug	http://tompat3:8080/WorkIte...	0	0
102	Bug86, Filed day 9	robot_test_1_7	Active	Regression	1	Bug	http://tompat3:8080/WorkIte...	0	0
103	Bug87, Filed day 10	robot_dev_1_11	Resolved	Fixed	3	Bug	http://tompat3:8080/WorkIte...	0	0
105	Bug89, Filed day 10	robot_dev_1_9	Active	Regression	2	Bug	http://tompat3:8080/WorkIte...	0	0
107	Bug91, Filed day 10	robot_dev_1_11	Active	Regression	3	Bug	http://tompat3:8080/WorkIte...	0	0
109	Bug93, Filed day 11	robot_dev_1_6	Resolved	Fixed	3	Bug	http://tompat3:8080/WorkIte...	0	0
110	Bug94, Filed day 11	robot_test_1_6	Active	Regression	3	Bug	http://tompat3:8080/WorkIte...	0	0
111	Bug95, Filed day 11	robot_test_1_6	Resolved	Fixed	2	Bug	http://tompat3:8080/WorkIte...	0	0
117	Bug101, Filed day 13	robot_test_1_5	Active	Regression	1	Bug	http://tompat3:8080/WorkIte...	0	0
118	TestMethod1: Bug cre...	Tom Patton	Active	New	2	Bug	http://tompat3:8080/WorkIte...	0	0
119	TestMethod3: Bug cre...	Tom Patton	Active	New	2	Bug	http://tompat3:8080/WorkIte...	0	0
120	TestMethod4: Bug cre...	Tom Patton	Active	New	2	Bug	http://tompat3:8080/WorkIte...	0	0
125	Bug106, Filed day 15	robot_test_1_6	Active	Regression	1	Bug	http://tompat3:8080/WorkIte...	0	0
129	Bug110, Filed day 16	robot_dev_1_2	Active	Regression	2	Bug	http://tompat3:8080/WorkIte...	0	0
133	Bug114, Filed day 17	robot_dev_1_6	Active	Regression	1	Bug	http://tompat3:8080/WorkIte...	0	0
136	Bug117, Filed day 19	robot_dev_1_7	Resolved	Fixed	3	Bug	http://tompat3:8080/WorkIte...	0	0
138	Bug119, Filed day 19	robot_pm_1_2	Active	Regression	1	Bug	http://tompat3:8080/WorkIte...	0	0

FIGURE 9.17   Underlying data structure for the Work Items report.

CUSTOMIZING REPORTS

Custom reports allow you to gain additional insight into the project status. You can tailor them to suit your unique organizational needs. You may choose to tweak existing reports or create new ones from scratch, depending on your requirements. Either way, you'll leverage SQL Server 2005 Reporting Services for report authoring, processing, and distribution. For more information on SQL Server 2005 Reporting Services, check out Microsoft Web site at *http://www.microsoft.com/sql/technologies/reporting/default.mspx*.

Editing Built-In Reports

In order to modify existing reports, you'll need to edit the corresponding report definition files (RDL files). To locate these files, export the MSF for Agile Software

Development - v4.0 process template (see Chapter 3, "Leveraging VSTS and Customizing MSF Agile," regarding how to export a process template). The RDL files are located in the Reports subfolder.

Alternatively, launch SQL Server Management Studio and connect to Reporting Services (see Figure 9.18). Expand the appropriate project node in Object Explorer, right-click the report you are interested in changing, and choose Edit Report from the drop-down menu (see Figure 9.19). Save the RDL file in a local folder.

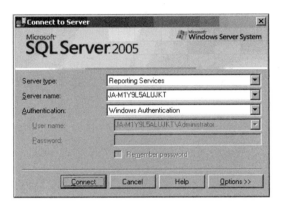

FIGURE 9.18 Connect to Reporting Services to view published reports.

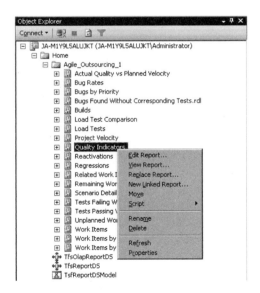

FIGURE 9.19 Choose Edit Report to save an RDL representation of the selected report.

Once you have the RDL file, create a new Report Server Project in SQL Server Business Intelligence Development Studio (see Figure 9.20).

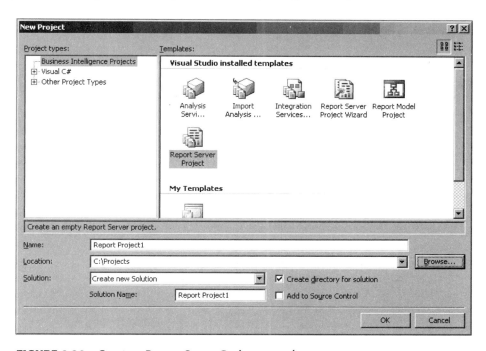

FIGURE 9.20   Create a Report Server Project to author reports.

Create two data sources (see Figure 9.21)—one named TfsReportDS for connecting to the relational database (see Figure 9.22) and another named TfsOlapReportDS for connecting to the multidimensional database (see Figure 9.23). Once the RDL files are added to the project, your solution will look similar to Figure 9.24. You can navigate to the Data and Layout tabs of the Report Designer and make changes as needed. The Preview tab shows a quick output based on your changes.

FIGURE 9.21   Data sources allow reports to connect to relational and multi-dimensional databases.

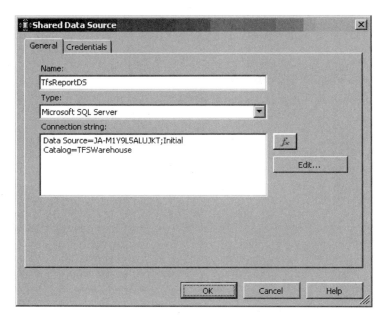

FIGURE 9.22   Choose Microsoft SQL Server as the data source type for TfsReportDS data source.

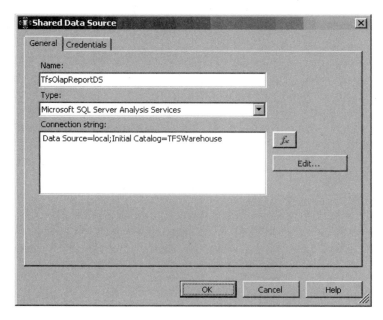

FIGURE 9.23   Choose Microsoft SQL Server Analysis Services as the data source type for TfsOlapReportDS data source.

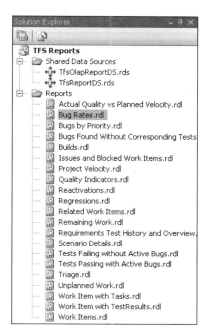

FIGURE 9.24   Default TFS reports loaded in a report server project.

When you are ready to publish your changes to the report server, first make sure that the deployment properties for the project contain correct values. On the Project menu, click (Your_Project_Name) Properties, and specify the deployment properties in the (Your_Project_Name) Properties dialog box (see Figure 9.25). To publish all reports as a group, right-click the top-level project node in Solution Explorer and select Deploy. The data sources will be optionally updated (depending upon deployment properties, as shown in Figure 9.25). Individual reports can also be published one at a time by right-clicking a specific report and selecting Deploy.

Creating New Reports

The process of creating new reports from scratch is similar to editing existing reports, as described in the previous section. Create a new Report Server Project and add data sources and reports. You can create new reports using the Report Wizard, or you can use a blank Report template (see Figure 9.26). For more information on report authoring, check out the MSDN "Designing and Creating Reports" topic at *http://msdn2.microsoft.com/en-us/library/ms159253(en-us,SQL.90).aspx*.

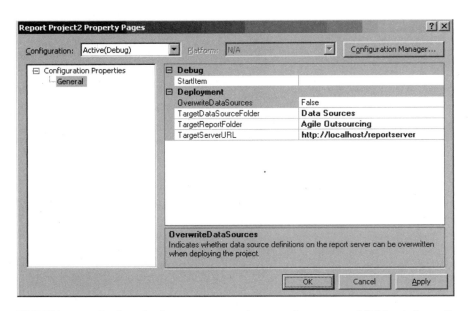

FIGURE 9.25 Project deployment properties contain report-publishing information.

FIGURE 9.26 Reports can be created from scratch or by using the Report Wizard.

SELECTED CUSTOM REPORTS

In this section, we create a few custom reports to gather additional insight into project health and progress. For outsourced projects, these reports take on added importance, since you have fewer informal avenues to feel the 'pulse' of the project. The full source code of the custom reports is available on the CD-ROM.

Average Bug-Fixing Time

Although bugs vary in complexity and scope, project managers are often interested in how long it takes a developer to resolve bugs, on the average. Given a reasonably long operational history, this information helps evaluate a developer's performance as well as provides a ball-park estimate of the time required to resolve currently outstanding bugs.

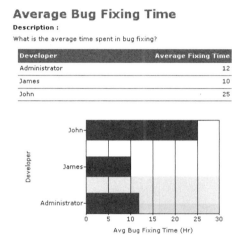

Average Bug Fixing Time

Description :

What is the average time spent in bug fixing?

Developer	Average Fixing Time
Administrator	12
James	10
John	25

FIGURE 9.27   Screenshot of the Average Bug Fixing Time report.

How it Works

- To determine the average bug-fixing time, calculate the average of the [Actual Duration] measure (this field was introduced in the Agile Outsourcing custom process template). Specify [Resolved By] as one of the slicing dimensions to break out the figures by developer. Filter the selection by the bugs that were resolved as fixed.
- Area and Iteration can be specified to further constrain the output.

Figure 9.28 shows the query design, and Figure 9.29 shows the structure of the underlying dataset for this report (row variable is Resolved By).

Effort Variance

The Effort Variance report shows the accuracy of estimates. Being able to come up with reasonably accurate estimates is a key success factor in any project. This report displays the extent to which actual implementation time varies from estimated time, in percentage terms. A large variance figure will alert you to deeper execution problems, such as unexpected roadblocks, volatility of requirements, technology challenges, morale or training issues, and so on.

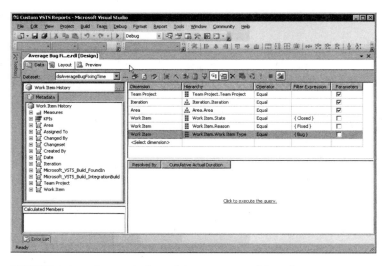

FIGURE 9.28 Query design of Average Bug Fixing Time report.

	Cumulative Actual Duration
Administrator	12.0
James	10.0
John	25.0

FIGURE 9.29 Underlying data structure for the Average Bug Fixing Time report.

Effort Variance

Description :

What is mismatch between estimated and actual effort?

Developer	Effort Variance
James	67%
John	32%
Potter	81%
Tina	0%

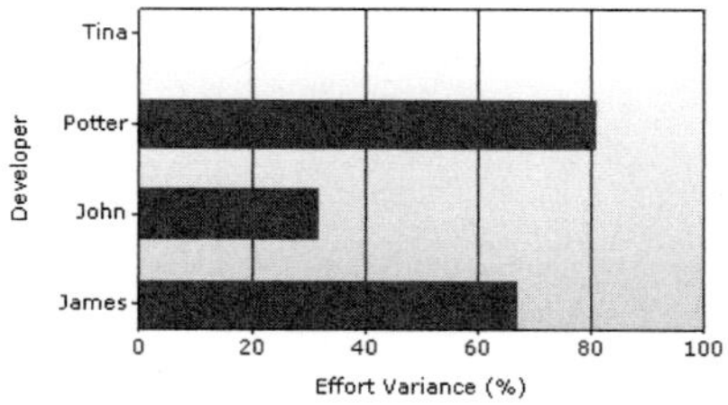

FIGURE 9.30 Screenshot of the Effort Variance report.

How it Works

■   To calculate effort variance, create a dataset containing [Actual Duration] and [Estimated Duration] measures; specify [Resolved By] as a slicing dimension so that we can break out the numbers by developer. In the graph, the variance is calculated as per the following formula:

```
((Actual Duration - Estimated Duration)/Estimated Duration) * 100
```

■   Area and Iteration can be specified to further constrain the output.

Figure 9.31 shows the query design, and Figure 9.32 shows the structure of the underlying dataset for this report (row variable is Resolved By).

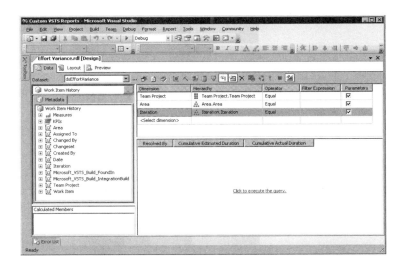

FIGURE 9.31   Query design of Effort Variance report.

	CRM_Outsourcing_Scheduling_ActualDuration	CRM_Outsourcing_Scheduling_EstimatedDuration
James	140.0	84.0
John	70.0	53.0
Potter	76.0	42.0
Tina	20.0	20.0

FIGURE 9.32   Underlying data structure for the Effort Variance report.

Defect Density

A Defect Density report enables you to identify hot spots in your applications. By looking at the distribution of reported bugs by area, you can quickly get an idea about the relative stability of the modules. This information will provide guidance regarding where to focus SQA and development efforts. You'll also be able to decide whether you should stick to the release date or drop certain unstable features.

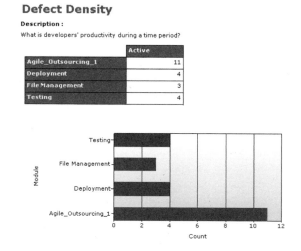

FIGURE 9.33   Screenshot of the Defect Density report.

How it Works

- To calculate the incidence of bugs by module, create a dataset containing the [Current Work Item Count] measure; use [Area] as the slicing dimension so that we can get the values for each module. Filter the selection by active bug.
- Iteration can be specified to further constrain the output.

Figure 9.34 shows the query design, and Figure 9.35 shows the structure of the underlying dataset for this report (row variable is Area).

Missed Schedule WorkItems

A project gets late one day at a time. Periodically, you may find it valuable to do postmortem analysis on the project and determine which work items missed their deadline dates. Although not all work items need to have deadlines, many important ones do. If deadlines are being missed, you need to be alerted so that you can

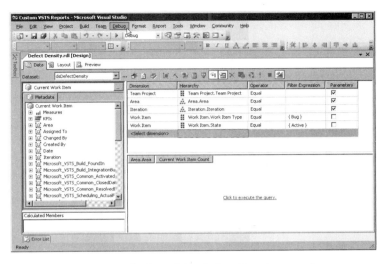

FIGURE 9.34   Query design of the Defect Density report.

		Current Work Item Count
Agile_Outsourcing_1	Active	11
Deployment	Active	4
File Management	Active	3
Testing	Active	4

FIGURE 9.35   Underlying data structure for the Defect Density report.

dig deeper and try to resolve the underlying causes. Missed deadlines need to be taken seriously, and investigations should be launched early.

How it Works

- Delayed work items can be found by comparing a work item's [Actual Finish Date] with its [Deadline Date] (the Agile Outsourcing process template introduces both of these fields). Create a dataset containing [Work Item Id], [Priority], [Deadline Date], and [Actual Finish Date]. Filter the dataset for those work items whose actual finish dates extend past their deadline dates. Specify the filter expression in the Filter tab of the dataset; the dataset will be filtered by Reporting Services *after* the query is run. Specify Resolved By as one of the slicing dimensions so that we can evaluate the performance of individual developers.
- Area and Iteration can be specified to further constrain the output.

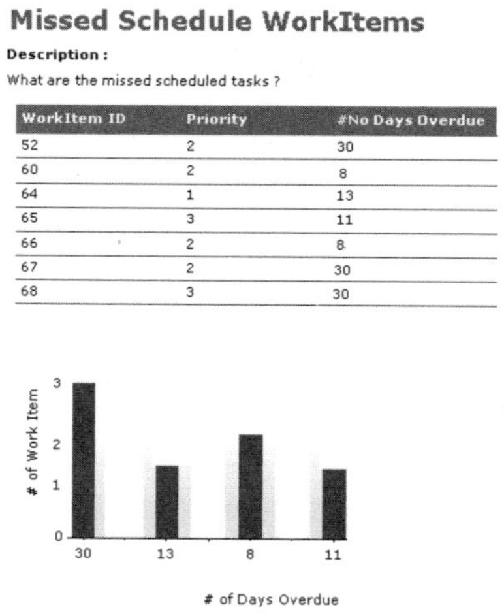

Missed Schedule WorkItems

Description :

What are the missed scheduled tasks ?

WorkItem ID	Priority	#No Days Overdue
52	2	30
60	2	8
64	1	13
65	3	11
66	2	8
67	2	30
68	3	30

FIGURE 9.36 Screenshot of the Missed Schedule WorkItems report.

Figure 9.37 shows the query design, and Figure 9.38 shows the structure of the underlying dataset for this report.

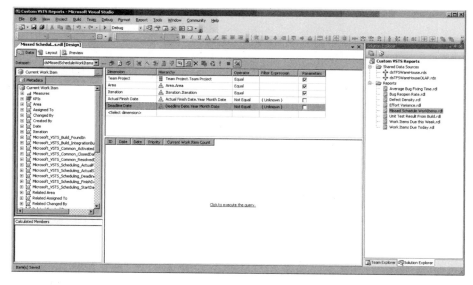

FIGURE 9.37 Query design of the Missed Schedule WorkItems report.

ID	Date	Date	Priority	Current Work Item Count
52	2/1/2006	1/2/2006	2	1
60	2/12/2006	3/31/2006	2	1
64	4/12/2006	3/30/2006	1	1
65	4/11/2006	3/31/2006	3	1
66	4/8/2006	3/31/2006	2	1
67	4/12/2006	5/12/2006	2	1
68	7/12/2006	8/12/2007	3	1
69	5/12/2006	5/25/2006	2	1
70	11/11/2006	12/12/2006	2	1
71	4/12/2006	3/31/2006	3	1

FIGURE 9.38   Underlying data structure for the Missed Schedule
WorkItems report.

DELIVERING REPORTS

When it comes to receiving updated reports in a timely manner from your offshore
development center, you do not need to rely on the offshore project manager's
memory and efforts. You can view the reports using the project portal and nothing
more than a Web browser. Moreover, you can configure Reporting Services to deliver the reports via email to various stakeholders at scheduled intervals. Report
consumers can subscribe to reports individually, on a per-report basis (see Figure
9.39). Alternatively, reports can be distributed based upon a data-driven list.

We find this capability to be of great value in the offshore scenario. Reports can
be scheduled to run at the end of the day at the offshore location and delivered to
your inbox before the start of your day. You can get summary as well as detailed
snapshots of what happened during the previous workday, with zero friction or
manual intervention. Achieving this kind of visibility makes a big difference in
terms of reducing offshore execution risks.

FIGURE 9.39   Report subscriptions can be created on a per-user
basis or based on a data-driven list.

OVERVIEW OF THE TEAM SYSTEM CUBE DESIGN

The TFSWarehouse OLAP database contains a single cube named Team System. The cube is designed as a high-performance Multidimensional OLAP (MOLAP) cube with proactive caching turned off by default (see Figure 9.40).

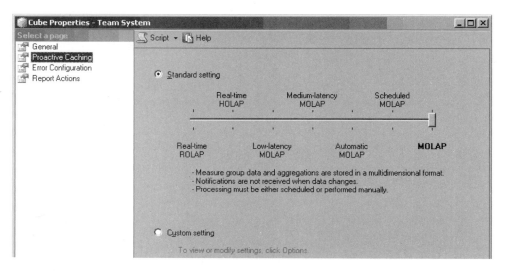

FIGURE 9.40   Default properties of the Team System cube.

Measure Groups

For scalability and performance, the cube comprises multiple measure groups (see Figure 9.41). Instead of having a single huge fact table, measure groups allow the cube to contain multiple fact tables at different levels of granularity—enabling better query optimization, cube maintenance, and data partitioning. Each measure group is usually associated with a subset of the dimensions defined in the cube.

In order to view the individual measures contained in each measure group, right-click the Team System cube and click Browse from the drop-down menu. Expand the measure groups and take a look at individual measures, as illustrated in Figure 9.42.

Dimensions

The Team System cube's shared dimensions can be viewed in Object Explorer. The Browse view displays both shared and private dimensions (see Figure 9.43). To view the dimension members, expand the dimension node in Browse view. You'll

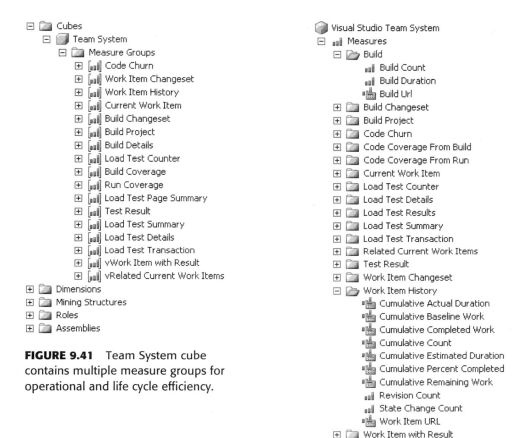

FIGURE 9.41 Team System cube contains multiple measure groups for operational and life cycle efficiency.

FIGURE 9.42 Expand measure groups in the Browse window to see individual measures.

notice that not all the members defined in the project templates are listed in the tree. As you *instantiate* various types in your team projects, the new members get added to the dimension tree. For example, in Figure 9.44 notice that the Work Item Type dimension does not contain the Requirement work item type defined in the Agile Outsourcing process template, although we have created a team project based on the custom template. The Requirement work item type will be added when we actually *create* a requirement work item in the team project. There is no way for the cube to learn about new dimension members unless they physically exist in the corresponding tables in the relational database.

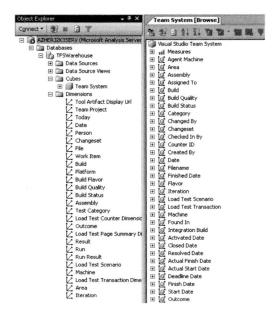

FIGURE 9.43   Partial listing of dimensions in Team System cube.

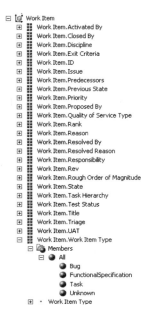

FIGURE 9.44   Only dimension members that actually exist in a team project are included in the dimension tree.

Perspectives

Perspectives provide a scaled-down, coherent context for users by displaying an interrelated subset of measures, dimensions, attributes, and calculations. Since the Team System cube contains a large number of measures and dimensions, you can obtain a more focused view of the area you are interested in by choosing the appropriate Perspective from the Browse view (see Figure 9.45). Perspectives appear as separate cubes to front-end applications, like Excel. Perspectives are available in SQL Server 2005 Enterprise Edition only.

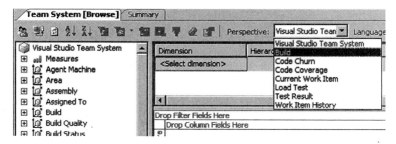

FIGURE 9.45   Choose an appropriate Perspective to view a limited set of data.

EXAMINING CUBE STRUCTURE IN DETAIL

If you are interested in studying the design of the Team System cube in greater detail, you can generate and inspect the scripted XMLA file (see Listing 9.1). Right-click Team System cube in Object Explorer and choose Script Cube As, Create To, New Query Editor Window. You can learn about dimension attributes and hierarchies, dimension usage in measure groups, perspective definitions, calculations, MDX queries used, as well as a wealth of other information associated with the Team System cube.

LISTING 9.1 Partial Listing of Team System Cube Definition Showing Selected Elements

```
<!-- Partial Listing Containing Key Features; Many Elements
    Omitted for Brevity -->
<Create xmlns="http://schemas.microsoft.com/analysisservices
    /2003/engine">
 <ParentObject>
  <DatabaseID>TFSWarehouse</DatabaseID>
 </ParentObject>
 <ObjectDefinition>
  <Cube xmlns:xsd="http://www.w3.org/2001/XMLSchema"
      xmlns:xsi="http://www.w3.org/2001/XMLSchema-instance">
   <ID>Team System</ID>
   <Name>Team System</Name>
   <Annotations>
    <Annotation>
     <Name>Owner</Name>
     <Value>Microsoft.VSTS</Value>
    </Annotation>
   </Annotations>
   <Language>1033</Language>
   <Collation>Latin1_General_CI_AS</Collation>
   <Translations>
    <Translation>
     <Language>1033</Language>
     <Caption>Visual Studio Team System</Caption>
    </Translation>
   </Translations>
   <Dimensions>
    <Dimension>
     <Annotations>
      <Annotation>
       <Name>Owner</Name>
       <Value>Microsoft.VSTS</Value>
      </Annotation>
     </Annotations>
     <ID>Tool Artifact Display Url</ID>
```

```xml
<Name>Tool Artifact Display Url</Name>
<Translations>
 <Translation>
  <Language>1033</Language>
  <Caption>Tool Artifact Display Url</Caption>
 </Translation>
</Translations>
<DimensionID>Tool Artifact Display Url</DimensionID>
<Visible>false</Visible>
<Attributes>
 <Attribute>
  <AttributeID>Tool Artifact Display Url</AttributeID>
 </Attribute>
 <!-- Other Attributes Omitted -->
</Attributes>
</Dimension>
<!-- Other Dimensions Omitted -->
</Dimensions>
<CubePermissions>
 <CubePermission>
  <ID>TfsWarehouseDataReaderCubePermission</ID>
  <Name>TfsWarehouseDataReaderCubePermission</Name>
  <RoleID>TfsWarehouseDataReader</RoleID>
  <Read>Allowed</Read>
  <ReadSourceData>None</ReadSourceData>
 </CubePermission>
</CubePermissions>
<Perspectives>
 <Perspective>
  <ID>Code Churn</ID>
  <Name>Code Churn</Name>
  <Dimensions>
   <Dimension>
    <CubeDimensionID>Date</CubeDimensionID>
    <Attributes>
     <Attribute>
      <AttributeID>Date</AttributeID>
     </Attribute>
     <!-- Other Attributes Omitted -->
    </Attributes>
   </Dimension>
   <!-- Other Dimensions Omitted -->
  </Dimensions>
  <MeasureGroups>
   <MeasureGroup>
    <MeasureGroupID>Code Churn</MeasureGroupID>
    <Measures>
     <Measure>
```

```xml
     <MeasureID>Lines Added</MeasureID>
    </Measure>
    <Measure>
     <MeasureID>Lines Deleted</MeasureID>
    </Measure>
    <!-- Other Measures Omitted -->
   </Measures>
  </MeasureGroup>
 </MeasureGroups>
 <Calculations>
  <Calculation>
   <Name>[Measures].[Total Churn]</Name>
   <Type>Member</Type>
  </Calculation>
  <!-- Other Calculations Omitted -->
 </Calculations>
</Perspective>
<!-- Other Perspectives Omitted -->
</Perspectives>
<MeasureGroups>
 <MeasureGroup>
  <ID>Code Churn</ID>
  <Name>Code Churn</Name>
  <Annotations>
   <Annotation>
    <Name>Owner</Name>
    <Value>Microsoft.VSTS</Value>
   </Annotation>
   <Annotation>
    <Name>Microsoft.VSTS.Measures</Name>
    <Value>Code Churn Count;Lines Added;Lines Modified;Lines
        Deleted;Net Lines Added;LastChild Total Lines;</Value>
   </Annotation>
  </Annotations>
  <Translations>
   <Translation>
    <Language>1033</Language>
    <Caption>Code Churn</Caption>
   </Translation>
  </Translations>
  <Measures>
   <Measure>
    <ID>Code Churn Count</ID>
    <Name>Code Churn Count</Name>
    <AggregateFunction>Count</AggregateFunction>
    <DataType>Integer</DataType>
    <Source>
     <DataType>Integer</DataType>
```

```
    <Source xsi:type="ColumnBinding">
     <TableID>Code_x0020_Churn</TableID>
     <ColumnID>__ID</ColumnID>
    </Source>
   </Source>
   <FormatString>#,#0</FormatString>
   <Translations>
    <Translation>
     <Language>1033</Language>
     <Caption>Code Churn Count</Caption>
    </Translation>
   </Translations>
  </Measure>
  <!-- Other Measures Omitted -->
 </Measures>
 <StorageMode>Molap</StorageMode>
 <ProcessingMode>Regular</ProcessingMode>
 <Dimensions>
  <!-- Tags Omitted -->
 </Dimensions>
 <Partitions>
  <!-- Tags Omitted -->
 </Partitions>
 <ProactiveCaching>
  <!-- Tags Omitted -->
 </ProactiveCaching>
</MeasureGroup>
<!-- Other MeasureGroups are Omitted -->
</MeasureGroups>
<Source>
 <DataSourceViewID>
  TFSWarehouseDataSourceView
 </DataSourceViewID>
</Source>
<MdxScripts>
 <MdxScript>
  <ID>DefaultMdxScript</ID>
  <Name>DefaultMdxScript</Name>
  <Annotations>
   <Annotation>
    <!-- Tags Omitted -->
   </Annotation>
  </Annotations>
  <Commands>
   <Command>
    <Text>CALCULATE;</Text>
   </Command>
   <!-- Other Commands Omitted -->
```

```
      </Commands>
      <CalculationProperties>
       <CalculationProperty>
        <CalculationReference>
         LastChild Total Lines
        </CalculationReference>
        <CalculationType>Member</CalculationType>
        <Translations>
         <Translation>
          <Language>1033</Language>
          <Caption>LastChild Total Lines</Caption>
         </Translation>
        </Translations>
        <AssociatedMeasureGroupID>
         Code Churn
        </AssociatedMeasureGroupID>
       </CalculationProperty>
       <!-- Other CalculationProperties Omitted -->
      </CalculationProperties>
     </MdxScript>
    </MdxScripts>
    <ProactiveCaching>
     <SilenceInterval>-PT1S</SilenceInterval>
      <Latency>-PT1S</Latency>
      <SilenceOverrideInterval>-PT1S</SilenceOverrideInterval>
      <ForceRebuildInterval>-PT1S</ForceRebuildInterval>
      <Source xsi:type="ProactiveCachingInheritedBinding" />
    </ProactiveCaching>
   </Cube>
  </ObjectDefinition>
</Create>
```

Viewing the Cube Definition in Designer

Although the XML dump in Listing 9.1 provides detailed information regarding the underlying structure of the cube, given its size and complexity, the information is difficult to visualize. An easier way to comprehend the cube structure is to look at it in cube designer. Open SQL Server BI Development Studio and create a new Business Intelligence Project; select Import Analysis Services 9.0 Database from Visual Studio Installed Templates (see Figure 9.46). Enter the server and database information in the wizard screen (see Figure 9.47). VSTS will import the Team System cube definition and display it in the cube designer (see Figure 9.48).

Once the cube is imported into the designer, you can drill down and inspect the cube's fact tables, measure groups, measures, dimensions, perspectives, and calculations using various tabs.

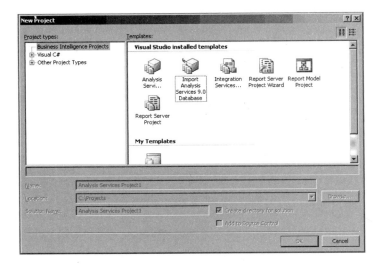

FIGURE 9.46 Create an Import Analysis Services 9.0 Database Project to view the Team System cube in Designer mode.

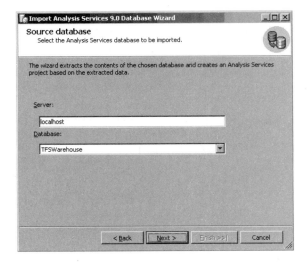

FIGURE 9.47 Enter server and OLAP database information in the project wizard.

Let's begin by looking at the relationships between the fact tables, as displayed in the Data Source View (see Figure 9.49). The fact tables are related via dimension tables. As discussed earlier, multiple fact tables (and corresponding measure groups) help improve the organization, scalability, and security of the Team System

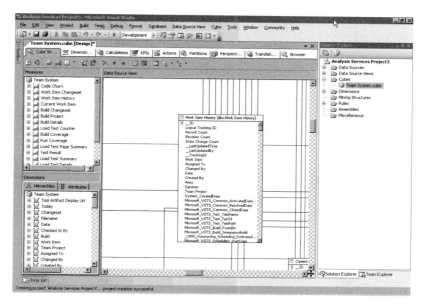

FIGURE 9.48   Team System cube definition displayed in Cube Designer.

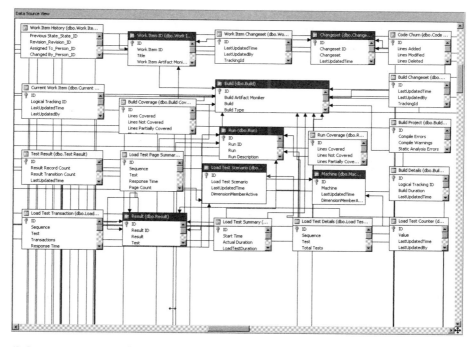

FIGURE 9.49   Fact tables in Team System cube are related via dimension tables.

cube structure. You can browse the underlying fact table rows by right-clicking a fact table and choosing Explore Data; the data can be displayed in tabular, pivot table, as well as chart format (see Figure 9.50 and Figure 9.51).

ID	Logical Tracki	Record Count	Transition Co	LastUpdatedT	LastUpdatedB	TrackingId	Work Item ID	State_State_I	Previous Stat	Revision_Revi	Assigned
1	2005/11/07 0	1	1	2005-11-07 0		1|1|1	1	1	(null)	1	1
2	2005/11/07 0	1	1	2005-11-07 0		2|1|1	2	1	(null)	1	1
3	2005/11/07 0	1	1	2005-11-07 0		3|1|1	3	1	(null)	1	1
4	2005/11/07 0	1	1	2005-11-07 0		4|1|1	4	1	(null)	1	1
5	2005/11/07 0	1	1	2005-11-07 0		5|1|1	5	1	(null)	1	1
6	2005/11/07 0	1	1	2005-11-07 0		6|1|1	6	1	(null)	1	1
7	2005/11/07 0	1	1	2005-11-07 0		7|1|1	7	1	(null)	1	1
8	2005/11/07 0	1	1	2005-11-07 0		8|1|1	8	1	(null)	1	1
9	2005/11/07 0	1	1	2005-11-07 0		9|1|1	9	1	(null)	1	1
10	2005/11/07 0	1	1	2005-11-07 0		10|1|1	10	1	(null)	1	1
11	2005/11/07 0	1	1	2005-11-07 0		11|1|1	11	1	(null)	1	1
12	2005/11/07 0	1	1	2005-11-07 0		12|1|1	12	1	(null)	1	1
13	2005/11/07 0	1	1	2005-11-07 0		13|1|1	13	1	(null)	1	1
14	2005/11/07 0	1	1	2005-11-07 0		14|1|1	14	1	(null)	1	1
15	2005/11/08 0	1	1	2005-11-08 0		15|1|1	15	1	(null)	1	1
16	2005/11/08 0	1	1	2005-11-08 0		16|1|1	16	1	(null)	1	1
17	2005/11/08 0	1	1	2005-11-08 0		17|1|1	17	1	(null)	1	1
18	2005/11/08 0	-1	0	2005-11-08 0		17|1|-1	17	1	(null)	1	1
19	2005/11/08 0	1	1	2005-11-08 0		17|2|1	17	2	1	2	1

FIGURE 9.50 Tabular view of underlying fact table data.

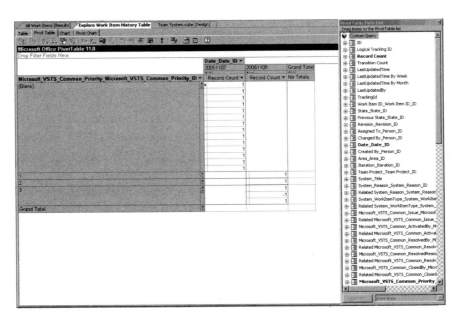

FIGURE 9.51 Pivot table enables creation of custom views of the underlying fact table data.

To analyze dimension information, right-click a dimension in the dimension pane and choose Edit Dimension from the drop-down menu; this action brings up the dimension editor (see Figure 9.52). You can review various attributes and hierarchies associated with the dimension. Each dimension also has an associated key field. To view the underlying data, right-click the dimension table in the Data Source View pane and choose Explore Data. To see tables related to a dimension, right-click the dimension table (in the Data Source View pane) and choose Show Related Tables. For example, in Figure 9.53 we can see that Work Item History, Work Item Changeset, and Current Work Item fact tables are related to the Work Item ID dimension table. The dimension table holds the primary key; Work Item ID is used as the foreign key in the three fact tables.

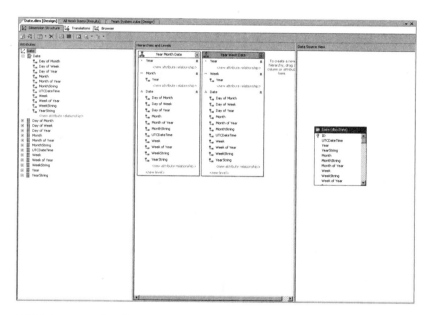

FIGURE 9.52 The dimension editor reveals the internal structure of a dimension.

Click on the Dimension Usage tab in the main cube design window. The Dimension Usage map shows the dimensions are used in various measure groups (see Figure 9.54). Bundling a subset of dimensions with each measure group provides a more focused context for the cube's users. You'll find this information useful when designing custom reports.

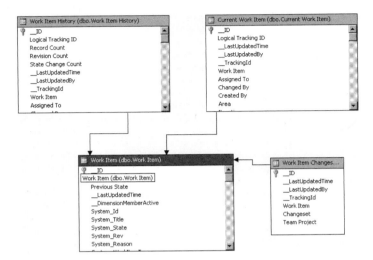

FIGURE 9.53 Related tables displayed in the dimension editor's Data Source View window.

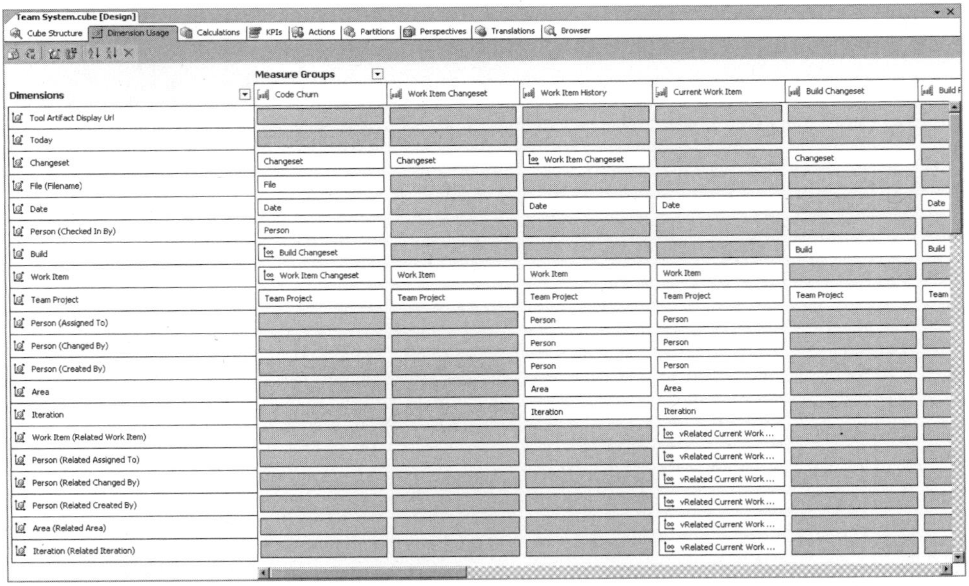

FIGURE 9.54 Dimension Usage map shows the dimensions included in various measure groups.

Click on the Perspectives tab in the main cube design window. The screen shows measure groups and dimensions used in various perspectives (see Figure 9.55). Like measure groups, perspectives provide a meaningful context to the end user by providing a limited and focused view of the cube data.

Cube Objects	Object Type	Perspective Name — Code Churn	Perspective Name — Work Item History	Perspective Name — Current Work Item	Perspective Name — Build	Perspective Name — Load Test	Perspe — Code Cove
Team System	Name	Code Churn	Work Item History	Current Work Item	Build	Load Test	Code Cove
	DefaultMeasure						
Measure Groups							
Code Churn	MeasureGroup	✓					
Code Churn Count	Measure	✓					
Lines Added	Measure	✓					
Lines Modified	Measure	✓					
Lines Deleted	Measure	✓					
Net Lines Added	Measure	✓					
LastChild Total Lines	Measure	✓					
Work Item Changeset	MeasureGroup						
Work Item Changeset Count	Measure						
Work Item History	MeasureGroup		✓				
Record Count	Measure		✓				
Revision Count	Measure		✓				
State Change Count	Measure		✓				
LastChild Record Count	Measure		✓				
_CRM_Outsourcing_Scheduling_E...	Measure		✓				
_CRM_Outsourcing_Scheduling_A...	Measure		✓				
_CRM_Outsourcing_Scheduling_P...	Measure		✓				
_Microsoft_VSTS_Scheduling_Rem...	Measure		✓				
_Microsoft_VSTS_Scheduling_Com...	Measure		✓				
_Microsoft_VSTS_Scheduling_Bas...	Measure		✓				
LastChild _CRM_Outsourcing_Sch...	Measure		✓				
LastChild _CRM_Outsourcing_Sch...	Measure		✓				
LastChild _CRM_Outsourcing_Sch...	Measure		✓				
LastChild _Microsoft_VSTS_Sched...	Measure		✓				
LastChild _Microsoft_VSTS_Sched...	Measure		✓				
LastChild _Microsoft_VSTS_Sched...	Measure		✓				
Current Work Item	MeasureGroup			✓			
Current Work Item Count	Measure			✓			
Current Work Item _CRM_Outsou...	Measure			✓			
Current Work Item _CRM_Outsou...	Measure			✓			

FIGURE 9.55   Perspectives include a subset of measure groups and dimensions.

Custom Measures and Dimensions

In Chapter 3, "Leveraging VSTS and Customizing MSF Agile," we created a custom process called Agile Outsourcing. We modified various work item types to include custom fields and transitions. TFS automatically updates the data warehouse schema to include the newly added custom fields.

The WarehouseController.asmx Web service running on the application tier adds the custom measures and dimensions to the data warehouse so that they are available for reporting. The data warehouse schema gets updated when the first team project (based on the custom process template) is created.

The custom measures and dimensions are added to relational as well as multi-dimensional databases. Select the TFSWarehouse relational database and expand the Columns nodes of Current Work Item and Work Item History tables. You'll find that the three measures have been added to these fact tables (see Figure 9.56). Notice that additional columns corresponding to the custom dimensions have also been added to the tables. To view the new measures in the OLAP database, browse the Team System cube under the TFSWarehouse analytical database. Expand the Current Work Item and Work Item History measure groups (see Figure 9.57); you'll see that the custom measures have been added.

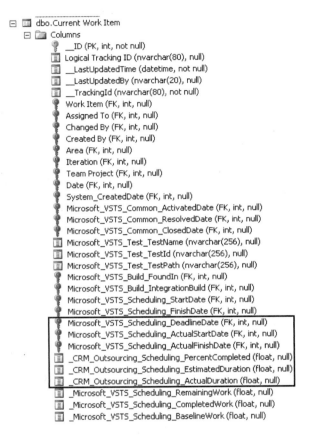

FIGURE 9.56 Partial column listing showing custom measures and dimensions added in the TFSWarehouse relational database.

Refreshing Cube Data

As discussed earlier in the chapter, an application tier Web service named WarehouseController.asmx is responsible for periodically refreshing the relational and analytical databases from various operational databases. Both the schema and content of the database may be updated. Although the default refresh frequency is set to one hour, the interval can be changed to update the data warehouses less or more

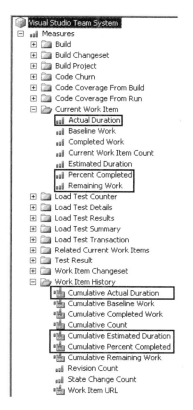

FIGURE 9.57 Custom measures added
in the TFSWarehouse OLAP database.

frequently. However, before making the interval shorter, you need to consider the
load associated with refreshing the data stores, and strike a balance between latency
and system resource consumption. To change the interval, follow these steps in the
application tier machine:

1. Click Start, point to Administrative Tools, and then click Services. Stop the
   TFSServerScheduler service.
2. Navigate to the WarehouseController Web service using your browser. If
   you don't know the URL of this Web service, launch Internet Information
   Services Manager, expand the Team Foundation Server Web site node, expand the virtual directory node named Warehouse, and look up the Web
   service under the folder named v1.0 (see Figure 9.58). Right-click the .asmx
   file and select Browse.

3. Click the ChangeSetting Web method on the Web service page.
4. On the Web method page, enter "RunIntervalSettings" in the settingID text box, and enter the desired refresh interval (in seconds) in the new-Value text box (see Figure 9.59).
5. Restart TFSServerScheduler service.

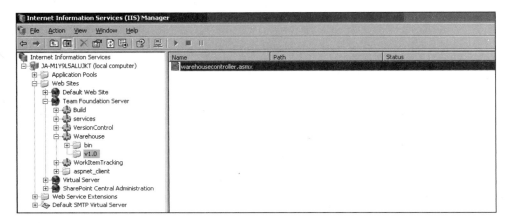

FIGURE 9.58 WarehouseController Web service is responsible for refreshing the data warehouses.

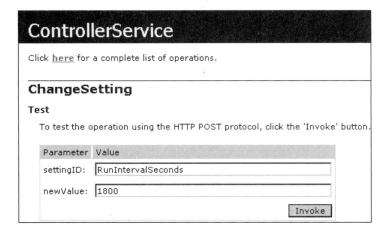

FIGURE 9.59 Enter a new refresh interval value in the ChangeSetting Web method page of ControllerService.

You can also refresh the databases immediately by invoking the Run method of the WarehouseController Web service (see Figure 9.60). After executing this method, invoke the GetWareHouseStatus method to determine the processing status. The valid responses from this method are the following:

- Idle
- Blocked
- RunningAdapters
- ProcessingOlap

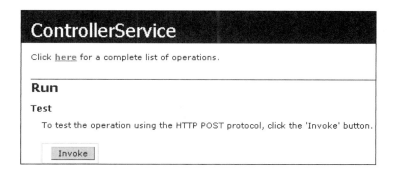

FIGURE 9.60   Invoke the Run method to force an immediate refresh.

CONCLUSION

In this chapter, we looked at the data storage and analysis infrastructure provided by TFS. We studied in detail the design of the analytical data warehouse. We also reviewed selected built-in reports as well as a number of custom reports. Finally, we saw how custom fields defined in the Agile Outsourcing process template show up in the relational and multidimensional databases.

We believe that the open architecture for data access and reporting provides a compelling value proposition. By leveraging the capabilities of SQL Server 2005 Analysis Services and Reporting Services, you can access, process, analyze, render, and distribute project-related information to suit your organizational needs. You can also mirror or cluster the back-end databases for disaster-recovery purposes using built-in SQL Server 2005 and Windows 2003 features.

You can expose the reports via the Windows Sharepoint Services-based project portal, enabling anyone with a browser to view project status information in near time from anywhere in the world. For offshore projects, the browser-based reporting capability provides tremendous benefits. The friction associated with obtaining timely and accurate status information from offshore locations is substantially reduced.

If the offshore implementation team follows the development process faithfully, the process of capturing key metrics becomes a by-product of their routine activities. The information is automatically propagated through various data warehouses and processing steps, and is seamlessly delivered to the stakeholders. The idea is simple, but is one that has the potential to transform the way you manage and execute offshore projects.

10 Using the Project Portal

In This Chapter

■ Overview of the Project Portal
■ Project Portal Features
■ Customizing the Project Portal

INTRODUCTION

The reach and the power of the World Wide Web is a key facilitator of offshore software development. Although limited outsourcing was still taking place in the pre-Internet days, widespread access to the global information superhighway set the stage for an explosive growth in outsourcing. About one billion people worldwide are estimated to have access to the Internet today. About 85 percent of Internet users use Microsoft's Internet Explorer Web browser.

It is therefore obvious that given its widespread availability, the Web browser provides a powerful application platform. VSTS automatically creates a project portal—containing reports, announcements, tasks, discussion groups, and so forth—when a team project is created. In this section, we discuss how the Web-based project portal can be leveraged to facilitate communication between distributed teams and stakeholders. The goal is to put everyone 'on the same page' so they can share critical project information from a central Web site. Even stakeholders who do not have VSTS can simply navigate to the project Web site and get access to the latest metrics, reports, documents, announcements, and discussions. It is a simple but effective way to collaborate with globally distributed team members.

OVERVIEW OF THE PROJECT PORTAL

The project portal is based upon Windows SharePoint Services. It is automatically generated when you create a team project (see Figure 10.1). In the offshore scenario, where you frequently work with people without ever meeting them face to face, a shared project site improves coordination and provides a central repository for project-related information. What we find especially compelling in the offshore scenario is the portal's ability to act as a gateway to current information from remote locations.

You can use the project portal to access the same reports that are available from Team Explorer (see Chapter 9, "Enterprise Reporting," for additional information about the Team Foundation Server data stores and reports). The report-integration functionality is based upon the capabilities of SQL Server 2005 Reporting Services, which provides Web-based access to stored reports in the Report Server. Easy access to reports on project health, task assignments, project planning, execution status, and so forth—without firewall problems, downloading special software components, or depending on manual efforts—reduces day-to-day operational friction, improves visibility, and mitigates offshore execution risk. Easy access to timely information is a key enabler of success.

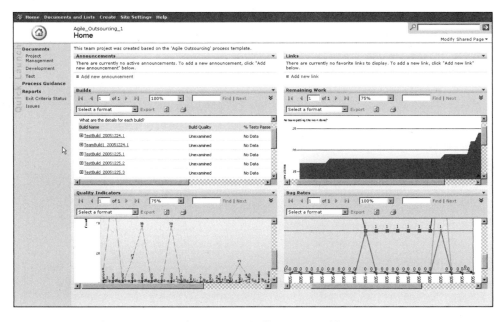

FIGURE 10.1 The project portal is automatically generated by VSTS.

PROJECT PORTAL FEATURES

The project portal is based on a standard SharePoint team site. As such, it contains a number of built-in features for team communication and collaboration. The primary functionality related to Team Foundation Server is access to team reports. However, you can create custom Web Parts to provide additional integration with Team Foundation Server, such as input forms for entering work items, synchronizing SharePoint documents with those stored in TFS Version Control, updating the SharePoint event calendar with work item scheduling information, and so on. In this section, we review selected out-of-the-box functionalities that are useful from an offshore development standpoint.

Document Management

No matter how small or large your outsourced project happens to be, you'll need to manage and share documents. Depending on organizational practice and project complexity, a variety of documents (e.g., business requirements, functional specifications, work breakdown structure, test cases, status reports, etc.) need to be created, distributed, and updated. Clearly, using a shared folder somewhere on the network is suboptimal for all but trivial cases. In offshore projects, accessibility is also an important consideration. Sending documents via email is not too efficient, either; you lose version control and change history, face potential difficulties with size and format (depending upon restrictions imposed by the recipient's email system), and often fail to find relevant documents amid the email clutter. You need something simple and practical.

The project portal contains several predefined document libraries (see Figure 10.2). The content and the structure of these libraries is the same as those of the corresponding Documents node in Team Explorer (see Figure 10.3). The document libraries and their constituent files are specified in the process template's WssTasks. xml file (located in the Windows SharePoint Services folder of the exported process template). Refer to Chapter 3, "Leveraging VSTS and Customizing MSF Agile," for how to export the process template to a set of XML files. You can modify the WssTasks.xml file to customize the content and the structure of the document libraries. Your changes will be reflected in new project portals that are created based on the modified template.

To create additional document folders in an existing site, navigate to the Documents and Lists screen and click Create. Click any folder to go to its file contents page. You can upload documents or create new documents using the toolbar options.

Document Libraries	Description	Items	Last Modified
Development		0	3 days ago
Process Guidance	Process Guidance for the team documents	396	3 days ago
Project Management		5	3 days ago
Requirements	Documents for the business analyst team	5	3 days ago
Security	Documents for the architect team	1	3 days ago
Templates	Templates for the team documents	0	3 days ago
Test		1	3 days ago

FIGURE 10.2   Predefined document libraries in the project portal.

FIGURE 10.3   Contents
of the Documents node in
Team Explorer.

Team members who are allowed to modify documents can check out a document for editing. Hover over the filename with the mouse and click the drop-down icon. Choose Check Out from the drop-down menu (see Figure 10.4). Checking out the documents keeps others from modifying the document, preventing change conflicts. Click Edit in Microsoft Office Word (or click Edit in Microsoft Office Excel, depending upon the file type) from the drop-down menu. The document will be opened in Microsoft Word (or Excel) for editing. Note the Shared Workspace pane. You can use various buttons in this pane to interact with the project portal without having to switch back and forth between the Office application and the SharePoint site.

When you are finished making the changes, click the Check In link on the Shared Workspace pane (or choose File/Check In) to upload the modified document to the project portal (Figure 10.5). Keep in mind that the rudimentary version control support offered in SharePoint is distinct from the Team Foundation Version Control (TFVC) system.

If you plan to make significant changes to the document in collaboration with distributed team members, create a separate site exclusively for that purpose. Select a document and choose Create Document Workspace from the drop-down menu. SharePoint will create a subsite for collectively modifying the specified document

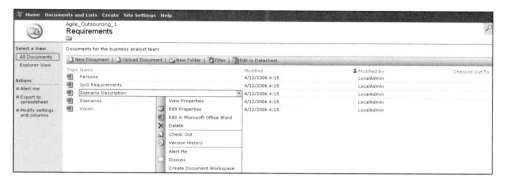

FIGURE 10.4   SharePoint provides basic version-control features for collaborative work.

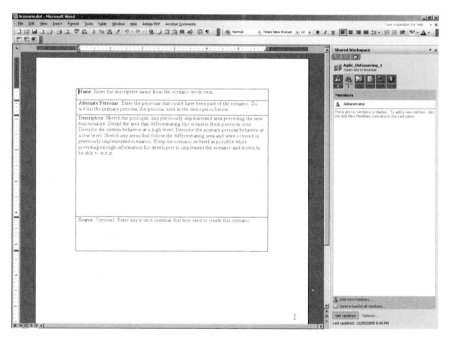

FIGURE 10.5   The Shared Workspace pane in Office applications provides seamless interoperability with SharePoint.

(see Figure 10.6). The subsite contains a separate task list and document repository. When the changes are finalized, bring up the document's context menu and click Publish to Source Location; this action will upload the modified document to the original project portal.

FIGURE 10.6 A document workspace allows distributed team members to work on a document and upload the final version to the original site.

Change Notifications

SharePoint email alerts keep you informed regarding specified changes in the site. When working with distributed teams, this feature is a simple, yet useful, mechanism to keep everyone in the loop. Few people have the time to periodically return to the portal site and look for changes; it is more efficient to notify them when changes take place in their areas of interest.

To create individualized alerts, click Site Settings in the site toolbar and select My Alerts on This Site. On the My Alerts on This Site screen, click Add Alert; you'll be directed to the New Alert screen (see Figure 10.7). On the New Alert screen,

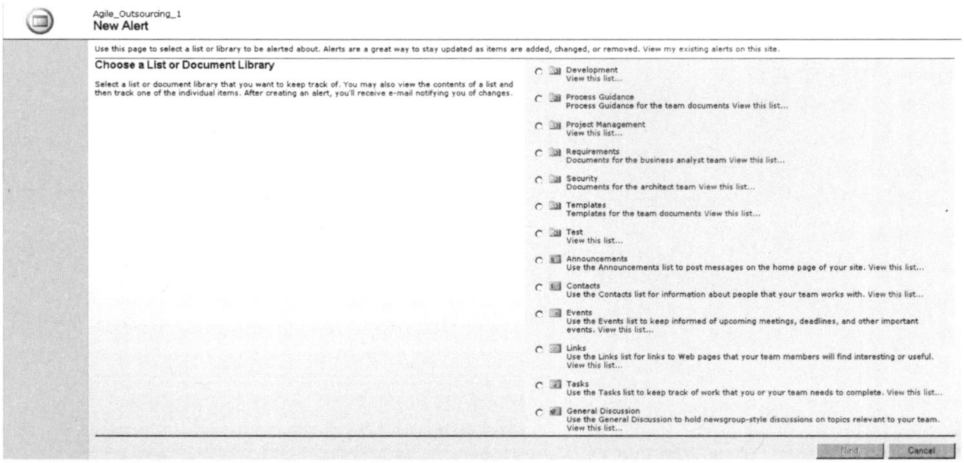

FIGURE 10.7 SharePoint allows you to specify lists or libraries to monitor for changes.

select the document library or list that you are interested in monitoring for changes. In the next screen, specify the alert type and frequency (see Figure 10.8). You can choose to be alerted of all changes or selected changes; you can also select whether you would like to be notified immediately when a change takes place, or whether you would like SharePoint to accumulate the changes and send you a daily or weekly summary.

Agile_Outsourcing_1
New Alert: Requirements: All items

Use this page to create an e-mail alert notifying you when there are changes to this item. More information on alerts.

| **Send Alerts To** | My e-mail address is: |
| Specify the e-mail address where your alert results will be sent. | developer35@offshorecompany.com |

Change Type	Alert me about:
Specify the type of changes that you want to be alerted to.	⦿ All changes
	○ Added items
	○ Changed items
	○ Deleted items
	○ Web discussion updates

Alert Frequency	Alert me how often:
Specify whether you want to be alerted immediately when there is a change, or if you would rather receive a daily or weekly summary message.	⦿ Send e-mail immediately.
View my existing alerts on this site.	○ Send a daily summary.
	○ Send a weekly summary.

OK   Cancel

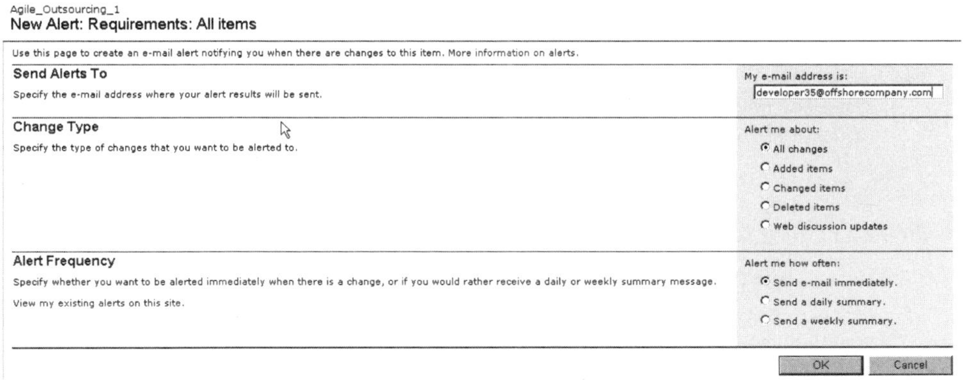

FIGURE 10.8   Alert options allow you to fine-tune email notifications.

You can further narrow your preferences and choose to be notified of changes to only a single item. Hover the mouse on the item and bring up the drop-down menu; click Alert Me. In the next screen, specify the alert type and frequency. SharePoint will alert you of changes only to the specified item.

Web Discussions

No matter how comprehensive your specifications are and how detailed your weekly meetings happen to be, we feel that ad-hoc, 'out-of-band' communications add significant value if managed properly. The popularity of thousands of Internet newsgroups attest to the usefulness of open communication and the strategic value derived from collective brain-share. A discussion board encourages distributed team members to express their ideas and concerns, as well as to request for clarifications. This kind of grass-root-level feedback, if allowed to be expressed freely, provides useful insight into the inner workings of the project. The project portal makes this possible with no additional effort.

The project portal contains a discussion board named General Discussion. You can create additional discussion groups to conduct more-focused discussions. To navigate to the discussion group, click Documents and Lists in the site toolbar, and click the General Discussion link under Discussion Boards. You can create topics as needed and conduct threaded discussions (see Figure 10.9).

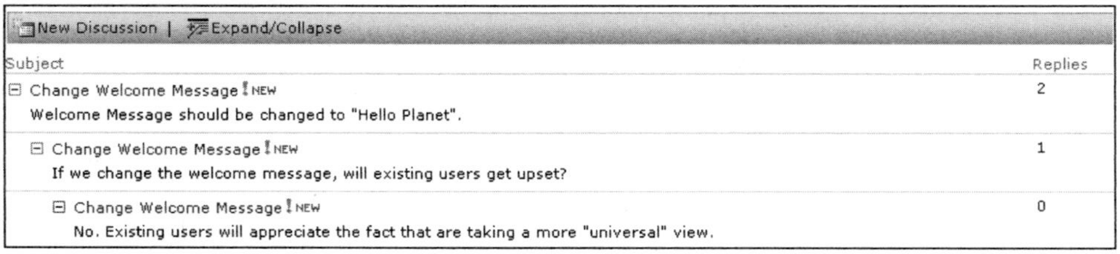

FIGURE 10.9 Threaded discussions allow distributed team members to exchange ideas and receive clarifications.

Reports

In addition to the reports available in the Quick Launch bar on the home page, you can view additional custom, as well as predefined, reports stored in the Report Server. Click the Reports link on the Quick Launch bar; you'll be directed to a Report Manager page containing a list of all available reports in the team project (see Figure 10.10).

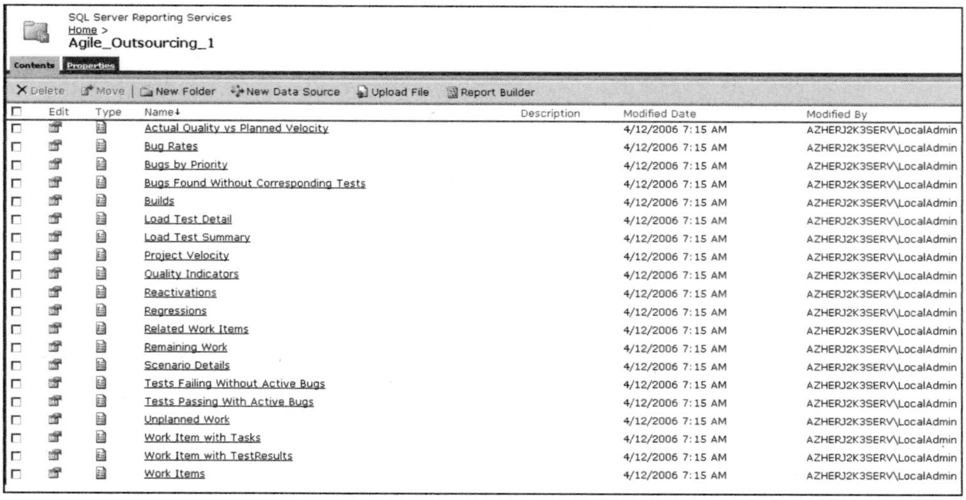

FIGURE 10.10 All reports associated with the team project are available from the portal site.

You can also insert links to critical reports directly on the home page. Click Add New Link under the Links section. On the Links: New Item screen, enter the name of the report as well as the URL. You can find out the correct URL by clicking any of the reports, such as those shown in Figure 10.10. The URL will be in the following format: *http://<your server name>/Reports/Pages/Report.aspx?ItemPath=%2f<your project name%2f<report name>.*

You can also use the Report Explorer and Report Viewer Web Parts to display reports in the project portal. You can connect the two Web Parts so that when a report is selected using Report Explorer, it is automatically displayed in Report Viewer. For more information regarding how to use these Web Parts, please visit Microsoft Web site at *http://msdn2.microsoft.com/en-us/library/ms159772(SQL.90). aspx.*

Meeting Workspaces

Meeting workspaces facilitate virtual meetings with globally distributed team members. The meeting agenda, relevant documents, meeting notes, action items, and so forth can be stored in a meeting workspace. All participants can share the stored resources and collaboratively work with them as needed. Instead of sifting through voluminous email messages and attachments, distributed team members can have access to a central location to review background information and follow-up tasks.

A meeting workspace can be created in a number of ways. One of the common ways is to generate it when creating meeting requests in Outlook. Launch Outlook; on the File menu, point to New, and click Meeting Request. Fill out the meeting information as appropriate (see Figure 10.11). Click the Meeting Workspace button, and Outlook will bring up the Meeting Workspace pane (see Figure 10.12)

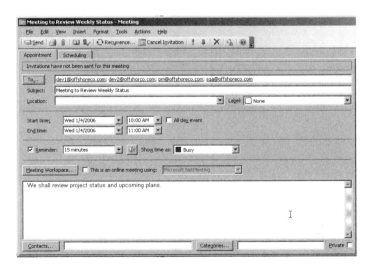

FIGURE 10.11   You can use the meeting request form to schedule virtual meetings with distributed stakeholders.

FIGURE 10.12 You can create a Meeting Workspace in the project portal from Outlook.

On the Meeting Workspace pane, click the Settings link to adjust the settings as needed, and then click Create (you could also link to an existing meeting workspace instead of creating a new one from scratch). A new meeting workspace will be created and its link automatically inserted into the meeting request (see Figure 10.13). Click on the link to open the SharePoint Meeting Workspace. You can upload relevant documents to the site and create appropriate agenda items so that the participants can view all background information from a single location (see Figure 10.14). During the meeting, participants can collaboratively edit and share documents using the site. You can post meeting notes, follow-up action items, and other information on the site for easy access by the team, both during the meeting as well as subsequently.

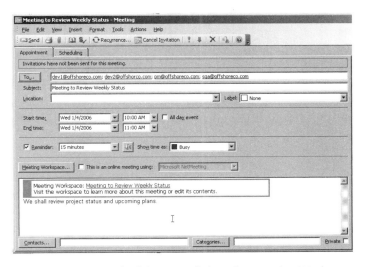

FIGURE 10.13   Outlook inserts a link to the Meeting Workspace in the meeting request.

FIGURE 10.14   The Meeting Workspace in the project portal hosts all information related to a meeting.

CUSTOMIZING THE PROJECT PORTAL

SharePoint provides built-in capability to modify team sites. On the home page, click the Modify Shared Page link and bring up the drop-down menu (see Figure 10.15). Available options are as follows:

■ Click Add Web Parts to search Web Parts installed in various galleries, as well as to import new Web Parts (DWP files). A wide variety of Web Parts are available from Microsoft as well as third-party providers.

- Click Design this Page from the drop-down menu to display an editable page where you can rearrange the interface by dragging Web Parts. You can click the drop-down icon on the header of individual Web Parts to modify them.
- Click Modify Shared Web Parts to change the appearance, location, and other properties of individual Web Parts.
- Click Shared View or Personal View to apply customizations for yourself or for all users. SharePoint is capable of displaying a personalized portal view for each user.

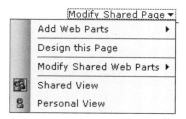

FIGURE 10.15 Modify Shared Page contains various customization options.

Additional portal customization options are available by clicking Site Settings in the site toolbar and selecting the appropriate links in the Customization section (see Figure 10.16).

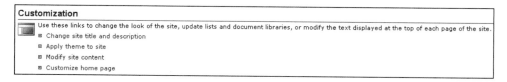

FIGURE 10.16 Customization options available in the Site Settings page provide additional choices to modify the site.

However, as of this writing, in version one in VSTS, there is a known bug that prevents customizations to the home page using the methods described in this section. You can, of course, create new custom pages and link them to the site. Microsoft is expected to release a hotfix soon to resolve the issue.

You can also use FrontPage 2003 to customize the project portal. FrontPage 2003 allows you to make substantial changes beyond what is possible from the portal site. Possibilities include editing text and graphics, changing menu options, filtering lists, adding Web Parts and Web Part zones, connecting Web Parts, modifying the Quick Launch bar on the home page, and other changes.

Modifying the Site Template

You can change the design of all new team sites by modifying the process template. Export the process template to a set of XML files (see Chapter 3, "Leveraging VSTS and Customizing MSF Agile," for how to export the process template). Open the WssTasks.xml file located in the Windows SharePoint Services folder. Listing 10.1 shows the contents of the file.

LISTING 10.1   Contents of the WssTasks.xml File Created from the MSF Agile Process Template

```
<tasks>
 <task id="SharePointPortal" name="Create Sharepoint Portal"
    plugin="Microsoft.ProjectCreationWizard.Portal"
    completionMessage="Project site created.">
  <dependencies />
  <taskXml>
  <Portal>
   <site template="VSTS_MSFAgile" language="1033" />
   <documentLibraries>
    <documentLibrary name="Security"
       description="Documents for the architect team" />
    <documentLibrary name="Test"
       description="Documents for the test team" />
    <documentLibrary name="Project Management" description=
       "Documents for the project management team" />
    <documentLibrary name="Templates"
       description="Templates for the team documents" />
    <documentLibrary name="Requirements"
       description="Documents for the business analyst team" />
    <documentLibrary name="Process Guidance"
       description="Process Guidance for the team documents" />
   </documentLibraries>
   <folders>
    <folder documentLibrary="Process Guidance"
       name="Supporting Files" />
    <folder documentLibrary="Process Guidance"
       name="Supporting Files/Code" />
    <folder documentLibrary="Process Guidance"
       name="Supporting Files/CSS" />
    <folder documentLibrary="Process Guidance"
       name="Supporting Files/EULA" />
    <folder documentLibrary="Process Guidance"
       name="Supporting Files/images" />
```

```
     </folders>
     <files>
      <file source="Windows SharePoint Services\Process Guidance
         \Supporting Files\ProcessGuidance.htm"
         documentLibrary="Process Guidance" target="Supporting
         Files/ProcessGuidance.htm" />
      <file source="Windows SharePoint Services\Process Guidance\
         Supporting Files\Glossary.htm"
         documentLibrary="Process Guidance"
         target="Supporting Files/Glossary.htm" />
  <!-- COMMENT: Other  Process Guidance related files omitted -->

      <file source="Windows SharePoint Services\Requirements
         \QoS Requirements.xls" documentLibrary="Requirements"
         target="QoS Requirements.xls"
         queryId="All Quality of Service Requirements" />
      <file source="Windows SharePoint Services\Requirements
         \Scenarios.xls" documentLibrary="Requirements"
         target="Scenarios.xls" queryId="All Scenarios" />
      <file source="Windows SharePoint Services\Project Management
         \Project Checklist.xls" documentLibrary="Project
         Management" target="Project Checklist.xls"
         queryId="Project Checklist" />
      <file source="Windows SharePoint Services\Project
         Management\Triage List.xls"
         documentLibrary="Project Management"
         target="Triage List.xls" queryId="Untriaged Bugs" />
      <file source="Windows SharePoint Services\Project
         Management\Issues.xls" documentLibrary="Project
         Management" target="Issues.xls" queryId="All Issues" />
      <file source="Windows SharePoint Services\
         Requirements\Vision.doc"
         documentLibrary="Requirements" target="Vision.doc" />
      <file source="Windows SharePoint Services\
         Requirements\Persona.doc"
         documentLibrary="Requirements" target="Persona.doc" />
      <file source="Windows SharePoint Services\
         Requirements\Scenario Description.doc"
         documentLibrary="Requirements"
         target="Scenario Description.doc" />
      <file source="Windows SharePoint Services\Security\Template
         Sample - Web Application Threat Model.doc"
         documentLibrary="Security" target="Template Sample - Web
         Application Threat Model.doc" />
```

```
        <file source="Windows SharePoint Services\Project
            Management\Test Development Plan.mpp"
            documentLibrary="Project Management"
            target="Test Development Plan.mpp" />
        <file source="Windows SharePoint Services\Project
            Management\Development Project Plan.mpp"
            documentLibrary="Project Management"
            target="Development Project Plan.mpp" />
        <file source="Windows SharePoint Services\Test
            \Test Approach.doc"
            documentLibrary="Test" target="Test Approach.doc" />
      </files>
    </Portal>
    </taskXml>
   </task>
</tasks>
```

As discussed earlier, you can customize the WssTasks.xml file to create additional document libraries by modifying the contents of the <documentLibraries> node. Pre-populate the folders with the files of your choice by editing the contents of the <files> node.

The look and feel of the site can be changed by creating the portal based on a custom SharePoint site template. Note from Listing 10.1 that VSTS uses a template named "VSTS_MSFAgile" to create the project portal. You can create a custom SharePoint site template and change the <site template="VSTS_MSFAgile" language= "1033" /> line in the WssTasks.xml file, replacing "VSTS_MSFAgile" with your custom template name. All team project portals created subsequently will be based on your custom design. The detailed steps involved are as follows:

1. Customize an existing team site or create a new SharePoint site from scratch, based on your preferred design, and save it as a template. Click Site Settings in the site toolbar, click Go to Site Administration, and click Save Site as Template. The template will be saved as an .stp file. Site templates include custom themes, Quick Launch bar, Web Part pages, document folders, lists, and so forth.
2. Open a command prompt window in your application tier machine and navigate to the directory containing the stsadm.exe tool (e.g., Program Files\Common Files\Microsoft Shared\Web Server Extensions\60\Bin).
3. Type the following line in the command prompt window to view the list of installed templates:

```
stsadm -o enumtemplates
```

4. The output will be something like the following (the exact output will depend on the SharePoint templates installed in your machine):

```
VSTS_MSFAgile - Language: 1033 - Site Template:
    _GLOBAL_#1 - Template Id: 1
VSTS_MSF_CMMI - Language: 1033 - Site Template:
    _GLOBAL_#2 - Template Id: 1
```

5. Add your site template to the central template gallery by typing the following line in the command prompt window:

```
stsadm -o addtemplate -filename <your custom template name>.stp
    -title <your template title> -description
    <your template description>
```

6. Verify that the template has been uploaded by typing the following command again:

```
stsadm -o enumtemplates
```

7. At this point, the custom template is uploaded to SharePoint. Now modify the following line in the WssTasks.xml file and replace "VSTS_MSFAgile" with the name of your custom template:

```
<site template="VSTS_MSFAgile" language="1033"/>
```

8. Import the modified process template into VSTS (see Chapter 3, "Leveraging VSTS and Customizing MSF Agile," for how to do this). Now, all new project portals will be based on the custom site template.

CONCLUSION

Easy access to timely information increases transparency of offshore execution. Development organizations are under constant pressure to reduce delivery time, improve quality, and provide more visibility. As discussed in Chapter 2, "Development Process—What Really Works," software development is unlike many 'hard' engineering disciplines where, given a set of initial frozen requirements, the outcome can be predicted with high certainty. Very few things remain constant in the life of an enterprise software project—changing market conditions, requirements, technology shifts, and the like result in the need for course corrections, compromises, and approximations. In order to be able to manage an ever-changing set of realities, you need relevant, timely information. Without knowing the real facts, you'll find it hard to handle shifting priorities and perform dynamic resource allocations.

Offshore execution becomes difficult, because discovering the underlying facts and conducting load-balancing is not easy when you're sitting halfway around the world. The process, people, and technologies involved in the communications channel cause bottlenecks and slow down the information flow. The Internet is still not a substitute for face-to-face communication, although it'll probably get there someday.

If you set it up right, you'll find the project portal to be a useful tool for discovering the raw facts regarding project health—without errors in interpretation, translation, or rendition. Furthermore, since the data is automatically captured as a by-product of routine development activities, there is little additional overhead associated with data gathering, processing, and reporting. For larger projects, the portal can also evolve into a community site where members can learn from one another and grow as a team. For far-flung team members, a central site facilitates mental cohesion, peer learning, and provides a sense of shared mission. Ideas emerge, productivity improves, and the execution process becomes more transparent. An effective, self-evolving project site reduces friction and improves visibility.

T he CD-ROM contains full source code for the examples presented in the book.

SYSTEM REQUIREMENTS

- ■ Visual Studio 2005
- ■ Visual Studio 2005 Team System

The hardware and software requirements for installing VSTS can be found in Visual Studio 2005 Team Foundation Installation Guide, which can be downloaded from Microsoft web site at *http://www.microsoft.com/downloads/details.aspx? familyid=E54BF6FF-026B-43A4-ADE4-A690388F310E&displaylang=en# Requirements*.

To run the code samples in Chapters 3, you will need
- ■ Microsoft Office Excel 2003

To run the code samples in Chapters 4, you will need
- ■ Microsoft Office Project Standard 2003

To run the code samples in Chapter 5, you will need
- ■ Microsoft Office Outlook 2003
- ■ Visual Studio 2005 Tools for Office (VSTO)

To run the code samples in Chapter 6, you will need
- ■ Microsoft Office Communicator 2005
- ■ Microsoft Live Communications Server 2005

Index